DAVID
HIS LIFE & CHARACTER

David
His Life & Character

George Lawson

CountedFaithful

DAVID: HIS LIFE AND CHARACTER
Originally published posthumously as *Discourses on the History of David* in 1833
This edition © Counted Faithful, 2018

COUNTED FAITHFUL
2 Drakewood Road
London SW16 5DT

Website: http://www.countedfaithful.org

ISBN
Book: 978-1-78872-111-0
ePub: 978-1-78872-112-7
Kindle: 978-1-78872-113-4

David: His Life and Character is a work in the public domain. Some minor updating of language and formatting has been undertaken to make this work as accessible as possible. Please respect the time and effort invested in preparing this work by not reproducing or transmitting any part of it in any form or by any means, electronic or mechanical, without permission in writing from the publisher.

Contents

1. On the General Excellence of His Conduct   7
2. Of David's Faith in the Pardoning Mercy of God   21
3. Of David's Repentance   33
4. David's Love to God   45
5. David's Confidence in God   57
6. Of David's Love to the Word of God   69
7. David's Meditations on the Word of God   77
8. Of David's Obedience to the Revealed Will of God   87
9. David's Afflictions and Fears   103
10. Of David's Behaviour in the Time of Trouble   117
11. David's Thanksgiving for His Deliverance   135
12. Of the Justice of David's Behaviour   149

1
On the General Excellence of His Conduct

And he did that which was right in the sight of the Lord, according to all that David his father had done. (2 Chronicles 29:2)

THE name of David is renowned in the church, and will be renowned whilst the world stands. He is the model of good princes. Of most of his successors in the kingdom of Judah, it is said that they did, or that they did not, according to what David had done.

There is one great benefit which we derive from the history of David, that it affords excellent lessons to princes in the government of their subjects. It may be reasonably believed that much of that virtue which has been practised by the Christian princes, as well as by the good kings of Judah, was learned from David. How glorious is that king of Israel who has taught so many illustrious men those lessons which made them blessings to thousands and millions of their fellow-creatures.

It is to be regretted, however, that there have been a greater number of princes of whom it may be said that they did not, than of those who did, that which was right in the sight of the Lord like David. But our chief business is to enquire whether we ourselves are walking in those good old ways in which he travelled to the land of blessedness. He was one of the most eminent of those men whose faith and patience we are commanded to imitate. I shall endeavour:

I. To show what it is to behave like David.

II. To suggest some motives for such behaviour.

I. What is it to behave like David.

He did that which was right in the sight of the Lord. He made the will of God the rule of his conduct, in the whole course of his life, and never turned aside from following the Lord save in the matter of Uriah the Hittite.

A man may do what is right in the sight of the Lord, without a perfect heart. This is the character of Amaziah given in one passage of Scripture. In another passage his character is given in these words of the same import – "He did that which was right in the sight of the Lord, but not like David his father," (*2 Chronicles 25:2; 2 Kings 14:3*).

It will be in vain to follow his steps in our outward conduct, if we do not imitate him in the dispositions of our hearts. Amaziah was conscious in the beginning of his reign that his prosperity depended on his good behaviour, and therefore he resolved to make the Law the rule of his conduct. But his heart was not right in the sight of the Lord. He turned out a hypocrite, and fell by his apostasy from God.

Let us at present take a general view of the graces and virtues in which David excelled. And may God bestow that grace upon us by which he was enabled to exhibit such a bright pattern of goodness. We may say of him that he exercised himself always to have a conscience void of offence both towards God and towards man.

1. His piety towards God was eminent above that of the greatest part of the saints whose names are mentioned with honour in the Bible.

He was an eminent pattern no less than Abraham of that faith by which we are justified. After Paul had proved the doctrine of justification by faith, from a passage which speaks of Abraham's justification, he adds a passage from David in which he describes the blessedness of the man to whom the Lord imputeth righteousness without works, saying, "Blessed is the man whose iniquity is forgiven, and whose sin is covered. Blessed is the man to whom the Lord will not impute sin." In the passage to which the apostle refers, David speaks of the transcendent excellency of this blessedness from his own experience. His confidence was not built on his own eminent virtues. He did not set them in opposition to his sins, as if he thought that the balance would lie on the favourable side in consideration of the singular service which he performed to God and to his generation, but looked to the sovereign mercy of God in the promised atonement as

On the General Excellence of His Conduct

the ground of his confidence. "If thou, Lord, shouldest mark iniquity, O Lord, who shall stand? But there is forgiveness with thee, that thou mayest be feared. I wait for the Lord, my soul doth wait, and in his word do I hope." "Purge me with hyssop, and I shall be clean: wash me, and I shall be whiter than snow," (*Psalms 130 and 51*).

He trusted in God with an unshaken confidence for everything that was good, and for the averting of everything that was evil. He committed his soul, his body, his fortunes, his family, his kingdom to God, being fully persuaded that all which God had spoken, he was able to perform. "The Lord," says he, "is my strength and my song; my heart trusted in him and I am helped: therefore my soul greatly rejoiceth, and with my song will I praise him," (*Psalm 28:7*).

He trusted in God not only in the day of prosperity, but in his extremest distresses, and amidst the most formidable enemies. When danger appeared, it was a signal to him to flee into his stronghold, the name of the Lord. Almost all his psalms are filled with professions of his faith and confidence in God. "What time," he says, "I am afraid, I will trust in thee." When deep was calling unto deep, and all God's waves and billows were passing over him, the language of his heart was, "Why art thou cast down, O my soul, why art thou disquieted within me? hope thou in God, for I shall yet praise him who is the health of my countenance and my God. The Lord will command his loving-kindness in the day time, and in the night his song shall be with me, and my prayer to the God of my life," (*Psalms 42, 43 and 56*).

Although God did not presently communicate his help, he was not greatly discouraged. He sometimes indeed felt the workings of despondency. Who can wonder at it? Which of us would not have been crushed by those strokes of calamity which sometimes made him stagger? But he soon recovered his strength and spirit. It was only in his haste that he said, "All men are liars – I am cut off from before thine eyes – I shall one day perish by the hand of Saul." He waited patiently for the Lord in all his numberless distresses, and the Lord heard him, and brought him up out of the deep pit and miry clay, and set his feet upon a rock, (*Psalms 40, 62*).

Although great troubles cannot destroy the confidence fixed on God, yet it may be thought almost impossible to hold it fast under the consciousness of great sins. And certainly great sins call for deep repentance. We are stubborn offenders if we do not mourn bitterly at the remembrance of our transgressions. No offender could weep more bitter tears of sorrow than David shed at the remembrance of his iniquities. When God forgave him, he could not forgive himself. "His sin was ever before him, and he caused his bed to swim with tears." His penitential Psalms are yet on record for the encouragement of broken-hearted sinners, and for the conviction of the unhumbled. (*Psalms 6, 32, 38, 51*).

Yet his confidence in God was not overthrown. He believed the word of forgiveness when he deplored his need of it. He believed that, notwithstanding of all that he had done to provoke the Lord to anger, the Lord would redeem his soul from all adversity. His flight from Jerusalem when Absalom rebelled against him, was the cause of many tears to all his friends, but his own tears were his meat day and night when he thought on his sin in the matter of Uriah, and on these words of Nathan – "Thus saith the Lord, Behold I will raise up evil against thee out of thine own house." Yet even then he could say to God, "Thou art my shield and my glory, and the lifter up of mine head." It was as a sword within his bones when his enemies said unto him, "Where is thy God? the Lord hath brought the evil thou hast done to others upon thy head, thou bloody man." Yet even then he could say to his soul, "Hope thou in God, for I shall yet praise him for the help of his countenance." His enemies were plotting to surprise him by night, and to take away his life from the earth by an unexpected stroke, but he laid him down and slept; he awaked, for the Lord sustained him, and he would not have been afraid if ten thousand men had set themselves in array against him.

His love to God was ever fervent, and it was kindled into a flame by every new instance of the divine goodness. He loved the Lord even when he was under the divine hand trying him by adversities, or chastening him for his iniquities. Then did he breathe after God, and long for his return in mercy to his soul. It was when he fled from Absalom, that he said to the Lord, "As the hart panteth after the water brooks, so panteth my soul after thee, O God. He is the health of my countenance, and my God." When he obtained deliverance from trouble, his love poured out the language of praise and thanksgiving. "I will love thee, O Lord, my strength. I love the Lord because he hath heard the voice of my supplication."

On the General Excellence of His Conduct

He loved the law of the Lord, the whole revelation of his will concerning man's duty and the divine mercy. "O how love I thy law, it is my meditation all the day!"

Meditation was his delight. He prevented the dawning of the morning that he might meditate on God's statutes. His delight in the Lord made meditation on the excellencies, the law, the works of God, delightful to his soul. "My meditation of him shall be sweet, and I will rejoice in the Lord."

He took delight in all the ordinances of the Lord. He was a man of prayer, and cried to God in the morning, the evening, and at noon. Praise was pleasant to his holy soul. Whilst he lived he praised the Lord. Whilst he had a being in this world, he gave thanks to his name. And now he not only praises God in heaven with Abraham and Israel and the holy angels, but he is still praising God on earth by the mouths of the saints in all the churches. He enjoys this pleasure above almost all the heavenly choir, that his songs which he wrote by the Spirit upon earth are still sung through every part of this world with acceptance, and please the Lord better than the oxen, the sheep and the incense that were in ancient days presented on his altar.

With great joy David joined in the service of the sanctuary. He "loved the habitation of God's house, and the place where his honour dwelt." And when he was an exile from his own house and country, he did not so much lament his bereavement of the comforts of domestic life and friendship as of sanctuary institutions. His soul was poured out in him when he thought of the multitude with whom he had formerly kept the holy day.

The carnal ordinances of the law were delightful to him, because he viewed them with a spiritual eye, and looked forward to the end of them, and expected fellowship in them with his God. He prayed that God would send forth his light and truth, that he might go to the altar of God, to God his exceeding joy, and employ his harp to praise him.

He was far from repining at the many afflictions allotted to him by the providence of God, but patiently and submissively endured sickness, reproach, exile, and every calamity that is painful to human nature. He was dumb, he opened not his mouth, when he was traduced, reviled and persecuted, because the Lord did it. He could even rejoice under tribulation, in the faith that God would bring it to a happy conclusion, and bring good out of all that he suffered.

He saw the goodness of God in the management of his condition, and when he was brought down to the lowest parts of the earth, he did not despond, he did not fret, for he believed that God would yet make him to see his goodness in the land of the living.

He made the will of God in all things the rule of his conduct, and therefore God, who knows the hearts of men, gives him this testimony, that he was a man who would do all his will. Saul did a part of the will of God, but when his interest and passions came into competition with the will of God, he chose rather to violate his conscience than mortify his inclinations. But David subjected his own will to the will of God, and maintained a constant respect to all God's commandments.

He devoted himself and all that he had to God. When he had built a magnificent palace for himself, he was grieved that the ark of God dwelt between curtains, whilst he himself dwelt in a house of cedar. God would not suffer him to build a house for his name, but he consecrated the greater part of his immense spoils taken in war to the honour and service of God. Although Solomon had the honour of building the temple, yet David's preparations and directions enabled him to build it in such splendour that nothing equal to it was seen in any nation.

He persevered in his religion to the end, amidst the dreadful trials to which he was exposed. Although he often found it necessary to ask favours from heathen princes, and even to take shelter with one of them, he always abhorred strange gods, and would not take their name into his mouth.

He swore, and he performed it, that he would keep all God's judgments, and that he would keep them continually for ever and ever.

He was animated with a fervent zeal for the glory of God, for the salvation of men, and the extirpation of wickedness. Horror took hold upon him because of the wicked that sought not God's law. It was zeal for God that dictated his awful prayers against wicked transgressors.

Thus was David an eminent example of piety, devotion, obedience, submission to God, and of all those holy endowments which have God for their immediate object. Happy are all those who love God and delight in his service. But let none pretend that he loves the God whom he has not seen, if he does not love his brother whom he hath seen, or that he walks in the way of the Lord, when he does not behave righteously towards men.

2. David was no less righteous than devout, and kept a conscience void of offence towards men as well as towards God.

"I have done justice," he says, "to all men." How *few* can speak such words with truth. David certainly did not mean that he was perfect in virtue any more than in devotion. It is too well known to be denied, that in some things he greatly offended against men as well as against God. Whether he had committed that dreadful wickedness in the matter of Uriah, in which he turned aside from following the Lord, at the time when he wrote these words, may be questioned; but certain it is, that it was his endeavour, in the general course of his life, to walk righteously. When he offended he was more displeased with himself than any other man could be, and did everything that was in his power to repair the injury. He rashly gave the inheritance of Mephibosheth to Ziba, but easily suffered himself to be undeceived. When he said, "Thou and Ziba divide the inheritance," he did not mean that Ziba was to possess the half of it as his own property, but that he was as formerly to transact the business of Mephibosheth, and enjoy those advantages of factorage which he had formerly enjoyed. It seems indeed strange that a just man should not have rather turned Ziba out of his former employment, and punished him as an evil speaker, according to his own resolution concerning persons of such a character. But we know not all the circumstances of the case. This we know, that David was an honest man. God bears testimony of him that he did justice and judgment to all his people.

He was not only a just but a good man. He entertained a warm charity for his fellow-men, "especially those that were of the household of faith," (*Psalm 16:3*). He earnestly desired the conversion and salvation of sinners, (*Psalm 51:13*). We find him indeed sometimes praying for the destruction of his enemies, and some have inferred from these prayers that he was a man of a revengeful spirit; but he presented them to God, under the unerring direction of the Spirit, who knows the secret counsels of the will of God, and it was not from a principle of revenge, but from a sincere regard to the glory of God, the vindication of oppressed innocence, and the welfare of the church, that he called down the vengeance of God upon men, hardened in their hearts beyond all hope of repentance. When he was not impelled by influences from on high to seek the destruction of his own enemies, the enemies of his God, he prayed "for them that despitefully used him and persecuted him," (*Psalm 35*). He mourned for their distresses as if he had been their brother or son.

In every different relation of life he deserved the highest praise. His filial affection is evident from the care he took to secure his parents from the violence of Saul, and to preserve them from the hardships to which he was himself exposed. His funeral elegy on Jonathan, and his affectionate behaviour to Mephibosheth, are proofs of his fidelity and generous kindness to his friends. No subject was more faithful to the best of princes than David was to his great enemy, whom he served with heroic courage, whilst he was allowed to serve him, spared and preserved from the vengeance of his followers, when that prince was in his power, and lamented him when he suffered the punishment due to his iniquities.

When he was advanced to the throne he did not sleep after his toils, but laboured with unwearied diligence to promote the welfare of his people, for whose safety he often exposed his life in bloody battles, till they almost compelled him to be more careful of his own safety that he might not quench the light of Israel.

When, after the noblest services to his people, the greater part of them revolted from his government, and conspired to destroy him, he was under the necessity of fighting the battles of justice and religion in his own defence, he spared as much as possible the blood of his subjects, and retained no traces of resentment against them, after he had by his wise and kind behaviour recovered them to a sense of their duty. When they were visited with the pestilence for their own sins as well as his, he wished to have the whole weight of the punishment laid upon himself and upon his father's house.

It was his chief care to make his subjects happy, and especially to make them holy. For this reason he took care to have the ark of God brought home to himself, with the concurrence of all the people, and gathered the chiefs of all the tribes to attend its removal with the voice of joy and praise. He wrote many Psalms to excite devout affections in his people. He did all that he could to recommend religion by his exhortations and example, and he took effectual measures to establish good order in the ministrations of the sanctuary.

On the General Excellence of His Conduct

He was exemplary in private life. He walked within his house with a perfect heart. He returned to bless his house, when with the assembled multitude from all Israel he had brought the ark to Zion. He spake the language of sharp reproof to Michal his wife, but open reproof is better than secret love. She not only merited it, but duty to himself required it. That love is deadly hatred which suffers sin upon the wife of one's bosom.

If David deserved censure for any part of his domestic behaviour, it was for too much lenity. He certainly commanded his children to keep the way of the Lord, but he was deficient in admonition and reproof. The bad behaviour of Amnon, of Absalom and Adonijah, appears to have been in some degree occasioned by the excess of his paternal fondness.

David has been by some severely censured for excess of severity to his enemies. But from his behaviour to Saul it appears that he was far from being of a revengeful spirit. His severities to the enemies of Israel were a necessary and a salutary infliction of just vengeance, and as far as we know, deserve as little blame as the strict execution of justice by the civil magistrate. His behaviour to the Ammonites indeed is highly censurable, if our translation of the passage which gives an account of it is just. But some very learned men are of the opinion that he did not destroy those insolent enemies with saws and harrows of iron, but punished them with well-merited infamy by causing them to pass under saws and harrows of iron, as the Romans afterwards caused some of their prisoners to pass under the yoke. This opinion seems to be well-founded. How could it be said that he never turned aside from following the Lord, save in the matter of Uriah the Hittite, if he was chargeable with an almost unexampled act of barbarity towards the Ammonites? Men cannot turn aside from the Lord into more crooked ways than those of unrelenting cruelty and barbarous revenge.

We cannot after all say that David was altogether unblemished through every part of his life. He was an eminently just man, but there never was a just man upon the earth, except the great Son of David, who did good and sinned not. He sometimes violated the laws of strict truth, but it was in circumstances of extreme distress and danger. He abhorred the way of lying. He fell shamefully in the matter of Uriah and Bathsbeba, and yet we may safely affirm, that he possessed the virtues of chastity, humanity and integrity, to a far higher degree than those who are most forward to censure him, although they have been preserved all their life long from any violations of the sixth, seventh, or ninth commandment, that would bring disgrace upon their name.

If David sometimes offended, he was deeply sensible of his offences. He condemned himself with greater severity than his enemies could do, and confessed that his transgressions were a burden too heavy for him to bear. He could not undo what he had done. He could not expiate his transgressions by any sacrifices which it was in his power to offer. But what he could do, he did. He presented unto God the sacrifice of a broken heart, and his broken and contrite heart God did not despise.

All his graces and virtues were adorned with humility. Some thought he was a high-minded man, who aspired to a higher station than that to which he was born. He was indeed a man of a noble spirit, who looked forward to the throne when he was in a private station, and even in a state of banishment. "But shall I not possess," said Jephthah, "that which the Lord my God giveth me to possess?" And was it not David's duty to lift his eyes to a throne that God had promised him? He was so far from wishing for the death of Saul, to obtain possession of his crown, that he carefully guarded his life when it was exposed to danger. He could appeal to the Searcher of hearts as his witness, that his heart was not haughty, nor his eyes lofty, and that he did not deal in great matters, or in things too high for him. He always showed due reverence to his superiors, and condescended to men of low degree. Before God he humbled himself to the dust, and accounted himself less than nothing and viler than the earth.

His piety was not stained by bigotry, nor by cruelty to men of false religions. It is plain that towards neighbouring princes he behaved in such a manner as to command their esteem and affection, when their minds were not embittered by prejudice or self-interest. He gained the cordial esteem of Achish king of Gath, of Hiram king of Tyre, of Nahash king of the Ammonites, and probably of Talmai king of Geshur, and Toi king of Hamath. Araunah, who treated him with profound respect, had once probably been king of the Jebusites.

He was a blessing to his people – a blessing even to his conquered enemies, except those who despised their own mercies. His kind

On the General Excellence of His Conduct

offices were extended beyond the bounds of his own dominions, and it is probable that Hiram king of Tyre learned from him the fear of the God of Israel.

He served his generation by the will of God, and fell asleep; but he served every succeeding generation likewise by the order which he established amongst the priests and Levites, by his preparations for the building of the temple, and the exhortations and instructions which he gave to his son and his people on that subject, and especially by the rich legacies of devotional compositions which he left to the church.

We praise David as one of the best of men. But our praises will be our own condemnation if we do not walk in his ways.

II. To suggest some motives to walk in his ways, was the second thing proposed. Consider,

1. The excellency of his practice.

What is that course of life which the greater part of men pursue? They employ their time and their powers of body and mind in seeking gratification to their desires of present enjoyment; and these mistaken views of self-interest lead them on to the habitual indulgence of those corrupt propensities by which they procure misery and destruction to themselves.

David had his views directed to the chief end of man, the glorifying and enjoying of God. These views directed, sanctified and beautified every part of his life. His days were employed in wise and holy efforts to advance the best of all interests. Whatever things were honourable, just, true, lovely, and of good report, if there was any virtue, if there was any praise, he thought on these things.

Most men live like the beasts, intent only on those things that perish. Should they gain all that they wish to gain, what would be their advantage? "Surely every man walketh in a vain shew, he heapeth up wealth, and knows not who shall gather it." If he should even employ his days in collecting treasures of knowledge whilst he is ignorant of God, he is but labouring for the wind. But the days of those who, like David, do that which is right in the sight of the Lord, are spent in the improvement of those talents which God hath put into their hands, in doing the will of God on earth as the angels do it in heaven.

See then and ask for the old way, what is the path in which the good men of former times walked, if you desire to live the life of angels rather than of beasts or of devils.

2. The happiness of such a life is a powerful recommendation of it. Why do men walk in the ways of sin? They expect happiness without doubt. But what can be more daringly presumptuous than to expect any advantage from doing that which is evil in the sight of the Lord? He is the fountain of joy as well as of everything that is desirable. And can joy spring out of that which displeases him? We may with better reason expect life to spring out of death. Whilst men follow their lusts, destruction and misery are in all their ways, and the way of peace they know not.

Was Saul or David happier in the course of their lives? Saul was continually labouring to secure and advance the glory of his family. But he lived in perpetual vexation. In the first years of his reign he fought successfully against the enemies of Israel. The advantage and glory gained to himself and his people, were then some compensation for the toil and danger to which he was exposed; but David, exposed to the same toils and dangers, was consoled and filled with joy by the faith of God's effectual aid, and by the sweet reflection that he was fighting the battles of his God. In the last part of Saul's reign he suffered miseries from the consciousness of guilt, and from his own tormenting passions, which the pleasures of a forfeited royalty could little alleviate. David's heart, amidst all his afflictions, was filled with gladness from the light of God's countenance, from the faith of his promises, from the testimony of a good conscience.

But why should we compare the happiness of Saul with that of David, when they were both occupying the same exalted station? When we confine our views to the present life we may safely assert that David was far happier in his most unprosperous state. He was incomparably happier in exile, in danger, in necessities, in reproaches, than Saul upon the throne, surrounded with flattering dependants who endeavoured to minister to all his pleasure. Whilst Saul in his palace was racked with remorse, envy and dismal forebodings of the evils that were to come upon him and upon his family, David, in caves and deserts, rejoiced in hope. When he knew not whence the next supply for his necessities would come, he was satisfied with marrow and fatness, when he remembered the Lord upon his bed, and meditated upon him in the night watches. Many were the afflictions of this righteous man, but the Lord delivered him out of them all. When deliverance was at a distance, he knew that it would come. When he sat in darkness, the Lord was a light unto him.

But let us turn our thoughts to the present state of the holy man. Although he is dead, he yet lives unto God and with God. He enjoys all those transcendent felicities which he looked for when he was on earth, and unspeakably greater felicity than ever came within the compass of his thoughts. He now knows what neither the light of grace nor the light of inspiration could teach him of those joys which are in God's presence, and that fulness of pleasures which are for evermore at his right hand.

Do you wish for joys on earth of a pure, satisfying and permanent kind? – follow the example of David, and of all the holy men of former days. They could speak from experience of the pleasures to be found in the ways of wisdom. "This poor man cried, and the Lord heard him, and delivered him out of all his troubles," and he calls to us to come and taste and see that the Lord is good, and that all who trust in him are blessed. Neither sufferings nor death could make him unhappy, for he knew, and on his death-bed he was able to say with joy, that the Lord had made with him an everlasting covenant, ordered in all things and sure, for this was all his salvation and all his desire.

Blessed are they that dwell in God's eternal house in the heavens, and blessed is the man in whose heart are the ways which lead to that eternal habitation. But upon whom cometh that blessedness? Is it possible that such sinful creatures as we can attain to such felicity? Yes.

3. Whatever we are at present, we may walk in the ways of David and attain to those felicities which he now enjoys.

I do not say that it is in your own power to turn from the ways of sin to the ways of God. But I call to your remembrance those words of our Lord Jesus Christ – "With men indeed it is impossible, but with God all things are possible." David could never have entered into the ways of God, if the Lord had not set him in the way of his steps. He could not have kept the good path of the Lord, had not God kept him by his own power. He could not have advanced a step, if the Lord had not led and strengthened him. Of his need of divine grace he was fully aware, and daily prayed for new supplies of it. "O that my ways were directed to keep thy statutes. Then shall I not be ashamed when I have respect to all thy commandments."

God is not less gracious than he was three thousand years ago. The rich grace bestowed upon David is an encouragement to us to seek all that grace which we need. David's prayer for grace are words put into your mouths. O that God would enable us all to present to him David's prayer with David's spirit. Then we would all find occasion like that holy man to give daily praises to the Hearer of prayer.

When we look for grace from God, we must not neglect the means of grace. "A day in God's courts is better than a thousand." It is better to be door-keepers in the house of our God than to dwell in the tents of wickedness, "for the Lord God is a sun and shield: he will give grace and glory."

You are chargeable with many sins, so was David, but he did not on that account despair of mercy. The greater his sins were, he prayed for mercy with the greater earnestness. He lived before the time when the Son of God appeared in the world to put away sin by the sacrifice of himself; but he saw the redemption of Christ afar off, and lifted up his voice to God for a share in its blessings. "Purge me with hyssop, and I shall be clean: wash me, and I shall be whiter than snow."

Think upon your ways, and turn your feet unto God's testimonies. Let it be your firm resolution to keep the ways of the Lord, and your ardent desire and prayer unto God that you may be led by his good Spirit unto the land of uprightness.

Remember that the eye of the Lord is upon all your ways. Whether you do good or evil, it is in the sight of the Lord. If you were always under the eye of a beloved or revered friend, you would certainly avoid everything offensive to him, and endeavour to please him by your conduct. It is a matter of less consequence to you to approve yourselves unto men, than to God who searches the hearts and tries the reins of men. "Let the wicked forsake his way, and the unrighteous man his thoughts, and turn unto the Lord, and he will have mercy upon him; and to our God, for he will abundantly pardon."

2
Of David's Faith in the Pardoning Mercy of God

DAVID was a sinner like ourselves. In that large history which is given us of his life, we find an account of some things in his conduct which no wise man will attempt to justify or excuse, and no doubt he was chargeable with many other evils to which his own heart was privy. But he knew that the God whom he served was a merciful God, and by the prayer of faith he had recourse to the throne of mercy, and obtained complete relief from all that guilt which he contracted in the course of his life, as well as from that which be brought with him into the world. Let us consider,

I. The account which is given us of his faith in the pardoning mercy of God.

II. Apply to our own use the instructions afforded by this illustrious pattern of God's long-suffering.

I. Let us consider David's faith in God's pardoning mercy.

1. He was deeply conscious of his need of this mercy. Some hope that God will be merciful to their transgressions because they do not think there is any great harm in them. They know that they have not done everything they ought to have done, and that they have done many things which they ought not to have done. What then? If they are to be damned because they are not perfect, who can escape? Thus they make themselves easy in their minds, not because God is

wonderful in mercy, but because they believe a very moderate share of mercy is sufficient for them. If God should punish them for their transgressions, they think he would show less mercy to his creatures than themselves would do to their fellow-sinners.

David was indeed aware that all mankind must perish as well as himself, if God should mark iniquity, but he did not think that God was therefore under any obligation to pardon either himself or any other sinner. "If thou, Lord, shouldest mark iniquity, O Lord, who shall stand?"

He thought likewise that though other sinners were pardoned, God might justly mark his own iniquity and make him an eternal monument of wrath. "My transgressions," he says, "are gone up above mine head. They are a burden too heavy for me to bear." He did not say to God, "O Lord, pardon mine iniquity, for it is little, it is excusable from the frailty of my nature, and from the concurrence of unhappy circumstances which have entangled my feet, and overthrown my steps:" but he says, "For thy name sake, O Lord, pardon mine iniquity, for it is *great*." The sense which he had of the greatness of his iniquity did not deter him from the throne of grace, but inflamed his desires of mercy. The greater his sins were, his need of mercy was the greater. The deeper sense he had of the greatness of his sins, he was the better prepared to ascribe glory, and honour, and praise to that mercy in which he trusted.

There was a time when David was too much disposed to extenuate his sin. "When I kept silence," he says, (*Psalm 32*) "my bones waxed old, because of my roaring all the day long." How did he keep silence and yet roar? He kept silence concerning his sin, but he roared by reason of the inquietude of his heart. His sin in the matter of Uriah and Bathsheba was so atrocious that he could not bear the thought of it, and when it forced itself into his mind, he endeavoured to extenuate it to the utmost of his power; but in this way he found no peace. His bones waxed old, his moisture was turned into the drought of an oriental summer, which is frequently unmitigated by any drops of rain. Never did he taste comfort till he said he would confess his transgression unto the Lord, and then the Lord forgave the iniquity of his sin.

The kind of faith which is exercised towards God by an unconvinced sinner, gives no honour to God, and does no good to the soul but

Of David's Faith in the Pardoning Mercy of God

much hurt. It is the fountain of innumerable abominations. It is easy to sin, and to seek pardon, if pardon is to be had as a matter of course. Men may gratify any licentious desire at their pleasure, if they have nothing to do when they have sinned, but to fall on their knees and say, 'Lord, take away my sin.' When, like David, we feel bitter anguish on account of our offences, we will see nothing in the pardoning mercy of God that gives the least encouragement to sin, but everything that can tend to create an aversion to that abominable thing, which only infinite grace can remove.

This holy man was deeply conscious not only of the evil of those gross sins that tarnished his life, but of the malignity of those lesser evils that are unseen by the world. When he contemplated the glory of the divine holiness, and considered the perfection of the law, he cried out, "Who can understand his errors? Cleanse thou me from secret faults. Innumerable evils have compassed me about, they are more than the hairs of my head."

He considered not only his actual transgressions, but his inherent corruption, and saw it to be out of measure sinful. When he lamented his guilt in the matter of Uriah the Hittite, he traced it up to its spring in that corruption of heart, which was the source of all his sins, and which would have produced as much evil in his life as ever appeared in the life of the most graceless of mortals, if God had not restrained its workings. "Behold, I was shapen in iniquity; and in sin did my mother conceive me." In these words David certainly was not confessing the iniquity of his parents, but his own. He was not extenuating his offence, but bewailing the loathsome distemper which made him appear hateful in his own eyes. He was spreading it out before God, and imploring that relief through the pardoning and sanctifying grace which God only could bestow.

2. Under a sense of his guilt David looked to the mercy of God for pardon. "Have mercy upon me, O God, after thy loving-kindness; according to the multitude of thy tender mercies blot out all my transgressions."

'My guilt is very great,' says one. 'If God should lay righteousness to the line, I am undone – and why should I doubt whether he will put the highest value on the life of an egregious offender, or on his own righteousness?' David had perhaps as much reason as any man to stand in fear of the justice of God, for his crimes exposed him according to the law not only to punishment in the next world, but to death in this world. Yet he despairs not of mercy. His sins were great, but he believed that the mercy of God was greater. They were many, but not equal to the multitude of God's tender mercies. According to the multitude of these tender mercies he hopes and prays that God would blot out all his transgressions, would wash him throughly from his iniquities, and cleanse away all his sins.

David seems to have employed many of his thoughts upon that name of mercy which is recorded *Exodus 34:6, 7*. From that name he borrows pleas for the pardon of his sins, and when he obtained assurance of pardon he gave glory to that name. "Rejoice the soul of thy servant: for unto thee, O Lord, do I lift up my soul, for thou, Lord, art good, and ready to forgive; and plenteous in mercy unto all them that call upon thee." "The Lord is merciful and gracious, slow to anger, and plenteous in mercy," *Psalms 86, 103*.

Through his confidence in the mercy of God, he was like a green olive tree in the house of God. Although his moisture was sometimes turned into the drought of summer by apprehensions of wrath, yet when he was enabled to look again to the mercy-seat, he revived as the corn and grew as the vine, and his scent was like the wine of Lebanon. When we are disquieted with a sense of our own guilt, although we cannot be humbled too low, let us never forget that despondency can be no part of our duty whilst we are in the world where God delights to show forth the riches of his grace in his kindness towards men through Christ Jesus.

3. David was not ignorant of the atonement that was to be made for sinners of his own days as well as of later times. It cannot be supposed that a man who was so eminent a type of a suffering and a glorified Saviour, and one who prophesied so clearly of the sufferings of Christ and of the glory that should follow, was unacquainted with the counsel of God concerning the manner in which sin was to be taken away by the offering of the body of Jesus Christ once for all.

The disciples of our Lord could not bear the prophecies of his sufferings and death uttered by his own mouth, and yet they were believers in that promise which was the hope of their fathers, that the Seed of the woman should bruise the head of the serpent, whilst his own heel was bruised by the serpent. They believed the prophecies concerning the sufferings and the glory of Christ, although they had but very obscure views of their meaning. Such was the faith of the generality of saints under the Old Testament. But some of them had their minds elevated by the Spirit to sublime contemplations, and brightened with clearer conceptions of the plan of redemption than others. Such a man was David. We cannot suppose that he understood his own prophecies so well as we may understand them, but he surely derived light from them, whilst he diligently considered their meaning.

In *Psalm 51* we find him saying in one place, "Thou desirest not sacrifice; else would I give it;" and yet in another place he says, "Purge me with hyssop, and I shall be clean: wash me, and I shall be whiter than snow." What was that blood sprinkled by hyssop from which he expected purification from his guilt? Not surely the blood of bulls and of goats. He knew that the blood of bulls and of goats could take away no sin, and that no use was to be made of such blood in the cure of such sins as those that now excited his chief concern. That blood which he had in view must have been that which the blood of the ancient sacrifices represented.

David knew that God was just as well as merciful, but he knew also that justice and mercy would meet together in that salvation which God had provided for men. He looked forward with eager joy, like his father Abraham, to that seed in which Jews and Gentiles, the believers of the times then present, as well as of future times, were to be blessed with pardon and with life everlasting.

4. The Psalmist hoped in God's Word. "There is forgiveness with thee, that thou mayest be feared. I wait for the Lord, my soul doth wait, and in his word do I hope." It was in the Word of God that he found the doctrines and the promises of forgiveness. *Exodus 34:6, 7; Numbers 23*. In the history contained in it, he found a complete verification of that name of the Lord, the God of pardons. *Nehemiah 9:17*. And in the institutions enjoined by it, he saw that great atonement represented by which the transgression was to be finished and an end put to sin.

In the Word of God he found a sufficient ground laid, not merely for a general belief that pardon was with God, but for a dependence upon God for pardon to himself, for the remission of all his offences, however great in themselves, however aggravated in their circumstances. He could not have hoped in God's Word for deliverance from those depths into which he was sunk by sin, if it had not emboldened him to trust in God for the pardon of his own offences. Sin is the greatest of our miseries, and no faith can give rest to the mind that does not inspire us with the cheering hope that we shall never suffer those awful penalties which are the certain portion of unpardoned sinners.

5. He waited by faith for the more full manifestation of God's pardoning mercy. "I wait for God, my soul doth wait, I hope in his word." Although he found rest and peace in believing, yet he waited for new communications of divine light and grace to establish his heart and to diffuse joy through his soul.

When Nathan said to him, "The Lord hath put away thine iniquity – thou shalt not die," he believed that it should be even as God had spoken to him, and yet the agitations of his soul were not wholly terminated. He thought it almost incredible that such good tidings could be true. The pardon of such grievous offences seemed almost an impossibility to boundless grace, because it can never interfere with the law of eternal righteousness. A thousand anxious thoughts presented themselves to his mind, yet he held fast his faith; he rejoiced in the hope that the bones which had been broken would be completely healed, and would rejoice.

The intimation of pardon was joined with a threatening full of awe. The sword was never to depart from his house. But the fear of this sword did not destroy his confidence in God. He knew that his soul was safe although his house was to suffer, and he lived in the animating hope that God would support and cheer his heart, amidst all that he might suffer, with the assurance of his loving-kindness.

Absalom's rebellion was one part of the execution of the sentence that was gone forth against him. Many said to him that there was no succour for him in God, and no doubt his own conscience spoke harder things to him than his enemies could say; but still he waited on God for new proofs of that mercy which had blotted out his sins. "Thou, O Lord, art my shield, and my glory, and the lifter up of mine head. Why art thou cast down, O my soul? and why art thou

Of David's Faith in the Pardoning Mercy of God

disquieted within me? Hope thou in God: for I shall yet praise him, who is the health of my countenance, and my God."

Whilst he waited, he prayed. The patience of faith is not a merely passive grace. It is attended with the rigorous use of all proper means for obtaining what we wish from God. *Psalm 51* is a specimen of David's prayers, when he heard and believed the words of Nathan. Although he was assured of pardon, he prayed for it, for he never could hear too often the voice of God saying to his soul, "I am thy salvation." He prayed that he might be throughly cleansed from the pollution of sin, that he might be preserved from the bitter effects of that sin which had been forgiven. He prayed that no damage might result from it to Jerusalem. There is no true faith when the mouth and the heart are not opened to prayer.

6. His faith was attended with sanctifying effects. It was not like that confidence of pardon, too common amongst us, which disposes men to sin that grace may abound. It was a faith which purified his heart, and inspired him with zeal for good works. He loved the Lord who heard the voice of his prayer and his supplication. All that was within him blessed the holy name of the Lord, who forgave all his iniquities, who healed all his diseases, who redeemed his life from destruction. It was as impossible that a man whose heart was penetrated with such lively gratitude should continue in sin, as that a man in his sober senses should stab the heart or vilify the reputation of his dearest friend, to whom he had been indebted for the highest favours.

"Thou hast delivered my soul from death, and mine eyes from tears, and my feet from falling. I will walk before the Lord in the land of the living."

When God delivered David's eyes from tears, he saw the special love of God, and the glory of his pardoning grace in his deliverance. He resolved to walk before the Lord in the way which would be pleasing in his sight, and testify his grateful sense of the benefits received, and he wished to turn as many sinners as he could induce, by his example and advice, out of the ways of destruction, into that good path in which he found peace. "Cleanse me from blood-guiltiness, O God, thou God of my salvation: so shall I teach thy ways unto transgressors, and sinners shall be turned unto thee," (*Psalm 51*).

II. Let us now call upon you to follow David's example. Abraham was the great ancient pattern of living by faith in the promised seed. The apostle Paul speaks at great length of that faith by which he was justified, and calls upon us all to walk in the steps of his faith. But he does not overlook the example of David also, who describes, from his own experience, the blessedness of the man to whom the Lord imputeth righteousness without works. Let us now consider the following things:

1. That we cannot pretend to be better men than David. If Abraham could not be justified by works – if David could not be justified by works – if they had nothing of which they could glory before God, shall we pretend to glory in his sight?

"If any man might glory," says Paul, "I could glory also." David might have found as good reasons to glory in the flesh. He was an Israelite of the noblest of the tribes, and prince of the noblest family of the tribes, and king of all Israel. He was adorned with every virtue and every accomplishment. He was richer in good works than almost any man that ever lived. His good works were accepted of God, "who recompensed him according to his righteousness, according to the cleanness of his hands appearing in the eyes of the Lord." Yet he durst not trust in his righteousness. His faith of acceptance to his works did not embolden him to think that he could be justified by his own righteousness. "If thou, Lord, shouldest mark iniquity, O Lord, who shall stand? But there is forgiveness with thee." He could confidently appeal to God as his righteous judge when he was oppressed by men, and expected from him a sentence suited to his behaviour; but he was far from thinking he could obtain the pardon of any one of his sins as the reward of his best works. Observe all his pleas for pardon. He does not say, 'Lord, I have done many good works, let them be put into the balance with my bad works, that I may obtain favour:' but, "Have mercy upon me after thy loving-kindness: according to the multitude of thy tender mercies blot out all my transgressions."

Weigh those good works on which you value yourselves, against David's works. May it not be feared that they will be found as light as feathers, or as air weighed against gold? Will you then pretend to greater merit than this illustrious saint, or advance pleas before God,

Of David's Faith in the Pardoning Mercy of God

which he would have trembled to produce? 'Lord, if David could not stand before thee, where shall I appear? If the best of saints found it absolutely necessary to seek a righteousness without works, I must perish for ever, if the Lord enter into judgment with me.'

2. You have the same ground with David to seek righteousness through faith in the great Redeemer.

You see that David trusted to the free grace of God, and that grace is not diminished. It is not less free than in the days of old. His ways are everlasting. All the high commendations given by this holy man to the mercy of God, are as true at this time as they were three thousand years ago, and they were written for every generation to come, that they might set their hope in God.

"Cleanse me from blood-guiltiness, and I will teach thy ways unto transgressors, and sinners shall be turned unto thee." David was a teacher not to his own age only, but to all ages. He still teaches us, and God teaches us by what he did for him, to depend on that mercy which pardons iniquity, transgression and sin. Read *Psalm 130*. After telling us that his soul waited on God, he calls upon us all to wait on God for that mercy which we all need. "Let Israel hope in the Lord; for with the Lord is mercy, and with him is plenteous redemption; and he shall redeem Israel from all his iniquities."

David hoped in God's word, and we have the same word that David had for the ground of his hope. None of those sacred books are lost in which David found such transcendent pleasure. There is only one sentence in the sacred book that could give to David any better ground of hope in God's pardoning mercy than to any other believer. "The Lord hath also put away thine iniquity; thou shalt not die." The other particular promises made to him respected his royal dignity, and his relation to the Messiah according to the flesh; and everyone that doth the will of the Father stands in a relation to Christ more highly valued by him, than even that of his mother, whom all generations have called, and will call, a blessed woman. And although these words to David, "The Lord hath put away thine iniquity," were spoken by Nathan to him alone, they were written for the benefit of us all. David's heart leapt within him for joy when he heard the prophet utter them, and should not our hearts also leap for joy when we read them. They are an expression of that boundless grace on which we are called to rely for the remission of our sins. Even murder and adultery, for which no sacrifice was appointed by the law, are expiated through that blood of which the blood of ancient sacrifices was only a faint shadow.

The promises made to David, concerning the King and the kingdom of grace, are grounds of faith to us as well as to David. So we are taught by Jeremiah, "Behold the days come that I will raise up unto David the Branch of Righteousness, and a king shall reign and prosper. In his days Judah shall be saved and Israel shall dwell prosperously, and this is the name whereby he shall be called, The Lord our Righteousness."

I might have said that our encouragements to live by the faith of a Redeemer, are in some sense richer than David's. David longed for the day when the redemption of Israel should come out of Zion. It *is* now come. The apostles saw what righteous men in ancient times desired to see, but did not see; and have transmitted to us some accounts of what they saw. God hath provided for us some better things than he provided for the Old Testament saints. Our prayers are no more to be directed to God for the redemption of men, but for the more full extension of the knowledge of salvation through the remission of our sins by the blood of the great Sacrifice already presented to God, and for the consummation of all things. We have promises too of a more abundant effusion of the Spirit of light and grace. We live under a dispensation concerning which it was said of old by God, "I will pour out my Spirit upon thy seed, and my blessing upon thine offspring. The wilderness and the solitary place shall be glad for them, and the desert shall rejoice and blossom as the rose." Having such promises, let us apply our hearts to the precious discoveries made to us by the appearance and gospel of our Lord Jesus Christ. Let us wash ourselves and be clean, for a fountain is opened to us for sin and for uncleanness. Let us pray that God may verify in us his promise, "I will sprinkle clean water upon you, and ye shall be clean; from all your filthiness and from all your idols will I cleanse you."

3. Let us consider where David now is. He hath long ago received the end of his faith, the salvation of his soul. When his spirit returned to God who gave it, it would have been found naked if he had not

Of David's Faith in the Pardoning Mercy of God

been clothed with that righteousness which is by faith. That blessedness, which he describes in his Psalms, of the man to whom the Lord imputeth righteousness without works, is now enjoyed by him in all that perfection which belongs to the intermediate state; and he looks forward with joy to the still happier state which commences at the resurrection from the dead. Whilst he lived, he believed that God would receive him, and deliver him from the power of the grave. His hope hath not deceived him. If he was not one of those blessed saints that rose with Christ at the resurrection, his dust is still asleep with Jesus, and will rise up with a glory like to that of the body of his Son and Lord.

Is it our wish to be forever joined with that illustrious society of which he is a distinguished member? Then let us walk in the steps of his faith. "We through the Spirit do wait for the hope of righteousness by faith, that we may, in due time, attain the end of our faith, even the salvation of our souls."

3
Of David's Repentance

I will declare mine iniquity; I will be sorry for my sin.
(Psalm 38:18)

THERE was one eminent grace of which our Lord Jesus Christ did not set us an example, I mean, repentance for sin. He felt the weight of sin to a greater degree than any man or any devil ever felt it. None ever hated sin with such a perfect hatred, or mourned for it more bitterly than Jesus; but the sins for which he mourned were not his own in any other way than by a just imputation. David was a sinner like ourselves. He was permitted to wound his soul by some gross offences, and no saint spoken of in the Bible sets us a more distinct example of repentance in all its exercises.

1. He entertained a just sense of his sins; for he thought upon his ways in the light of the divine law, and turned his feet to God's testimonies.

There are too many whose eyes are so little turned to their past conduct, or who have such indistinct views of the law of God, that although they cannot deny that they are sinners like other men, they think their sins are not very many, and that they are very excusable. Many have been worse, and yet have died in peace and hope, and why may they not hope for peace also in their latter end, without putting themselves to any great trouble about their condition? David studied the law of God, and understood the true nature of sin. In the light of the law he viewed his own sinfulness, and saw that, without a pardon, which infinite grace alone could bestow, he was for ever undone.

"Against thee, thee only, have I sinned." These words may appear very strange to those who have never seen nor felt the evil of sin. What greater wrong could any man do to his fellow-creatures than to rob them of their honour or of their life?

He had robbed Bathsheba of that which was the glory of her sex. He had robbed Uriah and some gallant men with him of their precious life. How can he say that he had sinned against God only, as if no man or woman had suffered any injury by his behaviour?

David doubtless felt bitterly the wrong he had done to Uriah and those who perished with him, to Bathsheba, to the whole nation in the matter of Uriah; but all was a mere nothing to the indignity done to God by his conduct. He had despised the commandment of the Lord, which was neither less nor more than to despise God himself, (*2 Samuel 12:9*). As is the difference between God and mortals, so in his estimation was the difference between the injury which he had done to men, and that which he did to the Most High.

If this was the notion which he entertained of the nature of sin, he saw the evil – not only of those iniquities which are detested by men as wrongs to society, but of every transgression of the divine law – of vain and vile thoughts as well as actions. He knew that God was the Maker and Lord of his soul as well as of his body, that he understood all the imaginations of the thoughts of the heart of man, and that he will bring down the haughty heart and the proud look, as well as those that magnify themselves against him by blasphemies and by the persecution of his people.

"Who can understand his errors?" He saw himself obnoxious to the vengeance of the law not only for his known iniquities, but for many that he had forgotten, or to which he had never adverted. (*Psalm 19*).

"Behold, I was shapen in iniquity; and in sin did my mother conceive me." He traced up all his iniquities to their poisonous source in the corruption of his nature, and longed for deliverance from the body of death.

Thus was David deeply aware that he was a vile creature, a lost sinner, compassed about with innumerable evils, a brand exposed to the fire of wrath. "Against thee, thee only, have I sinned; that thou mightest be clear when thou judgest." God had threatened awful calamities as the just chastisement of his offences. He acknowledged that God was righteous in all that came upon him, in all that would ever come upon him, in all that must have come upon him through endless ages, if his sin had not been blotted out from the book of God.

2. He was penetrated with grief on account of his sins. He not only saw them to be many and great, but he felt the weight of them upon his heart. "My transgressions are gone up above mine head; as a heavy burden, they are too heavy for me to bear." If horror took hold upon him when the wicked forsook God's law, with what horror was he seized when he thought upon his own iniquities?

He not only mourned for the evils which he brought upon himself and upon his family by his sins, but he mourned still more for the dishonour be had done to God. "Against thee, thee only, have I sinned." I have broken thy commandment, I have insulted thine authority, I have grieved thy Spirit, I have given occasion to the enemies of the Lord to blaspheme. I have been blessed with the best blessings by the sovereign mercy of God. Do I thus requite the Lord? O foolish creature and unwise!

David's grief for his sin was not lessened by the discoveries which he obtained of pardon. When his terrors were abated, his grief was purified but not diminished. He knew that forgiveness was with God, not that he might be insulted with impunity, but that he might be feared. He saw the baseness of his sins in the light of God's loving-kindness, and when God was pacified towards him, he could not open his mouth for shame. Before Nathan came to him after he had sinned in the matter of Uriah the Hittite, he had mourned sore like a bear roaring under the anguish of some deadly wound. He mourned like a dove of the valley, after it was said unto him, "The Lord also hath put away thine iniquity." *Psalm 51* is a proof that he could not forgive himself although God forgave him. "His sin was ever before him."

"They shall look upon me whom they have pierced, and shall mourn for him." Jesus was not yet pierced for the sins of men. Yet David looked forward by faith to the wounds of the Redeemer, by which his stripes were healed, (*Psalm 51:7*). His need of divinely precious blood to cleanse his sins must have impressed the malignity of them deeply upon his heart. His faith in that blood which should be shed for the remission of his sins, must have melted his heart with sorrow for those iniquities that required such mysterious mercy to forgive them.

The grief of sinners too often rests on the surface of their souls, and is speedily effaced by business, by amusements, or by time. David's grief for his sins was deep and permanent. He caused his bed to swim with his tears. Many of his days and nights were spent in tears and sighs for his sins, or for those troubles in which he saw God punishing him for his iniquities. Through life he retained his sense of the evils that he had done. His penitential Psalms show that he did not forget his abominations when God remembered them no more, but still continued to present unto God the sacrifice of a broken and a contrite spirit.

3. He hated sin. He was not only grieved to his heart that he had transgressed against the Lord, but he hated and abhorred that abominable thing which God hated. He abhorred himself and repented in dust and ashes, and sought the destruction of that principle of corruption which had been productive of such horrible effects. For a thousand worlds he would not again have done what he did when temptation prevailed against him. A man who finds that his bones are broken by falling from the top of a house, will not be induced by any consideration again to throw himself down from the same place. David's bones were broken, and he could never forgive that cruel enemy of his soul who had broken them. He hated the work of them that turned aside, and resolved that it should never cleave to him. He hated not only open works of sin, but all the pollutions of the heart. "I hate vain thoughts, but thy law do I love." It was impossible, when he entertained such a dear regard to the law of God, that he should love sin. A man who wishes to be for ever with Christ will as soon love eternal death. He will as soon desire to dwell for ever both with God and with the devil, as love sin whilst he loves the law of God.

David esteemed all God's precepts concerning all things to be right, and therefore he hated every false way. If you love any sin, you must esteem that part of the law which forbids it to be wrong. Although David was sometimes taken in the snare of sin, yet he hated those very iniquities which ensnared him. We find him sometimes drawn by imminent danger to make a lie his refuge; yet he hated and abhorred lying, and would not suffer liars to abide in his sight. He was chargeable once with murder, and once with adultery, but he cried to God to "create in him a clean heart and to renew a right spirit within him," and his prayers were heard. The acts of sin in unregenerate men, lead them on to the habits of sin; these are attended by a delight in iniquity, which renders reformation hopeless. But when David was drawn away by his lust into any sin, he bitterly repented. He thought upon all the intolerable malignity of his particular offences, and conceived an implacable hatred to those evils which now appeared out of measure grievous in his eyes.

Wherever he saw sin he hated it. He hated in some sense the persons guilty of it. "Do not I hate, O Lord, all them that hate thee; can I but be grieved with those that rise up against thee?" But his hatred of the haters of God was not a cruel, but a merciful hatred. The charity of bad men is impure, and often cruel; the hatred of good men is holy, and often charitable. David hated the wicked, not as God's creatures, but as God's enemies. He prayed that God might not be merciful to any wicked transgressor, but he prayed also for the conversion of sinners, and desired grace for himself that he might teach transgressors God's ways, that sinners might be turned unto him.

It was a determined and irreconcilable hatred which David entertained towards sin. All his days he was at war with it, for he determined to keep God's law continually for ever and ever. Although iniquities sometimes prevailed against him, and made him to stray like a lost sheep, yet he did not forget God's commandments; and as long as a man remembers these with delight, he will continue to hate every false way. (*Psalm 71; 2 Samuel 23*).

4. He confessed his sins, his original sin, his actual sin. He confessed himself guilty of many sins which he could not reckon up, and he confessed with sorrow those particular iniquities which he remembered. He confessed them to God, and he confessed them to men, when it was expedient to confess them. When Nathan reproved him he did not reckon the reproof a poisonous draught, but a precious oil that would not break his head. "I have sinned against the Lord." These words were few, but the heart of the penitent was in them. It was probably so full that he could say no

more, till he had obtained more composure of spirit. Judas said, "I have sinned, in that I have betrayed innocent blood." Pharaoh said, "I and my people are wicked." Saul said, "I have sinned, for I have transgressed the commandment of the Lord, and thy words." But the words of these men are not expressive of the sentiments, the gracious affections, the shame, the self-loathing, the piercing grief for sin itself as well as its miserable consequences, which dictated the words of David. The Lord heard the words of all these men, and he knew those affections of heart from which they proceeded. He did not hear with a favourable ear the words of Judas or Pharaoh or Saul. Their confessions were extorted from them by a mere sense of the mischiefs they had brought upon themselves. He heard with delight the confession of David, for it presented before him the sacrifice of a broken and of a contrite spirit, which thou, O Lord, wilt not despise.

You confess that you are sinners. What thanks have you for confessing what you cannot deny, and what is common to you with all the rest of mankind? You can no more be praised for acknowledging that you are a sinner, than for confessing that you are not an angel of heaven. You must confess your sins, and not merely that you are sinners. And you ought not only to confess them to God, but to confess them, likewise, to men when edification requires it. Paul readily confessed that he erred through ignorance in what he said to the high priest in the council. David confessed his sin not only to God but to Nathan, and to all Israel, and to all the generations of the saints. He confesses and bewails his adultery and murder in *our* ears. He knew that every age would hear of his sin, and he wished that every age should hear of his repentance. He was deeply ashamed that he had sinned, but he was not ashamed to confess his sin. He was very unlike some who sin without shame, but are ashamed to bring forth the fruits of repentance. Their nice and ill-regulated sense of honour spreads and perpetuates their disgrace.

David's name would have sunk under his crimes if he had continued to use unhallowed shifts to hide his iniquity, but his confessions have fully retrieved his character. We are not ignorant of the baseness of his conduct in the matter of Uriah, but who will ever think of comparing with this holy man that king of Galilee who cut off John the Baptist's head for reproving his adultery? The blameless Samuel and Daniel have not left a sweeter memorial than David who greatly sinned but greatly repented, and left behind him his confessions to be the model of ours.

5. David's repentance operated in fervent supplications. If we have a just sense of sin, and just views of our own sins; if we are ashamed of our iniquities and hate them with irreconcilable aversion, we will earnestly desire to be completely delivered from them and from all their bitter effects. But who shall deliver us from these worst of all evils, or rather these only evils? All evil consists in sin and in its bitter consequences. None can deliver us but God only, and to him will the true penitent seek for this all comprehensive deliverance with all the desire of his heart.

To God we find David often seeking, with all earnestness and importunity, for deliverance from the guilt of sin, from the pollution of sin, from the sorrows and distresses into which sin had brought him.

Although the Lord said unto him by Nathan, that his iniquity was put away, yet he prays (*Psalm 51*) again and again that God would have mercy upon him and blot out his iniquities. He did not call in question the truth of God's assurance, but desired more full assurance of his pardon, that the bones which God had broken might rejoice.

He was afraid that the malignant influence of the sins he had committed might still cleave to his heart to dispose him to new instances of misconduct, and to obstruct the exercise of grace in his soul. He therefore prays that God would work in his heart and subdue his iniquities with the same exceeding greatness of power which he usually displays when he begins a work of grace in the soul. "Create in me a clean heart, O God; and renew a right spirit within me."

He saw that God hated iniquity with an invariable and infinite hatred. He was afraid that after such provocations as he had given to the Holy One, he might never again be admitted to the enjoyment of those delicious pleasures that he had often tasted in his intercourse with heaven, and therefore he earnestly begged that God would restore to him the joy of his salvation, and never take his Holy Spirit from him.

He was afraid that the malignant influence of his sin might extend to the people and to the sanctuary of the Lord. When he prayed for pardon for himself, he expressed his ardent desire that sinners might be turned to the Lord, that God would do good to Zion in his good pleasure, and build up the walls of Jerusalem. Most devoutly he desired that none who waited upon the Lord might be ashamed for his sake, and when the hand of the Lord was stretched out against Jerusalem for his sin, he prayed that the hand of the Lord might rather be upon himself and upon his father's house.

6. His repentance appeared in all its proper fruits. David was not one of those men who sin and repent, and sin again, as if their repentance made full amends for their former debts, and left them at liberty to contract new debts to be paid off with equal ease. David committed adultery, but he was more chaste than many of those sober men who say, 'God, I thank thee that I am no adulterer.' Never did he return to the abominable iniquity, when he was purged from it. He hated sensual impurities with a more deadly hatred than those saints who were never permitted to pollute their bodies with the gross evil of unchastity.

He endeavoured to undo what he had done by removing all that offence which he had given, and as he had yielded his members as instruments of unrighteousness unto sin, he yielded himself to God like a person recovered from sin, and his members as instruments of righteousness unto holiness. Conscious of his own weakness, his prayer was to the God of his life, "that his feet might be kept from falling, to walk before God in the light of the living."

"Who can understand his errors? Cleanse thou me from secret faults, keep back thy servant also from presumptuous sins. Let them not have dominion over me. Then shall I be righteous and innocent from the great transgression." His sense of his past sins fired him with indignation against sin, and opened his mouth in ardent supplications, attended with suitable endeavours that he might not be suffered any more to fall by the power of those lusts which warred against his soul.

When his conscience was purged from guilt, his lips were opened to declare the righteousness and the truth of God, that sinners might be turned unto him. It is a good sign of real penitence to seek and

Of David's Repentance

labour to bring other sinners to repentance. It is to be feared that we have all done those evils by our example which we cannot repair. Let it be our endeavour to do at least as much damage as we have ever done service to the kingdom of Satan.

When Theodosius the Emperor was not admitted by Ambrose, bishop of Milan, to his ordinary place in the church, because in a fit of anger he had given unrighteous orders to destroy some of the inhabitants of Thessalonica, he pleaded the example of David for his excuse. 'You speak of David's sin,' said the good bishop, 'Let us see David's repentance, and then expect to have your privileges restored.' The Emperor could not deny the justice of the admonition. He exhibited satisfying proofs of the humblest penitence, and recovered both his place in the church and the esteem of men.

You have all sinned like David, although none of you have ever performed the half of his good works, or any good work with his ardour of spirit. Follow then the example of David's repentance. Think upon your ways, and turn your feet to God's testimonies with a sincere abhorrence of your former ways.

David was brought to repentance of his guilt in the matter of Uriah, by Nathan, who reminded him of the great things God had done for him, and set his iniquity before him in the light of God's commandments. Consider what great things God has done for you, and whether you have given due proofs of your gratitude by obedience to God's law. God gave David a kingdom. He hath done infinitely greater things for us all than if he had conferred upon us the monarchy of the whole earth. "He spared not his own Son, but delivered him up for us all." Let us look upon him who was pierced for us, and mourn as one mourneth for his only son. What infinite goodness do we see in the cross of Christ! To this infinite goodness we have made the most ungrateful returns. We have poured insufferable contempt upon Him who sent his Son to die for us, upon Him who gave his precious life to save us from destruction, upon that eternal Spirit through whom Christ offered himself for us a spotless sacrifice. Be astonished, O heavens, and let the earth be horribly afraid. The dwellers on the earth have rebelled against him who left the Father and came into this world to save them from destruction by bearing their curse. Through the blood of Jesus I obtain forgiveness for all those enormities by which I have provoked the God whose mercy is so high above the heavens. I will never forgive that old man which is corrupt according to the deceitful lusts, that body of sin which raised my hand against my God and Saviour, which nailed my Lord to the cross, which made my death inevitable if he had not died for me an accursed death.

David saw only at a distance the accomplishment of our redemption. Like the other ancient prophets he searched diligently what or what manner of time the Spirit of Christ which was in them did signify, when it testified beforehand the sufferings of Christ and the glory that should follow. But he knew and foretold that when that redemption was accomplished, all the ends of the earth should remember and turn to the Lord. Let us all seek to be found in the happy number of them in whom this prophecy shall have its accomplishment.

Think of the vileness of that abominable thing which could not be washed away but by the blood of the Son of God. Think of that awful justice, which would not suffer the least sin to escape unpunished. Consider in how many instances you have transgressed that holy law which was magnified and made honourable in the death of our Redeemer. Seek the pardon of all your innumerable offences through that precious blood, and beholding the glory of those perfections which you have dishonoured by your sins, manifested in the method of your salvation, be ashamed and confounded because of your ways. Hear the voice of God speaking peace to your souls, and turn not again to folly. By seeing and hearing what the prophets of ancient times were not permitted to see or to hear, you have advantages above them to balance those advantages which they enjoyed in the privilege of inspiration. Inspiration did not give them such clear views of the atonement as many without inspiration have obtained under the Gospel. And although by the law is that knowledge of sin which strikes terror into the heart, yet by the Gospel we have the clearest views of that abominable vileness in sin which should inspire us with detestation, and the Gospel alone gives us those views of the mercy of God which dispose us to mourn for sin after a godly sort. We know far more clearly than the saints in David's time, or perhaps than David himself, what is the meaning of these words, "There is forgiveness with thee, that thou mayest be feared." Who would not fear God, and stand in awe of offending him, when he hath set forth his own Son to be a propitiation through faith in his blood? The best of men must perish for ever without the atonement, otherwise Christ must have died in vain.

As we ought through life to bring forth the fruits of repentance, so when we are left to fall into any wilful sin, we ought to follow David's example, in mourning, in confessing our iniquity, in imploring pardon, in waiting and longing and crying for the manifestations of God's pardoning mercy. Think not that when you have fallen into grievous sins you have nothing more to do than to mention your sin in your prayers, and then recover your usual serenity of spirit. You have little of David's spirit if sin appears such a slight matter. Remember how David's soul was poured out within him, what sighs and groans he uttered under the impressions of those evils into which he was drawn by the power of lust.

David seems to have continued long under the power of murder and adultery before he repented after a godly sort. But his heart was in the interim harrowed with remorse. He never tasted true joy till he returned to God, with much weeping and with importunate supplication. (*Psalm 32, 51*).

4
David's Love to God

"THOU shalt love the Lord thy God with all thine heart, with all thy soul, with all thy strength, and with all thy mind. This is the first and great commandment," and no saint under the Old Testament gave clearer evidence of an ardent and supreme love to God than David. His soul appears to have been made for love. Dearly he loved his children, his friends, his subjects; but whom had he in heaven but God, and there was none on earth that he desired besides him. – Let us consider:

I. The nature of this love.

II. The reasons of it.

III. Some of the expressions of it.

I. Let us consider the nature of this love.

Some think that there cannot exist such an affection as love to the invisible God in the heart of man. He is unseen by us. He is high above us, and they think that all pretensions to the love of a being so incomprehensible to us must be mere imposture or enthusiasm. 'Let us be virtuous,' say they, 'and do all the good we can to our fellow-men. This is all that love to God which he expects from the dwellers of the dust: their goodness cannot reach to him.'

David was a man of like passions with us, and yet he loved God with an affection pure and holy, far removed from that enthusiastic ardour of false devotion, which may have been too justly attributed to some blind devotees, and which has been falsely attributed to many of the true saints of God.

1. David's love to God was founded in just apprehensions of his amiable character.

We cannot love an object that is utterly unknown, and we can never love God so much as he deserves to be loved, because we know him but in part. It was but little that even David knew of him, but he knew so much as to be fully persuaded that he was the best as well as the greatest of beings, and that his loveliness was equal to his grandeur.

In *Psalm 36* he speaks with indignation of the wickedness of profligate transgressors; but he was cheered by turning his thoughts to God, and contemplating the beauties of his nature. "Thy mercy, O Lord, is in the heavens; thy faithfulness reacheth unto the clouds. Thy righteousness is like the great mountains; thy judgments are a great deep. O Lord, thou preservest man and beast. How excellent is thy loving-kindness, therefore the children of men put their trust under the shadow of thy wings. For with thee is the fountain of life: in thy light shall we see light."

It is certain that God dwells in light inaccessible, but it is no less certain that his beauty is displayed in his Word and in his works, to the astonishment of every wise beholder. David surveyed the works of God which men behold; he saw the mercy of God filling the earth. He found himself encompassed on every side with goodness unutterable. He could not lift up his eyes to the sun and to the stars without admiration of that benignity which caused the sun to rule by day, and the moon by night. When he meditated on the law of the Lord he found still greater reason to admire that mercy which spares transgressing mortals, and gives them the hope of salvation through the remission of their sins.

But God appeared to him amiable in the rectitude and purity as well as in the benignity of his nature. He did not consider the just God as a severe and inexorable tyrant, but was fully satisfied with his character as the righteous judge, who will not suffer transgressors always to rejoice in impunity, but will render to every man according to his works, (*Psalm 62:12*). Because the righteous Lord loveth righteousness, he rejoiced in his name, and teaches us all to rejoice, not only because he dispenses the blessings of his grace to the unworthy, but because he sits on his throne judging righteously and making the rebellious to inherit a dry land. (*Psalm 9, 68*).

2. David delighted in God and in all the discoveries which he made of his goodness.

It was his joy that God is what he is, and nothing but what he is. He was so well pleased with the character given of God in his own Word, that he would rather have died a thousand times than wished the least alteration in it. He felt much disconformity in his own heart to the law and to the holiness of God, but he neither thought nor wished that God were such as he was, but he ardently wished to be more like to God, and more conformable to his holy law. "Thy word is very pure, therefore thy servant loveth it." Those who falsely call themselves God's servants, do not love the law because it is very pure. They would love it better were it less pure than it is. They would love God better than they do if he were less inflexible in his demands of perfect purity; but the true saint esteems all God's precepts, every part of his Word, concerning all things, to be right. He gives thanks at the remembrance of God's holiness; he sees an infinite beauty in those perfections which are the terror of selfish men. Jesus Christ, the image of the invisible God, is to him altogether lovely, and his highest delight is to contemplate with joy those excellencies which are the everlasting subject of the songs of angels and saints.

He delighted in God as his own God, and his portion. He said unto the Lord, "Thou art my refuge, O Lord, and my portion in the land of the living." Whilst some trust in horses and chariots, whilst others say to the gold, Thou art our hope, and to the fine gold, Thou art our confidence; whilst others place all their happiness in earthly friends, it was David's happiness that he could say to the Lord – "I will love thee, O Lord, my strength. The Lord is my rock, and my fortress, and my deliverer, my God, my strength in whom I will trust, my buckler, and the horn of my salvation, and my high tower."

Such joy in God cannot certainly exist when there is no faith in God, as our own God, and therefore it is evident that the same commandment which requires us to love the Lord our God with all our heart, requires us also to trust in him. Every commandment must require all that is essentially necessary for performing that obedience which it requires.

We joy in God through our Lord Jesus Christ. David rejoiced in God through the promised Saviour. He saw that there was mercy with him, and plenteous redemption. He trusted in that mercy which the word of promise revealed, and placed all his happiness in the favour of God, which was better to him than life – than all those enjoyments which render life desirable. In his favour is life. "Because thy loving-kindness is better than life, my lips shall praise thee."

3. Earnest desires of more intimate fellowship with God possessed the heart of this holy man.

He was often driven from his dwelling. On these occasions he did not so much regret his exile from his country or from his house, as his banishment from the sanctuary of the Lord. "If they be the children of men who have stirred thee up against me, cursed be they before the Lord, for they have driven me out this day from abiding in the inheritance of the Lord." "When I remember these things I pour out my soul, for I had gone with the multitude; I went with them to the house of God, with the voice of joy and praise, with a multitude that kept holy day," (*1 Samuel 26:19; Psalm 42:4*).

He longed at such seasons to behold again the sanctuary in which the Lord dwelt, to see the face of the men who took pleasure in the institutions of God, to converse with them about everlasting things. But what he desired above all was to see the glory of God manifested in his ordinances. "O Lord, thou art my God; early will I seek thee: my soul thirsteth for thee, my flesh longeth for thee in a dry and thirsty land, where no water is, that I may see thy power and thy glory as I have seen thee in the sanctuary."

You have perhaps been astonished to read some of David's ardent expressions of love to the sanctuary of God. Although Christian ordinances excel in glory and utility over the ordinances of the law, yet there are few Christians whose hearts are inflamed with a love so ardent to the institutions of Jesus as David felt for the ordinances of Moses. But God was enjoyed by true believers in the ancient institutions. It was this that rendered them precious in their eyes. "I have loved the habitation of thine house, and the place where thine honour dwelleth. A day in thy courts is better than a thousand. I had rather be a door keeper in the house of my God, than to dwell in the tents of wickedness." Why? For "the Lord God is a sun and shield: he will give grace and glory: he will withhold no good thing from them that walk uprightly."

When David desired re-admission to the sanctuary, it was not the ordinance that drew his regard any further than as it was a means of fellowship with God. "O send forth thy light and thy truth: let them lead me and bring me to thy holy hill, even to the place of thy tabernacles; then will I go to the altar of God, to God mine exceeding joy," (*Psalm 43:3, 4*).

As David earnestly desired fellowship with God on earth, he doubtless looked forward with earnest expectation to the more perfect enjoyment of God in a better world. "Thou shalt guide me with thy counsel, and afterward receive me to thy glory," (*Psalm 73:24*).

These were probably the words of Asaph, but Asaph was not more spiritually-minded than David. He firmly believed "that God would redeem him from the power of the grave," or of the invisible world, (*Psalm 49:15*). Amidst the distresses of the present life, it was his joy that a day was coming in which he would be admitted to the full enjoyment of God. "With thee is the fountain of life: in thy light shall we see light. As for me I shall behold thy face in righteousness: when I awake I shall be satisfied with thy likeness."

4. David was zealous for the honour and interests of God.

Zeal for God is essential to the character of a saint. How can we say that we love any man if his interest or honour is a matter of indifference to us? And if we love God above all creatures, nothing will be of so much consequence to us as the glory of God and the advancement of his dearest interests in the world.

David had learned the chief end of man. He made it his great business to glorify God in all things, and nothing gave him deeper concern than the dishonours done to God by ungodly men. "The zeal of thine house hath eaten me up" (*Psalm 69:9*). These words are applied to our Lord Jesus Christ, (*John 2:17*). But they were true of David himself, as well as of David's Lord. Horror took hold upon him, because of the wicked that forsook God's law. Rivers of waters ran down his eyes at the sight of the transgressions of the wicked.

He no doubt was attentive to his own interest. He was attentive to the interests of his people; but his dearest interests were those of the kingdom of God. He was not so much grieved at the indignities and wrongs done by his enemies to himself, as at the indignities done by them to his God. He prayed, he laboured with unceasing perseverance for the advancement of religion. He gloried in the title of God's servant, and was constantly devoted to his fear.

II. Let us consider the reason of David's ardent love to God.

That question is easily answered, Why we all ought to love the Lord with all our hearts. The reasons are so plain and clear that nothing but extreme depravity of heart can be given as the reason why anything earthly should occupy that place in our hearts which is due to God only. Yet none of us will truly love God till our natural enmity is subdued by the power of his grace through the Word of truth.

1. David knew and believed the love of God to himself.

While God appears to us as an enemy, we will hate him. It is not in human nature, or in any nature whatsoever, to love one who appears in the light of an enemy, determined and able to destroy. Christians are indeed enabled to love their enemies, but they know that their enemies can do them no lasting hurt, and that all their malevolence will tend to the furtherance of their salvation when they are enabled to love them for God's sake.

David believed the word of grace revealing the mercy of God to men, and laying a just and firm foundation for his confidence, and his heart was inflamed with grateful love. "Because thy loving-kindness is better than life, my lips shall praise thee," (*Psalm 63:3*).

Although the Son of God had not yet appeared in human flesh to pay the price of our redemption, David, in the faith of the promise, knew and believed the love of God to himself, and to others of the sons of Adam whom he was to deliver from their sins. "Many, O Lord my God, are the wonderful works which thou hast done, and thy thoughts which are to us-ward, they cannot be reckoned up in order unto thee: if I would declare and speak of them, they are more than can be numbered," (*Psalm 40:5*). The wonders of divine mercy far transcended his thoughts and his praises, yet he could not withhold himself from making mention of the chief of God's ways

David's Love to God

of grace, the expected appearance of his Son to put away sin by the sacrifice of himself. It is in the person of Christ himself that he speaks, when he introduces the council of peace between him and his Father concerning our salvation. "Sacrifice and offering thou wouldest not, but a body hast thou prepared me. In burnt offerings and sacrifices for sin thou hast had no pleasure. Then said I, Lo, I come; to do thy will, O my God, I take delight; yea, thy law is in my heart," (*Psalm 40:6-8*).

Through the promised Saviour he believed in God for the remission of his sins, and life everlasting, and he could not but love and bless and praise the author of such precious benefits. "Bless the Lord, O my soul: and all that is within me, bless his holy name. Bless the Lord, O my soul, and forget not all his benefits: who forgiveth all thine iniquities; who healeth all thy diseases; who redeemeth thy life from destruction; who crowneth thee with loving-kindness and tender mercies," (*Psalm 103:1-4*).

"Oh how great is thy goodness, which thou hast laid up for them that love thee, which thou hast wrought for them that trust in thee before the sons of men." In the view of all that unutterable blessedness prepared for believers in God, the holy Psalmist calls upon them all to give Him their whole hearts, "O love the Lord, all ye his saints," (*Psalm 31:19-23*). A flame was kindled in his own breast, and he wished that every saint might feel a like ardour of devotion.

2. To the faith and hope of the Psalmist was added rich experience of God's kindness. He not only hoped in God's Word and waited for the accomplishment of it, but actually found it in part accomplished to him, both in the state of his soul, and in his outward circumstances.

All that light and purity, all those spiritual comforts which he enjoyed, were ascribed by him to God, the giver of every good thing, and therefore we often find him giving thanks to God for teaching him, for quickening him, for lifting up the light of his countenance upon him.

All the deliverance from trouble, and all the signal mercies which he enjoyed during the course of his varied life, inspired him with gratitude to God, and enlarged his views of that mercy and righteousness in which he so greatly delighted. "I will love thee, O Lord, my strength. I love the Lord, because he hath heard the voice of my supplications.

I will praise thee with my whole heart, for great is thy mercy unto me, and thou hast delivered my soul from the lowest hell."

It is too usual with us, whatever mercies we have received, to lose our sense of them in the troubles which are mingled with our felicities. Thus our gratitude to God is repressed, and we lose the chief benefit of the good things which we enjoy because we do not improve them as incentives to the love of God. But David had a very different way of viewing the good and the bad incidents of his life. He was not only conscious that every benefit he enjoyed was the fruit of undeserved mercy, and that the evils which he endured were the fruit of his own misconduct, but he considered the evil things of life as favours from God, as the corrections of a father, intended to make him a partaker of God's holiness. He saw that all the paths of God towards him were mercy and truth, and that all the varied dispensations of providence were one continued trait of mercy that had been following him all the days of his life.

3. Think not that David's love to God was mercenary and selfish. He loved God as all true believers will do, because God first loved him; but he did not love God merely because God loved him, but because God was infinitely lovely in himself. He saw the amiableness of the divine nature in that goodness which was showed to himself. "I love the Lord because he hath heard my voice and my supplications ... Gracious is the Lord, and righteous; yea, our Lord is merciful. The Lord preserveth the simple: I was brought low, and he helped me," (*Psalm 116:1, 5, 6*).

We cannot know God any other way than by the discoveries which he hath made of himself to us. And what discoveries of God are more endearing to our hearts than the benefits which he bestows on ourselves, especially those glorious blessings which he bestows on our souls in Christ Jesus? When we know the love of God to us in Christ, we see God to be love itself, and when the Spirit of faith works powerfully in our hearts by these discoveries, we love the Lord with all our heart and soul and strength and mind, because he appears infinitely lovely in his own nature as well as being the giver of every good and perfect gift.

David contemplated the beauty of the Lord not only in the favours granted or promised to himself, but in all that profusion of bounties with which the creation is filled. *Psalm 104* is a proof amongst others of his holy compositions, that his soul was ravished with admiration, and that his heart often overflowed with joy at the consideration of what God has done and is ever doing not only for his creatures of the human race, but for all the creatures that have life, and of those impressions of goodness that we may behold even in the face of the inanimate creation. "The glory of the Lord shall endure for ever: the Lord shall rejoice in his works ... I will sing unto the Lord as long as I live: I will sing praise to my God while I have my being. My meditation of him shall be sweet: I will be glad in the Lord," (*Psalm 104*).

But it was chiefly in the sanctuary that David beheld the beauty of the Lord, and therefore this one thing he desired above everything else, "to dwell in the house of the Lord all the days of his life, to behold the beauty of the Lord, and to inquire in his temple." Charmed with the discoveries he there obtained of the power and glory of the Lord, he anticipated the joys of heaven, and felt his heart enlarged and inflamed. He saw not everything in the institutions of the law which we may see in them by the light of the Gospel; but it is plain that he saw, both in the writings and in the institutions of Moses, much more of the beauty of the Lord than the greater part of us see in the more spiritual institutions of the New Testament, and in the richer displays of grace now made to the church by the appearance of Jesus Christ.

All the discoveries made in the works and Word of God are unavailing to us without the Spirit. Without his illuminating influence we cannot understand them. Without his sanctifying influence they cannot impress the heart. David was blessed with rich communications of the spirit of faith, and we having the same spirit of faith will find our love to God increased by every view that is given us of the grace, of the holiness, of all the incomparable excellencies of God. To know him aright is to love him, and the more we know and think of him, we will love him the more; for everything in him is lovely, and there is nothing lovely wanting in him with whom is the fountain of life and goodness. – Let us now consider:

III. How David's love to God operated on his heart and life.

It is certain that where love exists it will work. If we love our neighbours we will endeavour to contribute to their happiness. We cannot contribute to the happiness of the Almighty. Our goodness cannot reach him. Yet love to him where it exists is strong as death, and will not be buried in the heart. It is stronger if it be genuine, than that love which we have to any of our fellow-creatures. We do not love him at all, if we do not love him as the infinite God whose beauty and goodness can admit of no comparison.

1. When we entertain a warm affection to any person we think of him with pleasure. David's thoughts were daily and nightly occupied by the perfections, the works and the law of his God. Such meditations were delightful to his heart. They afforded him pleasure when his condition appeared to be utterly deplorable and desperate. When he was in a dry and thirsty land where no water was, he was satisfied as with marrow and with fatness whilst he remembered God upon his bed and meditated on him in the night watches.

2. When we love any person we take pleasure in the enjoyment of his company, and David took pleasure in every means of fellowship with God. He delighted in reading and studying the Word of God – in prayer, in the institutions of the sanctuary. Whilst others said, "Who will shew us any good?" the language of David's heart was, "Lord, lift thou up the light of thy countenance upon us." Whilst other men diligently employed every method to obtain the gratification of their reigning desires, David did the same. His reigning desire was that God might be glorified, and that he might be happy in the enjoyment of God. This prevailing temper of his soul gave the direction to the whole course of his life. A day spent where he might hope to meet with God, was better to him than a thousand. A thousand years without the enjoyment of God, though spent amidst all the pleasures of this world, would have been to him a dreary blank in existence, for there was none on earth that he desired besides the Lord. All his salvation and all his desire were concentrated in the everlasting covenant that God had made with him.

3. We endeavour in all things reasonable to please those whom we love. David in all things endeavoured to please God, and therefore God himself bore witness of him, that he was a man according to his own heart.
"Ye are my friends," says Christ, "if ye do whatsoever I command you." We may be the friends of men when we disobey them. Our best

friends ought not to please us any further than our wishes are consistent with reason and religion; but none of God's commandments ought to be disputed. His will is invariably wise and righteous, and true love must show itself in obeying. Such was David's disposition: he made it his constant business to walk so as to please God. "I have sworn, and I will perform it, to keep thy righteous judgments." It must be confessed that David's obedience was not absolutely perfect. It was too high a compliment paid him by the widow of Tekoah when she said, "My lord the king is wise as an angel of God to know all that is done in the earth." And we would pass too high a compliment upon him if we should say that the will of God was as well done by him as by the angels in heaven. Yet it was undoubtedly the reigning desire of his heart, and the habitual endeavour of his life to yield an unreserved obedience to the will of God. His own will was disregarded by him when it stood in competition with the commandment of the Lord. He sometimes erred through inadvertency. Once he turned aside from following the Lord; but when he came to himself he was pierced with sorrow for his transgression. He would rather have died a thousand times than return to folly.

4. Love is expressed by dissatisfaction at everything injurious or offensive to its object. Sin is the only thing that God hates. Sin alone is injurious to his honour and interest. Although it cannot diminish in the least degree his blessedness, it does what it can to bring him down from the throne of his glory, and therefore will be hated by all who love him. David makes it a sign of depravity when men do not abhor evil, (*Psalm 36:4*). And his own hatred of sin was an evidence that he was a sincere lover of him whose glory lies in the absolute perfection of his holiness. He hated sin in himself, and carefully he kept himself from his own iniquity. He hated sin wherever he saw it, and would not suffer it in his house or in his sight, (*Psalm 101*).

5. Sincere love to God is manifested by an affectionate regard to every thing and to every person loved by God.

God loves the gates of Zion, and David loved the habitation of God's house. God loves holiness in all its extent, and David above all things wished to be perfect in holiness. The Lord loveth mercy, and David took pleasure in showing mercy to his fellow-men. God loveth his saints, and David was the companion of all them that fear and obey him. God loves the stranger in giving him food and raiment; David praised God for his goodness to the stranger, the fatherless and widow, and was a follower of God in this as well as in other instances of his mercy. Joab knew this part of David's character when he employed a widow of Tekoah to move his compassion on behalf of Absalom, (*2 Samuel 14*). Ittai the Gittite, though a stranger, was one of David's favourites.

6. David's love to God showed forth its power in those praises and blessings which were continually proceeding from his mouth.

By such instances of conduct David made it evident that he loved God, not in word or in tongue, but in deed and in truth. Let us pray to God that he may circumcise our hearts, like his, to love the Lord our God with all our heart and with all our soul. It is only the Spirit of God that can subdue the selfishness, the earthliness, the sensuality of our spirits, that we may set our hearts on God as the great object of our love. But whilst we implore the grace of the Spirit, let us not neglect the means by which he works upon the heart.

David thought upon all the various manifestations which God had given to his ancient people of his goodness and beauty. We are blessed with brighter displays of that grace which ought to attract our hearts. God has now fulfilled the great promise which was the hope of David and of all the ancient saints. "He hath showed forth his righteousness and salvation in the sight of the nations. All the ends of the earth have seen the salvation of our God. Greater love hath no man than this, that a man lay down his life for his friends. Hereby perceive we the love of God, because he laid down his life for us." Are not our hearts harder than the adamant, if they are not melted by the love of God in Christ Jesus who died for us? Hath God given us the pardon of all our sins? Hath he received us into the number of his children, and given us a right to life everlasting? "We love him because he first loved us." We love him with a supreme, a steady, an inextinguishable love. He loved us and gave his Son for us when we were enemies, when we were abominable in his sight. May God shed abroad his love in our hearts; then will we give him our whole hearts, and testify our love in all holy conversation and godliness.

5
David's Confidence in God

HAPPY is the man who hath a true friend, in whose kindness he can place an unreserved confidence. His afflictions are consoled and his blessings are sweetened by the pleasing intercourses of love. But our earthly friends may fail us in the time that we most need their assistance. They may die. Their hearts may be alienated from us. Their sympathy in many cases may be of little use. But happy is the man who hath the God of Jacob for his refuge. If all his earthly friends should, like Job's friends, prove miserable comforters in the day of his distress, the Lord will ever be a present help in the time of trouble.

It was David's happiness that he could say of the Lord, "He is my light and my salvation, he is my refuge and my God, and in him will I trust." Let us learn from his example how to trust in the Lord at all times.

I. David had just views of those sure grounds of confidence by which he was encouraged at all times to put his confidence in God.

"They that know thy name will put their trust in thee." But how can these men put their trust in God, who know not his name? If they hope for good from him, how do they know that they are not deceiving themselves? We read of men that looked carefully for good, but evil came down to them from the Lord of hosts. Not every man who hopes to receive the blessing from the Lord shall actually receive it, but he whose hope is built upon a sure foundation. The Lord will fulfil all the promises which he hath made, but he will not fulfil those promises which self-flattering sinners make to themselves.

"Remember," says David, "thy word unto thy servant, on which thou hast caused me to hope." The Word of God must be a stable ground of hope, for it is for ever established in the heavens. The pillars of heaven may be overturned, but the Word of the Lord endureth for ever.

We are sinful creatures. David was by nature a sinner like ourselves, and his heart was privy to much iniquity, that must have proved fatal to him if it had not been taken away by the pardoning mercy of God; but from the Word of God he learned that with the Lord is mercy, and with him is plenteous redemption. He learned from the Word and institutions of God that sin was to be taken away by a great Sacrifice of atonement, to be offered in due time for the sins of men. And therefore though the law had appointed no sacrifice for murder and adultery, yet under the consciousness of these crimes he could cry to the Lord, "Wash me, and I shall be clean; sprinkle me with hyssop, and I shall be whiter than the snow."

Every perfection of God revealed in his Word and in his works was a firm ground of confidence to his soul. He trusted in the power, in the faithfulness, in the righteousness of his God. When we know that a man is at once able and willing to help us, we place in him all that confidence that can be placed in a human creature; but we are fully assured in the Scripture that the kindness of God is as much superior to the kindness of a father, as his power is superior to that of an arm of flesh. "This God is our God for ever and ever. Our safety cometh from the Lord who made heaven and earth. As we have heard, so have we seen, in the city of the Lord. His right hand is ever full of righteousness."

David's faith in God was confirmed not only by the manifold proofs which God had given of his power and faithfulness to his people in every age, but by what he had seen and tasted of God's goodness to himself. Although his hope was in God's Word, which he accounted abundantly sufficient to establish an unwavering confidence, yet his experience of the truth of God's Word strengthened his hope. "Because thou hast been my refuge, therefore in the shadow of thy wings will I rejoice."

II. The holy man's confidence in God was unlimited. He committed to the Lord his soul, his body, his outward circumstances, his family, and everything that was dear to him, in the confidence that the Lord would perfect all that concerned him.

Conscious of his sins he trusted in divine mercy for the free and full pardon of all his iniquities. Although his transgressions were red like crimson, he believed that through divine grace they should be white like snow or wool.

He trusted in God for light and grace, to carry on and perfect the work of his sanctification. In this confidence we find him praying that God would enlighten him more and more, in the knowledge of his Word, create in him a clean heart, and renew a right spirit within him, uphold him by his free Spirit, and lead him by it to the land of uprightness.

In his distresses of every kind he trusted in the Lord that he would deliver him. When he walked through the valley of the shadow of death he did not cast away his confidence, but believed that God would quicken him and bring him again from the lower parts of the earth.

When he was called to expose his life and his army in the high places of the field, he remembered that to God the Lord belong the issues of death; and whilst heathens trusted in horses and chariots, he remembered, and taught his people to remember, the name of the Lord their God.

When he was in a low condition he remembered the promises of God concerning his exaltation to power and glory. He believed that however desperate his condition was in the eyes of men, not one good thing that God had spoken of him would fail of accomplishment. "Thou, Lord, who hast showed me great and sore adversities wilt quicken me, and bring me again from the depths of the earth." This is much – it is wonderful, but it is not all. "Thou wilt increase my greatness, and comfort me on every side."

He could trust God for his seed as well as for himself. He was charmed, he was transported with the promises made concerning his seed for a great while yet to come, and did not doubt of the faithfulness of the promises. "Great deliverance giveth he to his king, and showeth mercy to David his anointed, and to his seed for evermore."

All his people were dear to him. Jerusalem was his chief joy, and he trusted in God for the performance of all the glorious things that were spoken concerning the city and people of the Lord. "As thou hast confirmed to thyself thy people Israel to be a people unto thee for ever, and thou Lord art become their God."

Happy was this holy man. Amidst all the cares that pressed on his mind, he could commit all his concerns to one who was able and gracious to take the entire direction of them, and who knew how to bring good out of all the evils that befell him in the course of his life. Let us follow his example and his advice, or rather the counsel of God; "Cast thy burden upon the Lord, and he shall sustain thee. He will not suffer the righteous to be moved."

III. David held fast his confidence at all times.

When iniquities prevailed against him he still looked to the pardoning mercy of God, (*Psalm 65:3*).

There was a time indeed when the magnitude and terrible aggravations of his guilt filled him with anguish and drove him to the brink of despair. No wonder. His behaviour was scandalous to the highest degree. His iniquities were some of the blackest which an abandoned sinner could commit, and the aggravations were unexampled. His bones waxed old because of his roaring all the day long, and his moisture was turned into the drought of summer. Yet his faith did not utterly perish. At last, he said he would confess his transgression unto the Lord, and the Lord forgave the iniquity of his sin. His bones had been broken, but the God of hope gave him joy and peace, and all his broken bones, healed by the mercy of God, were made to say, "Lord, who is like unto thee!"

He was deeply conscious of the power of sin which dwelt in him, and was sure that without divine grace, he must one day perish by the power of those lusts which warred in his members, assisted by temptations from the devil and the world; but he committed himself to that grace which was able to keep his feet from falling, that he might walk before the Lord in the land of the living. "Hold up my goings in thy paths, that my footsteps slide not. I have called upon thee, for thou wilt hear me, O God."

Confiding in God he could encounter the most extreme dangers without terror. A giant that made the hearts of the mightiest men in

David's Confidence in God

Israel tremble within them, could not terrify David. When he was yet a stripling, unfit to carry the armour which appeared necessary for the preservation of his life, he met him in battle with his sling and a few smooth stones, for he doubted not that the Lord who had delivered him, when he was feeding his sheep, from a lion and a bear, would deliver him from the hands of the Philistines who defied the armies of the living God.

David was afterwards exposed to the fierce wrath of the king who armed against him the thousands of Israel. He was driven to dens and caves, and what was still more dangerous, he was driven to the bed and city of that champion whom he had killed in battle, who had left several brothers almost equal to himself in stature and strength to revenge his quarrel. He was like a lamb chased into the dens of the lions. Yet still he trusted in God, and believed that he should yet see the goodness of the Lord in the land of the living. "What time I am afraid, I will trust in thee. In God I will praise his word, in God I have put my trust; I will not fear what flesh can do unto me," (*Psalm 56:3, 4*).

When he was driven from Jerusalem by his unnatural son Absalom, he was again forced to leave the place which God had chosen to put his name there. He might have carried with him the chief symbol of God's presence in his sanctuary. This would have been a rich consolation to him in his banishment, yet he chose to leave it in the place appointed for it, expecting that God would bring him again to see both it and his habitation; or if God should not think fit to grant him this favour, committing himself into the hand of the Lord, to do with him as seemed good to his divine wisdom. Many at that time said of David, 'There is no succour for him in God;' but this was not the language of David's own heart. He said unto the Lord, "Thou art my strength and my glory, and the lifter up of mine head." Sometimes he felt his soul almost overpowered by the dismal thoughts that crowded into his mind, but in the multitude of his thoughts within him the comforts of God delighted his soul. "Why art thou cast down, O my soul? why art thou disquieted in me? Hope in God; for I shall yet praise him, who is the health of my countenance and my God. O my God, my soul is cast down within me; therefore will I remember thee from the land of Jordan, and of the Hermonites, from the hill Mizar. And I will say unto God my rock, Why hast thou forgotten me?"

David's distresses were often embittered by circumstances that would have crushed the spirit of a valiant man. When he was persecuted by Saul he was not only driven from the bosom of his beloved wife, but she was given to another man, after he had bought her with a hundred foreskins of the Philistines. What was still more grievous to him, he had by his imprudence, or by the shifts which necessity compelled him to use for bread and for life, been the occasion of the death of the most eminent of the priests of the Lord. Yet the dangers and extremities of distress to which he was reduced in the time of Saul were far from being attended with such unpleasant reflections as those which embittered his flight from Absalom. He was formerly persecuted by his father-in-law, now by his son who proceeded from his own bowels, and the sufferings which he endured from this unnatural monster were the punishment of his own offences against God. Because of his sin in the matter of Uriah, the Lord had said to him that the sword should not depart from his house, and that the Lord would bring evil upon him out of his own family. This threatening was not inconsistent with the assurance of pardon that was given him by Nathan, or with the everlasting covenant which was all his salvation and all his desire. While he humbly submitted to a chastising God, he held fast the faith of his love. He believed that the same God who afflicted him with the rod of men, loved him with a divine love, and that he would not make void his covenant.

Death did not destroy David's confidence in God. He believed that the God who had been his God unto death, would be his God beyond death, and would show him the path of life in that land which deserves much more than this earth to be called the land of the living. "Although my house be not so with God, yet he hath made with me an everlasting covenant ordered in all things and sure; for this is all my salvation and all my desire."

Any man will trust God, or rather imagine that he trusts God in the day of prosperity, but trials of faith are allotted to men by God, that they may know whether they really trust in him or not, and whether their confidence is weak or strong. No man's confidence was more severely tried than David's, but the trial of his faith afforded proofs not only that his confidence was well-founded, but that it was firm and strong. Like his father Abraham he could believe in hope against hope. Sometimes indeed his heart was shaken with

David's Confidence in God

fears. He said in his haste, "I am cut off from before thine eyes – All men are liars – One day I shall perish by the hands of Saul," – but he soon unsaid what he said in his haste. When he recollected who he was, in whom he believed, he said, "The Lord is my light and my salvation, whom shall I fear? The Lord is the strength of my life, of whom shall I be afraid?"

IV. The fruits of his confidence in God were salutary and pleasant.

Some pretend to trust in God, but their confidence is the snare of their souls. They trust as they imagine to the mercy of God, but they insult that goodness on which they presume. They take liberty to sin because grace abounds. They neglect the means that God has prescribed for obtaining what they desire, because God has promised to supply all their needs. But David's confidence in God was joined with reverence, and animated his activity both in the service of God, and in the care of his own interests.

David never expected that God would work miracles for him, when he had no warrant to expect them. When his child by Bathsheba was sick he prayed and fasted, for who could tell him whether God might not repent of the evil and save the child; but when the child was dead, he was far from hoping that God would stretch out his hand to the chamber of death to recall it to life. He diligently used means when means might be of use – when they could be of none, he quietly submitted to the will of the Most High.

When he was persecuted by Saul he trusted in God to preserve him for the kingdom, and in this confidence he diligently used every proper method for his own security. He did not sit in his house to wait for Saul's messengers of death in the hope that God would wither their arms before they could strike the fatal blow, or furnish him with wings like those of a great eagle to flee into the wilderness from the face of the dragon that sought to devour him. He fled to Samuel, and when he could no longer be safe with the prophet, he fled to other places. God was his refuge and his salvation, yet he took shelter in caves and deserts till the tempest had spent its fury.

But he would use no unhallowed means for safety. His faith in God secured him against temptations to stretch out his hand against the Lord's anointed. To try his integrity, providence put Saul into David's power. His friends would have persuaded him that he had now a divine warrant for killing his enemy. But his constant rule of conduct was the Word of God. "As the Lord liveth, the Lord shall smite him, or his day shall come to die, or he shall descend into battle and perish. The Lord forbid that I should stretch forth mine hand against the Lord's anointed."

It must be confessed that David sometimes used shifts unworthy of his character and piety to save his life. He did not speak the truth to Ahimelech when that priest asked him why he was come alone. But the reason of such instances of misconduct was the imperfection of his faith. He sorely regretted his lie when he found how little it served him and what damage it did to his friends. "I have occasioned the death of all the persons of thy father's house."

From David's example it clearly appears that nothing can have such a happy influence in animating and invigorating men to the use of all proper means for their own safety and advantage than confidence in God, and at the same time that it has a no less happy influence in preventing the use of all unwarrantable means. Consider the desperate condition to which he was often reduced. Despair must have greatly impaired or have utterly annihilated his powers of action, if he had not been supported by his faith in God. He had fainted unless he had believed to see the goodness of the Lord in the land of the living. If any sinful means to extricate himself from his difficulties occurred, the faith and the fear of God were equally powerful preservatives from the temptation. When men are persuaded that all good and all evil come from God, they will not accept of help from the devil in their most urgent distresses.

David could be happy as well as active in his most extreme distresses. He rejoiced in hope, when he had every reason to think himself miserable unless the Lord had been his powerful protector. "My heart trusted in him and I am helped; therefore my heart greatly rejoiceth, and with my song will I praise him."

Do you wish to be happy only at some times? When your confidence is in creatures you can be happy only when your circumstances wear a smiling appearance. Or rather you never can be happy, because smiling appearances are little to be trusted. Do you wish to be happy at all times? Trust in the Lord; wait on the Lord, and he shall strengthen your heart. None who trust in him shall be desolate. They may be brought very low, but they shall not be utterly cast down. They may be stripped of every earthly enjoyment, but they cannot be bereaved of the light of God's countenance; or if he should hide his face from them, the ground of their confidence is as stable as ever. The source of their joy can never be exhausted. How could a man be reduced to more deplorable circumstances than David at Ziklag, when the Philistines drove him out of their army, when the Amalekites had taken and burnt Ziklag, and carried off all his family, all his substance, the wives and children of all his fellow exiles, and when the companions of his banishment spake of stoning him as if he had been the author of all their miseries? His own heart probably told him that although they had no reason to stone him, they had too much reason to be dissatisfied. Yet even in that time of desolation and danger and cruel reflections, David encouraged himself in the Lord his God.

Let us learn from this holy man to place our dependence on God continually, and to commit to his care every concern respecting either our outward or inward man. Consider how well God dealt with him in this world, and how happy he is at present in the better world. Those who opposed David trusted in an arm of flesh, or in their crooked counsels which terminated in their own destruction. When they fell never more to rise, he was raised to the summit of felicity, and yet all his earthly glory was not worthy to be compared with that glory to which he is now exalted, and to which he will be exalted at the resurrection of the just.

Consider our Lord Jesus Christ, who gave his life for our redemption. He finished transgression and made an end of sin, and brought in an everlasting righteousness, that invested with it we might have confidence towards God. "Ye believe in God," says Christ, "believe also in me." Without faith in Christ we cannot believe in God. Sinners must deal with God by a mediator, and there is no mediator but Christ, and we need no other. Having our conscience purged by his blood, we may expect everything from the power and grace of his Father. "He who spared not his own Son, but delivered him up for us all, how shall he not with him also freely give us all things?"

The covenant made with David was a sure ground of hope in God. Living and dying he believed that the covenant should stand fast with him. But this covenant is revealed to us also that we might set our hope in God. "Hear," says God, "and your souls shall live, and I will make an everlasting covenant with you, even the sure mercies of David."

This everlasting covenant secures to us all the mercies that we can desire – pardon of sin, peace with God, sanctifying influences of the Spirit, a happy event to all our chastisements – all temporal blessings as far as they can be of real use, life everlasting in heaven. What more can we desire, or what better security can we possess?

Our trials are not like David's. Nothing befalls us but what is common to men. If he could quietly repose his confidence in God when he was persecuted by the king or forsaken by his subjects, when his life was sought by an unnatural son assisted by the force of the nation, when he was suffering under the displeasure of God, and under the natural and just consequences of his own great transgressions, what pretence have we at any time for alleging that there is no succour for us in God? The foundation which God hath laid in Zion is sure. The mercy of God is everlasting. In the Lord Jehovah is everlasting strength. The blood of his Son can never lose its value, his promises can never fail those who trust in them.

Those whose happiness depends on their present enjoyments and on their visible prospects must spend a considerable portion, if not the greatest part, of their lives in misery, for they will rarely be without something to disquiet them, and they have nothing to which they can trust for relief, because they have built their foundation upon the sand. But the man is blessed whose hope is in the Lord his God. When David was an exile, he could say without hesitation, "Gilead is mine, Manasseh is mine, Ephraim is the strength of mine head, Judah is my law giver." Everything that God had promised to give him was already his own. The promise of God was to him performance, because his faith was the substance of things hoped for, the evidence of things not seen. This happiness is to all the saints in proportion to their faith. When they are poor, they are rich; when they are sick, God is the health of their countenance; when they dwell in the wilderness, their souls dwell in a paradise; when they sit in the region of the shadow of death, they sit in heavenly places in Christ.

Think of the power and mercy, of the eternity and the inviolable faithfulness of God. Think of the works that he hath done, his wonders and the judgments of his mouth. Beware of violating the

David's Confidence in God

commandments of the Lord, and of everything that may damp your confidence. When you have sinned, turn your eyes to the atonement. Show forth your faith in God by your endeavours to please him in all things. Hold fast your confidence against every temptation. Remember David and Paul and all the noble army of believers and martyrs. These all trusted in God and were delivered; they cried to him in their distresses and were not confounded. "O Lord God of hosts, blessed is the man that trusteth in thee," but cursed is the man that trusts in anything below the sun.

6
Of David's Love to the Word of God

WHEN we read so many expressions of ardent love to the Word of God in the writings of David, we are surprised how he could taste such delight in a small part of the Word of God, and in a part of it in which Christians taste less delight than in other portions of Scripture written since the days of David. Let us, in accounting for this affectionate regard of David to the Word of God, consider:

I. What was that Word of God in which he so greatly delighted.

II. What was the reason why he so much delighted in it.

I. Let us consider what that book was in which he so much delighted.

The books of Moses were at that time the principal part of the Scriptures. They contain the history of the church for some thousands of years, the laws of worship instituted by Moses as well as the moral law binding on men in every age.

The *Book of Job* is probably not less ancient than the writings of Moses. This book some suppose to have been written by Moses himself, or to have been communicated by him to the church. It was doubtless of admirable use to David who was, like Job, tried by severe sufferings, and patiently endured till God was pleased likewise to turn his captivity.

A portion of the historical books that follow the writings of Moses was likewise bestowed on the church before or in the days of David. The *Book of Joshua* was probably written by Joshua himself, and the books of *Judges* and *Ruth*, with a part of *1 Samuel*, were written by Samuel the prophet.

One of the best portions of the Word of God contained in *2 Samuel* was communicated first to David himself, and was never forgotten by him. It was his joy in all the afflictions of his subsequent days of life and on his death bed, that God had made a covenant with him to establish his seed for ever, and to build up his throne to all generations.

He was the writer of many of the Psalms, and doubtless tasted as much sweetness in his own inspired compositions as in those of other holy men of God. Whilst he was feeding others, he was himself fed with those words which are sweeter than honey to the taste.

But David had not the happiness of reading some of the most pleasant prophecies in the Old Testament concerning our Redeemer, far less did he enjoy the rich discoveries that are made to us in the New Testament of the life and death and doctrine of Christ. He was one of those prophets of whom our Lord speaks when he says, "Many prophets and righteous men have desired to see those things which ye see, and have not seen them, and to hear those things which ye hear, and have not heard them."

If David so highly esteemed and so dearly loved the Word of God, what excuse is left for us if we treat it with indifference, when to those books which David had the opportunity of reading, so many books are added in which the precious truths contained in the ancient revelations made to the church are placed in such a clear light, that the light of the moon is now become as the light of the sun, and the light of the sun is seven-fold as the light of seven days? – Whilst we consider:

II. The reasons why David delighted so much in the Word of God, let us consider at the same time the reasons of superior force which should draw our regard to the Scriptures.

1. David loved the Lord, and therefore he loved his Word. Should any man whom we highly respect, favour us with a letter, we would certainly think that gratitude required us to peruse it with attention, and make that use of it which was intended by the writer. But when God himself is pleased not only to speak to us, but to write to us

Of David's Love to the Word of God

the great things of his law and covenant, we must be chargeable with extreme impiety, with the basest ingratitude, if they are accounted by us a strange thing. "God hath spoken in his holiness," says David, "I will rejoice." When he calls upon all the powers of his soul to bless the Lord, he forgets not to mention amongst those other benefits which demanded his warmest gratitude, that the Lord had made known his ways to Moses and his acts to the children of Israel. The words of God, he says in another place, "are pure words, they are like silver that hath been purified seven times in an earthen furnace." If God is infinitely pure, righteousness and eternal, righteousness must be in his testimonies. His Word is the image of himself. Let us hear what God the Lord hath spoken, and let us walk in his light. The law of God's mouth will be better to all that love him than thousands of gold and silver.

2. The Word of God was valued above gold and silver by David, because of its precious contents.

What is all the gold and silver in the world, compared with the knowledge of God. "This is life eternal," said Jesus, "to know thee the only true God, and Jesus Christ whom thou hast sent." This knowledge is to be learned only from the Word of God. The heavens indeed declare the glory of the Lord, and the firmament showeth his handiwork, but they give us no information concerning Jesus Christ, or concerning that saving mercy which is exercised towards men through a mediator. The everlasting righteousness through which we are justified in the sight of God, was witnessed by the law and the prophets, and is now manifested in the Gospel. In the law and in the earlier prophets David learned the doctrine of the atonement, of which he frequently speaks in his inspired writings when he is describing his own exercise, (*Psalms 51, 130*).

God revealed his name to Moses, and by Moses to the church, as "the Lord God, merciful and gracious, long-suffering, abundant in goodness and truth, forgiving iniquity, transgression and sin." This blessed name of God was well-known to David. In different passages of his Psalms he mentions it. In *Psalm 103*, after he had mentioned God's kindness in making known his way to Moses, he proceeds to speak of the mercy of God, and of his pardoning grace, in language which seems to have been suggested by the name revealed to Moses, (*Psalms 6, 8 – 13*).

How we may walk so as to please God, is an inquiry of infinite importance, which cannot be answered by fallen creatures without a divine revelation. The light of nature cannot inform us whether an offended God will ever receive men again into his favour; far less can it tell us how we are to seek his favour, and how we may order our steps so as to hear that joyful voice from him, "Well done, good and faithful servants." But from the Bible we learn what is "that good and acceptable and perfect will of God. Moreover by them is thy servant warned, and in keeping of them there is a great reward."

Some will be displeased with the Word of God for that reason which rendered it delightful to this holy man. They would be glad to have a rule for their conduct, every way agreeable to their inclinations; but they hate a book which requires them to do so many things they are unwilling to do, and forbids so many things which they wish to do. They are like a sick man who would be glad to enjoy health, and yet rejects the physician whose salutary prescriptions are disagreeable to his taste. David was deeply aware of the diseases of his soul, and he loved the Word of God because it discovered to him all his distempers, and prescribed the proper remedies. He did not wish any alteration to be made in the Scripture. All the alteration that he wished was in himself, for he esteemed all God's precepts concerning all things to be right, and therefore he hated every false way. Having contemplated the excellencies and requirements of the divine law, he cried out, "Who can understand his errors? Cleanse thou me from secret faults, keep back thy servant also from presumptuous sins; let them not have dominion over me: so shall I be righteous and innocent from the great transgression."

3. The happy effects of the Word of God on the heart and life were attractions to David's love. He was converted, enlightened, comforted, sanctified by it. He had thought upon his ways in the light of the law, and turned his feet unto God's testimonies. The entrance of God's Word gave him light and understanding. It made him wiser than the ancients, wiser than his teachers, wiser and wiser as he proceeded in studying it. By taking heed to his way according to God's Word, he cleansed it from the pollutions of the flesh and of the spirit. His heart was filled with joy and gladness by the promises of God's Word, and in all his trouble it revived him. From his own experience

he speaks in these high commendations given to the Word of God: "The law of the Lord is perfect, converting the soul; the testimony of the Lord is sure, making wise the simple; the statutes of the Lord are right, rejoicing the heart; the commandment of the Lord is pure, enlightening the eyes; the fear of the Lord is clean, enduring for ever; the judgments of the Lord are true, and righteous altogether. More to be desired are they than gold, yea, than much fine gold, sweeter also than honey and the honeycomb."

In all his straits he was directed, revived, enlarged by the Word of God. He must have perished if the statutes of the Lord had not been his delight. All his hopes for this world and for the next were founded upon it. No wonder that he valued it above gold, above honours, above the most delicious pleasures of the world, above life itself.

There are some who can read the Bible with some pleasure, to gratify their curiosity, or to enlarge their knowledge, and yet there are many things better to them than the Bible. But David's life lay in the favour of God, and therefore his love to the Word of God was vigorous, permanent and active, for it was by means of it that he knew and believed the love of God. By means of it his own love to God was inflamed. Through the discoveries it made to him of the will and of the grace of God, he enjoyed all the pleasures of the spiritual life. The world to him without the Word of God would have appeared a dark and comfortless habitation, in which he would have gone mourning without the sun.

If David so dearly loved the Word of God, you cannot pretend to be animated by his spirit, if it is valued no more by you than a human composition. And if you love the Scripture, let it be made evident that you love it, by such proofs as this holy man gave of his high regard to that part of it which he possessed.

He meditated on the Word of God day and night. For this purpose he prevented the dawning of the morning, and the night watches. He often mingled meditations on the law of God with the business of the day, and redeemed many hours from business and sleep to think of God and of his Word. So great was his delight in this exercise that when he awaked he was even with God. At the seasons when covetous men think of their wealth and of the means of increasing and securing it, he was thinking of those precious discoveries which God makes to men of his grace and of his will. "O how love I thy law, it is my meditation all the day!"

David did not meditate on the Word of God merely to increase the treasure of his knowledge. There was no knowledge that he valued like that which he obtained from the Bible, but he valued it chiefly from its happy influence on practice. He desired to know the grace of God, that his faith and love might be increased. He desired the knowledge of his duty, that he might practise it. "I understand more than the ancients, because I keep thy precepts. I have refrained my feet from every evil way, that I might keep thy word. I have not departed from thy judgments: for thou hast taught me." (*Psalm 119:100-102*).

He daily prayed to God for light and grace, that he might understand and observe the law of the Lord. He was conscious that there were treasures of wisdom in the Scriptures which he had not yet discovered, and that however desirous he was of standing perfect and complete in all the will of God, he had not yet attained. He therefore earnestly besought the Lord to open his eyes, that he might see wonderful things out of God's law, and give him understanding to keep God's commandments. These prayers were the expressions of fervent desires. His soul breaks within him for the longing that he hath to God's judgments at all times.

To these prayers were joined thanksgivings and praises for God's goodness in giving his law to his people, and for giving the knowledge of it to himself. "Bless the Lord, O my soul. He hath made known his ways unto Moses, his acts to the children of Israel. I will rise at midnight to praise thee. Seven times a day will I praise thee, because of thy righteous judgments."

As he was still breathing after a more perfect conformity to the Word of God, he earnestly recommended it to others. He trained up his children in the knowledge of the Scripture and in the love of that wisdom which it teaches, and doubtless it was one of his sorest afflictions that so many of them turned aside from that path in which he commanded them to walk. "I was my father's son," says Solomon, "tender and only beloved in the sight of my mother. He taught me also, and said unto me, Let thine heart retain my words: keep my commandments and live. Get wisdom, get understanding; forget it not, neither decline from the words of my mouth," (*Proverbs 4:3-5; 1 Chronicles 28*).

Of David's Love to the Word of God

From David's love to the law of God let us learn, while we set a just value upon our superior privileges, not to undervalue that portion of the Bible which to some seems almost to be superseded under the Christian dispensation. Every word of God is precious. The writings of Moses are precious as well as the writings of Paul and John. Whilst we read with delight the wonderful things that Jesus spake, and did, and suffered for our salvation, let us not forget the wonders of creation, the wonderful dispensations of God in the early ages of the church, the law published by Moses, and those ordinances of worship in which were prefigured the works and sufferings of Jesus, and the blessings which he obtained for us by his death. We cannot understand the apostles without knowing what Moses and the prophets wrote. The law was the schoolmaster of the church until Christ, and still the church may learn much of Christ from the law, or may learn much more from the prophets and apostles together, than from either separately.

"Open thou mine eyes that I may see wonderful things out of thy law." David already saw in part the mysteries to which the law referred, and he wished in the light of God to see more of them. Through divine mercy we may see more than the clearest sighted saints beheld, for the darkness is past and the true light now shineth. Paul hath explained Moses, but to understand his comments we must know the text.

One reason of David's high regard for the Word of God was its veracity and faithfulness. David was a witness of the faithfulness of God's Word, and could say from his own experience, "As for the Lord, his word is tried." Yet he did not live to see what we have seen, or what these faithful witnesses saw, who have declared unto us what they saw and heard, that our fellowship might be with them, as their fellowship was with the Father and his Son Jesus Christ.

We are our own enemies if we do not make God's testimonies our counsellors, the subjects of our thoughts by day and by night, the rule of our belief, and of every part of our practice. By what means shall we cleanse our way? By taking heed thereto according to God's Word. May God write his laws in our hearts, and order our steps in his Word. If we abide in Christ, and his Word abide in us, we shall bring forth much fruit. (*Colossians 3:16; Psalm 119*).

7
David's Meditations on the Word of God

YOU are not lovers of the Word of God if you take no pleasure in meditating on the precious truths which it contains. As out of the abundance of the heart the mouth speaketh, so out of the abundance of the affections of the heart the thoughts of men receive their direction. We often think of our beloved friends. We would reckon it a grievous calamity to be hindered from thinking on any person or anything that is very dear to us. How then is it possible that any real Christian can think that a grievous task is imposed upon him when he is required to employ many of his thoughts about his blessed Saviour and the things that belong to his peace. "O how love I thy law," says David. What proof does he give of his ardent affection to it? "It is my meditation all the day." – Let us consider:

I. The subject of David's meditations.

II. The time when he meditated on God's law.

III. His reasons for so constantly meditating on it.

I. What was the subject of David's meditations is our first enquiry.

"How sweet unto my taste are all thy words of truth." There was nothing in the Word of God that did not afford him a subject of profitable meditation, although doubtless there were some parts of it in which he found more pleasant subjects of thought than in other passages. The circumstances of his life, and the varying tempers of his mind, would give a different direction at different times to his mind. Yet there were truths in which he daily found delightful nourishment to his soul.

He was never weary of meditating on the loving-kindness of the Lord. "Thy loving-kindness is better than life, therefore my lips shall praise thee. My soul shall be satisfied as with marrow and with fatness, and my mouth shall praise thee with joyful lips, when I remember thee upon my bed, and meditate on thee in the night watches."

All the revealed properties of the divine nature were delightful subjects of his meditation. Those attributes which to stubborn sinners are terrible, were pleasant to David. Because God is righteous, he knew that his malicious enemies would be destroyed, and that all the promises made to himself should be fulfilled. He rejoiced no less that the righteousness of God was like the great mountains, than that his mercy is in the heavens, and his faithfulness reacheth unto the clouds. The Lord was David's rock, the horn of his salvation and his high tower, and therefore every perfection of the divine nature was to him a source of gladness.

The promised Redeemer was a delightful subject of his meditations. Like his father Abraham he saw the day of Christ afar off. The apostle Peter tells us that when he spake of God's Holy One, who should not be left in the state of death, he had in his view that blessed Seed that was according to the divine promise to see no corruption in the grave, (*Acts 2*). It was from the earnest expectation of his soul that he taught the church to pray that God would send out of Zion the redemption of Israel.

The precepts of God were likewise the daily subject of his thoughts. He examined by them his heart and his ways. He was pleased with himself only in so far as he found a conformity in his temper and conduct to these precepts, and it was his constant desire and prayer that his ways might be more completely directed to keep God's statutes. He rejoiced in those precepts to which he found most contrariety in himself. It was his delight to cleanse himself more and more from the pollutions of the flesh and of the spirit, by attention to the law of God, that he might attain that perfection of holiness which he esteemed the perfection of happiness. He doubtless felt much pain in the view of his own deficiencies, which appeared in a clear light to his conscience whilst he contemplated the purity and sublimity of that holiness which the law required. Yet such contemplations gave him far more pleasure than pain, because he knew that the God who had begun the work of grace would finish it in his own time. The law gave him not only a view of what he was, but a pleasant view of what he would one day be, when God should make him as holy as the law required him to be. "As for me I shall behold thy face in righteousness; when I awake, I shall be satisfied with thine image."

The works of God afforded him many pleasant meditations which inflamed his heart with love, and excited him to praise the Lord, who had made him glad with his works. His meditations on the works of creation were regulated by the Word of God. We have several specimens of them in his Psalms. In *Psalm 8* when he expressed his transport at the sight of the glorious luminaries of heaven, he shows at the same time what improvement the Scripture history of the creation taught him to make of this visible display of the divine glory. How wonderful was it in his eyes, that he whom the moon and the stars proclaim so wonderfully great should have showed such favour to man in his best estate. How much more wonderful is it, that he should show such favours to the fallen sons of Adam, and restore them to their ancient glory, and more than restore them in the person of Christ. In him these words are verified in their full extent of meaning: "Thou hast put all things under his feet." Here there is nothing excepted that is not put under him, except him who put all things under him.

Psalm 104 contains some pleasant meditations of David on the works of nature, in which he takes for his guide the account which he found of the creation in the *Book of Genesis.*

The works of divine providence recorded in the Bible afforded many pleasant and profitable meditations to David as well as to other writers of sacred song. He knew that God's ways are everlasting, and that the saints in every age will be blessed with the same privileges, and have all their affairs managed by that kind providence which ensured the happiness of their fathers. When David complained that his prayers were not heard, he rejoiced in the hope that he would not at least find himself neglected by that God who was known in every former age as the hearer of prayer.

The divine dispensations towards himself were not forgotten by him. He thought of God's dealings with him in childhood and youth, and was cheered with the hope that the God on whose care he had been cast from the womb, and who had caused him to hope on the knees of his mother, would not cast him off when he was old and grey headed, (*Psalm 71*).

As he thought upon the times that were past many ages before him, he turned forward his views to future ages, and rejoiced in the prospect of the redemption of Israel, and the illumination of the Gentiles. Glorious things were spoken of the city of God, and he knew that none of these glorious things were forgotten, although they were not accomplished as soon as some expected.

In the light of faith he could look forward to the resurrection of the dead, and entertain his soul with the prospect of the glories that were to be revealed in the saints. "God shall deliver me from the power of the grave, for he shall receive me." – Let us:

II. Consider the season when he meditated on God's law – "All the day."

How was it possible that David could find any time through the day for meditating on God's law? He had the care of a great kingdom to engross his hours. He was frequently engaged in wars, the events of which were so successful as to add greatly to his labours by increasing his dominion.

Servants and common labourers will perhaps be able to redeem some time for meditation from their work, because their minds are free from care. They may even mingle religious thoughts with the exercises of their hands. But those whose business it is to inspect many labourers, and to transact a multitude of affairs that render attention indispensable, can find almost no time through the whole day from the rising of the sun till his going down to think of God. And yet the cares that come upon them are trifling to the cares that came upon David. A wrong step in his conduct caused by inattention, might have done incalculable mischief not to himself only but to the Israel of God.

"Let every man in the calling wherewith he is called therein abide with God." He must not on pretence of any religious duty neglect the business of his station. This would not be consistent with the direction to abide in his calling. But let him not exclude necessary religious duties under pretence of necessary business. This would not be consistent with the direction to abide with God in his calling.

That business cannot consist with religion which excludes religion. The remembrance of God and of the duty which he requires, will not interfere with the right performance of any duties which we owe to our fellow-men, or to ourselves, but animate and direct us in our exertions, and fortify us against temptations to indolence, or to wrong conduct. What king ever reigned with more advantage to his subjects or with more comfort to himself than David? He did judgment and justice to all his subjects. He was the minister of God to them for good, attending continually upon this very thing, at the same time that he was meditating continually upon God's law. His meditations enlightened his mind and made him wiser than his enemies, because God's judgments were continually with him. His meditations were an incentive to activity in the service of his people. His meditations cheered his soul under the pressure of that multiplicity of cares which lay upon his mind. He remembered God's judgments, and his heart was comforted, his hands were strengthened, and his feet were swifter than the hinds' feet to run in the path which duty prescribed. He remembered God's judgments, and saw plainly that no advantages could be gained from turning aside into the ways of crooked policy. They were a lamp to his feet and a light to his path. The happy effects of that pleasure which he took in meditating on God's statutes, were enjoyed by all that happy people that enjoyed the benefit of his government.

He did not neglect his business to enjoy his intellectual pleasures. The Word of God taught him what he owed to his subjects. But as worldly thoughts intrude into the minds of the lovers of the present world when they pray, so spiritual meditations spontaneously presented themselves to David's mind, whilst he was engaged in the businesses of the world, and he redeemed time from the hurry of his affairs to employ his thoughts about God and his law. When any question arose about his present duty, the testimonies of the Lord were the men of his counsel. When any advice was offered to him in which more regard was paid to his feelings or to his present interests than to the laws of justice and piety, his continual recourse to his best counsellors repelled the temptation. They convinced him that strict integrity was his true interest, and that nothing could more effectually destroy his happiness than a deviation from the path of duty, whatever present pleasures or advantages it might promise.

But if David had not leisure by day to invigorate his soul by the marrow and fatness which he found in the Word of God, he redeemed time from his sleep to enjoy his favourite refreshment. He remembered God's name in the night, and kept his law. He prevented the dawning of the morning, that he might meditate on God's statutes. He could live longer without sleep or food to the animal part of his nature, than he could live without supplies of nourishment to his soul from the Word of God. And when his eyes were debarred from rest, the darkness and silence of the night were more pleasant to him than even the light of day was to those who count it a pleasure to spend their hours in the pleasures of sense.

III. The reasons why David meditated so frequently or constantly on the law of God are now to be given. And it is not difficult to produce them.

He was no doubt conscious that it was his duty to meditate on God's Word. The commandment given to Joshua is a commandment to all, and to the higher powers as much as to private persons, to meditate on the law day and night. If God gives us a book to inform us of the truths most needful to be known by us, we are chargeable with extreme ingratitude and impiety if we do not carefully endeavour to learn what it contains. The bare reading or hearing of it is not sufficient. God has commanded us to keep his precepts diligently. But to the diligent keeping of them daily meditation is requisite, that they may be on every occasion present to our minds.

But David was not actuated by a mere sense of duty. He took pleasure in the work, for God had written his law upon his heart. If we must be dragged to this duty it is too plain that the law of God was never inscribed upon our souls by the regenerating grace of the divine Spirit. "I will never forget thy precepts: for with them thou hast quickened me," (*Psalm 119:93*).

If we are partakers of the grace of God, our affections will no longer be engrossed by present things. The things of the Spirit of God are loved when they are known, and the love of those things that are above will give a direction to the thoughts of the heart. "I have chosen thy testimonies to be mine heritage for ever, for they are the rejoicing of mine heart." "Where the treasure is, there will the heart be also," (*Psalm 119:11; Matthew 6:21*).

David's Meditations on the Word of God

The pleasure that David tasted in religious meditation was very great. It was heaven begun in his soul. "I have rejoiced in the way of thy testimonies, as much as in all riches. I will meditate on thy precepts, and have respect unto thy ways. I will delight myself in thy statutes: I will not forget thy word," (*Psalm 119:14-16*).

The advantages which he found in meditation, greatly recommended it to this holy man. His understanding was enlightened, his faith was strengthened, his love inflamed, all his virtues were invigorated by it and fitted for exercise. "Through thy precepts I get understanding: therefore I hate every false way." "By the words of thy lips I have kept me from the path of the destroyer," (*Psalm 119:104; 17:4*).

In all his distresses he was preserved from sinking into despondency, and from turning aside into the ways of sin, by means of God's Word which was ever present to his view. "The wicked have waited for me to destroy me: but I will consider thy testimonies," (*Psalm 119:95*). "My soul is continually in my hand: yet do I not forget thy law. The wicked have laid a snare for me: yet I erred not from thy precepts," (*Psalm 119:109,110*).

Do you wish to be happy and to be holy? Follow the example of David, and comply with the advice of his wise son, and of that divine Wisdom which spake by his mouth. "Bind them (my commandments) upon thy fingers, write them upon the table of thine heart. Say unto wisdom, Thou art my sister; and call understanding thy kinswoman," (*Proverbs 7:3, 4*).

Who would live on chaff or feed on poison, when the most salutary and delicious provision is placed on a table before him? You may roll, if you please, the delights of sin in your minds – you may, if you choose, keep your mind open to the disquieting and anxious cares of life. They will supply you with an inexhaustible abundance of materials for thought. But what pleasure or what advantage will you derive from such employment to your mind? If you wish to be wretched in this world and in the next, let your mind take its natural course. Let the lusts of the flesh and of the mind afford constant business to your musing faculty. But if you wish to be happy, learn to meditate on the doctrines and promises, the precepts and histories of the Word of God. Life and death are set before you; choose that which is good, and abide by your choice.

Thoughts pleasing to the flesh will be constantly seeking admittance. But remember that the pleasure of sin is momentary and its pains everlasting.

Thoughts of a painful and tormenting kind will be often springing up in your minds under the influence of disappointed desires and of malignant passions. Banish them, they are destroyers both to body and soul. Do you take more pleasure in thinking on what men have done to vex you, than what God has done to save you? on what poisons your life, than on these delightful truths which are the food, the medicine, the life of the precious soul?

That we may meditate with pleasure and advantage on the doctrines of the Lord, it is necessary to have a heart, like David's, cleansed from the pollutions of sin and inflamed with holy love. We all take pleasure in thinking on those objects that have the chief place in our hearts, and think with reluctance or with pain on the objects of our aversion. We are naturally disaffected to God and his law. The power of our enmity can be broken only by the power of the Spirit of God, and the faith of the Gospel is the means by which he works. Blessed are the people that know and believe the joyful sound. They walk in the light of God's countenance, and the Word of God is to them the joy and rejoicing of their hearts.

We ought to beware likewise of placing too much of our affections on any earthly object. The well-regulated love of our friends is worthy of praise, nor is it inconsistent with the Christian temper to exercise a due care about those things of the world that are necessary for our comfortable subsistence. But the danger is that these things to which some place must be given in our minds, may usurp too much room, whilst we are not aware of the danger, and exclude better things from that room which they should occupy. Let Christians consider whether the things of the present world do not often engross their thoughts when they should be otherwise employed, and whether they do not often steal into the mind, when it wishes to be free from them. Mortify your earthly affections if you desire to enjoy the delicious pleasures of heavenly contemplation. "Lord, turn away our eyes from viewing vanity, and quicken us in thy way," (*Psalm 119:37*).

That we may not be embarrassed in our religious meditations we ought to learn the patience and meekness required by the law of Christ and recommended by his example. When the evils of life overwhelm our spirits, when bad usage from men rankles our hearts, it will be hard for us to meditate without distraction on divine things. Yet the defects of our meekness and patience must be remedied by meditation. When we find our hearts oppressed with grief, or embittered by angry passions, let us immediately apply our thoughts to those sources of consolation, and to those powerful motives to a charitable and satisfied frame of spirit which meet us in every part of the Bible. "Why art thou cast down, O my soul, and why art thou disquieted within me? Hope thou in God: for I shall yet praise him, who is the health of my countenance, and my God," (*Psalm 42:11*). Whenever David heard of the snares that his enemies were laying for him, he meditated on God's Word and comforted himself.

When we have been entangled in the snares of sin, we will find no pleasure in any kind of meditations that are not fitted to our condition, nor can we find pleasure even in those without the proper improvement of them. When we think of God we will be troubled, if we lie under guilt unpardoned. It is indeed fit to think of those perfections of God that will inspire us with an awful sense of the necessity of sound and bitter repentance, as well as those which are springs of consolation to a heart humbled by conviction. Consider how infinitely holy our God is, that you may be awakened to repentance. Consider how infinite his mercy, that you may not despair of pardon. Those meditations that might be profitable and pleasant at other times must give place for the time to the consideration of those truths that are best fitted for the recovery of that peace which has been banished by sin. David could not take his ordinary delight in God and in his laws while he endeavoured to erase from his own conscience the criminality of his conduct in the matter of Uriah. He tasted no true joy till he said that he would confess his iniquity to the Lord. The Lord then forgave the iniquity of his sin, and he could again delight himself in the contemplation of that mercy which pardoned his sin, and of all those excellencies which were the fountains of his felicity.

That you may expatiate with ease and pleasure in your holy meditations, endeavour to attain a comprehensive knowledge of the Word of God, and to treasure up large portions of it in your memories. If David found an inexhaustible fund of devout contemplations in those few books of Scripture which were given in his days to the church, what inexhaustible treasures do we possess! He meditated on the writings of Moses, and Joshua, and Samuel, and Job, and his own, and never found himself at a loss for pleasant and useful subjects to occupy his leisure hours either in the day or in the night. Besides these holy books we have the writings of Isaiah, of Jeremiah and all the other prophets, the charming compositions of Solomon, the precious histories of the life and death of God our Saviour, the epistles of the holy apostles, and the revelation of future things given to the church by the beloved disciple who saw the visions of Christ. Can we be excused if we ever have recourse for filling up our time, to those amusements that waste time and corrupt the heart? We know not what pleasures are to be found in religion if we complain that our days and nights move heavily along, when no heavy affliction is laid upon our bodies or our minds. And heavy must that affliction be, the griefs of which cannot be dispelled by meditating on the loving-kindness of the Lord, and the joys of heaven. Who was ever tried by sorer afflictions than David? But in the multitude of his thoughts within him, the comforts of the Lord delighted his soul.

8
Of David's Obedience to the Revealed Will of God

I have sworn, and I will perform it, that I will keep thy righteous judgments. (Psalm 119:106)

IT would be worse than vain, it would be a direct falsehood, to pretend that we love the Word of God, and that we often meditate upon it, if we do not make it the rule of our conduct through life. The tree must be known by its fruits. David, a tree of righteousness of high stature, planted in the house of God, whose leaf was almost always green, brought forth fruit, abundance of fruit in due season. He came under solemn engagements, and he never forgot them, to walk worthy of the Lord unto all pleasing, by obeying all his commandments. "I have sworn," he says, "and I will perform it, that I will keep thy righteous judgments." – Let us consider:

I. The obligations under which he brought himself to be obedient to God.

II. The care with which he performed his engagements.

I. The obligation under which he brought himself to obey God as his master by keeping his righteous judgments.

We read of several vows that David made concerning particular services which he designed to perform to the Most High. "He swore unto the Lord, and vowed unto the mighty God of Jacob; Surely I will not come into the tabernacle of my house, nor go up into my bed; I will not give sleep unto mine eyes, or slumber to mine eyelids, until I find out a place for the Lord, an habitation for the mighty God of Jacob," (*Psalm 132:2-5*). How well he performed this vow, we find in the history of his life. He often vowed to bring sacrifices of praise to the house of the Lord, and he never grudged the expense or the trouble of performing these vows, but thought himself happy to be called to perform service, so pleasing to his soul, (*Psalm 66*). He vowed to give a very large portion of his acquisitions to the service of God in the building of the temple, and he did not enjoy half the pleasure in having his family rich as in the consecration of the largest share of his substance to him from whom he had received all, (*1 Chronicles 29*).

But the vows of which he speaks in this place, are his general engagements to walk in all the commandments and ordinances of the Lord. To do this he was bound independently of any engagements which he could lay upon himself. The command of God binds us all to perfect obedience whether we choose or whether we refuse. Yet it is no vain thing for us to bind our consciences by solemn vows to do what he requires from us. Some have alleged that it is unwarrantable and presumptuous to promise or vow to the Lord that obedience which his law demands. But this certainly was not the mind of David, or of the other holy men of God whose example is set before us in Scripture. The patrons of the above-mentioned opinion allege that it is the fruit of a self-righteous or a self-sufficient spirit to come under such engagements. And it must be allowed that the vows of too many professors of religion justly come under this imputation. But it is only too clear that multitudes of professors perform every religious service in which they are engaged, with a proud reliance on their own strength or merits. We read of men who sought of God the ordinances of justice and took delight in approaching to him, and then complained if they did not receive the rewards which they thought they had merited. "Wherefore have we fasted," said they, "and thou seest not? Wherefore have we afflicted our souls, and thou takest no knowledge?" But we do not think it vain or sinful to pray and fast in the manner in which we are called to perform these duties, because others have added to their guilt by their unhallowed manner of performing them. Let us follow David's example, and our dedication of ourselves to the Lord will

Of David's Obedience to the Revealed Will of God

be a service acceptable to him, and a useful preparation for all other services which God requires at our hands.

If we are prompted only by a sense of the necessity of obedience without any delight in it, it will be vain for us to hope that we will fulfil the engagements which we propose to take upon ourselves. Our wills must be sanctified as well as our consciences, that we may perform any action well-pleasing to God. David was not only aware that the ways of sin were pernicious, but that the commandments were all holy and just and good. He esteemed all God's precepts concerning all things to be right. He delighted in the law of the Lord after the inward man, and therefore with pleasure he could bind himself by indispensable engagements to make it the rule of every part of his behaviour, (*Psalm 119:99, 111, 128*).

If we should hope to merit the favour of God by our own works of righteousness, our vows of obedience would be detested by God, as expressions of that pride of heart against which he will have indignation for ever. But nothing was further from David's heart than a presumptuous opinion that he could merit anything at the hand of God. "Enter not into judgment," he says, "with thy servant, for in thy sight shall no man living be justified." He trusted in that righteousness without works which he describes in many passages of his Psalms, and came under solemn engagements to testify his gratitude to the God of his salvation by holy obedience. "What shall I render to the Lord for all his benefits towards me? O Lord, truly I am thy servant; I am thy servant, and the son of thine handmaid; thou hast loosed my bonds."

It would be presumptuous to depend on our own strength, or our good dispositions for the performance of our engagements. When David was left to himself he gave a melancholy proof of the weakness of the best of men. But he maintained a habitual sense of his own inability either to preserve himself from the snares of vice, or to walk onward in the way of God's commandments. When he swore that he would keep God's righteous judgments, his dependence was placed on the promised grace of the Most High. He knew and believed the promises of the covenant, which was his great comfort in life as well as in death. He trusted in the God of his fathers as his own God, as the rock of his salvation, the God who gives strength and power to his people. To him he looked and daily prayed for grace to perform his vows. "Hold up my goings in thy paths, that my footsteps slide not. Teach me, O Lord, the way of thy statutes, and I shall keep it unto the end. Give me understanding, and I shall keep thy law; yea, I shall observe it with my whole heart. Make me to go in the path of thy commandments, for therein do I delight."

In the strength of promised grace he promised with the solemnity of an oath that he would keep God's righteous judgments. – Let us now:

II. Consider his performance of this engagement.

The history of David is given us at great length in Scripture, and therefore we know more both of his virtues and defects than of almost any other saint. From this history it appears that David frequently stumbled in his path, and that he once turned aside from following the Lord, and brought great calamities both on himself and on his kingdom. Can it then be said that he kept his engagements, to walk in the ways of God?

To this the reply is not difficult. David often testifies of himself in his Psalms that he had kept the way of the Lord, and had not wickedly departed from his God. We cannot, indeed, in ordinary cases admit a man's testimony for himself; but although David bears testimony concerning himself, his testimony is true, because it is the testimony of the Holy Ghost by his pen. Besides, God himself bore testimony of him by Samuel and by other prophets. "I have found David the son of Jesse," said the Lord to Samuel, "a man after mine own heart, who shall fulfil all my will." "And it shall be," said God to Jeroboam by Ahijah, "if thou wilt hearken to all that I command thee, and wilt walk in my ways, and do that which is right in my sight, to keep my statutes and my commandments, as my servant David did; that I will be with thee, and build thee a sure house, as I built for David, and will give Israel unto thee," (*Acts 13:22; 1 Kings 11:38*).

1. David laid the testimonies of the Lord before him as the rule of his conduct. When the question was, what was to be done or left undone, he did not consult with flesh and blood. He did not consider what line of conduct would be most agreeable to his own inclinations or to his own interests; but what the Lord his God required of him. He did not seek to please men any further than the pleasing of them was consistent with the will of God. He resolved to walk in

Of David's Obedience to the Revealed Will of God

that good path in which he saw the footsteps of the saints who had lived in former times, because he knew that their course of life had been well pleasing to God. Yet he would not have thought himself justified by their example in doing anything forbidden by God.

Concerning the works of men, he says, "By the word of thy lips I have kept me from the path of the destroyer. Hold up my goings in thy paths, that my footsteps slide not. I have kept the way of the Lord, and have not wickedly departed from my God; for all his judgments were before me, and I did not put away his statutes from me."

There are some who could not, without exposing themselves to painful remonstrances from their own consciences, wilfully do what is forbidden in the Scriptures, if they know the voice of the law; but they have no desire to know anything that might interfere with the gratification of their own wills, and therefore they are at no pains to obtain a complete knowledge of sin and duty, as if their ignorance would be their justification when they do what is wrong. But David was not more careful to do what he already knew to be his duty, than to obtain a more perfect knowledge of the will of God. For this reason he daily meditated on the testimonies of the Lord, and prayed with unceasing importunity for divine illumination, not only that he might know the things which were freely given him of God, but that he might know how to stand perfect and complete in all the will of God.

2. He held fast his purpose of obeying God through every different period of his life, (*Psalm 119:44*).

His circumstances at different times were very different, but his disposition and his course of behaviour was still the same. He was poor, afflicted, and persecuted in the reign of Saul. But his distresses did not unsettle his mind, or banish from his remembrance the commandments of the Lord, (*Psalm 119:83*). It is well-known and too commonly seen, that sore affliction tends to engross men's thoughts and leave them scarcely the power of calling up to view those holy principles which are necessary for counteracting the temptations attendant on adversity, especially such adversities as David suffered, from which he might in appearance have found protection or relief by departing in some measure from that undeviating course of holy behaviour, which he had planned out for himself. When he was driven to the countries where false gods were worshipped, his persecutors tempted him to go and worship them, or at least to dissemble his zeal for his own religion, that he might obtain that protection from strangers which he could not find in the land of Israel. "But I will speak," he says, "of thy testimonies before kings, and I will not be ashamed. Their sorrows shall be multiplied that hasten after other gods; their drink-offerings will I not offer, nor take up their names into my mouth."

He might have in all appearance put an end at once to his trouble from the persecution of Saul by killing him, when the Lord had put him in his power. "Behold," said David's men, "the day of which the Lord said unto thee, Behold I will deliver thine enemy into thine hand, that thou mayest do unto him as it shall seem good unto thee," (*1 Samuel 24*). It is accounted not only lawful, but a necessary duty, for a man to defend his own life at the expense of the blood of his enemy, when he can find no other means of security. But it might have appeared necessary for David, not only for his own safety, but for the safety of all his men, to take away the life of their implacable enemy, whose fury they had no visible means of restraining, whilst they suffered him to live above the ground. Besides, God had now given David an opportunity which, if not improved, might never be recovered, of securing his own life, and the life of all his friends, by destroying a bloody man who scrupled no means for destroying the innocent. He would be thought by his own people careless of their safety as well as his own, and unthankful to God, who had furnished him with the means of performing such a necessary and important service to himself and to them, if he did not seize the opportunity to put an end to their fears and his own, when the day was come of which the Lord had said, "he would put his enemy into his hand to do he what pleased with him." But the question with David was not how he might best secure his own life, and the lives of his dependants; how he might please the men that followed his fortunes; but what it was his duty in the present circumstances to do. The Lord had delivered his enemy into his hand to do what seemed good to him, and thus tried him whether it seemed good to him to trust God in the path of duty, or to take the method that his followers urged him to do for delivering them from their fears. The path in which he was called to go was clear, and it was not a matter of discussion with him whether he should please men or please God; whether he should

Of David's Obedience to the Revealed Will of God

revenge himself with his own hand when it was in his power, or leave vengeance to him to whom it belonged. He cut off the skirt of Saul's garment, but he would not for a thousand kingdoms have stretched forth his hand against the Lord's anointed.

There are some whose consciences will not suffer them to stretch forth their own hands to do an evil thing that promises pleasure or advantage to them, yet they will not be sorry that another should do what they scruple to do. But David not only withheld his own hands from the blood of the king, but the hands of all his followers, amongst whom there were not wanting many who would have been bold enough to perpetrate an action which they recommended to their captain. But he acted as if he had been stationed to guard the tyrant who sought his destruction, at a time when he seemed to be forsaken both by God and men. Nor was it once only but a second time that he showed a tender care for the life of his enemy, when he might have destroyed him, and when he incurred the danger of turning the *few* friends that were left him into enemies, by seeming to prefer the safety of their common enemy to the safety of his followers and his own. Abishai earnestly begged David's leave to put an end at one blow to the life of that tyrant who had already imbrued his hands in the blood of the innocent priests of the Lord, and who had given too much reason to believe that he would never rest till he had extirpated the name and memory and friends of David from the face of the earth. But David was steadfast and unmoveable. He was the same man at the hill of Hachilah, that he had been in the wilderness of Engedi. And if Saul had come ten times into his power, it was his determined purpose to leave him to the judgment of the great King whose name is the Lord of hosts. He had no hope of melting the heart of Saul into kindness, or at least of working such a change in his temper as to permit him to enjoy tranquillity and safety in his own country. He would rather seek a refuge for himself among the aliens, whose enmity he had procured to himself by the most important services to Saul. He would rather run the continual hazard of perishing one day by the hand of Saul, than revenge himself upon his great enemy, or suffer one of his dependants to execute revenge on his behalf. He knew him who said, "Vengeance is mine; I will recompense it, saith the Lord." "The Lord judge," said he to the king, "between me and thee, and the Lord avenge me of thee;

but mine hand shall not be upon thee; as saith the proverb of the ancients, Wickedness proceedeth from the wicked; but mine hand shall not be upon thee."

When David was in constant and extreme danger of his life, he was so far from taking unhallowed methods for his security, that if God called him to expose himself to still worse dangers, he was ready to encounter them. When he heard that the Philistines were fighting against Keilah, and robbing the threshing-floors, he called on his men at God's command to come with him to fight against the Philistines, and save Keilah. His men were very unwilling to encounter new dangers in addition to those to which they were already exposed from their own king and countrymen. Why should they venture their lives in the service of a king who sought their destruction? Had they not already too many enemies that sought their blood continually? "Behold we are afraid here in Judah; how much more then if we come to Keilah against the armies of the Philistines?" David himself saw that he was multiplying dangers to himself and to his followers, and that if he had made the rules of worldly policy his guide, it was his interest rather to make friends of the Philistines, whom he had already irritated by fighting with success the battles of an ungrateful master against them. But still he considered it his duty to fight the battles of the Lord against the enemies of his people. He enquired of the Lord yet again, and the Lord answered him and said, "Arise, go down to Keilah, for I will deliver the Philistines into thine hand; so David and his men went down to Keilah and fought with the Philistines." And when Saul intended to come against him to Keilah after he had chased away the Philistines, he obeyed the command of God in leaving it, and went whithersoever he would go.

When David was in the cave of Adullam, where he hoped to hide himself and his followers from his persecutor, he did not place his confidence in concealment, in the strength of any of these strongholds in which he could shelter himself, but in the God of his salvation; and therefore was always ready to change his situation when he knew that God required him to do it. And therefore when the prophet Gad brought him the command of God to leave his hiding place and go into the land of Judah, he was as ready to yield obedience as Abraham his father when he was called to leave his native country, and go unto a place that he knew not. (*2 Samuel 2*).

Of David's Obedience to the Revealed Will of God

Many were David's afflictions in the days of his persecution from Saul. Not only was his own life threatened, but his friends were menaced with destruction for his sake; and therefore he found it necessary to solicit the protection of the king of Moab for his father and mother. The enmity of Saul procured him the enmity of all that wished to enjoy the smiles of royalty, and deprived him of the benefits of the friendship of all that were afraid of exposing themselves to the king's resentment. He was a reproach among all his enemies, but especially among his neighbours, and a fear to his acquaintances. They that did see him without fled from him. He was forgotten like a dead man out of mind, he was like a broken vessel. But amidst all the temptations of his afflicted state, he did not forget the great principle of conduct which he had laid down, and to which he determined, whatever should be the case, to cleave. Slanders without number were everywhere disseminated against him, and were the readier to gain belief that his circumstances appeared so desperate as almost to compel him to have recourse to sinful methods for his relief; but he could appeal to God, the Searcher of hearts, for the purity of his principles and the integrity of his conduct, at the very times when he was under the most dangerous temptations, and when he laboured under the most cruel suspicions. "Lord," he says, "my heart is not haughty, nor mine eyes lofty, neither do I exercise myself in great matters, or in things too high for me. Surely I have behaved and quieted myself as a child that is weaned of his mother: my soul is even as a weaned child." And when he composed a Psalm of praise to God for his deliverance from the hands of all his enemies, and from the hands of Saul in particular, he could appeal to God for the righteousness of the whole course of his life amidst the temptations to which he was continually exposed by the malice and craft of his enemies. "The Lord hath rewarded me according to my righteousness, according to the cleanness of my hands hath he recompensed me. For I have kept the ways of the Lord, and have not wickedly departed from my God. I was also upright before him, and I kept myself from mine iniquity."

The Lord recompensed him according to his righteousness, and advanced him to that high condition to which he had been appointed. But greater temptations, though of a very different kind, cleave to a prosperous, than to an adverse condition. How often do we see men who seemed to fear God whilst they moved in a humble sphere of life, behave like men who have no fear of God before their eyes, when they are elevated above their former equals. David, however, was still the same, or if there was any difference in him, it was that he was more careful than ever to please God who had done so great things for him. He considered himself as much the servant of God as ever, and still continued to meditate on the statutes of the Lord, that he might approve himself faithful, in all his administration, to the Lord who had set him on high above all his adversities, and made him his king on the holy hill of Zion.

When the way seemed to be opened to the throne by the death of Saul, although he was a long time before anointed by the prophet Samuel, yet he would take no steps to attain the actual possession of the throne, till he had an express discovery made to him of the will of God, that he should go up to one of the cities of Judah. When he was seated on the throne, he still used the proper means for knowing God's pleasure concerning the different steps of his conduct in war and in peace. He resolved when he should receive the congregation, to do everything in his power to promote piety and righteousness. He determined that none should serve him who did not make the revealed will of God the rule of his conduct. In his last days or hours of life, he described the model of a good king agreeably to the principles on which he himself had acted in the course of his whole administration. "He that ruleth over men must be just, ruling in the fear of God." Happy would it be for all the nations to whom the light of the Bible comes, if their princes would model their conduct by his example and precepts. (*Psalm 75, 101; 2 Samuel 23*).

When David came to the throne, his troubles were far from being at an end. He was tried at once by some of the most powerful temptations both of adversity and of grandeur when his son Absalom rebelled against him, and prevailed on the greater part of the people to favour his traitorous designs. The history of the rebellion contains many shining instances of David's unshaken virtue, and of the regard which he still entertained for the statutes of the Lord as the rule of his conduct. When one of his bitterest enemies exposed himself by the outrageous fury of his malice, to the vengeance of David, a conscientious regard to what David believed to be the mind of God, not only withheld his hands from vengeance, but made him the protector of the insolent ruffian. God had said unto him, "Curse David;

Of David's Obedience to the Revealed Will of God

and who shall say unto him, Why dost thou so?" But it will no doubt be remembered by all who have read the history of the life of David, that there were not only blemishes in his conduct, but one or two very shameful instances of disobedience to God, by which he greatly stained the lustre of his virtues. And some will allege that he was far from having fulfilled his vow of keeping God's righteous judgments, when he brought upon himself the guilt of some of the worst crimes which a man can commit.

It is indeed undeniable, and David himself was far from denying, that he sinned greatly in the matter of Uriah, and in the numbering of the people. Nor were these the only sins which he found reason to lament. He acknowledges that innumerable evils took hold of him, and earnestly prays that God might cleanse him from secret faults.

But we would form a very false and uncharitable judgment of the good man if we should suppose that his vows were treacherous, or that he took too much upon him when he said that he would perform his vow. It has been already observed, and must appear plain to every man who is a reader of the Bible, that David made his vow in dependence on the grace promised in that covenant which is the only ground of hope for sinners. He could not mean by his vow that he would yield such a perfect obedience to God as the old covenant requires as the condition of eternal life. He was not so ignorant as not to know that such obedience can be performed by no man in the present life, and that it would be presumptuous in any man to promise the performance of it. That obedience which he promised was that sincere obedience which, though imperfect, is acceptable to God according to the tenor of that covenant which was all the salvation and all the desire of the holy man.

There can be no doubt but David's great transgressions were greatly aggravated by the solemn obligations under which he had brought himself, to keep God's righteous judgments; and he was doubtless deeply humbled under the view of his unfaithfulness to that God whose authority he had solemnly recognised in these transactions. Yet these sins of the good man did not affect the sincerity or the sanctity of his engagements. Although he came far short of his own hopes in keeping his promise, his promise was good and holy. He did not repent of making it, but of not keeping it so well as he might have done; he had indeed no reason to repent of making it, but reason rather to rejoice that he had done his duty at one part of his life, though he erred in another part of it. He had not sworn with a double, but with a perfect heart, and was accepted of God in this expression of his love to the law. His vows were a means in the general tenor of life of promoting his sanctification. After his great transgressions as well as before them, he remembered and recognised his vows, and rejoiced that he had sworn to the Lord, although he greatly mourned that he had so shamefully violated his oath in some parts of his conduct.

On the whole David deserves praise for his behaviour, first, in swearing; then, in renewing his promise to God; and lastly, in keeping it through life. And the honour we give to his memory is very consistent with our just detestation of his abominable uncleanness with Bathsheba, and of the atrocious murder of his gallant servant Uriah. But of those iniquities he sincerely repented, and they were graciously forgiven by God. His prayers were heard. The Lord washed him thoroughly from his iniquity, and cleansed him from his sin, and made him whiter than the snow, and bears testimony concerning him to all generations, that he was a man after his own heart who did all his will.

Follow David's example, 1. In vowing to the Lord that you will keep his righteous judgments. But you are far from imitating David, if you make this vow under transient impressions of the necessity of obedience without a firm and determined resolution that, whatever befalls you, it shall be your earnest desire and endeavour to walk in the statutes of the Lord blameless. When David swore unto the Lord, he left no secret resource for lying, or for uncleanness, or for any iniquity to which he might be tempted. He hated and abhorred lying and every false way. He loved the law of the Lord, and with joy he put his neck under the easy yoke of his God and his Redeemer. (*Psalm 119:104, 128*).

You are not called to make a new covenant of works with God on easier terms than the old covenant. You are called to trust in God who pardons iniquity, transgression, and sin, through an atonement already made for sin. But whilst you trust in the Lord Jesus Christ as your Saviour, you are called to promise obedience to him as your King; and you are called to promise no more than you engage to do if you call him your Lord. For why do you call him Lord, Lord,

Of David's Obedience to the Revealed Will of God

if you do not the things which he says? If you are afraid to promise obedience to him, you should be afraid likewise to confess that you were baptised, for your baptism brought you under indispensable obligations to obey him. For the same reason you should decline obedience to his dying commandment, "Do this in remembrance of me." For in obeying this part of his law you engage yourselves to obey every precept of his Word. (*Matthew 28:19, 20; 1 Corinthians 11*).

The children of Israel at Horeb promised that all that God had spoken they would do and be obedient. But God saw that their hearts were not right with him. Their words were good, but, "O," said God, "that there were such an heart in them that they might hear me for their own good, and for the good of their children after them." He would have been well pleased with their words if they had been spoken with pure hearts. He delights in the professions and vows of those who, like David, love his testimonies and are devoted to his fear. "Also the sons of the stranger that join themselves to the Lord, to serve him, and to love the name of the Lord, to be his servants, every one that keepeth the Sabbath from polluting it, and taketh hold of my covenant, even them will I bring into my holy mountain, and make them joyful in my house of prayer; their burnt-offerings and their sacrifices shall be accepted on mine altar."

Do you believe in Christ as made of God unto you righteousness? Believe in him also as made unto you sanctification. Your faith cannot be sound if you depend not in him for strength as well as pardon. And therefore the most humbling sense of your own weakness ought not to deter you from yielding yourselves to the Lord. "I beseech you, therefore, brethren, by the mercies of God, to present yourselves to him as a living sacrifice, holy and acceptable to him through Jesus Christ."

2. Often recognise your engagements to keep God's righteous judgments. We are too apt through the selfishness of our hearts to forget that we are not our own masters, but the servants of him who hath bought us with his own blood, and to whom we have devoted ourselves. We find David often calling to mind his indispensable engagements to the service of God, and renewing his vows, (*Psalm 16:2; 116:8, 9*). And doubtless his frequent remembrance of what he had said to the Lord, as well as of what God had spoken to

him, was a happy means of the great improvements he made in the spiritual life.

If you are left to fail in your course of obedience after vowing to the Lord, you ought to be greatly humbled. You cannot be too deeply humbled. You may find reason to question the sincerity of your heart when you came under your solemn obligations, although failures are no sure proof of the point, as you see in the instance before us. Never was one more sincere and cordial in swearing than David, that he would keep God's righteous judgments, although few saints have been left to fall into such abominable iniquities. He was left to himself for a proof to us all how greatly we need preserving grace from God.

But if you should see reason to confess, in searching your hearts and ways, that there has been something essentially wrong in your manner of vowing to the Lord, that you would be his servants, think not that you are loosed from your obligations because they were not entered into with pure hearts. God hath no pleasure in fools. Pay that which thou hast vowed. Seek from God that truth in the inward parts which he requires, and which he alone can work within you, that from henceforth you may perform your engagements. And however cordial you may have been in your engagements to the service of God, it will still be your great advantage to search and try your hearts, whether you can with cheerfulness and unfeigned pleasure renew your engagements. Can you ever have any reason to repent of your repentance from dead works? If after coming under engagements to the service of God you have been left to turn aside, leave your complaint where it ought to be left. The fault is not in these engagements, which it was certainly your duty to take upon yourselves, but in that corruption of your own hearts, which has tempted you to prove unfaithful to God. You certainly did well in swearing with uprightness of heart that you would approve yourselves faithful servants to God. But you have done very ill in forgetting for a moment that the vows of God are upon you. God might justly cast you out of his sight, and fill you with your own ways. But he is not a man like you. He is not the son of man. He is faithful to his engagements even in dealing with his people who have dealt unfaithfully with him. The assurance of his faithfulness ought to increase the abasement of your spirits before him, but at the same time to encourage you to return unto him, with new professions, and even with new promises, of care to please him, and of vigilance against those temptations that might again turn your steps out of his holy paths. Take away all iniquity, and receive us graciously, so will we render the calves of our lips. We will no more return to our former follies, for in thee the fatherless findeth mercy.

3. Perform your engagements to the Lord. "I have opened my mouth to the Lord, and I cannot go back," said one of the ancient believers when he believed that his vow obliged him to sacrifice his dearest hopes for this world. But your vow binds you to do nothing but what duty and interest would have required you to do, if you had never opened your mouths to the Lord. "The ways of wisdom are pleasantness, and all her paths are peace." But those who refuse to walk in them can never find peace, and least of all can those find peace who turn aside out of them to walk in the ways of sin.

"Keep your hearts with all diligence." Stand at a distance from all temptation. Call frequently to mind the powerful motives which should influence every part of your behaviour, and those powerful motives that will recommend to your hearts those particular duties which you are called daily to perform. Live by the faith of the Son of God, through whose grace you must be fitted for every instance of obedience, and preserved in the day of temptation from falling, or recovered when you have been so unhappy and so unwise as to yield to temptation.

Pray with all prayer and supplication for grace to perform your engagements. "Thy vows are upon me, O God: I will render praises unto thee. For thou hast delivered my soul from death: wilt not thou deliver my feet from falling, that I may walk before God in the light of the living?" (*Psalm 56:12, 13*).

9
David's Afflictions and Fears

The sorrows of death compassed me, and the floods of ungodly men made me afraid. The sorrows of hell compassed me about: the snares of death prevented me. (Psalm 18:4, 5)

WE never can be duly thankful to God if we forget the troubles which we have suffered, and the distress of our souls when they were pressing us down. Never was a man on earth more deeply penetrated than David with gratitude to the Lord for the deliverances which he had received, and never did he forget those embittering circumstances of his troubles which endeared to his heart his gracious deliverances.

"I will love thee, O Lord, my strength. The Lord is my rock, and my fortress, and my deliverer; my God, my strength in whom I will trust, my buckler, and the horn of my salvation and my high tower." Why does the holy man heap up so many expressions of delight and joy in the Lord when giving thanks for his deliverances from the hands of all his enemies? Because his distresses had been exceeding great and to all appearance desperate, and the exceeding riches of the grace of God had been marvellously displayed in sending from above, and taking and drawing him out of the many waters which threatened to overwhelm his soul.

"The sorrows of death compassed me, and the floods of ungodly men made me afraid." When Paul speaks of a great deliverance bestowed upon him in Asia, he says that God had delivered him from so great a death. In another passage he protests that he died daily. David through a considerable part of his life had good reason to say that he was in deaths every day. He felt the sorrows of a man who knows himself to be in a dying condition. Through the restless malice and power of his enemies he was exposed to the same dangers and fears as a man swallowed up in deep waters and forcibly hurried along with the torrent. The sorrows of hell compassed him about. He was environed on every side with deadly danger, and nothing but wonderful interpositions of divine providence could preserve him from being chased out of the world to mingle with the congregation of separate spirits. The snares of death prevented him. He was like a bird caught unexpectedly in the snare of the fowler. And if the Lord had not, by methods wondrous in David's eyes and in the eyes of all who heard of them, wrought deliverance for him, his life must have been cut off from the earth. – Let us speak:

I. Of the great distresses and dangers of David.

II. Of his sorrows and fears under his afflictions.

III. Of the reasons why God suffered him to be brought into such calamitous circumstances.

I. Of the great distresses and dangers of David.

David probably enjoyed such happiness and tranquillity as this evil world can afford before he was anointed by Samuel to be king over Israel; but almost from that time, whilst he was yet in early youth, his troubles commenced. He was indeed for a little time a favourite with Saul, but from the day when he killed Goliath, and was celebrated by the daughters of Israel as the champion of their country, he became an object of restless jealousy to a tyrant who scrupled no wickedness to wreak his malice on the innocent.

He was employed in the duties of his office as a servant of the king, when his master cast a javelin at him to take away his life, and he avoided out of his presence twice. Had not the Lord been on his side he must have perished, and his death would have been ascribed not to Saul, but to that temporary insanity with which Saul was frequently seized.

He was afterwards honoured to be the king's son-in-law. But this honour was intended for his destruction. It was granted on a condition which the insidious prince hoped would prove fatal to a youth

David's Afflictions and Fears

of an ambitious temper, as he supposed David to be, and of a courage that rose to a blind temerity. He was to give for the dowry of the princess a hundred foreskins of the Philistines. It was expected that in the ardour of his desire to be united in marriage with the royal family, he would expose himself to danger, from which he could not be expected to escape with his life; or if he did escape the swords of the Philistines, it was expected by Saul that his own daughter under his direction would be a snare to him from which he could not long escape. When Saul found that his daughter would not become such a passive instrument as he expected, for the destruction of her husband, his fury broke through every restraint of decency and shame. He gave general orders to his servants and to his son Jonathan, to murder an innocent man who had wrought with God in a great salvation to Israel. Many doubtless of Saul's servants were well disposed to gratify his passions. How then was it possible for him to escape? His own house was no refuge for him. The college of the prophets, with the venerable prophet at their head by whom Saul was anointed king, could not protect him. Thither Saul not only sent messengers, but went in person to kill David, and was prevented only by a very singular interposition of divine providence from executing his bloody purpose.

David was compelled to seek refuge in dens and caves of the rocks and mountains. But Saul had so many cringing slaves through every part of the country to discover David's haunts, that if God had not shielded him in a very singular manner he must have soon been swallowed up. At Sela-hammahlekoth he was like a lamb almost in the mouth of the lion; and no hope seemed to be left for him unless wings had been given him like the wings of an eagle, to flee far away that he might be at rest, till the Philistines, his mortal enemies, were unconsciously made the instruments of his escape, by an incursion into the land which compelled the tyrant to call off his forces for a different service. In a cave at Engedi David seemed to be in almost as great danger, till God put his enemy into his power by leading him, without knowing it, apart from his own army into the midst of David's troops, who were all secreted from view in the clefts of the rocks and dark caverns of the earth. By a dead sleep which seized upon Saul and all his army, David was again miraculously preserved from destruction in the wilderness of Ziph. Never was a lion more eager to seize a defenceless lamb than Saul was to seize on David; and it was the care of the people in whose country he was, to deliver him up into the hands of the king.

After such remarkable deliverances, and after the remarkable proofs which David found means to give, that he was one of Saul's best friends, it might have been expected that he would be permitted to breathe from persecution, and to revisit without danger the sanctuary of the Lord, which he so dearly loved. But he knew Saul too well to trust to his justice or gratitude, or warmest professions of friendship; and therefore he thought he could not do better than to retire into the land of the Philistines, to a place where he had once been put into such fear of his life, that he had been glad to put on the appearance of insanity, that if possible their hatred of him might be swallowed up in pity or contempt.

Through the humanity or policy of Achish he found a shelter in the land of the Philistines for a time; but there too he was encompassed with dangers, for they were the inveterate enemies of Israel, and David was a sincere lover of his country. Such were the perils of his condition, that although he hated and abhorred lying, he was strongly tempted to make use of equivocation, which is a species of lying, in more than one instance. Nor could his mean shifts have saved him from the rage of the Philistines when he was coming with them to the battle, if God, who has the hearts of all men in his hands, had not overruled their counsels, when the lords of the Philistines said to Achish, "Make this fellow return to his place. Is not this David the king of the land, of whom they sang one to another in dances, saying, Saul slew his thousands and David his ten thousands?" David had reason to wonder that they did not say, Let us destroy this destroyer of our famous champion, this man who bought a princess to himself with the blood of our people; let us extinguish in his blood that great name which he acquired by the slaughter of our people, and appease their ghosts by chasing him out of the world.

David was involved in inextricable perplexity when he followed Achish to the war against Israel. He could neither fight for nor against his kind benefactor, nor refrain from action, without exposing himself to incalculable dangers of life or reputation. Perhaps the terrors of the shadow of death never appeared more dismal to him than those perplexities to which he was now reduced by the shifts which

David's Afflictions and Fears

his distressed circumstances had compelled him to use. He was a happy man when the wrath of the lords of the Philistines was kindled to such a degree as tended to extricate him from his embarrassment, and to no higher degree. Yet he had scarcely escaped from this snare when he found himself entangled in another scarcely less dreadful. The Amalekites had made a spoil of all his substance, and of the substance of all his followers, and had carried their wives and children captive, whilst he was following the banners of the king of Gath. His people, not without the appearance of reason, laid the blame of this heart-rending calamity upon him, and whilst their souls were grieved for their sons and their daughters, they spake of stoning him. What condition could appear more deplorable! The Israelites drove him out of their land; the Philistines expelled him from their army; the Amalekites plundered him of his substance and his family. If he looked to the right or to the left hand, all refuge failed him; no man cared for his soul, and there were many who sought his precious life.

Such was the spite of his great persecutor, that when he could not find an opportunity to execute his rage on David himself, he put to the sword the best and the greatest men who had the courage to show him any kindness. What must the good man have felt when fourscore and five priests of the Lord were butchered, for a kindness shown to him by one of their number, and when even the sucking children and the oxen and sheep of those who were suspected to be his friends were not spared? Cursed was the wrath of his enemies, for it was fierce; and their wrath, for it was cruel. It is probable that the father who begat, and the mother who bare him, would not have escaped if he had not committed them to the protection of the king of Moab till his calamities were overpast.

His sore distresses were not at end when he was advanced to the throne. The greater part of the tribes of Israel carried on war against him for some time under the command of a very illustrious captain. The Philistines were exasperated when they heard that the man whom one of their princes had protected in his distress, and all of them had spared, when he was a fugitive amongst them, was now advanced to the throne of that nation which they had long hated with a cruel hatred. They hoped to destroy, by the hands of some of their giants, the man who had made himself famous by destroying their Goliath, and he would have been killed by Ishbi-benob, of the race of the giants, if God had not graciously strengthened Abishai the son of Zeruiah to be his preserver.

But the greatest of all his dangers after his advancement to the kingdom was that to which he was exposed by his unnatural son Absalom, and his treacherous counsellor Ahithophel. David's life was what above all things they sought, because he appeared to be the only obstacle to the accomplishment of their designs. "I will come upon him," said Ahithophel, whose counsel was reputed equal to an oracle, "I will come upon him while he is weary and weak-handed, and will make him afraid; and all the people that are with him shall flee; and I will smite the king only, and I will bring back all the people unto thee; the man whom thou seekest is as if all returned; so all the people shall be in peace." This saying of Ahithophel pleased Absalom well, and all the people of Israel. They thought it expedient that one man should die, that all the people might enjoy peace. How was it possible that David could escape the snares laid for him by the greatest politicians in Israel or in the world, with the approbation of all the princes, and of the man whom they had chosen to be their king? He was deeply conscious of his danger. He saw that without extraordinary interpositions of divine providence he would soon be cut off from the earth. His heart was sore pained within him, and the terrors of death fell upon him. Fearfulness and trembling came upon him, and horror overwhelmed him.

The short summary which we have given of David's afflictions is chiefly taken from the history of his life and reign. Much might be added to it from his own Psalms, in which many particulars are brought to view, which a short account of his life could not properly comprise. We learn from them that his enemies were very many, very malicious, very unreasonable, and that they had cast off all fear of God, and all regard to truth or justice, in the slanders which they published, and the arts which they employed for his destruction. Severe and dangerous sicknesses are sometimes mentioned among his other complaints, and those may well be believed to be natural consequences of his other untoward troubles and the attendant anxieties of his mind. Troubles of various kinds often concurred to embitter his days and to spread a gloom over his mind. God seemed to his distressed soul to have forgotten him, or to have called to remembrance his iniquities, to render unto him the deserved recompense of his works. "Deep calleth unto deep at the noise of God's waterspouts; all his billows and his waves passed over him." And he was under strong temptation to say that he was cast off from God's eyes, and set up as a monument of his displeasure.

II. But the consideration of the state of his mind under his troubles, was the thing proposed.

1. Great *sorrow* often obtained possession of his soul. When he says, "The sorrows of death compassed me," we are put in mind of what was said by one whose sorrows as far exceeded the sorrows of David as he excelled him in the sanctity of his life, and in the dignity of his person. "My soul is exceeding sorrowful," or encompassed with sorrow even unto death. And as David was an eminent type of that blessed person, his sorrows may be considered as an emblem of those inexpressible and unequalled sorrows which seized on our Redeemer when he was bearing our iniquities.

Poverty, exile, reproach, and danger of life, are evils which make a deep impression of grief upon the minds of most men, especially when they meet together; and David, though a wise and a holy man, was not exempt from the feelings of human nature.

He was reduced to great poverty when he was driven from home, and declared to be an enemy to his prince, whom it would be treasonable to relieve or assist. If we were in absolute poverty, we might hope to find relief from the charity of well-disposed neighbours. But David was often compelled to dwell amongst men who without cause were his enemies, (*Psalm 56*). And his friends were afraid to perform the offices of friendship. They knew what Ahimelech had brought not only on himself but on his family and kindred by a single instance of hospitality to David. It is indeed surprising that David could find subsistence and his four hundred or six hundred men, without the use of means which his soul abhorred, although necessity might seem to justify them. Doubtless his soul was often wrung with sorrow at the thought of the persecutions which his followers were compelled to endure, and with anxiety about the means of making such necessary provision for them as to restrain them within the bounds of honesty.

But exile is more distressing to a lover of his country than poverty. It was peculiarly distressing to an Israelite indeed, who could not leave his country without leaving behind him the sanctuary of his God. David was for years driven from his house, from his beloved wife, who was given to another man, and from the tabernacle of the Lord. He was driven for a year and four months out of the Lord's land. How deeply he was affected with grief we learn from his complaints. "They have driven me out this day from abiding in the inheritance of the Lord, saying, Go serve other gods. Woe is me that I dwell in Meshech, and sojourn in the tents of Kedar."

His heart was broken with reproach whilst he heard the slanders of many, and had good reason to think that they made an impression much to his disadvantage on the minds of those whose friendship and esteem were most highly valued and most necessary for him, (*Psalms 35, 126*).

Continual dangers to himself and to his adherents could not fail to fill his mind with great uneasiness. He had indeed promises which assured him of a happy event to himself, but there is no wonder that his faith of these promises was sometimes shaken. Besides, these promises did not secure him from the danger of losing some of his most faithful friends. His dearest friend was lost to him before the end of his troubles, and it might almost be said that he lost the half of himself when his wife, whom he had purchased at the great risk of his life, was forced to become the wife of another man.

The distress of his mind from these and many other concurrent circumstances pressed very heavily upon him, at those times especially when his body was weakened by sickness and his mind enfeebled by apprehensions of God's displeasure on account of his sins. When he composed some of his Psalms, he was oppressed with such anguish from a complication of the most grievous afflictions, that he made his bed to swim with his tears, (*Psalms 6, 31, 38*).

But to his grief for himself, and for his friends, let us add what he felt for his country, for the indignities done to his God, and even for the guilt and misery which his enemies were bringing upon themselves, and we shall see that he drank deeper than most other men have done in any age of the cup of affliction.

David, from his early days, was an ardent lover of his country, and doubtless his unction by Samuel, which gave him the prospect of the throne, gave him a livelier interest in all its concerns. He could not but feel the deepest regret when the land was dissolved, with all that dwelt therein, by the corrupt administration of Saul; when the faithful decayed from among the sons of men, when vile men were high in place, and the wicked walked on every side, and lifted up their horn on high.

He hated and abhorred every false way, and therefore he was pierced with grief at the sight and hearing of that wickedness which everywhere abounded. The wickedness of his enemies gave him much disquiet for the trouble and danger to which he was exposed by it, but still more, perhaps, for the mischiefs that he saw them bringing on their own heads, and most of all for the dishonour they were doing to God, by the violation and contempt of his holy law. Horror took hold on him, because of the wicked who forsook God's law. Rivers of waters ran down his eyes, because his enemies sinned so grievously against his God in the wrongs they did to him. His own feelings and condition, however important to him considered by themselves, were not of great consequence in comparison with the indignities done to him whom he loved far more than his life. It was as a sword within his bones when his enemies said daily to him, "Where is thy God?"

Thus was David penetrated with the deepest grief. His soul clave unto the dust. His heart was melted with heaviness.

2. Great *fear* often seized upon him. The floods of ungodly men made him afraid. But of whom was he afraid? Did he think that the Lord had forgotten to be gracious, and had in anger shut up his tender mercies? Surely he was a firm believer in the mercy and faithfulness of God. And yet his faith had a great fight to endure. It was sore tried by many enemies and by hard dispensations of providence. He could not seriously doubt of the veracity of God. He was sure that if the promises on which he rested should fail, there could be no fault, no change of mind, no want of power or goodness in the Most High. Yet he frequently found great difficulty in making use of these precious truths for the support of his own hope in God. An overwhelming tract of afflictions holds the mind captive, and almost forcibly excludes those thoughts of the principles of truth believed by the heart which are necessary to give them their proper effect. Even an Abraham could say, "They will kill me for my wife's sake," although his life was at that time under the security of a promise

from God that he should have a numerous seed, (*Genesis 13:16*). "One day," said David, "I shall perish by the hand of Saul," although by divine designation and promise he was to succeed Saul on the throne of Israel.

God will not, he cannot lie. The conclusion from this sure principle was plain, that all the promises made to David would most certainly be accomplished. But whilst he held the principle, he was not always able to hold fast the conclusion. When he was in his usual temper of mind he could say, "God hath spoken in his holiness, I will rejoice." But sometimes in his haste he said, "All men are liars." He never would have said, God is a liar. But when he said, "All men are liars," he did not except the prophets who had spoken unto him the word of God.

In days of great temptation it is very difficult to restrain those corrupt reasonings by which faith is embarrassed. The promise of God was certainly faithful and true. But David might think that the truth of God would not be impeached, although he came short of the promised mercy on account of his iniquities. He found himself in circumstances of such danger, that he could not, without extraordinary succour from above, hold fast his integrity. His steps had almost slipped, his feet were almost gone. He had even on some occasions been left so far to himself as to take unworthy means for preserving himself from danger. These things pressed sore upon his mind. The heart knoweth its own bitterness. The heart of a saint alone knows the bitterness felt by a right sense of the evil of sin and of divine displeasure on account of it. David, remembering his sins and the errors of his youth, and his miscarriages under pressing danger, was overwhelmed with confusion and fear. What if he had made God his enemy? He surely deserved to be rebuked in God's indignation, and chastised in his sore displeasure. God was true to his word, but his faithfulness was not sullied by destroying in the desert that generation which he brought out of Egypt, although they had the promise of entering into God's rest, which would have been fulfilled to them if they had not come short of it through their own unbelief.

Such might be the workings of David's mind at the times when a deep consciousness of guilt, and a terrifying sense of divine displeasure, discomposed his mind, although during the greater part

David's Afflictions and Fears

even of the days of tribulation he could glorify God by an unshaken confidence. No man is always himself. David could often say, "The Lord is my light and my salvation; whom shall I fear? The Lord is the strength of my life; of whom shall I be afraid?" But at other times he cried out in the agony of his soul, "I am cut off from thine eyes; I am poor and needy, and my heart is wounded within me; I am gone like the shadow when it declineth; I am tossed up and down as the locust." – It was proposed to enquire:

III. Why God suffered the holy man to be brought into such calamitous situations. May we not reasonably hope, that those men whom God blesses with his special favour will be preserved from those sorrows and fears which are the just portion of the wicked? Can he not by his divine power, by which he rules over the whole world, set them high above all their enemies, and fill their mouths at all times with songs of triumph? Undoubtedly he can, and undoubtedly he would do it, if he saw that it would tend to their best advantage; for all his paths are mercy and truth unto them that fear him. But whatever David might think of the awful circumstances in which he was often placed at the time when he was enduring the blows of God's hand, and the contradiction of sinners, yet, when he afterwards took a review of all God's dealings with him, he declares that it was good for him that he had been afflicted.

1. His faith was tried and approved. We are called to count it all joy when we fall into divers temptations, knowing this – that the trying of our faith worketh patience. Some remains of unbelief were found in David when his faith was tried as it were by fire. But it was good for him to be brought to the knowledge of those evils that were in his heart. And on the whole, his faith, when it was tried, was found to be unto praise and honour and glory. (*Psalm 27:13, 14; 118*).

2. His sore afflictions were means for quickening his devotions. Never was there a more fervent supplicant at the throne of grace. Many of his prayers are on record, and we cannot but observe the effect of his great and sore adversities in awakening his heart to devotion and inflaming his desires.

3. He learned from his sore adversities the value of the Word of God. He learned the value of its promises, its precepts, its warnings,

its histories. He made it his rule, when trouble came upon him, to turn his attention to the Word of God, and he always found in it direction, support, consolation, warning, and arguments to enforce his prayers, (*Psalm 119*).

4. Those graces were improved in him by his afflictions, to the exercise of which he was to be called in the days of his prosperity – his humility, his meekness, his humanity and tenderness of heart to the poor and afflicted. David would not have been such an excellent model for kings as he was, if he had obtained the throne like his successors, by hereditary right, without passing to it through a great fight of afflictions. The experience of misery taught him to pity and succour the miserable. The experience which he had of the mischievous effects of Saul's corrupt administration and of the views of his ministers, taught him the necessity of curbing the wicked, and of promoting the interests of virtue and piety by his example and authority. (*Psalms 75, 101*).

5. His great and sore afflictions prepared the way for those marvellous loving-kindnesses which inspired him with joy and praise. He would not have spoken so rapturously on many occasions of the salvations wrought for him by the God of his salvation, if he had not tasted the bitter dregs of the cup of affliction. He never thought he could sufficiently praise that mercy which had delivered him from great and sore adversities, or that he could do enough for that God who had done such wonderful things for him. (*Psalms 116, 71*).

6. He was designed to be an eminent type of our Lord Jesus Christ in his sufferings and in his exaltation. Many of his Psalms speak of the sufferings and glory of Christ under the figure of his own sufferings and glory. This was a great honour to him, to be, by anticipation, conformed to the image of his blessed Son in his afflictions, in his griefs and fears, in his behaviour under his sufferings, and in the happy event of them. (*Psalms 22, 69; Acts 2:25-31*).

7. The church in every age was to derive unspeakable benefit from David's sufferings. The devout exercises of his soul in the days of his distress have directed and animated the devotions of the afflicted in every age. (*Romans 15:4*).

Improvement 1. Think it not strange that you must endure many chastisements and trials in the world. Are your afflictions equal in number or greatness to David's? (*James 5*).

Thank God that you see the footsteps of the saints before you in the valley of humiliation, and in the valley of the shadow of death. But thank God especially that our Lord Jesus Christ is set forth before you afflicted, persecuted, crucified, bearing your curse, that your afflictions may be turned into blessings.

2. Admire the providence of God. He knows how to execute his purposes by means which seem calculated to defeat them. Clouds and darkness are often round about him, but righteousness and judgment are ever the habitation of his throne. Whilst David was tempted to think that God had forgotten his promises, he was taking measures for the more signal accomplishment of them. He can make death the means of life, and turn darkness into light.

We ought not therefore to judge of the end of a thing from the beginning or progress of it, in opposition to the word of God. What God hath said will be done, although every appearance should be against it. (*Hosea 6:1-3*).

3. Be ready to meet with every occurrence in the course of your lives. You do not know what evil shall befall you; but you know that man is born to trouble. You know that the best of men have met with great tribulations in the way to the kingdom of heaven. You are very unwise if you are not prepared for changes. Collect from the Word of God those precious truths which will be useful for your support in a day of evil, and endeavour not only to know but to believe them, and to have them in constant readiness for use. It will be of great advantage with this view to have the Psalms of David familiarised to your minds.

What if troubles should befall you, which will bring death into your immediate view? How terrible will it be to be prevented by the snares of death, if you are not found in Christ? If you are found in him, and live by the faith of him, an unexpected death will not be a loss, but a gain to you. You will then only close your eyes on this world, to open them in that world where you will see, not the pleasant light of day, but the brightness of the divine glory, and be for ever satisfied with his image.

David: His Life and Character

Whilst you enjoy peace and quietness, be thankful but not secure. You must certainly die, although you should escape these changes in the course of life which are so common in the world. You know not how soon the cords of death may take such hold of you, as to put a final period to your present life. "But if a man keep my savings," says Jesus, "he shall not see death," (*John 8:51; 11:25, 26; Romans 8:11*).

10

Of David's Behaviour in the Time of Trouble

They had almost consumed me upon earth; but I forsook not thy precepts. (Psalm 119:87)

DAVID was not only persecuted and harassed by his enemies, but almost consumed by them. They would have made an end of his earthly life, if God had not, by wonderful methods, preserved him when he was apparently in the jaws of death.

This was a very trying condition. What multitudes are there who behave well, as far as men can judge, when they meet with no extraordinary temptation, and yet in the day of sore trial put forth their hands to iniquity. But David's conscience bare him witness in the Holy Ghost that he adhered steadfastly to the great rule of duty in the most trying circumstances in which he was placed by the malice of his enemies. "They had almost consumed me upon earth; but I forsook not thy precepts." Before his troubles came upon him he had chosen the way of truth. He had laid down the principle that in all the businesses and circumstances of his life he would make the testimonies of God his counsellors, and to this resolution he adhered not only when he entered on his long course of tribulation, but during the whole time of its continuance. At the times when he found his dangers multiplied and in appearance desperate, he would not, to save his life, have wilfully turned aside out of the good path. He considered what was the will of God concerning his behaviour in present circumstances, and regulated by it his steps, whatever consequences might have been apprehended as the result.

David: His Life and Character

This passage will give us occasion to consider:

I. David's holy conduct under his troubles; and,

II. What his reasons were for so invariably adhering to his duty.

I. Let us consider how David behaved in extreme distress. He did not forsake God's precepts, but constantly behaved under his trials, according to their prescriptions.

1. In the time of his trouble the precepts of God were the constant subject of his thoughts. Most other men in his condition would have suffered their thoughts to be engrossed by the unpleasant circumstances of their condition, by the inconveniences to which they were put by the persecutions they endured, by the pains they felt, by the dismal prospects before them, by the wickedness of their enemies, by the coldness or treachery of their friends. Thus they would have added to their own misery, and seconded the malice of their enemies. But David was too wise to give his thoughts leave to fix themselves on subjects so unpleasant and so hurtful. He found such delight and such advantage in meditating on the Scriptures at all times, and especially in times of distress, that he would not suffer his mind to be diverted from them by any other subject that pressed upon him. He could not help contemplating at times the magnitude and the various embittering circumstances of his distresses. But his unpleasant feelings and thoughts were powerful motives to turn his mind to that blessed Book which presented to his view unfailing springs of consolation. The statutes of the Lord were his song in the house of his pilgrimage. O how did he love the law of the Lord! It was his meditation night and day, not only when he was at rest in his house, and flourishing in his palace, but when he was chased like a partridge from mountain to hill, and compelled to seek refuge in dens and caves of the earth. It was his wisdom, when princes sat and spake against him, to make God's testimonies his counsellors. We rejoice in days of danger and trouble if we have found a friend who can advise us how to take measures that will effectually extricate us from every embarrassment, and bring a happy termination to our distresses. The Wonderful Counsellor was David's friend, who made him to know the way of God's testimonies, and he learned from them how to counteract all the malicious designs of his persecutors,

Of David's Behaviour in the Time of Trouble

how to escape from every snare, how to extract advantage from all the innumerable afflictions by which he was so frequently pressed down. (*Psalm 119*).

2. He was careful under all his troubles to walk in the way wherein he was directed by the Word of God to walk. It is one thing to know, even in the times of prosperity, the way wherein we should go, and another thing to walk in it. But in times of distress the best men find it very difficult to observe the rules of conduct which they have learned, and which they earnestly wish to reduce to practice. When you are well, you can with great fluency exhort a sick man to be patient, and a dying man cheerfully to commit his spirit into the hands of a gracious Redeemer. But when you are yourselves stretched on a bed of affliction, you feel that your arguments have no force upon yourselves unless God be pleased to give them efficacy on your hearts. Yet you will find it no vain thing to have your duty presented to your minds, and to have your purpose firmly established in your minds, to make the will of God, and not your own understanding or feelings, the rule of your behaviour. David was a man of like passions with us. He was not always himself. To will, however, was present with him. He swore, and he performed it, to keep God's precepts in adversity as well as in prosperity. His patience and perseverance were not absolutely perfect. But his attainments were very great, and he is an eminent example to us of the exercise of suffering graces. His faith in God continued firm and vigorous under all his sufferings. The providence of God seemed to set itself in opposition to his promises. A glorious high throne was promised to him, and yet he was driven from his house to dwell in caves and deserts. From those too he was driven to a strange land. And yet he still believed that nothing would fail of any good thing that God had promised to him. Sometimes indeed he found a powerful impulse in his mind to think that God had forgotten him, and that his promise failed for evermore. But he would not so far give place to the devil, as to suffer thoughts so detested by him, to obtain the possession of his heart. When he was himself he could say, "God hath spoken in his holiness, I will rejoice; I will mete out Shechem; I will divide the valley of Succoth. Ephraim is mine, Manasseh is mine." The whole land of Israel is mine. I shall be made head of the heathen. "The word

of the Lord is sure." It is as certain that I shall one day enjoy all the power and grandeur that are promised to me, as if I were already in possession of them.

When he was stripped of all his possessions, when his house was burnt, when his wives and children were carried captives, and his people reduced to such extremity of distress, through a rash step which he had been unwise enough to take, that they spake of stoning him, his faith did not fail. He knew that his people would not be permitted by God to stone him, and that the Lord who had showed him so great and sore troubles, would quicken him and bring him up from the lower parts of the earth, and would accomplish all the promises made to him in their utmost extent of meaning. David encouraged himself in the Lord his God. He had taken hold of the covenant which is ordered in all things and sure, and could say of the Lord, "He is my refuge, and my fortress, and my God, and in him I will trust."

The faith of David was so far from being weakened by his manifold distresses, that it was greatly improved and strengthened. The more his troubles abounded, the more were his thoughts turned to those testimonies which comforted him against all his sorrows; and the more he thought of them, the more deeply he was penetrated with the conviction that they excelled in faithfulness. When all refuge failed him, and no man cared for his soul; when his enemies were fearfully increased in number, and when his very friends were greatly tempted to think that his condition was desperate, he still said to the Lord, "Thou art my refuge, and my portion in the land of the living. Thou art my shield and my glory, and the lifter up of mine head. I will both lay me down in peace, and sleep, and awake in tranquillity; for thou, Lord, sustainest me," (*Psalms 3, 31, 142*).

Nor was his faith in God subverted by the consciousness of much sin which might have justly provoked the Lord to cast him out of his sight. He was humbled to the dust at the remembrance of his iniquities. He acknowledged that he could not stand before God in judgment, but he knew that there was forgiveness with the Lord, and therefore hoped in his mercy for every blessing promised to him in the present life, and for the richer blessings of eternity in the life to come. (*Psalms 51, 65, 130, 143*).

Of David's Behaviour in the Time of Trouble

3. He patiently submitted to the will of God in all his persecutions and tribulations. He knew that wicked men could do nothing to his prejudice without divine permission, and he was persuaded that the Lord was righteous and good, not only in what he did with his own hand, but in what he permitted to be done by the hands of men. When Shimei cursed him, he would not suffer Abishai to take off the head of the man who had poured out the vilest slanders and the most virulent imprecations against the man who had well deserved the veneration and gratitude of all Israel. The Lord had bidden him curse David, who then shall say unto him, "Why hast thou done so?" (*2 Samuel 16*).

Faith and patience are frequently conjoined in Scripture as graces so intimately connected with one another that they cannot be separated. If we are firmly persuaded that God will perfect all that concerns us, we will patiently bear all that he is pleased to lay upon us, because we know that no evil can befall us which will not have a happy termination. David patiently waited the end of his calamities, because he was persuaded that the words spoken by God would be all fulfilled in their season. And he calls upon us all to follow his example: "Commit thy way unto the Lord; trust also in him; and he shall bring it to pass. And he shall bring forth thy righteousness as the light, and thy judgment as the noonday. Rest in the Lord, and wait patiently for him: fret not thyself because of him that prospereth in his way, because of the man who bringeth wicked devices to pass," (*Psalm 37:5-7*). "He that believeth shall not make haste," (*Isaiah 28:16*).

4. David's patience was attended with meekness of spirit and behaviour towards the instruments of his calamities. If we see and revere the hand of God in the evils that come upon us, we will entertain no fierce resentments against the men whom God employs for our correction or trial. We ought rather to pray for than to hate the poor men that are doing hurt to themselves and good to us. Our corrections are eventually beneficial to us of whatever kind they are, if we patiently endure them; but the benefits resulting to us are no diminution of the guilt of the instruments employed by providence in inflicting them.

We cannot but remember how meekly and charitably David behaved towards his great enemy Saul. When that tyrant was in his power, he not only spared but protected him, and addressed him in the language of reverence and love, when he remonstrated with him concerning the cruel treatment which had been given to him. He could not do justice to himself without asserting that he had been unjustly persecuted; yet he will not load his king with the injustice of his own hands, but seems to take it for granted that he had been prompted to what he had done by wicked counsellors. (*1 Samuel 24, 26*).

When that tyrant perished by the hands of the Philistines and by his own, he was far from insulting his memory by triumphing in his destruction, but sincerely bewailed his fall; and taking pleasure to speak of those parts of his character that tended to his praise, cast a veil over what was bad. "Saul and Jonathan were lovely in their lives, and in their death they were not divided. Ye daughters of Israel, weep over Saul, who clothed you in scarlet, with other delights," (*2 Samuel 1:23, 24*).

That David practised the same generous virtue towards his other enemies we learn from his behaviour to Shimei, to Amasa, and others who had conspired with Absalom against him, and from several passages in his Psalms, wherein he appeals to God as his witness that he had been a true friend to his bitter enemies. (for example *Psalm 35*).

It will, however, be said, that in several Psalms of David we find him praying to God against his enemies, and even imprecating the most signal vengeance against them. Hence it will be alleged, can this consist with that meekness of which he at other times makes so high professions?

There is no inconsistency between that meekness which we ought to show to all men, and that care of our own safety, and that zeal for the public welfare, and for the glory of God, which are not less essential than meekness of behaviour to the character of a wise and good man. David had many enemies, whose destruction was necessary, not only to his own safety, but to the welfare of the nation, and the glory of the great King who sits upon his throne, and ministers judgment in righteousness to his people, and to their enemies, (*Psalm 9*). We must not, however, think ourselves entitled to pray for such calamities to our enemies as those which David imprecated against his persecutors. We have not the same means of knowing that our enemies are irreclaimable, and that God has determined to glorify himself not by their reformation, but by their destruction. David was not only a saint but a prophet, and had the Holy Spirit given to him not only as a spirit of grace and supplication, but likewise as the spirit of prophecy. And his prayers on several occasions were prophecies put into his heart by that Spirit who taught him, and who teaches us what to pray for as we ought. He prophesied not only of the destruction of his own enemies, but of the destruction of the enemies of another king who was his Son and his antitype. There are none of the Psalms in which more awful imprecations are uttered against the haters of David than *Psalm 109*, and the predictions of this Psalm were fulfilled in Judas and the other enemies of Jesus. (*Acts 1*).

No man ever resembled Jesus in meekness more than the apostle Paul, and yet we find him praying that the Lord might reward Alexander the coppersmith, who had done him much evil, according to his works. But unless we can make it to appear that we know the mind of Christ about particular persons as well as Paul did in many instances, we must be cautious not to depart from the general rule, "Love your enemies, bless them that curse you, pray for them that despitefully use you and persecute you." This Jesus taught us to do by his example as well as by his doctrine; "Father, forgive them, for they know not what they do."

5. David maintained his uprightness under all the temptations of adversity and persecution. He resolved to use no crooked means to extricate himself from his distresses, and he kept his resolution as well as could be expected in the present state of human nature. We have already heard how averse he was to methods of violence against the head and chief of his persecutors. Had he permitted his warm friend Abishai to put forth his hand but once against Saul, the great obstruction to his safety and honour would have been for ever removed, for God had declared him to be Saul's successor. But he would rather have died a thousand times by the hands of violent and cruel men, than brought upon himself the guilt of one cruel action. "The day will come that he will die; God will smite him, or he will descend to battle, and perish." but I will not on any consideration kill him, or suffer him with my consent to be killed.

But here too an objection meets us. Did not David on some occasions lie or prevaricate to save his life, or to extricate himself from difficulties? When he was fleeing from Saul, and came to the house of Ahimelech, he pretended to be sent on a message by the king. When he made invasions on the enemies of Israel, he told Achish that he had been making them on the south of Judah. These words might have been explained into a meaning consistent with truth, but that was not the meaning in which he wished or expected them to be understood. He gave the same prince reason to hope that he would fight on his side, against his own people, although nothing was further from his heart; "Surely thou shalt know what thy servant can do." Achish was certainly made to know what David could do, but in a sense very contrary to what he had reason from David's profession to expect. To those instances of dissimulation in his own conduct, we may add the advice he gave to Hushai to pretend friendship to Absalom with a design of betraying him: "If thou wilt go and say to him, As I have been thy father's friend, I will be also thy friend; then mayest thou for me defeat the counsel of Ahithophel."

What shall we say to those instances of conduct? If they were not direct violations of the law of truth, did they not, at least, plainly infringe it in a manner fit only for cowards, but detested by every man of honour?

Far be it from us to justify sin even in a righteous man. Dishonest arts even for saving one's life ought to be abhorred, and death ought to be chosen rather than life, when it cannot be saved without dishonest artifices. The righteous man hates and abhors lying in all cases; and David hated it as much as any of us can do. Yet he certainly was impelled by cruel circumstances and by the remaining corruption of his heart, to make use, on some few occasions, of lies for extricating himself from those sore perplexities in which he was involved.

If we are Christians we have laid it down as a maxim of conduct never to deviate on any account from truth. Yet we cannot answer for ourselves what we might be driven by the violence of temptation to do, if we were placed in circumstances half so trying as those in which David was often placed. "If one of you be overtaken in a fault, ye who are spiritual restore such an one in the spirit of meekness; considering yourselves, lest ye also be tempted." We do not judge equitably of those who have been drawn or driven into sin, if we do not place ourselves in circumstances similar to theirs. We do not judge equitably of David's faults, if we do not consider how sore his

Of David's Behaviour in the Time of Trouble

adversities were, how greatly they were multiplied, how long they continued, and how little leisure he was allowed, on some pressing occasions, to consider how he was to speak or to act. When we must speak without a moment's consideration, and when life or death may be in the words that we speak, we will think it our duty as well as our wisdom, to go to the bounds of what is lawful to be spoken for our safety. But at such seasons it will be surprising if we have sufficient presence of mind to go to the utmost bound of what is lawful without overstepping it.

David sinned in the instances of behaviour we have mentioned, and in some others which are likewise on record, to which no doubt others would have been added by himself, if he had been called to confess before the world the evils of his life. In his confessions to God he acknowledges himself chargeable with many offences, for which he implored forgiveness. "There is not a just man upon earth that doeth good and sinneth not." But there is not a just man who does not earnestly endeavour to do good without sinning, and who does not mourn for his offences before God, and implore grace from him that he may stand perfect and complete in all the will of God. "O that my ways were directed," says David, "to keep thy statutes; then shall I not be ashamed when I have respect to all thy commandments. Remove from me the way of lying, and grant me thy law graciously."

Some may call in question the integrity of David in the means which he used to provide subsistence for himself and his followers, from the vengeance which he vowed against Nabal the Carmelite for refusing to supply his necessities. But we are assured by David himself, speaking by the Spirit of God, that he did justice to all men. And he was so well assured, by the testimony of the Spirit of God with his own spirit, of the rectitude of his behaviour, that he could make use of it as a plea for preservation from his oppressors. This testimony to his integrity is confirmed by the testimony of Nabal's servants. Notwithstanding of that indigence of his circumstances which constrained him to become a petitioner to a man of Belial, he was so far from suffering any depredations to be committed on the numerous flocks and herds of that wretched man, that David's troop was a defence to them from every plunderer. For his good services he had a right to expect a liberal reward from Nabal. His intention to revenge the insult which he received must be confessed to have been a plain violation of the laws of meekness and justice. We need not labour to excuse an instance of conduct which David himself deplored. God did not give him grace to prevent his sinful vow, but he gave him grace soon to repent of it, and to bless the Lord who had prevented him from executing it.

6. David served God and his country in the best way that he could when he was restrained from serving them as he wished to do. He could not in his banishment serve God in the sanctuary, but he held fast his religious profession, and his practice was uniformly correspondent to his profession. When he was under an apprehended necessity of seeking shelter among the Philistines, he did not profess any respect for Dagon, but prayed to God to preserve him from the infection of idolatry whilst he was dependent on the favour of the worshippers of idols. It was at least probable that he was going to dwell amongst heathens, when he prayed to the Lord that his heart might not be inclined to any evil work, to practise wicked works with men that work iniquity, or to eat of their dainties. (*Psalm 141*).

He was excluded from the public assemblies of God's worshippers, and his heart was poured out within him when he thought of the multitude that kept the holy days, with whom he had once enjoyed delightful communion. But it was his joy that those who banished him from the sanctuary, could not banish him from his God, for he knew that the presence of God was not limited to the sanctuary. When he remembered the Lord upon his bed, and meditated on him in the night watches, his soul was satisfied as with marrow and with fatness, and he praised the Lord with joyful lips. He could still pray, and he found that the Lord did not turn away his prayers. He could still consult God by means of his priest Abiathar or the prophet Gad. He could still speak of the greatness and glory of the Lord, and neglected no fit opportunities of doing it. We have reason to believe, although it is not expressly mentioned in the history of his life, that far from any mean compliances with the religious institutions of those heathen princes whose favour he found it expedient to conciliate, he rather sought and found opportunities of recommending to them his own religion. "I will speak of thy testimonies," he says, "before kings, and I will not be ashamed." When he asked protection to his parents from the king of Moab, he professed to that prince

Of David's Behaviour in the Time of Trouble

his humble dependence on his God for a termination to his calamities. From the intercourse of Hiram with Solomon, we find that that prince, who was even a lover of David, had conceived very high ideas of David's God. And we find Achish the king of Gath, swearing by the name of Jehovah, who was the God not of the Philistines, but of Israel, that David's behaviour had always been found by him good – as that of an angel of God.

When David ascended the throne of Israel his troubles were far from being at an end, though of a different kind from what they had formerly been; but still his heart was set upon the testimonies of God, and he did not make the urgent necessity of his affairs, when he was encompassed by deadly enemies, a pretence for neglecting any part of his duty. "Lord, remember David and all his afflictions: how he sware to the Lord, and vowed unto the mighty God of Jacob; Surely I will not come into the tabernacle of my house, nor go up into my bed; I will not give sleep to mine eyes, nor slumber to mine eyelids, until I find a place for the Lord, an habitation for the mighty God of Jacob," (*Psalm 132:1-5*).

He was not permitted by God, when he had attained rest in his palace, to build a temple for the Lord. But he determined by anticipation to share in the glorious service destined for his son Solomon, and took advantage, from the troubles to which he was put by the enemies of Israel, to provide materials for the noblest building which had ever been constructed by the hands of men. "Now behold," says he, "in my trouble, I have prepared for the house of the Lord an hundred thousand talents of gold, and an thousand thousand talents of silver, and of brass and iron without weight (for it is in abundance), timber also and stone have I prepared, and thou mayest add thereto."

His distress was very great when he was driven from his throne and capital by his unnatural son. He was banished from that habitation which he himself had prepared for the mighty God of Jacob, and his friends believed that nothing could give him so much comfort in his exile as to have the ark of God carried with him, wherever he might find it necessary to go; but he would not suffer the symbol of the divine presence to become again a wanderer like himself. "Carry back the ark of God," he said to his priests; "If the Lord take delight in me he will bring me again, and I shall see both it and his habitation:" but if he say thus, "I have no delight in thee, behold, I am in his hand, let him do unto me as seemeth good in his eyes." He was in no danger of forgetting his God, although the ark and the tabernacle in which he so much delighted, were at a great distance. When he awoke he was still with God, and believed that God would be still with him. "O my God, my soul is cast down within me; therefore will I remember thee from the land of Jordan, and of the Hermonites, from the hill Mizar."

Whilst he remembered his duty to his God, he could not forget his duty to his people. At the very time when he was persecuted by his king, and by many of his fellow subjects under the influence of the king, he did what he could for his country. He drove the Philistines from Keilah, although he was not long after under a necessity of seeking a refuge among them. The rich present he sent from Ziklag to many places of the land, was one of many proofs that his heart was not alienated from his own people, after all the instances of ingratitude which would have embittered to revenge the hearts of ordinary men. Although the king of Israel was his implacable enemy, and a great part of the people had the meanness to second his ill temper, or to give at least no discoveries of their dissatisfaction with the wrongs done to their champion, David still continued an Israelite indeed. He continued to love his people after the greater part of them had showed their monstrous ingratitude to their king and father, by taking part with the unnatural son who sought at the same time his life and his crown. Never was a prince worse rewarded for eminent services. Never did a prince either before or after such bad treatment set a nobler example of royal virtues. He must be confessed to have erred greatly when he numbered the people. God, displeased with the sins of Israel, left him to himself to bring upon them the pestilence. Yet in the time of the great calamity he prayed with sincerity and fervour, that the judgment might fall exclusively on himself, and upon his family. (*2 Samuel 24*). – We proposed:

II. To enquire why this holy man was so careful to keep the path of duty under all the temptations of his adversities; and it is scarcely necessary to give any other reason for it than the reality of that principle of religion by which he was animated. The seed of God remaineth in every man who is truly sanctified, and he cannot sin, because he is born of God. A double-minded man is unstable in all his ways, but an upright man is the same in prosperity and adversity. There may be changes in his behaviour, because the corrupt principle natural to men is not extinguished. He may fall, but he shall not be utterly cast down, for the Lord upholdeth him with his hand. The Spirit of God is the author and principle of the spiritual life, and it cannot be destroyed. Every man who is born of God, is kept by the power of God through faith unto salvation.

It will not, however, be unprofitable to mention some of those considerations which powerfully determined the mind of David to cleave to God's testimonies amidst all the persecutions and dangers of his eventful life.

1. He was fully persuaded that nothing happened or could happen to him without the permission of divine providence. He was persuaded that none could move a tongue or a hand against him any further than God had determined in his wise counsels to make them the instruments of his providence for good purposes. Men might behave very wickedly; but all God's ways are judgment. "I was dumb, I opened not my mouth, because thou didst it. Who is he that saith and it cometh to pass, when the Lord commandeth it not?" And if the Lord give commandment, who shall say unto him, What doest thou? Surely he will do nothing either by his own immediate agency, or by the hands of men, inconsistent with his righteousness or with his love to his people. (*Psalm 39; 2 Samuel 16*).

2. It was of incomparably greater importance in his view to behave dutifully under trouble, than to obtain deliverance from it. The loss of the greater part of sufferers is that their anxiety for deliverance from their distresses swallows up thoughts of infinitely greater consequence. They do not duly consider how they may glorify God and obtain benefit to their own souls from their distresses. David no doubt prayed fervently for divine interposition to rescue him from his tribulations; but he prayed with still greater fervour of spirit that the Lord might lead him in a plain path, because of his enemies, that his goings might be held up, and that he might be preserved from those iniquities by which he was in the greatest danger of being ensnared, (*Psalm 119*). If we are more solicitous about relief from troubles, than preservation from sin, or grace to perform our duty,

our temper is very different from that of David, and of all the ancient saints. They all sought in the first place the kingdom of God and his righteousness. They chose the testimonies of the Lord as their heritage for ever, and thought themselves incomparably happier when God lifted up the light of his countenance upon them, whatever their outward condition was, than the most prosperous transgressors when their corn and wine did most abound.

The heart knoweth its own bitterness. The heart of a saint finds more bitter than death the pains of a self-accusing conscience. David felt unspeakably more distress in the reflections of his own mind, upon some parts of his conduct, than he ever felt from the oppression of his enemies. If he had looked no higher than his own interest, he would have been careful in all his afflictions to keep a conscience void of offence both towards God and towards man.

3. David knew that his troubles would all come to a happy termination. He walked by faith and not by sight, and was assured that when he had endured the temptations assigned him, he should receive the promised crown. He took to him the shield of faith, and the helmet of salvation, and stood firm against the wiles of the devil, who doubtless used his utmost art and efforts to overthrow his goings. Had the holy man forsaken the path of duty in the day of trouble, he must have endured a sore rebuke from God, whose displeasure was infinitely more terrible in his view than the wrath of all the men on earth. But he was persuaded of the love of God to his soul, and knew that all his enemies would be confounded, and that he himself would be in due time more than a conqueror through him that loved him. "Hope thou in God," he said to his soul when it was disquieted with dismal apprehensions; "for I shall yet praise him for the help of his countenance. Deep calleth unto deep at the noise of thy waterspouts; all thy waves and thy billows have passed over me. Yet the Lord will command his loving-kindness in the daytime, and in the night his song shall be with me, and my prayer to the God of my life."

4. He knew that his troubles would turn to a good account through the grace of God enabling him to make the proper improvement of them. He knew that he should have good cause to praise God, not only for the event of his troubles, but for the troubles themselves,

Of David's Behaviour in the Time of Trouble

and that all the paths of the Lord to him were mercy and truth, even when they were encompassed with clouds and thick darkness. "I know that all thy judgments are righteous, and that thou in faithfulness hast afflicted me." We must surely view things in a very wrong light, if we leave the righteousness of the Lord, because he is doing us good in his own way, and not in the way that our own folly would prescribe. If we follow the example of the best saints we will not only continue patient, but count it all joy when we fall into divers temptations; knowing this, that the trying of our faith worketh patience, and that the trying of our faith will be found unto praise, and honour, and glory at the appearing of Jesus Christ.

By such motives as these David strengthened his holy resolutions of cleaving to God's testimonies in every different situation in which he might be placed. But he was conscious that his own firmest resolutions were not to be trusted in the day of trial, and therefore by daily prayers he committed himself to the protection of his God, who alone could preserve him from the snares of the destroyer. We must endeavour to fix upon our minds, and frequently to call up to our view, the powerful motives that ought to exert a continual influence upon our hearts. We cannot conscientiously pray for the grace of God to preserve us from falling, if we neglect the means furnished by himself to guard us against the dangers to which we are exposed. But we trust to ourselves and not to the Lord, if we hope that we can stand fast by the power of our best fortified resolutions, without the succours of that grace which we ought continually to implore.

You see how David behaved in the day of his calamity. You have not only prophets, but princes and kings for an example of suffering affliction and of patience. Think it not strange that you must suffer. Think it rather strange that your sufferings in this evil world are not greater than they are. Are your sufferings such as you deserve? Are they such as Job or David endured? They have left you an example. Follow the steps of those who through faith and patience inherit the promises. Consider the end of their course. David in his present state of glory and felicity remembers all his afflictions with joy and praise. He now knows more perfectly than he could know on earth, that it was good for him to be afflicted. He would not for a world have wanted any one of all the sufferings he endured on earth. All the happy inhabitants of these regions, in which there is no sin nor sorrow, bless God in strains of heavenly rapture because he managed all their concerns on earth not according to their own wishes, but according to the unerring counsel of his own will.

You will say perhaps, that you are not able to bear sufferings like these heroic believers who came out of great tribulation in ancient times. It is true, you are not girded with strength like theirs, but you are not called to endure such fights of affliction as they did. You have but a little strength, and you are not called to encounter such trials as the men who were clothed with extraordinary endowments. God is faithful and wise. He does not and he will not suffer you to be tempted above that ye are able; but will with the temptation make a way of escape, that ye may be able to bear it.

You are not yet come to your rest. You may be called to harder sufferings than any that you have yet endured. But you have promises of strength from above, suited to your exigences. "As thy days are, so shall thy strength be. My grace shall be sufficient for thee."

David was strong in faith, and in every virtue. But it is plain that he was enabled to hold on in his way, and that he waxed stronger and stronger, not by his own strength, but by the grace of God given unto him. He ran in the way of God's commandments, because God had enlarged his heart. If God had not been with him he could not have advanced a single step. He would have been constantly stumbling and falling, or turning aside from the Lord. "Blessed is the man who trusteth in the Lord." Even the youths who trust to themselves shall faint and be weary, and the young men shall utterly fall; but they that wait upon the Lord shall renew their strength. They shall mount up with wings as eagles; they shall run and not be weary, they shall walk and not faint.

Beware, however, whilst your trust is in the Lord, of provoking him by your own folly to withhold the needful supplies of his grace. Vigilance must be joined with your prayers. "I said I will take heed to my ways, that I sin not with my tongue. I kept my mouth with a bridle whilst the wicked were before me." These were the words of David, who says in another place, "Set a watch, O Lord, before my mouth; keep the door of my lips." At one time we find him saying, "I hate the congregation of evil-doers; I will not sit with them. Their sorrows shall be multiplied that hasten after another god. Their

Of David's Behaviour in the Time of Trouble

drink-offerings of blood will I not offer, nor take up their names into my lips." In another passage we find him saying to the Lord, "Let me not eat of their dainties." We trust in God that he will work in us both to will and to do of his good pleasure; and having this confidence we work out our salvation with fear and trembling.

How much easier is it to endure all that men may be permitted to do against us, than to endure the reflections of our own mind for sinning against the Lord, either by the neglect of duty or by doing what he hath forbidden? Of two evils the least is to be chosen, especially when by choosing the lesser evil it is turned into good. Affliction will always do good to those who choose it rather than sin, (*Hebrews 12:11-13*).

Look not at the things which are seen, and are temporal; but at the things which are not seen, and are eternal; and then your light afflictions which are but for a moment, shall work out for you a far more exceeding and eternal weight of glory.

11
David's Thanksgiving for His Deliverance

To the chief musician, a Psalm of David the servant of the Lord, who spake unto the Lord the words of this song in the day that the Lord delivered him from the hand of all his enemies and from the hand of Saul: and he said: – (Psalm 18, Title; 2 Samuel 22:1)

MANY songs of thanksgiving were composed by David. Perhaps it would be too bold for us to say that this Psalm excels them all; but we may say without hesitation that none of them excels this. It was composed on the occasion of his deliverance not from one, but from many troubles, and of a deliverance which set him on high from the fear of evil, if men could be said to be exalted in this world above fear. – I shall speak:

I. Of the great deliverances which gave occasion to this Psalm.

II. Of God as his deliverer.

III. Of the praises given to God in it.

I. Of David's deliverance from the hands of his enemies. In the early part of David's life he obtained signal instances of God's preserving mercy. A lion and a bear came to destroy a lamb of his fold; David had the courage to attack both these fierce animals in defence of the young of his flock, and the Lord delivered him both from the lion and the bear, and gave him the hope of deliverance in the after part of his life from lions and bears in human shape, (*Psalm 7*).

A great deliverance was granted to himself, and through him to his people, when the Lord delivered into his hand the terrible giant of Gath, who had boasted that "he would give his flesh to be meat to the fowls of heaven, and to the beasts of the earth," (*1 Samuel 17*).

Many and wonderful were the deliverances which he obtained from Saul. Who would not have thought that the implacable hatred of an unprincipled king would have soon proved fatal to the shepherd of Bethlehem, who was given out to be a traitor to his prince? Fourscore and five priests of the Lord were cut off by him in one day, because one of them had performed an office of friendship to David. The footmen of Saul would not put forth their hands against the priests of the Lord; but a wicked king never wanted wicked servants to gratify his malice. There were many Doegs in the land. Why was not one found to kill a man a thousand times more obnoxious to the king than Ahimelech? Surely there were hundreds and thousands who would have been glad to sacrifice their consciences and souls to the king. But David's soul was bound up in the bundle of life with the Lord his God. The king's palace and David's house; Naioth in Ramah; the caves of Adullam and Engedi; the rocks of the wild goats, and many other places of the land were witnesses of the amazing loving-kindnesses of the Lord to his persecuted servant. Often he was like a lamb within the grasp of the lion, but God never failed nor forsook him in the time of need. Often was he tempted to account himself free among the dead, like those who are cut off from God's hand, whom he has no more in remembrance. But the Lord redeemed his life from destruction. For a long course of months or years there was but a step between him and death. But precious in the sight of the Lord is the death of his servants, and he will not suffer them to be destroyed out of the land of the living till the time is come which he hath set for receiving them to himself.

David sometimes thought it necessary for himself to leave the Lord's land and to seek refuge among strangers, who were not such heathens as many of his own people. Among them too he found protection and obtained great deliverances. The king of Moab behaved to him with kindness so far as we know. Among the Philistines he was more than once in extreme danger. But the Lord was still his stay and his helper. After his advancement to the throne of Judah, he was under a necessity of carrying on war with a dangerous rival who

David's Thanksgiving for His Deliverance

reigned over the greater part of the tribes of Israel. If the Philistines at that time had vigorously prosecuted the advantages which they had gained in the terrible battle of Gilboa, they might to all human appearances have crushed both David and Ishbosheth under their feet. But the Lord moderated their counsels in such a manner that David enjoyed rest from them till he was put into a better condition to oppose them, and when they afterwards attacked him, the Lord broke in upon his enemies like the breaking in of water, and destroyed them before his anointed. In one of the battles which he fought with that nation, one of the mighty giants, in which it seems to have been fertile, thought to have slain David. His army trembled for his safety, and swore to him when the battle was over, that they would not suffer him again to go out to battle lest the light of Israel should be quenched.

When the Philistines were brought low by many terrible engagements, David was still exposed to great perils, but the Lord preserved him whithersoever he went. All nations compassed him about, but in the name of the Lord he destroyed them. They compassed him about like bees, but they were quenched as the fire of thorns, for in the name of the Lord he destroyed them. Neither Moabites, nor Ammonites, nor Syrians of different kingdoms, could stand before him, either singly or in conjunction, for the Lord taught his hands to war and his fingers to fight, and made his feet like hinds' feet, and set him on his high places. He was made the head of the heathen as well as of his own people, and peoples whom he knew not, were compelled to serve him.

But when the Lord had given him rest from his enemies round about, evil rose up against him out of his own kingdom and out of his own house. Never was he brought into deeper distress, or more perilous circumstances by Saul or by the idolatrous nations, than by his graceless son, and his perfidious friend, whose counsels he had regarded as oracles. Yet God was still with him, and redeemed his soul out of all adversities. Sheba rose up after Absalom to seek his life, but he soon lost his own as his predecessor in wickedness had done.

These were some of David's deliverances from his many visible enemies; and they were attended and sweetened by other deliverances, not less, but still more important. He was sometimes almost overwhelmed by fear and dejection of spirit. We are told that he feigned himself mad before Achish when he first fled to the land of the Philistines. Some think that the translation of the passage to which I refer ought to be altered. When it is said that he feigned himself mad before them, they would have the meaning to be that he really became mad, that is, that he was seized, by means of terror, with a fit of insanity, and scrabbled on the door posts, not through design, but because he knew not what he was doing. Certain it is that he published the praises of the Lord for deliverance from fears as well as from other troubles. "O magnify the Lord with me, and let us exalt his name together. I sought the Lord, and he heard me, and delivered me from all my fears. In the day when I cried, thou answeredst me, and strengthenedst me with strength in my soul."

He was often in great bodily distress; but he cried unto the Lord and was healed, (*Psalm 30*).

But the most dangerous of his troubles were those which he suffered from the law in his members, warring against the law in his mind, and bringing him into captivity to the law of sin which was in his members. Iniquities more than once prevailed against him in a very fearful manner. Never were his fears of Saul or of the giants of Gath half so distressing to his soul, as the terror produced in his heart by guilt. He roared all the day long, and his moisture was turned into the drought of summer. But the Lord revived, and recovered, and pardoned him after his loving-kindness, and thus he overcame, not only flesh and blood, but principalities and powers and the rulers of the darkness of this world. – We proposed to speak:

II. Of God as the deliverer of David. "Salvation is of the Lord," (*Psalm 3:8*). Everywhere we find him giving to the Lord the glory of the salvation wrought for him. "The Lord is my rock, and my fortress, and my deliverer; the God of my rock, in him will I trust: he is my shield, and the horn of my salvation, my high tower, and my refuge, my Saviour. Thou savest me from violence," (*2 Samuel 22:2, 3*). "For who is God, save the Lord? Who is a rock, save our God?" (*2 Samuel 22:32*).

We know that there were many heroes who obtained a just and glorious name for the valiant exploits which they performed in the defence of their king and country. One of them had the honour of preserving the life of David when the hand of a terrible giant was

David's Thanksgiving for His Deliverance

lifted up against him. And there were many besides his mighty men to whom he was greatly indebted for signal service. His life was at one time saved by the kindness and wit of his wife Michal, at another time by the good offices of Jonathan, and even the Philistines were at one time made the instruments of preserving the life of that champion of Israel who was to be the destroyer of their power.

But we never find David employing his fine genius in celebrating the exploits of these heroes to whom he was so greatly indebted. His talents were consecrated to the praise of the God of his salvation. Yet their exploits will not altogether be forgotten, because the most illustrious actions performed by them are recorded in monuments far nobler than the best of human compositions. But they were no more than instruments in the hand of God, who raised them up, who girded them with strength, who directed their steps, and crowned their efforts with success.

God is pleased for the most part to employ means and instruments in his works of mercy or of vengeance. But they do neither less nor more than God has intended to accomplish by them. "Who is he that saith, and it cometh to pass, when the Lord commandeth it not?"

It was God who made use of the Philistines for the salvation of David at Selah-hammah-lekoth. They were far from meaning so, neither did their heart think so. There was no man in the land except Saul whom they hated so much as David. They came into the country to destroy many of the Israelites, and to plunder their wealth. But God sent them, without their knowing it, to save the life of one of the illustrious saviours of Israel.

God employed not only men on earth, but the angels of heaven, for the deliverance of David from his enemies, and therefore in his commendations of the goodness of God to himself, he assures us that the angel of the Lord encamps round about them that fear the Lord, and delivers them. It is probable that when he heard the sound of a going upon the tops of the mulberry trees, he considered it as a signal that creatures whose dwelling was not in the earth were come by divine direction to help him, and to destroy his enemies. Thus *were* his prayers heard, "Let their way be dark and slippery: and let the angel of the Lord persecute them," (*Psalm 35:6*).

Thunder and lightning were ministers of divine providence, which seem to have been sometimes employed for the destruction of his enemies, as we know that they were employed against the enemies of Israel in the days of Samuel. "The adversaries of the Lord," said Hannah, in her prophetical song, "shall be broken in pieces; out of heaven shall he thunder upon them. The Lord shall judge the ends of the earth, he shall give strength unto his king, and exalt the horn of his anointed. The Lord also thundered in the heavens," says David himself; "and the Highest gave his voice, hailstones and coals of fire. Yea, he sent out his arrows and scattered them, and he shot out his lightnings and discomfited them."

Whatever were the means employed for the deliverances of David, no doubt was left in the mind of any reasonable man concerning the great Author of his salvation. The Lord gave as tangible proofs of his presence with David and of his indignation against his enemies, as if he had in the literal sense bowed the heavens and come down, attended by his heavenly ministers, causing the earth to tremble at his presence, and discovering the channels of the waters. Such marvellous works were accomplished, and such a combination of events took place, all of them contributing to the great work, that the man must have been completely blind who did not see and acknowledge the hand of the Almighty. David himself, in all the things that befell him, good or bad, saw the working of God, and in those seasons of his life when he was set on high from his afflictions, and placed in pleasant circumstances, he saw such a series of wonderful works of mercy towards him as filled him with admiration, love and praise. And ought we not all to observe the works of the Lord towards us with admiration, especially when we have been preserved from accidents that might have proved fatal, or delivered from sore afflictions from which nothing but the hand of God could save us? Had we hearts like David, we would often be rejoicing in God, and singing his praises, when our corrupt dispositions prompt us to utter complaints as if God had forgotten to be gracious, because he will not resign the management of all our affairs into our own hands.

III. Of this Psalm of thanksgiving to God for all his deliverances.

David was the sweet singer of Israel. He was the truly inspired poet who was raised up by God, to compose songs of praise to God, to charm and elevate the hearts of God's people, not only in his own age, but in every succeeding generation. One reason why he was so

David's Thanksgiving for His Deliverance

often humbled to the dust by afflictions of various, and of the most distressing kind, and why he was blessed with so many wonderful salvations, was that he might have occasion given him, from his own experience of every kind of distress and relief, to compose Psalms well adapted to the different circumstances of the people of God in every age of the world.

He composed many sweet songs of praise for the many deliverances he had obtained through the course of his eventful life. But this Psalm was composed on the review of manifold salvations wrought for him through a great part of his life, the result of which was, that he was now established in the kingdom of the Lord over Israel, and blessed with the happiest opportunities of doing such services to God, as few men in former ages were ever in a condition to perform. He might have enjoyed far more tranquillity and happiness in his original station than he could find after he was elevated to the sure hopes of royalty, if happiness were placed in personal or in domestic enjoyments. But it was the glory and felicity of David that he was not only blessed, but the chosen instrument of blessings to thousands and millions of the human race. – In this Psalm we find David expressing:

1. *The ardour of his love* to that God who had blessed him with so many and such wonderful deliverances. Dearly he loved the God of his salvation, before he needed any of the deliverances which gave occasion to this Psalm. But every new deliverance increased the ardour of his love. We ought to love God more for what he is, than for what he does to us. But we see what he is in what he does. In what he does for us, we see the infinite loveliness of his nature and his love to us, and we love him because he first loved us. (*Joshua 23:11; Psalm 116:1*).

2. We find him expressing *his firm reliance on God* as the God of his salvation. Before he incurred the resentment of Saul, he was a firm believer in God. "The God," he said to that prince, "who delivered me from the mouth of that lion and that bear which would have destroyed the lambs of my flock, shall deliver me from this Philistine." But his faith was powerfully invigorated by every new deliverance. When he had been blessed with so many glorious salvations, he

thought that he could not better express his gratitude to the God of his mercies, than by warm expressions of unbounded confidence in the Lord as his strength, his fortress, his rock, his deliverer, his God in whom he trusted, the rock of his salvation, and his high tower. We cannot please and glorify God better than by walking in the steps of our father Abraham. And would we not greatly dishonour him if we withheld from him our confidence after a thousand proofs of his special favour? (*Psalm 18:2, 3*).

3. He expatiates on the *greatness*, on the *grace*, on the *glory* of these salvations which had been wrought for him.

He illustrates the greatness of the salvations by representing the dreadful danger from which he was delivered. The terrors of death had fallen upon him. He was like a brand plucked out of the burning, or like a man raised out of the grave. He had as much reason to be astonished at his deliverance as if he had been in the belly of hell. (*Psalm 18:4, 5; Jonah 2*).

His deliverance was the answer of fervent cries addressed to God from the depths into which he was cast. "There was no day like that when the sun and the moon stood still in their habitations," says the writer of the history of the wars of the Lord, "when the Lord hearkened to the voice of a man," (*Joshua 10:14*). Yet the day of David's deliverance from the hand of all his enemies was a day that might well be compared to it. The Lord hearkened to the voice of David's prayers, and in his answers to them gave as signal proofs of his power and glory, as when at the voice of Joshua the sun stood still for the space of a whole day in Gibeon, and the moon in the valley of Aijalon, (*Psalm 18:6-9*).

In the sublimest strains he describes the steps of majesty of his king and his God, when he appeared for his salvation from these enemies that were too strong for him. We wonder at the boldness of his imagery, because we are too dim-sighted to behold the glory of the Lord in the ancient works of wonder wrought for his people and for his servants. But we ought to remember that it is the will of God to make himself known by the judgments which he executes, and by the mercies which he bestows. And the deliverance of David and the destruction of David's enemies were very distinguished acts of the providence of God, by which he intended to show forth to all generations how wonderfully gracious he is to all that love him, and how terrible an avenger he is to their enemies. We ought to remember too, that David was the chosen king, and the destined father of a race of kings, over God's peculiar people, and that he was the father and an eminent type of that greater King in whose sufferings and exaltation, God was to show forth his glory in such a manner as it never was formerly displayed, in the most excellent of his works in heaven or earth.

We are too much disposed to look with a careless eye on the great works of God. We have read the history of David's afflictions and deliverances in the books of Samuel, and can scarcely find anything in them corresponding to the description in this Psalm. But let us rather be ashamed of ourselves than ascribe blame to David for his high admiration of God's grace to himself, and his endeavours to make his praise glorious for the great things done for himself, and in him for his people, and for his seed. The more our eyes are opened to see the glory of God's works of mercy, the more will we admire them, the more will we praise them, and we will never think that we can sufficiently praise them, (*Psalm 18:8-17*).

4. *He celebrates the excellency of those divine perfections* which were manifested in his deliverance. He shows forth the glory of that righteousness which appeared in the gracious rewards bestowed on himself, and the vengeance inflicted on his wicked enemies. He speaks of his own righteousness not in the language of vain-glory, for he certainly maintained on his spirit a constant sense of his imperfections and sins, but to the praise of the great King of Israel, the Lord of hosts, who sat upon his throne judging right, between him and his enemies, and infers from what he had seen, and what the whole nation had seen, of the wonderful works of the Lord, that the Lord is pure to the pure, upright to the upright, that he will show his grace and kindness to the merciful, but will manifest irreconcilable displeasure against the froward.

He shows forth the glory of the Lord as the God of salvation, who had given striking and incontestable proofs of his saving power and grace in the salvations wrought for him. None of the gods of the nations had ever given any proofs of their power to save their worshippers that trusted in them. Never were such salvations wrought in the world, as those which were evidently accomplished for David and Israel, except those salvations which had been wrought by the same God for those who trusted in him, in the years of ancient times. Well then might he draw this conclusion to the praise of his great Saviour, and for an encouragement to trust in him, "As for God, his way is perfect; the word of the Lord is tried; he is a buckler to all them that trust in him; for who is God save the Lord, or who is a rock save our God?"

Great things God had done for David. David had himself performed wonderful things, and achieved victories that were to make him famous through all generations. But not to himself, but to his God was the praise due. It was his God that girded him with strength, and made his way perfect. It was God that taught his hands to war, and his fingers to fight. It was God that made his feet like hinds' feet, and set him on his high places. It was God that enabled him to crush his enemies under his feet, that subdued his people under him, and made him the lord of the heathen. Without God, neither he nor his mighty men could have done anything. The saving power which belongs to none in heaven or earth, but to the God of Israel, shone conspicuous in all these great actions and surprising events, by which the kingdom was established in David and in his family. And what he did for David, is a decisive proof that he is able, and gracious, and faithful to perform all his promises to all that trust in him.

5. He praises God and expresses his unshaken confidence in him, for the great things that were yet to be done for him, and for his seed after him. Although great and wonderful things had been already done, yet David did not reckon himself now so great and so happy, as to stand in no further need of help from God. He was blessed with exceeding great and precious blessings which filled his heart with joy and praise. But there were also given to him exceeding great and precious promises. And the blessings promised were already in effect given to him, for the word of the Lord was sure, and his faith gave a substance to the things hoped for. He was firmly persuaded that a people whom he had not known should serve him, that the strangers should submit themselves to him, that the Lord who had already highly exalted him would increase his greatness and his power on every side, and make him most blessed for evermore. "The Lord

David's Thanksgiving for His Deliverance

liveth; and blessed be my rock; and let the God of my salvation be exalted. He delivereth me from mine enemies: yea, thou liftest me up above those that rise up against me: thou hast delivered me from the violent man. Therefore will I give thanks unto thee, O Lord, among the heathen, and sing praises unto thy name. Great deliverance giveth he to his king; and showeth mercy to his anointed, to David, and to his seed for evermore," (*Psalm 18:46-50*).

David was not young when he composed this Psalm. He certainly did not confine his views within the bounds of that life which was drawing towards its conclusion, for God taught him to number his days, that he might know how frail he was. "We are strangers before thee and sojourners, as were all our fathers. Our days on the earth are as a shadow, and there is none abiding." These words addressed to God, near the close of his life, express the thoughts concerning his condition on earth, that had been formerly familiar to him, (*Psalm 39, 119*). What then did he hope for, when he was firmly seated on his throne? He believed that God would be still fulfilling his hopes when he was sleeping with his fathers, that he would be still receiving new testimonies of the faithfulness and goodness of his God in the persons of his posterity, and especially in the raising up of the great Messiah from his loins, and in the establishment, the glory, the universal extension and prosperity of his kingdom of grace.

David often spake of the Messiah when he appeared to be speaking of himself, and he knew that what he spake in his own person was to be verified chiefly in that righteous Branch, which in the fulness of time was to be raised up to him, (*Acts 2*).

The apostle Paul plainly teaches us that what David says of the submission of the nations to his government was a prediction of the conversion of the Gentiles to the faith and obedience of Christ. We may therefore fairly understand the words of the writer of this Psalm in a more exalted sense than that which at first view presents itself to our minds. "David being a prophet, and knowing that God had sworn with an oath to him, that of the fruit of his body, according to the flesh, he would raise up Christ to sit on his throne; he seeing this before spake of the resurrection of Christ, that his soul was not left in hell, neither his flesh did see corruption." These are the words of Peter commenting on some parts of *Psalm 16*. Are we not authorised by Paul to make a similar comment on a part at least of *Psalm 18?*

Seeing beforehand the universal extension of the kingdom of Jesus, he said, "For this cause, I will confess unto thee among the Gentiles, and will sing unto thy name," (*Psalm 18:49; Romans 15:9*).

In this view of the meaning of the Psalm, it is a song of praise to God, not merely for the deliverance of David from the hand of Saul and of all his enemies, but a song of praise for our deliverance from worse enemies than Saul or the giants of the Philistines, for our deliverance from the rulers of the darkness of this world, and our translation into the kingdom of God's dear Son; a sweet song of salvation to Gentiles as well as Jews, by the Branch of righteousness raised up unto David – by that Root of Jesse who was raised up to reign over the Gentiles, and to be the salvation of God to the ends of the earth.

On the whole we are taught by this Psalm what improvement we ought to make of the great works of God, recorded in his Word. If David saw and admired and celebrated in such strains of rapture his deliverance from the hand of his enemies, can we sufficiently admire the glory that shines forth in the whole train of providential administration recorded in the volume of inspiration. Manifold were the salvations wrought by God for Abraham and Jacob, for Moses and the people of Israel, and in all of them we see the power and the grace of God our Saviour. We ought especially to contemplate with increasing wonder and devotion, the wonders of grace to men, performed in the person of our Lord Jesus Christ. David's worst sufferings were but a faint shadow of the extreme abasement of our Lord Jesus Christ when he endured all the horrors of his Father's wrath for our iniquities. And all the grandeur to which David was exalted, is not to be compared with that glory to which our Lord Jesus Christ is raised at the right hand of his Father. "He hath ascended on high, he hath received gifts for men, yea, for the rebellious also, that the Lord God might dwell among them."

Great was the happiness enjoyed under the government of David by the people of Israel. But infinitely more precious are the blessings enjoyed by the spiritual Israel under the administration of our Lord Jesus Christ. If all true Israelites in the days of that glorious prince, would cheerfully concur in the high praises of God, for the salvation bestowed upon him, with what ardour of devotion ought we to praise the God and Father of our Lord Jesus Christ for bringing him again from the dead, and setting him at his own right hand, in

David's Thanksgiving for His Deliverance

the heavenly places, far above all principality and power, and might and dominion, and for giving him to be head over all things to the church which is his body, the fulness of him that filleth all in all.

Nor ought we to forget any of God's deliverances wrought for ourselves. We have never suffered such persecutions and tribulations as Paul endured, and we cannot be too thankful to that kind providence which has not suffered us to be tempted above that we are able to bear. Yet we have not been without our share of adversities. And unless the Lord had been our help, we had long ago been at rest in the house of silence. When we were brought low, he helped us, and with our songs, or with the songs prepared for us by the holy men of former times, we will praise him. Nor will we praise him with our lips only. Let our whole lives be consecrated to his praise.

Nor ought we to forget the obligations that lie upon us to praise God for our friends and brethren. What numberless deliverances has God bestowed upon us in our own persons, or in the persons of those who are dear to us, and whose life and happiness make a part of our own. Amidst Paul's tribulations he found many causes to bless God for deliverances, or for preservation granted to his friends. He was glad and he praised God when he was weak, if his friends were strong; when he was confined in prison if they enjoyed liberty. Whilst he was in prison at Rome, he could rejoice in God and bless his name, that the Word of the Lord was not bound, that there were many others that were enabled to publish it abroad whilst he was shut up in confinement. God's mercies to them were mercies to him. "Indeed he was sick," he says of Epaphroditus, "nigh unto death; but God had mercy on him, and not on him only, but on me also, lest I should have sorrow upon sorrow."

Perhaps some of you may allege that though God has been very kind to you, you have not such mercies as those of David to be the subjects of your songs. You have been delivered from sicknesses; you have been preserved in time of danger, but you have not been exalted like him to royal dignity. Your condition is not enviable. You have still many subjects of complaint, and are far from enjoying that happiness that would give you satisfaction, and open your mouths to praise.

It is true that God has not thought fit to place you on thrones. All men cannot be kings, and all men are not fit to be kings. Perhaps if you were made kings you would find yourselves further removed from prosperity than you are at present. David did not find himself at perfect ease upon his throne, and if he had not been better qualified to reign than most of us are, he would have found his royal dignity a snare and a trap, and not a pleasure or a benefit.

You are not raised to the dignity of kings like David. But if you are Christians you have obtained a deliverance infinitely more important than if you had been raised from a prison to a throne. You have been delivered from the power of darkness, and have been made kings and priests unto the God and Father of our Lord Jesus Christ. David's royalty on earth terminated within forty years. If he had not enjoyed the charming prospect of a kingdom which cannot be moved, he would not have thought himself a happy man with all the glory to which he was exalted on earth. He confessed that he was a stranger and a pilgrim on this earth. But God had made with him an everlasting covenant, ordered in all things and sure. This was all his salvation and all his desire. This was his joy in the view of leaving the world. And all of us are called to take hold of this covenant, and to claim all the blessings of it for ourselves. "Hear," says God, "and your souls shall live, and I will make with you an everlasting covenant, even the sure mercies of David. Behold I have given him for a witness to the people, for a leader and commander to the people."

12
Of the Justice of David's Behaviour

The Lord rewardeth me according to my righteousness; according to the cleanness of my hands hath he recompensed me. (Psalm 18:20)

IN concluding our examination of the life and character of David, we come to reflect on the justice of his behaviour in all his affairs. Let us consider:

I. David's righteousness.

II. God's respect to his righteousness.

III. His consciousness of his own righteousness.

IV. The sense he entertained of God's respect to his righteousness.

I. Let us speak of David's righteousness.

Righteousness consists in rendering to all their due, and the revealed will of God is the standard of it, (*Deuteronomy 6:25*). As we are under infinitely greater obligations to perform our duty to God than we can be under to perform any services to our fellow-men, righteousness includes in it that piety which has God for its object, as well as the performance of those duties to which our neighbours have a right. Yet it is not seldom used to denote the rectitude of our dispositions and conduct to our fellow-men, as godliness denotes right tempers and behaviour towards God. The grace of God which bringeth salvation to all men, teaches us to live soberly, righteously and godly in this present world. It teaches us that sobriety by which we regulate our passions and appetites; that righteousness by which we do to our fellow men what we would have them to do to us; that piety by which we love God with all our hearts and souls, and devote ourselves to his fear.

David laid it down as his settled purpose to walk in the law of the Lord, the great standard of righteousness, and through divine mercy he was enabled to keep his resolution inviolable through the course of his life. He did not pretend to perfection. He often confessed his sins to the Lord. Yet he had the testimony not only of his own conscience but of the Spirit of God, that he was righteous in the general course of his behaviour both towards God and towards men.

Of his righteous behaviour towards God, we have already taken occasion to speak in several discourses. He referred all his actions to the glory of God; he loved his testimonies with his whole heart, and took pleasure in the habitation of his house. He made use of all his power to advance the honour of his God, and valued his royal authority chiefly for the advantages it gave him to promote the interests of religion, and of the commonwealth of Israel, the people of the Lord. We shall speak at present of the righteousness of his behaviour towards men, which he seems chiefly to have in his view when he says that "the Lord rewarded him according to his righteousness."

He behaved righteously towards king Saul, his first and great enemy. Reports were industriously spread that he was an insidious enemy to that prince, and wished to deprive him of his throne and life in order to hasten his own elevation. But nothing could be more false and malicious. He could at all times appeal to the Searcher of hearts as his witness, that ambitious thoughts found no admission to his bosom. "Lord, my heart is not haughty, nor mine eyes lofty, neither do I exercise myself in great matters, or in things too high for me. Surely I have behaved and quieted myself as a child that is weaned of his mother; my soul is even as a weaned child." By divine providence he was furnished with more than one opportunity to show how scandalous the slanders were which were propagated against him. He not only spared, but saved the life of his master when it was in his power. He was so far from killing that implacable enemy when the Lord delivered him into his hand, that he would not suffer him to be killed, and even exposed himself to the resentment

Of the Justice of David's Behaviour

of his own followers by saving their enemy from that death which seemed to them the best security for their own life.

He was just to all his fellow-subjects whilst he lived under the government of Saul. He acquired a high reputation for the prudence with which he managed all his affairs, and he would not have attained this honest fame if he had not abstained from all appearance of evil. Those who afterwards turned out his bitter enemies, had no reason given them from any part of his conduct to hate him, but every reason to love him, for in the time of their troubles he had behaved as if he had been their friend or brother.

We have no reason to form the least doubt of the care that David took, when he was an outlaw and a fugitive, to keep his followers from using any unwarrantable means for the supply of their wants, although they must often have been in extreme poverty. We have a testimonial from Nabal's servants of the honesty of David's men, and even of their generous care of Nabal's substance, at a time when the good man was almost reduced to beggary. It is hard for us to say how he found the means of subsistence for so many hungry followers, or how he maintained sufficient authority to restrain a set of poor and discontented soldiers from acts of violence. Of this we are sure from his Psalms, and from the history of his life, that he would suffer no wicked thing before his eyes. The loving-kindness of God was still before his eyes, and he walked in God's truth. We have no reason to think that Abigail spoke the language of flattery when she said to him, "The Lord will surely make my lord a sure house, because my lord fighteth the Lord's battles, and evil hath not been found in thee all thy days."

We have no reason to doubt of David's rectitude of behaviour in all the dealings that he had with strangers. He had transactions in the time of his troubles with the king of Moab, to whom he committed the care of his father and mother when they could no longer dwell with safety at Bethlehem. We have no further account of any dealings with that prince, although we afterwards find David carrying on a bloody war with the Moabites. We have not the means of knowing whether the king of Moab had provoked this war by cruelty to David's father and mother; but we can have no doubt that the cause of the war was just on David's part. After the kind treatment which he received from the king of Gath, he took Gath out of the hands of the Philistines, but the Philistines themselves were the authors of the war. David in his government was a man of blood, but in his disposition he was a man of peace. A necessity was laid upon him to fight the battles of the Lord, and of the people of the Lord. And he was in his wars as well as in other incidents of his life, an illustrious figure of that great King of whom it is said, that in righteousness he doth judge and make war.

When he was advanced to the throne of Israel, it is testified of him that he did justice and judgment to all his people. He did justice and judgment without any partiality, to the poor and to the rich, to men of every tribe in Israel, without any partiality to his own tribe of Judah, as we learn from the contention between the tribes at the end of Absalom's rebellion. We pity and even censure David when we are informed of his indignant speech to Nathan at hearing his parable of the poor man's ewe lamb; yet we cannot but respect that zeal for justice which was expressed in it when he doomed to death the oppressor of his poor neighbour. He tells us in *Psalms 75* and *101*, how he intended to govern his family and his kingdom, and doubtless, as far as human infirmity would permit, he kept his resolution.

Gratitude may well be considered as an ingredient of justice. We owe returns of love and of the proper fruits of it to friends who love us, and who are glad to serve us according to the best of their abilities. David's gratitude to his benefactors was a remarkable part of his character. We find him sending presents of the spoils gained in battle to those places where he and his men were accustomed to haunt. When Saul was dead, he was so far from expressing resentment against him, that he enquired whether there were any left of his family, that he might show them the kindness of God for Jonathan's sake. It was indeed a very considerable time after his advancement to the kingdom before he made this inquiry; but we ought to remember that he had some dangerous wars, besides much other pressing business, to occupy his thoughts; and long before he was informed where he might find Mephibosheth, he had perpetuated the memory of his gratitude to Jonathan by the elegy which he composed on his untimely death, with that of his father. And many years afterwards he showed that Jonathan was not forgotten by him, when he took care to secure Mephibosheth from the destruction brought upon the family of Saul, at the requisition of the Gibeonites.

Of the Justice of David's Behaviour

He was grateful for favours even to those heathens from whom he received any kindness. Nahash, king of the Ammonites, showed kindness on some occasions to David, perhaps rather from hatred to Saul than good-will to the poor man whom Saul oppressed. Yet David showed kindness unto Hanun, the son of Nahash, for his father's sake. If he afterwards treated that weak ungrateful prince with severity, necessity was laid upon him.

Righteousness in a king will dispose him to an impartial execution of the laws against criminals. A wise king crusheth the wicked, and bringeth the wheel over them. Some princes, by an excess of lenity, have done as much hurt to their subjects, or exposed themselves to as much danger, as others have done by their rigorous severity. David was by natural disposition and by grace a merciful man. Yet it was a matter of conscience with him not to show mercy to the prejudice of justice, or in such a manner as to give encouragement to sin. "Whoso privily slandereth his neighbour, him will I cut off; him that hath an high look and a proud heart will I not suffer. I will early destroy all the wicked of the land, that I may cut off all wicked-doers from the city of the Lord."

But how was this consistent with the favour showed to Joab and to Absalom? Did he not know that God had forbidden any satisfaction to be taken for the life of a murderer. Yes, he knew it very well, and took measures even when he was dying, that Joab's grey hairs should not come down to the grave without blood. It is perhaps impossible entirely to justify him for suffering that bloody man to live so long above the ground. Yet never was lenity to a criminal more excusable. Seldom has a prince or a nation been more indebted to a subject than David and his people were to Joab for brilliant services. And it appears to have been almost impracticable to bring to condign punishment a man so popular, and of such power in the army as Joab. David himself made this excuse for himself when he said, "These men, the sons of Zeruiah, are too strong for me." We may observe likewise that David was once indebted for his own life to Abishai, the brother of Joab, who seems to have had some share in the blood of Abner. He might with some appearance of reason think that he owed a life to the family of his sister Zeruiah, or that at least he might incline to the favourable side when plausible reasons could be advanced for their exoneration. Similar reasons might be advanced to excuse, if not to justify, him for sparing his beloved Absalom. Absalom had killed a man, who deserved to die for his abominable conduct. Absalom, however, well deserved to die for killing him without legal authority. But he fled from the country, and put it out of his father's power to execute the laws upon him without first recalling him from banishment. But he could not have prevailed on his son to return to his country without an implicit promise of pardon. And the reasons which David had to recall him, even with this condition, were so very strong in themselves and so artfully pressed upon him, that we cannot wonder at David's compliance. He had his errors, but they leaned to the side of virtue. His humanity induced him to pronounce a sentence, which though it may be excused, yet it cannot be justified, in favour of the pretended widow's son who had killed his brother. His humanity (if it can be so called) prompted him to pass a sentence of a contrary kind on the case of the rich man in Nathan's parable. But who in the course of so many weighty affairs committed fewer errors, or displayed such a uniform course of shining virtues?

Some think that the Amalekite who pretended to have killed Saul was treated by him with unmerciful severity. But the Amalekite himself asserted that he had killed Saul. His excuse was that he saw it impossible for Saul to live. But would it be a sufficient excuse for any of us, if we killed a man who appeared to be in a dying condition, to say that we were sure he could not live? How was it possible for us to know that he would not recover? Would any upright judge exempt us from condemnation on such a plea?

David had only the man's own testimony that he had killed Saul, and it is very probable that the man lied against his own life. But as David justly told him, His blood was upon his own head. He put it almost out of David's power to dismiss him alive, without exposing his own fair character, and laying a temptation in the way of some other ruffian to imbrue his hands in the blood of the poor remains of Saul's family, in the hope of doing an agreeable service to his successor. Baanah and Rechab might with some appearance of reason have hoped for a reward from David for their nefarious deed, if he had given occasion to say that he testified little displeasure against a man who gave out himself to be the person who put an end to the life of Saul.

Of the Justice of David's Behaviour

At the first view of the history of Ziba and Mephibosheth we are disposed to censure David's conduct towards that young prince, the son of his kind and generous friend Jonathan. But the character of David is sufficient to raise him far above the suspicion of deliberate ingratitude. He had met with a very seasonable instance of kindness from Ziba, when he was ungratefully deserted by many, and when his life was sought by the very men who ought not to have counted their own lives dear to them in his cause. Ziba gave an account of the conduct of Mephibosheth which could scarcely fail to gain a temporary credit from the mouth of a man so polite and artful as Ziba, at the very time when Mephibosheth's crime, if he had been justly accused, must have appeared a venial fault compared with those of David's own son and of the friends in whom he had most reason to confide. David, in the hurry of his affairs and agitation of his mind, seems to have too readily believed Ziba. But infallibility of judgment never was pretended to by the good man, and there is no reason to doubt that he did complete justice to the injured prince as soon as he had leisure and opportunity to examine his case. It would be doing greater injustice to David than he ever did to Mephibosheth, or to any man except Uriah, to suppose that he would persist in doing injustice to the son of Jonathan. A good man may through ignorance or through some powerful temptation do a very bad thing, but when he is awakened to repentance, he will make all the reparation for it in his power. We find that David had almost done an irreparable injury to Nabal and his family; but he blessed the Lord who preserved him from such guilt; and doubtless he was no less happy that he had been preserved from doing any wrong to the son of Jonathan which he had it not in his power abundantly to repair.

We cannot pretend to vindicate his behaviour in the case of Uriah. But we cannot reprobate that part of his conduct in stronger language than David himself did. He bitterly repented, and the Lord forgave the iniquity of his sin. He was left to himself that he might know what was in his heart, and that we might all learn very important lessons both from his sin and from his repentance.

There is an expression used concerning this dreadful transgression which may be applied as a satisfying answer to other objections which have been made against David's conduct. It is said, that he "never turned aside from following the Lord, save in the matter of Uriah the Hittite." From this passage it appears evident that there must be a mistake in our reading of *1 Chronicles 20:3*. "And he brought out the people that were in it, and cut them with saws, and with harrows of iron, and with axes. Even so dealt David with all the cities of the children of Ammon." If David had carried his vengeance so far as these words seem to import, he would have turned as far aside from the Lord in the matter of the Ammonites as in the matter of Uriah the Hittite. He would have put many helpless innocents to death, without mercy, and to the most cruel kind of death, without such temptation as he had to the murder of Uriah. For what could the savage barbarity, perpetrated on multitudes of men that had no concern in the indignity done to his ambassador, have availed him, but to make his name hateful and his memory odious. By a change in one letter of the original, not greater than necessity requires to be made in some other places of the *Books of Chronicles*, we are furnished with another reading which is consistent with the known character of David. "And he brought out the people that were in it, and *put them under* saws and harrows of iron," etc. By this reading, the words express the same thing that is said in *2 Samuel 12:31*. The words too of this passage have been strangely misunderstood. Unless we can suppose that David in one part of his life was become worse than an infidel, the meaning of the passage can be no more than this, that he caused the Ammonite soldiers to pass under saws and harrows of iron set up above their heads, in the same way that the Romans caused their conquered enemies sometimes to pass under the yoke as a sign of their complete subjugation.

We may make the same observation concerning another instance of David's procedure, which has given occasion to criticisms of his conduct; I mean the charge given to Solomon concerning Shimei. "Behold thou hast with thee Shimei the son of Gera, a Benjamite of Bahurim, which cursed me with a grievous curse in the day when I went to Mahanaim: but he came down to meet me at Jordan, and I sware to him by the Lord, saying, I will not put thee to death with the sword. Now therefore, hold him not guiltless: for thou art a wise man, and knowest what thou oughtest to do unto him; but his hoar head bring thou down to the grave with blood," (*1 Kings 2:8, 9*).

We might have observed that fidelity in performing engagements is an essential part of justice in which it cannot be supposed that David

Of the Justice of David's Behaviour

would be deficient. But how could David observe his promise and oath to Shimei if he brought down the hairs of Shimei with blood to the grave by the hands of Solomon. A man is no less accountable for what he commands to be done, than for what he does with his own hands. Can we reasonably suppose that David on his death-bed would commit an act of wickedness for which his memory might be detested by all who feared an oath. In fact we find that the crime of cursing David at Mahanaim was not the ground of the sentence against Shimei, although the reason he had given by that crime to suspect his loyalty was the cause why he was laid under a prohibition of leaving Jerusalem under pain of death. But there is another reading of the last part of the charge equally agreeable to the words of the original, which clears the character of David from all blame. Neither bring down his grey hairs to the grave with blood; keep a strict eye over him as a man disaffected to my family; punish him for any new crime by which he may merit punishment, but let my oath be sacred, and bring not down his grey hairs to the grave with blood, for that crime which I sware by the Lord not to punish with death.

Another objection to David's character has been without reason drawn from his behaviour to the family of Saul, seven of whom he gave up to be punished with a cruel death by the Gibeonites for a crime not committed by themselves, although he had solemnly sworn to Saul that he would not cut off his seed after his death. But what proof is there that Saul's sons did not participate in the crime committed by him against the Gibeonites. Some must have participated with him, and the Gibeonites were not ignorant of these circumstances attending the bloody outrage against them that were fittest to determine their choice of victims to the ghosts of their murdered countrymen. But it is sufficient for the vindication of David to observe, that he undoubtedly had a divine warrant for what he did, as we learn with certainty from the consequences of it. The Lord's displeasure was averted, and plenty was restored to the famished country. Peter was thought by the most bigoted of his friends in Jerusalem to have made a sufficient apology for his conduct in baptising uncircumcised Gentiles, when he let them know that he could not have acted otherwise without attempting to resist God. David would have been the enemy of his country if he had set his oath to Saul in opposition to the means necessary for averting a dreadful calamity from his people. He had sworn that he would not cut off the posterity of Saul. The plain meaning of the oath was, that he would not cut them off in revenge of the injuries that were done to him by their father. But certainly Saul himself could not understand the oath to mean that he would never put them to death if justice should require their blood on other accounts, or that he would be bound by it to secure their lives against the vengeance of God, either for their father's sin or their own. David might with as much justice be censured for sparing Nabal and his family after his rash oath to destroy them, as for giving up Saul's sons to be slain and destroyed by the Gibeonites. God had in a very awful manner testified his pleasure that satisfaction should be made to them for the murder of their countrymen.

David was without question a man who at all times abhorred a false oath. His sense of the guilt and danger of perjury must have been deepened, if possible, by that event which gave occasion to the Gibeonites to demand the bloody sacrifice of the seven sons of Saul. If the heavy judgment of year after year of famine was brought upon the land by Saul's violation of an ancient oath sworn long before he was born, he could not expect that the judgment already inflicted would be removed by his own violation of an oath sworn by him in person. He must rather have stood in dread of new judgments on the people and on his own house, for well he knew that the God with whom he had to do was no respecter of persons.

But perhaps too much already has been said in vindication of charges that have been brought against David. And it would be tedious to say what might easily be said to clear his memory from another – his severity towards the enemies of Israel, on whom he appears to some to have inflicted too barbarous retaliations, for the injuries formerly done to his people. It is indeed true that he did not follow that code of military law which is now observed among civilised nations, and which was not known nor thought of in former times, before the world was humanised by the light of moral truth emanating from the Christian revelation. But he certainly practised all that justice and humanity in his wars, which he had been taught by the unerring rule of the Word of God. Otherwise God who detests all cruelty even to enemies, would not have so often commended him, as the model of kings. It is a small thing to be judged of man's judgment. He who is

Of the Justice of David's Behaviour

the Judge of all has pronounced a sentence upon David's behaviour, which the world will never be able to reverse.

Many were the reproaches and censures thrown out on David whilst he lived, and his memory has not been spared. But the more thoroughly his behaviour is understood, in most instances it will be the more admired. And if there are some particular parts of it which we cannot reconcile to his general character, we ought to remember that there may be many circumstances now unknown which would fully justify these instances of his conduct, for which we cannot account. We read of slaughters committed by him amongst conquered nations, that appear inconsistent with the laws of humanity which regulated the conduct of good men in every age. But we cannot tell what crimes on the part of his enemies might render such examples of severity needful and worthy of praise. We find that in this Psalm he speaks not with remorse or shame, but with exultation and praise of the vengeance which he inflicted on his enemies, who were also the enemies of God and of his people.

Charity is essential to justice. There are duties which we owe to all men, by the second great commandment of the law, the commandment to love our neighbour as ourselves. If David had not conscientiously observed this precept, he could not have so often appealed to God, the Searcher of hearts, as the witness of his inviolable regard to these divine testimonies, which were the light to his path, and the lamp by which his feet were guided in the way of peace.

II. We proposed to speak of God's regard to David's righteousness in the deliverances granted to him from his enemies.

Without all doubt, David ascribed all the rich favours he received from God to that sovereign and free mercy to which every saint of God must be infinitely indebted. (*Psalm 116:4, 5*).

He was aware like his father Jacob that he was not worthy of the least of God's mercies, and that there was no merit in the least of his works, (*Psalm 138:2, 3*).

But he knew at the same time that through the infinite mercy of God, the good works of his people are accepted and rewarded by him, and that it is his glory to show forth his love of righteousness by his kindness to those who endeavour to approve themselves in his sight, (*Psalm 11:7*).

Mercy and truth meet together in God, righteousness and peace kiss each other, and display their united glories in the administrations of his providence to his people. The Lord shows forth the exceeding riches of his grace in making them righteous, and when they are made righteous, he shows both his grace and his justice in rewarding them according to their righteousness. There is so much sin mingled even with their good works, that if they were still under the law they could not escape the condemnation at once of all their works, and of their persons likewise. But all their iniquities, and amongst other iniquities those which cleave to their holy things, are covered from God's sight. He sees no iniquity, neither does he behold any perverseness in them, because the blood of Jesus cleanses them from all sin, and he ever lives to make intercession for them. He is their advocate with the Father to secure them against the imputation of their guilt. He is their High Priest to recommend their sacrifices of righteousness to divine acceptance. Their good works therefore cannot but be well-pleasing to God, and richly rewarded by him. He will never be unrighteous to forget any of their works or labours of love, and therefore those who follow after righteousness shall have a sure reward. David therefore had good reason to plead the righteousness as well as the mercy of God for deliverance from his enemies when he was in trouble, and to praise the righteousness of God in dealing with him according to his righteousness, and the cleanness of his hands when he was delivered from trouble. "Judge me, O God, and plead my cause against an ungodly nation. O let the wickedness of the wicked come to an end, but establish the just, for the righteous God trieth the heart and the reins."

It was a source of rich consolation to the good man in the time of his sore persecution that Saul was not the supreme king of Israel. He knew that God sat upon the throne judging right. To him he committed his cause in the assurance that a righteous sentence would be pronounced and executed on his behalf. "The Lord therefore be judge, and judge between thee and me, and see and plead my cause, and deliver me out of thine hand," (*1 Samuel 24:1,2*). And when the Lord had given a decisive sentence in his favour, it was his duty to sing aloud of the righteousness as well as of the grace of his God and his king.

Of the Justice of David's Behaviour

David's enemies were wicked men. They were unrighteous in persecuting him and in making war upon him, for he had done them no wrong. To some of them he had done eminent services. But the Lord who reigns on high executes righteousness and judgment for the oppressed. The deliverances of the people of God from their enemies are called the righteous acts of the Lord to the inhabitants of his villages in Israel, (*Judges 7*). "Sing unto the Lord with thanksgiving because he lifteth up the meek, and casts the wicked down to the ground," (*Psalm 147:6, 7*).

But did not David glory in himself rather than in the Lord, when he spoke of his own righteousness in such high terms? This question leads us:

III. To consider David's consciousness of his own righteousness. He speaks with perfect assurance concerning the regard which God expressed to his righteousness. Is this the language of humility? Is it fit language for a sinful man, who knows that if he is saved, he must be saved by the sovereign mercy of God? And was there no danger of self-deception in the favourable judgment which he formed of his own behaviour?

It would indeed be very presumptuous to form and to express such a judgment concerning ourselves without searching our own hearts, without comparing them with the law of God, and without finding good evidence that our hearts are sound in God's statutes. But in none of these particulars had David been negligent.

1. He had searched his heart as well as his ways. "I thought," he says, "upon my ways, and turned my feet unto thy testimonies." He was far from thinking that his ways could be right unless his heart was right in the sight of God. "Thou desirest truth in the inward parts: and in the hidden part thou shalt make me to know wisdom. Judge me, O Lord; for I have walked in mine integrity: I have trusted also in the Lord; therefore I shall not slide. Examine me, O Lord, and prove me; try my reins and my heart," (*Psalm 51:6; 26:1, 2*).

2. His standard by which he tried himself, was the law of his God. He was fully aware of the folly of trying himself by any other standard. He well knew how vain it would be to form a good opinion of

himself from any comparison he could form of his own behaviour with that of other men. "O that my ways were directed to keep thy statutes! Then shall I not be ashamed, when I have respect unto all thy commandments," (*Psalm 119:5, 6*).

3. He found in his heart and ways a habitual conformity to the law of God. He was indeed constrained to acknowledge that in many things he had offended God. When he meditated on the admirable purity of the law, he cried, "Who can understand his errors? cleanse thou me from secret faults." Yet he could with confidence say that he had hoped for God's salvation, and done his commandments.

This conclusion he did not rashly form from the consideration of a few of his actions, or of the frame of his heart at some particular periods of his life. Many deceive themselves by forming a hasty judgment of themselves, founded on temporary impressions made upon their minds in some moments of seriousness, excited by some particular circumstance of providence, or by the transient influence of some divine truths. For there are awful or comfortable truths which at times rouse the most thoughtless sinner to consideration, or spread a temporary joy through their souls, when the Word of God has no permanent influence on their hearts. David from his youth up made God his hope, and the Word of God the rule of his conduct, and his conscience bore him witness in the Holy Ghost that he cordially loved the testimonies of God, and had chosen them as his heritage for ever.

He knew the deceitfulness of the heart of man, and that without divine illumination he might easily deceive himself. He therefore referred himself to God the Searcher of hearts, to preserve him from entertaining any false hopes of the goodness of his own condition, (*Psalm 139:23, 24*). God heard his prayers, was pleased with his sincerity, and gave him the testimony of his Spirit that he was righteous before him.

IV. We proposed to consider the assurance which David had of God's respect to his own righteousness in the deliverances granted to him by his gracious providence.

We must not place humility in an affected ignorance of what is true, either concerning our own personal righteousness, or concerning God's acceptance of it. Nothing could be more dangerous than the presumption that God is well-pleased with us if our way or our heart are perverse before him, (*Micah 3:10-12*). Nothing could be more unbecoming in a Christian than the forgetfulness of his infinite obligations to that grace which has blotted out his innumerable transgressions. Yet it is desirable for every child of God to be well assured of the cleanness of his hands in God's sight, and of the acceptance of his works as well as of his person. Paul was perhaps the most eminent believer and preacher of the gospel of the grace of God that ever lived, and yet he rejoiced greatly both in the testimony of his conscience to his own uprightness, and in the prospect of the gracious rewards which the Lord the righteous Judge would give him.

As it is our duty to pray to God for the acceptance of our services, it must be our duty likewise humbly and thankfully to acknowledge God's righteousness and grace in his dealings with us. Paul, to the praise of God, declares that the Lord had delivered him out of the mouth of the lion which would have torn him in pieces. Jacob asserted in the face of Laban, that the God of his father, the God of Abraham, and the fear of Isaac, had seen his affliction, and the labour of his hands, and had rebuked Laban for his unrighteous intention against him. (*2 Timothy 4:17; Genesis 31*).

The good Hezekiah blessed the Lord, who had in love to his soul delivered him from the pit of corruption, and had cast all his sins behind his back. He acknowledged that his preservation from going down to the pit was a wonderful instance of the mercy of God in forgiving his sins. And yet he had prayed that God might remember in goodness to him how he had walked before the Lord in truth, and with a perfect heart. His hope of the gracious acceptance of his works was not in any degree inconsistent with the fullest conviction that he was infinitely indebted to the riches of pardoning mercy for any favour that he received from God.

The riches of divine mercy appear in the acceptance of our works, and in the consequent rewards bestowed on them, as well as in the acceptance of our persons. Were it not that our iniquities are hidden from God's sight, such works as even David's could not have been rewarded by that God who is of purer eyes than to behold evil. David was conscious that many sinful defects were to be found in all his righteousnesses, but he knew that there was forgiveness with

God that he might be feared; and that whilst his face was hid from his iniquities, his eyes were open to every holy affection in his heart, to every humble attempt to serve God, and to that rectitude of disposition and behaviour towards men, by which he endeavoured to please God. "I know also, my God, that thou triest the heart, and hast pleasure in uprightness," (*1 Chronicles 29:17*).

"Go thy way," says Solomon, "eat thy bread with cheerfulness, and drink thy wine with a merry heart, for God now accepteth thy works." If God does not accept our works, we can have no well-grounded pleasure in the bounties of his providence. They come not to us attended with the blessing of God, that is the true source of satisfaction in any of the good things that we possess. David could not with integrity of heart have blessed God for his great deliverances, if he had not considered them as testimonies that God was his friend, and that his works were accepted by him. "He delivered me, because he delighted in me. The Lord hath rewarded me according to my righteousness, according to the cleanness of my hands hath he recompensed me."

On the whole learn, 1. The great advantage of walking in the ways of God. "The Lord loveth him that followeth after righteousness. Say ye to the righteous, it shall be well with him." You know not what is good or evil for you, if you are more solicitous to abound in wealth than to please God, in whose hand are your life, and breath, and all your ways. You must be happy or miserable, not by gaining or by coming short of the objects of pursuit to which you are prompted by your natural inclinations, but according to the will of God, who gives to a man that is good in his sight all those things that he knows to be good for him, and withholds those things that would be evil, although he should long for them.

What reason have we to adore that plan of mercy which allows us to hope for divine acceptance, and for the reward of our works done to please God, although they are so imperfect that we must daily seek from God the pardon of our iniquities. Do not think that Nehemiah was an admirer of himself when he prayed that God would remember the good and great things which he did for the people of the Lord. "Remember me, O my God, for good concerning this also, and spare me according to the greatness of thy mercy."

Of the Justice of David's Behaviour

2. God's people ought patiently to hold on in the way of righteousness amidst the most discouraging dispensations of providence. David had after all his dismal days a new song put into his mouth to magnify the Lord. If he had turned aside from the ways of the Lord, and wickedly departed from his God, iniquity would have been his ruin, but the judgments of God were before him, and the statutes of the Lord he did not put away from him. He was also upright before the Lord, and kept himself from his iniquity. Therefore the Lord recompensed him according to his righteousness, according to the cleanness of his hands appearing in his eyesight. From what God did to David and to David's enemies, good and bad men may learn the grace and righteousness of God's administration, and what they have to expect from him. "With the merciful thou wilt show thyself merciful, with an upright man thou wilt show thyself upright, with the pure thou wilt show thyself pure, and with the froward thou wilt show thyself froward."

3. When we obtain deliverances, it is our duty to consider how we behaved under our troubles. Thus we will find occasion never to be proud, yet to bless God with the warmer, greater, and with unmingled pleasure, if through his mercy we have been enabled to behave aright in the time of trouble, and to wait for its termination in the way of righteousness. If we have been impatient and fretful, or if we have used unhallowed means for relief, we have great reason for humiliation and fear. Sanctified troubles are better than unsanctified deliverances.

If you have been rescued from troubles that have done you no good, you have reason to stand in fear of *new* and heavier troubles, or of what is worse than any earthly distresses, – of being left to yourselves, to wander in your own counsels without restraint. What son is he whom the father chasteneth not? It were better to suffer, as Job did, all that the devil himself can inflict, than to be left without suffering under that terrible sentence. "Because I purged thee, and thou wast not purged, therefore thou shalt not be purged any more, till I have caused my fury to rest upon thee."

Yet we still ought to bless God for deliverances from trouble, although we should not dare to say that we have kept the way of God when we are under it. Whilst we lament our guilt and folly, let us thank God that we are not consumed, that he has granted us favours of providence which we ill-deserved, that he is continuing to give us space of repentance, and exciting us to it by his patience and forbearance and goodness. Kind as well as alarming dispensations of providence lead to repentance, (*Romans 2:4, 5*).

4. Let us give praise to God for the great salvation wrought for us by our Lord Jesus Christ. The deliverances of David were salvations to all Israel. All the people were blessed under his government, and therefore were bound to magnify the Lord with him, and to exalt his name together. But the salvation wrought for us by our Lord Jesus, when he subdued him that had the power of death, was the salvation of the world. If he had not risen from the dead, none of us could have been begotten to the living hope of the inheritance that is incorruptible, and undefiled, and unfading. In a sense far higher than his father David, he could say, "The Lord rewarded me according to my righteousness; according to the cleanness of my hands hath he recompensed me. He loved righteousness, and hated iniquity: therefore God, his God, hath anointed him with the oil of gladness above his fellows," (*Psalm 18:20; 45:7*). He hath brought in an everlasting righteousness for us, and therefore we are delivered from the guilt and power of sin, and shall in due time be delivered from the grave, and put in possession of glories and felicities that pass all understanding. We never can be sufficiently thankful for the many deliverances with which we are blessed in the course of our lives on earth. But the great salvation above all others ought to be the subject of our constant praises. (*Psalm 21; Hebrews 5:7*).

It is to be feared that many of us are totally destitute of righteousness. By nature there is none righteous, no, not one. If we are still in that state in which we came into the world, all our righteousnesses are as filthy rags. Should God reward you according to your righteousness, whilst you continue in your natural state, you are undone. Your best works are no less condemned by the holy law, than those which you confess to be your worst. When God makes mention of your righteousness and your works they shall not profit you.

What then will you do? Will you do your best to work out some better righteousness for yourselves? Alas! what can you do? They that are in the flesh cannot please God. Can dead men perform any works? Can they arise and praise God? Can they procure for

Of the Justice of David's Behaviour

themselves a title to life? Then may men who are dead in trespasses and sins procure for themselves a title to the favour of God, and to a happy resurrection.

Yet your condition is not desperate. There is a righteousness revealed and offered in the gospel, by which all who believe are justified. You are authorised to say, "Surely in the Lord have I righteousness and strength," (*Isaiah 45:24; Jeremiah 23:6*).

If you receive the righteousness of Christ by faith you will no longer live in sin. "Jesus is made of God to us wisdom, and righteousness, and sanctification, and redemption," (*Romans 6:3-5, 12, 13; Titus 2:13-15*).

Printed in Great Britain
by Amazon

Jésus

Alain Vircondelet

Jésus

Flammarion

© Flammarion, 2007.
ISBN : 978-2-0806-8871-2

Pour Antoine, Albertine et Aurélien.

« Cette obscure clarté qui tombe des étoiles. »

Pierre Corneille, *Le Cid*

Prologue

Chapitre 1

Où il est question du début du monde et du refuge de Dieu dans un trou noir

L'histoire commence bien avant Jésus, dans la nuit des temps, quand il n'y avait encore rien et qu'il y eut tout, quand le néant laissa la place au ballet bien réglé des planètes, et que surgit le monde, neuf, innocent, sauvage. Une histoire sans hasard dans le grand mouvement des astres et des mondes organisés, dans le vaste périple des étoiles.

Il faudrait remonter au début des temps, quand Dieu, dit-on, les instaura et qu'il voulut ensuite revenir sur le destin du monde qu'il jugeait imparfait. Une histoire incroyable qui inspira un nombre incalculable de livres. Si des milliards d'hommes ont renoncé à y croire, des milliards d'autres hommes y croient encore dur comme fer. Pas de chaos dans l'ordre de l'univers, disent-ils, pas davantage de coups de dés, aveugles et capricieux qui, sans conscience aucune, auraient jeté dans le monde les hommes, les animaux, les plantes, toutes les particules élémentaires, les moins douées d'intelligence apparente, les moins futées à se reproduire, les moins curieuses pour s'acclimater aux saisons incertaines, les moins tendres pour se couler dans les bras des autres espèces. Pas d'autre choix, dans l'évolution millénaire de l'univers, qu'une main tendue, suprême et douce, ouverte aussi, qui chercherait à s'allier à ce qu'elle a donné : le jour, la nuit, les lueurs de l'aube, les crépuscules roses qui s'étirent à l'horizon de toutes choses, le chaud du soleil, et les mers et les terres, les fleurs hybrides, les animaux qui connaissent mieux que quiconque le passage du temps, les hommes encore, jamais jetés dans le monde, jamais livrés à eux seuls, mais offerts au monde. Qu'une main immense, qui aurait donné ça, la vie, qui court et ruisselle partout. La vie, son désir, furieux, inassouvi, de rejoindre et d'unir. Et tout le champ des possibles livré par elle à tout ce qui vit, palpite et frémit, et ne peut être le fruit d'un système aveugle et sourd, qui roulerait, imbécile, seul, et misérable, et qui avancerait vers qui, vers quoi, sans but et sans regret. Pas jeté dans le monde, mais donné, aimé. Pourquoi ne pas vouloir y croire ?

La main de Dieu tendue dans la musique des étoiles et des comètes, dans le grand chant des vibrations cosmiques, la main ouverte, la paume visible, les doigts tendus, vers ceux de l'homme, vers les pétales de toutes les fleurs, les yeux de tous les chiens, les plis de tous les paysages. Ainsi aurait commencé le monde, l'incroyable parade des planètes, l'inexpliqué cheminement de la préhistoire, qui donne le tournis. La main de Dieu vers d'autres mains, d'autres yeux.

Du haut de son échafaudage, Michel-Ange n'en finit pas de concevoir le début de l'histoire. Sous les voûtes de la chapelle Sixtine, la main de Dieu rejoint celle de l'homme. Mais l'index de Dieu ne touche pas l'index de l'homme. Il influe, il magnétise, il irradie mais il ne touche pas, il ne prend pas : il crée la même main que la sienne, belle, large, ouverte, offerte. C'est ainsi, n'est-ce pas, que commence la vie de l'homme, Adam, si vous voulez. Dieu est en lui,

Dieu le traverse comme un courant, comme une onde qui vibre et le recharge. Dieu, c'est son nom, est ce courant, cette onde, ce mouvement qui brûle et réanime. On pourrait l'appeler aussi bien la foudre, le feu, le chant, la poésie, l'eau qui bénit la terre, le désir, Dieu ou encore Bach, Mozart, la musique en tout cas, qui traverse, parcourt, enfreint les barrières et les codes, oui, il pourrait s'appeler comme ça, Dieu, cette folie, cette force qui va vers les hommes et les anime, embrase leurs corps.

Donc le doigt de Dieu ne touche pas l'index de l'homme. Et Adam vibre et brûle du grand feu de Dieu. Mais Dieu est trop naïf, il croit qu'Adam saura rester à son image, belle, forte, vaste, ouverte. Bien qu'il soit Dieu, il ne sait pas qu'Adam va aimer les cendres de son feu, le noir des flammes, préférer la nuit qui resplendit d'autres feux, bleus, livides comme la mort, des feux froids, qui glacent et torturent, des feux de haine, de guerre, des brasiers de douleur.

C'est que Dieu ne veut pas retenir de force sa créature, il l'a voulue libre, libre de l'aimer, de vivre avec lui, dans sa paix, dans l'harmonie des saisons et des cycles, dans la douceur de miel des champs de blé, sous l'abondance des treilles, dans les vallons de lait qu'il avait créés. Mais rien de tout ce qu'il avait prévu ne se réalisa, les jardins immaculés et le bonheur d'être ensemble, d'être rejoint. Alors l'homme fut chassé et Dieu disparut.

Cependant Dieu veillait, il avait feint de se retirer, d'oublier les hommes. Des calamités s'accablaient sur le monde qu'il avait conçu, des déserts s'étendaient là où il y avait semé l'or des céréales et tendu la clarté verte des mers et des forêts. Partout, le chaos et les cités ensorcelées, comme si Dieu avait abandonné l'univers, comme s'il s'était retiré dans un trou noir, si profond que les plus grands savants du monde ne pourraient jamais le voir ni le débusquer. On en avait conclu qu'il n'existait pas, qu'il n'avait jamais existé, qu'il était une fable, une histoire de veillée pour adoucir la colère des hommes, leur faire craindre quelqu'un quand même, car ce n'était plus possible finalement de vivre toujours dans cette guerre, dans cette nuit. Dieu continuait pourtant le travail commencé. Dieu n'était pas mort car Dieu est le souffle, et le souffle ne peut se tarir. Dieu est le vent qui va et vient, indomptable, insaisissable, chaud et froid, sirocco et blizzard ou bien zéphyr qui tiédit les arbres fruitiers quand ils ne parviennent pas à bien mûrir.

Dieu souffle sur les malades, une brise qui passe sur eux et il les enlève, les emmène avec lui. Chaque jour qu'il a fait, Dieu ramène ainsi les malades. Et le souffle les sauve. Cette fois-ci, Dieu ne fait pas comme au début des temps, il serre la main des malades, très fort, et il ne la lâche plus. La route est longue, sidérale, pour rejoindre le lieu retiré de Dieu, le lieu obscur qui manque aux savants, sans lequel ils pourraient dire qu'il n'y a rien qu'un monde de hasard, qui n'a aucune force intelligente, aucun dessein, simplement une mécanique qui roule sur elle-même, livrée aux rouages tyranniques d'une machine infernale, toujours inconnue, insatiable et têtue.

Quelquefois encore, Dieu reste caché dans l'espace ignoré, il laisse les planètes poursuivre leur valse régulière, et se croiser des vaisseaux et des sondes qui veulent faire des passerelles entre elles. Dans ce lieu si reculé où Dieu observe le manège de l'univers, règne le vent qui brasse l'espace et régénère tous les êtres vivants qu'il a recueillis chez lui, tout ce brassage d'êtres, de molécules, devenus particules infinies et qui se pulvérisent dans l'air nouveau. Et ce grand mouvement rejoint le souffle de Dieu, sans visage, mais qui se fond en chacune des particules comme un courant d'amour. Une bénédiction.

Il ne faut pas croire, non, que Dieu reste étranger au sort de l'univers. Que des événements aléatoires, des accidents dans l'ordre des planètes, le dépasseraient, lui rendraient insurmontable le projet qu'il a conçu pour lui. Il sait tout cela. Il a promis cependant de sauver son œuvre, de ne pas la laisser à la dérive mais de rétablir l'alliance qu'il a toujours voulue, et cela de tout temps. De temps en temps il faut bien reprendre en main le grand dessein, en finir avec l'arrogance des mondes. Il l'a promis depuis longtemps : un jour viendra où il enverra son fils pour parachever son plan, sur cette terre où les hommes se livrent au chaos de l'intelligence, égarés qu'ils sont dans la nuit de Dieu qu'ils ne savent plus reconnaître, asservis de rites et de fausses lois, étourdis de fausses joies. Il enverra son fils pour racheter les hommes, pour leur permettre d'être sauvés, de le rejoindre. Parce qu'après leur mort terrible, qu'en adviendrait-il de cet esprit qu'il avait mis jadis en eux ? Au fond de quelle absurde fosse iraient-ils s'ensevelir au lieu de se couler à nouveau dans le grand souffle originel ? En tout cas, c'est ce que croit Dieu. Yahvé, le Vent, le Grand Souffle, la Musique, la Poésie, comme vous voulez. Mourir et renaître, assure-t-il. Vivre et mourir, et retrouver vie et renaître encore. Mais autrement cette fois. Dans le grand vent du lieu ignoré, dans la dernière citadelle qu'aucune onde, aucun radar ne pourront jamais repérer, loin, très loin, derrière les planètes, à des milliards de milliards d'années-lumière de notre système, dans le grand manteau de vent de Dieu.

Dieu envoya donc son grand souffle créateur pour que naisse son fils.

« Va, lui dit-il, qu'il retrouve les hommes, qu'il se mêle à eux, qu'il les instruise du grand lieu de son Père, de son Royaume et où je les attends, qu'il les rende enfin dociles. J'ai une peine infinie à le voir partir, parce que je l'aime, et que je ne veux pas le voir mourir, et pourtant il faudra bien qu'il meure. Va, mon fils, rassemble-les tous, annonce-leur la bonne nouvelle ! »

C'est ainsi que Dieu parla dans le grand jeu des vents, dans la musique qui se fait au passage des particules vivantes, heureuses et apaisées. Dans le ballet de tous ceux qui étaient jadis vivants et qui, fidèles à l'alliance ou infidèles, se retrouvent ici, dans la douceur de la maison de Dieu. Au cœur du Poème.

Chapitre 2

Où Jésus le Fils est annoncé à Marie

C'est donc de l'immensité biologique que viendrait Jésus, créé par son père dans le ventre d'une vierge, Marie de Nazareth. Il a suffi d'un jet de lumière, d'un rayon violent, magnésique, pour qu'il s'attache à son ventre et y prospère jusqu'à la nuit de Bethléem, nouveau-né réchauffé par le souffle des bêtes. L'histoire commence comme un conte mythologique, il faut de la foi pour y croire, au moins se laisser emporter par elle, renoncer à la raison, se faire petit enfant.

Dieu donc a choisi une jeune fille pure et modeste de Galilée, il aurait pu choisir d'autres jeunes filles mais il a voulu que cela soit ainsi. Ses voies sont impénétrables. Ce jour-là, Marie est dans sa chambre, elle s'est retirée, elle a revêtu pour s'endormir une longue robe blanche, elle s'est agenouillée au pied de son lit et elle a prié, afin que vienne enfin le Messie promis d'Israël, qu'il mette fin par sa venue au chaos et aux esclavages, que cesse la tyrannie de la violence et des blasphémateurs. Elle ne sait pas encore le projet de Dieu qui a dépêché un de ses anges de lumière pour porter l'éclair dans son ventre. Marie prie, elle semble chanter, elle psalmodie dans le silence de la nuit. La lumière surgit, elle auréole la chambre, elle en est effrayée et peu à peu discerne dans le halo de lumière la silhouette de l'ange.

Brentano, le poète allemand, est au chevet de Catherine Emmerich, la mystique stigmatisée qui, chaque vendredi que Dieu fait, entre en extase et revit la passion du Christ. Il est assis tout près d'elle, au bord du grand lit dont les taies si blanches, presque empesées, vont bientôt s'imbiber du sang qui coule du front et des tempes de Catherine. Il a un petit cahier sur ses genoux et il note toutes les paroles qu'elle balbutie, sans s'arrêter, comme un grand fleuve qui n'en finit pas de se déverser, un torrent qui fracasse et roule. Elle dit que l'ange parle à mi-voix à Marie, qu'elle ne peut pas les entendre, sauf à la troisième fois, quand Marie relève son voile et tend ses yeux vers l'ange. Catherine perçoit, de cela elle en est certaine, les paroles de l'envoyé, les mêmes que celles de l'Évangile : « Voici la servante du Seigneur », et la réponse de Marie : « Qu'il me soit fait selon votre parole. »

Elle dit encore qu'à ce moment-là le plafond de la chambre « paraissait enlevé, et le ciel se montrait ouvert sur sa tête ». Alors la lumière qui émanait de l'ange sortit en flots et envahit Marie, l'inonda à son tour de clarté, la rendit diaphane, presque irréelle. De ses mains ouvertes qui disaient oui jaillissaient de longs filets éclatants. Elle répétait inlassablement : « Qu'il me soit fait selon votre parole. »

La lumière ensemençait Marie, elle sentait en elle une coulée d'amour qui la remplissait, cette douceur presque sucrée, liquide, onctueuse, comparable peut-être, elle n'en pouvait rien dire, à ce qu'on racontait de l'amour entre les humains. Une coulée chaude, inconnue, toujours renouvelée, et dont elle percevait en elle le passage, comme le courant de l'eau dans les rivières.

Il y avait aussi le silence. Le plus difficile à expliquer, à reproduire. Fra Angelico le connaissait bien, ce silence, dans la cellule de son couvent de Florence, quand, à matines, il restait prostré sur le dallage de marbre, froid et lisse, à contempler la Sainte Face. Le même silence que celui du soir quand, juste après le *Salve Regina*, le père abbé venait bénir tous les frères, sans un bruit, seulement le murmure feutré des bures qui frôlent le sol. Par les petites fenêtres des cellules, il pouvait entendre le calme de la nuit qui monte du patio, un silence parfumé du sucre des bougainvillées et des lauriers roses lancés à l'assaut des murs. Il sait que, comme ici, l'Annonciation est d'abord silence. Il la veut ainsi : l'ange surgit dans la maison à arcades, il s'agenouille devant Marie, la lumière qui l'entoure nimbe à son tour la jeune fille, la presque enfant, elle la pénètre et l'auréole. Pas de paroles, c'est une nuit chaude de Galilée, peut-être, au loin, à peine perceptibles, le piétinement des ânes, inlassables au puits, et le pas des derniers caravaniers qui rentrent au village, fourbus mais apaisés.

Jésus est conçu dans ce silence parce qu'il en vient, du très lointain lieu de Dieu, où sont rassemblés des milliards d'années et des milliards de pensées fondues en lui. Il vient au monde pour lui dire qu'il doit se préparer à se réunir dans la loi d'amour où fusionnent toutes les consciences, où il n'y a plus d'individus, plus d'ego, plus rien que ce grand champ d'âmes anéanties dans la vague d'amour. Cette mer.

Marie n'a que quatorze ans. Elle ne sait rien de la vie, de l'amour, de ce que c'est que d'être mère, des montées de lait qui vont engorger ses seins, de son corps qui va changer, de ses nausées et de ses vomissements et aussi de ses fatigues soudaines. Mais rien surtout de cette douleur des mères qui doivent apprendre le délaissement de leurs enfants, les mettre sur la voie de leur mort. Jésus grandit dans son ventre, elle le sent tressaillir. Elle protège son ventre, elle dit : « Mon tabernacle. »

Voilà ce que Dieu, Yahvé, la Musique, le Souffle, le Poème voulait pour le monde qu'il avait créé. C'était le dernier grand mouvement de son dessein, l'ultime phase de son plan : appliquer la loi d'amour, s'en donner les moyens, puisque sans lui les hommes ne pouvaient que détruire son ordre, vaquer à leur folie. Son fils conçu dans le ventre intouché d'une vierge, qui viendrait ranimer les hommes, leur rendre le sel.

C'est un conte incroyable, une de ces histoires d'Orient où rien ne nous surprend, les tapis qui volent et les cavernes logées au cœur des montagnes qui s'ouvrent en deux quand on prononce des formules magiques. Une histoire féerique, avec des effets spéciaux, des anges qui surgissent, porteurs de lumière, scintillants comme des néons qui étincellent les snacks le long des autoroutes américaines, qui aveuglent comme les enseignes des casinos de Las Vegas, avec des naissances qui se passent d'étreintes, comme dans les romans de science-fiction de Bradbury.

Mais rien, n'est-il pas vrai, ne peut échapper **au désir de Dieu**, à sa volonté créatrice, à ses projets. **Voilà** qu'il a manigancé un plan inouï, un fils venu de son lieu vibratoire, de son espace pneumatique, un lieu qui aspire et fusionne. Ce lieu, le sien : l'amour. Cette force irrésistible, supérieure, et qui agence son monde.

Marie ne peut confier son destin à quiconque. Elle n'est encore que la fiancée de Joseph, promise à lui. Qui donc pourrait croire à cette fable ? Qui ? Qui pourrait admettre qu'elle porte un enfant qui n'a pas été le fruit d'une union charnelle ?

Dans le silence de sa maison, elle accepte pourtant peu à peu cette évidence. Elle porte, c'est l'ange qui le lui a dit, celui qui va sauver Israël et le monde. La nuit, quand elle monte sur la terrasse pour prendre un peu de fraîcheur, elle regarde la vallée entière et ses coulées de palmiers, et les petits cubes de maisons carrées enchevêtrées, son village. Elle voit le ciel clouté d'étoiles qui scintillent, elle n'a qu'une seule chose à faire, contempler sa grandeur, sa vastitude, offrir sa foi qui ne demande aucune explication. Ce qu'elle veut, c'est seulement ça : être ouverte à l'apparition.

Depuis peu, elle a vu l'ange. Elle n'ignore plus rien de son halo de lumière, de sa présence, de ses paroles qui n'en étaient pas vraiment et qu'elle comprenait quand même, lettres étincelantes qui sortaient de sa bouche. Oui, disait Catherine Emmerich à son fidèle Brentano, « c'étaient des lettres qui jaillissaient, lumineuses, stellaires ».

Cet enfant serait-il donc le sauveur d'Israël ? Sa renommée n'aurait-elle pas de limites ? Jusqu'où, le prodige ?

Ernest Renan qui ne croit à rien tant qu'à la raison fulmine dans son bureau. Il ne peut se soumettre, dit-il, au credo des contes de fées. Aux histoires abracadabrantes qui font de Marie l'épouse virtuelle de Dieu. Un temple vivant que Dieu aurait choisi, comme ça, au hasard. Le Dieu de Renan, presque abstrait, n'a aucune intention de mimer les hommes. Qui donc a pu inventer cette histoire ? D'où est-elle partie ? Jésus est né d'une union humaine, parce que c'est ainsi que naissent les hommes. Il a mené toute sa vie de prédicateur parce qu'il était doué d'un talent immense, thaumaturge qui guérissait les malades, faisait se lever les foules endormies. Où est le miracle divin ? Mais Renan, c'est saint Thomas. « Homme de peu de foi, il te faut donc des preuves. Les voici. Touche mon flanc, mets tes doigts dans mes plaies. Je suis Jésus le Ressuscité » : ainsi dut parler Jésus à Renan. Bien après sa mort, juste avant d'accéder dans le grand tout de son lieu, dans le vertigineux espace du Souffle à jamais vivant.

Chapitre 3

Où Joseph et Marie quittent Nazareth pour rejoindre Bethléem

Partir pour Bethléem, c'est défier le froid de l'hiver et les montagnes recouvertes de fine gelée blanche qui durcit jusqu'au fond des vallons et poudre le faîte des oliviers et des épineux que ne peuvent plus brouter les chèvres. L'édit de César Auguste qui exige à chacun de se faire recenser dans sa ville d'origine oblige Joseph et Marie à quitter Nazareth. La route est longue et Marie ne sait pas comment elle supportera le voyage. Joseph l'a installée sur son âne, ils marchent presque au pas, rejoignent ceux qui se disent de la maison de David, les hommes et les femmes, les enfants, les animaux qui braient, les chameaux qui se déhanchent lentement le long des pistes sableuses. La nuit, ils dorment dans des caravansérails toujours bondés, des lieux de passage et d'exil, où se croisent marchands et bandits, miséreux et voyageurs, voleurs et prostituées. Avant de dormir, ils chantent les psaumes qu'ils ont toujours sus, les vieux cantiques qui espèrent dans la venue d'un Sauveur qui les libérera de leur joug et leur rendra la terre promise de toute éternité. Bientôt, ils le croient, le Sauveur sera parmi eux et Yahvé soit loué, disent-ils, pour sa compassion !

Marie, instinctivement, protège son ventre de ses deux mains, elle est au terme de sa grossesse, redoute que les douleurs ne surviennent en route mais elle apaise ses craintes car elle sait que Dieu ne veut pas ça pour son fils. Alors elle va au pas de l'âne, elle se concentre sur les tressautements de son ventre, sur la respiration secrète qu'elle décèle et ressent là, précisément, au milieu de son ventre, un cœur qui bat. Elle seule le sait. La route continue. La longue file des voyageurs longe des champs encore meubles, mais la terre autour de Bethléem est riche en céréales, plus tard c'est l'or des blés qui va les recouvrir. Bethléem, c'est la ville du pain, dit-on, et celle des fruits. On la surnomme *Ephrata*, littéralement « riche en fruits ». Hâte d'y arriver, de trouver refuge dans la chambre d'une hôtellerie. Le petit village est un damier de cubes blanchis à la chaux. Des palmiers dattiers en surgissent et leurs palmes restent vertes malgré le froid. Joseph ne peut obtenir de chambre, depuis cette affaire de recensement l'hôtellerie est prise d'assaut. Il rassure Marie, la met à l'abri des regards et de la foule, lui demande d'attendre, le temps qu'il trouve un lieu. Il revient, préoccupé, et se rend dans une petite étable. Il y installe Marie et l'âne, dépose ses maigres bagages, et attend la nuit.

Elle vient, cette nuit, dans la clarté bleue des étoiles. Marie sent les premières douleurs. Elle sait que c'est cette nuit-là que tout va se jouer. Elle se souvient de l'ange, de la promesse qu'il lui a faite : « Ce sera un garçon, il sera le Messie et tu l'appelleras Jésus. »

Tout commence. Il vient, l'enfant, dans la douleur de Marie. Il n'y a pas de femme pour l'aider, que Joseph qui prie au seuil de l'étable, pas d'autre souffle que celui de l'âne qui diffuse sa chaleur de bête, comme s'il avait compris l'histoire qui se joue. C'est ainsi que naît Jésus.

Pourquoi les étoiles brillent-elles autant cette nuit-là, tels des repères dans l'obscurité, des voies tracées, des éclats du lieu de Dieu ?

Il semble à Marie que, pendant la délivrance, l'étable, qui n'est en fait qu'une grotte dont la façade a été bâtie d'un mur de roseaux tressés, se soit soudain illuminée, et que d'innombrables présences ont envahi le lieu. Ce sont les cohortes des anges qui viennent les réchauffer, clamer leur joie de leurs musiques secrètes. Dehors, la nuit est tranquille, d'une douceur de lait. On n'entend pas un cri, aucune colère ne résonne, aucune violence ne se fait. C'est une nuit épargnée de la douleur du monde, une sorte de trêve, de cessez-le-feu, et personne ne sait pourquoi il y a tant de douceur dans cette nuit. On dit que cela faisait penser à la douceur du jardin d'Éden, établi par Dieu et qui avait été trahi.

Il y eut d'autres nuits de Bethléem, bien après la mort de Jésus, dans l'interminable déroulement des siècles, où Dieu a fort à faire pour préserver l'ordre. D'autres nuits où Jésus naît de nouveau, où la clarté des étoiles est plus intense, étincelant d'une clameur vivace, surnaturelle. Nuits de Bethléem comme des nuits de résistance, des nuits d'avènement et d'espérance ! Au creux du gouffre, dans les ténèbres des camps nazis, Noël reste encore Noël pour les chrétiens déportés, il y a même des Juifs qui secrètement implorent Jésus de les délivrer. Où trouver de la force et de l'innocence, des raisons d'espérer et de célébrer quand tout autour de soi n'a plus de lien avec le monde, comme lâché dans le grand vide de la nuit, livré au mal ? Comment faire pour que Noël, même tu, même murmuré, s'élève comme un chant et fasse réapprendre le désir du don ? C'est la nuit de la Nativité, Bethléem il y a deux mille ans, Bethléem encore aujourd'hui. Nul ne pourra jamais s'y opposer. Ni ceux qui font les camps, ni ceux qui imaginent des trous immenses pour ensevelir des cadavres, des à peine morts, des encore vivants, des enfants et des mères, des vieux et des vieilles, des artistes, des chanteurs, des pianistes, des peintres, des tailleurs d'étoffes et de pierre, des mendiants et des débiles, des fous et des patriotes. Tous ceux qui continuaient le lien, tissaient la tapisserie.

Dans le baraquement ouvert au froid, aux clayettes de sapin qui laissent passer le givre et le gel, par moins trente degrés, il y en a qui se souviennent de la nuit de l'étable. C'est une autre crèche ici, et l'haleine des moins faibles réchauffe celui des leurs qui va mourir. Pour le mourant de Mauthausen ou de Birkenau, c'est Bethléem et le Golgotha à la fois. À mi-voix, tandis que les autres déportés, des Juifs pour la plupart, les écoutent, des voix s'élèvent, balbutient des chants oubliés, leurs mains se croisent et se serrent, et le souffle de Noël monte dans la nuit. Des étoiles sont accrochées au ciel noir, elles scintillent avec une dureté inquiétante, persistent dans leur éclat d'argent, indifférentes. Le chant se souvient des nuits de Noël dans les villages, des mots simples et naïfs, des histoires de hautbois et de musettes qui célèbrent la venue du « divin enfant ». Étrange nuit qui fait oublier les clameurs des chiens, les cris et les hurlements, les ordres et les mitrailles, la langue allemande, autrefois si douce quand elle chantait Bach dans les chapelles de bois et devenue si rauque, si barbare ! Il y en eut plusieurs de nuits de Noël à Mauthausen et à Birkenau, et jamais le petit chant de Bethléem n'a été oublié. Quelquefois des Juifs se convertissaient à leur douceur, comme une manière de revenir avant l'enfer. Vers quoi, vers qui ? Peut-être vers l'enfance, la toute petite enfance dans les bras des mères.

Il y eut aussi des nuits de Noël qui faisaient cesser le feu et la guerre, des nuits qui retrouvaient la grâce du silence et des chants enfantins, dans Jérusalem toujours déchirée. Même grâce qui faisait trêve à la souffrance de Thérèse dans son lit du carmel de Lisieux, à l'agonie de Bernadette à Nevers, de Jeanne dans son cachot ou de Jean de la Croix.

Dans tous les hôpitaux du monde, jusqu'au vertige, des humains naissent et meurent, la nuit de Bethléem. Les médecins et les infirmières se partagent la tâche. Même ceux qui ne croient en rien notent que l'enfant qui vient de naître est né la nuit de Noël, que l'homme qui vient de mourir cette nuit-là a comme une chance particulière, reçu une bénédiction. C'est que Bethléem est depuis la naissance de Jésus le lieu de l'espérance, d'un espoir infini qui rallierait d'autres mondes, d'autres joies.

Dans l'étable, Marie se repose, apaisée, irradiée. Il n'y a de place que pour la louange, que le temps ne peut plus mesurer. Depuis des siècles, dans les grands ordres monastiques, cette nuit-là n'a pas de prix. Elle brise l'ordre du temps, rétablit et accomplit le lien. Autour de l'étable, tout dort. Peu savent déjà la nouvelle, Joseph, Marie, eux la reconnaissent : à cette douceur qui préfigure le lieu de Dieu, à chaque fois retrouvée dans la naissance d'un enfant, quelque chose qui échappe à l'histoire, se vit par effraction, visible au rayonnement du visage de la mère, à l'apaisement immédiat de toute douleur, à l'oubli des choses du monde, aux larmes du père. Après, tout peut bien recommencer, mais il y a eu ce temps disponible. On va l'appeler le temps de Dieu.

Chapitre 4

Où se découvre la splendeur de cette nuit

Dans les maquis du Vercors, les nuits sont semblables à celles de Judée. Même silence rendu à d'autres réalités, à d'autres expériences. Au fond des bergeries, les résistants ne craignent pas les embuscades. Ils veillent et contemplent la clarté des étoiles qui profilent les vallons, dessinent les ravins, soulignent les arbres. Les étoiles sont des repères qui fixent les chemins, témoignent de l'ordre de l'univers. Quelquefois, certaines d'entre elles filent comme des comètes, avec leurs queues de lumière qui se pulvérisent. Elles semblent se décrocher de la voûte céleste et tomber dans le vide. Les maquisards souvent sortent de leur tanière et dorment, malgré le froid, à même le sol, les yeux face au ciel. L'endormissement ramène aux douceurs de la toute petite enfance, aux émerveillements. Le face-à-face dure longtemps, rien ne bouge, ni eux ni les étoiles : que cet éblouissement comme un signe de Dieu.

Dans la nuit de Bethléem, il fallut bien cependant que Dieu annonce la naissance du Sauveur. Les bergers de Gaza, dans leurs maisons, virent que les étoiles, cette nuit-là, étaient plus intenses que d'habitude. Brillaient avec plus de violence et semblaient tressaillir, vibrantes. Alors ils surent que quelque chose d'extraordinaire venait de se passer, quelque chose d'heureux. Ils se rassemblèrent dans la nuit et les étoiles scintillaient toujours plus, elles étaient devenues vibrantes, roulaient sur elles-mêmes. Nuit des prodiges. Dieu envoya ses anges, ils illuminèrent d'un éclat particulier une des plus grosses étoiles qu'ils placèrent au-dessus de la crèche. Tout peut survenir et surtout le poème, et la foudre de ses mots qui enchantent le monde et l'inaugurent. Et le prodige, le miracle, voulait dire à peu près cela : « Un enfant est né, le Messie promis aux enfants d'Israël qui viendra les sauver de leur misère et de leurs souffrances. Et ce Messie ne vient pas pour sauver une génération mais le monde dans sa totalité et pour l'éternité des temps. Cet enfant est né dans une crèche misérable, il est cependant le fils de Dieu et il viendra vous sauver tous, vous racheter de vos péchés, et vous garder toujours dans sa lumière, il vous ressuscitera comme il sera lui-même ressuscité. Et j'éclaire d'une lueur plus vaste, plus inouïe, l'étoile du berger, la plus grosse de tout le ciel que j'ai créé, pour vous guider dans la nuit et que vous alliez vers lui. Car dans cette nuit si rare, unique dans l'histoire de l'univers, vous apprendrez le bonheur d'être réunis, vous découvrirez la chance d'être sauvés du malheur, de connaître l'espérance. Il vous dira, cet enfant que je vous envoie, de ne plus avoir peur parce que je ne vous quitterai plus. »

Ainsi parla Dieu à travers les anges. Cela dut se proclamer par des chants, et tous quittèrent leurs maisons pour aller vers Bethléem s'assurer du prodige. Dieu, du fond de sa cachette, souriait de tant de confiance et de foi. C'est qu'il s'est fait fort, cette nuit-là, d'apporter un peu de miel à la souffrance, un peu de musique dans la détresse.

À lui, tout est possible et même la force de faire croire l'impossible. Au Cap Juby, sur la toute petite langue de terre et de sable où vécut un temps Antoine de Saint-Exupéry, la nuit de Bethléem revenait chaque soir. Près de sa cabane de tôle ondulée, il s'installait pour veiller, se couler dans l'immensité de la nuit, s'en laisser envelopper comme pour s'assurer de la présence de Dieu, pour s'associer au grand poème de la vie, en avoir sa part. Car chaque humain, chaque plante, chaque bête a cette liberté-là de se relier au mouvement permanent du temps, de faire partie de la voûte. Être de cette patrie de Dieu. Jamais autant que dans ces nuits étoilées Saint-Exupéry parvenait à se sentir solidaire du grand plan divin. Sans elles, sans ces nuits parfaites, il se disait lui aussi « lâché » sur la terre, abandonné au chaos obscur et incompréhensible, à l'inintelligibilité d'un monde dans lequel il ne se reconnaissait pas, à la misère aveugle d'un désert de sable qui ne laissait échapper que de la solitude. Et soudain c'était la nuit et, sous ses pas, « le luxe d'un sable épais », la nuit, cette demeure. Cette chambre d'écho d'où il pouvait capter, comme il le disait, des secrets d'ange.

Il y a dans la cathédrale d'Autun, en Bourgogne, un chapiteau de pierre qui raconte le sommeil des mages. Ils dorment sous les constellations, d'un sommeil apaisé, un ange bienveillant les recouvre de ses ailes étoilées. Depuis des centaines d'années, les pèlerins viennent l'admirer. Dans leurs yeux se devine l'envie d'être comme les bergers et les mages de Galilée, dans la confiance de la nuit, bordés par les anges.

À Bethléem donc, les bergers arrivent de nuit pour adorer l'enfant-roi. Ce sont des pauvres, de piètre réputation, pas les bons bergers de Jean Giono qui dorment à la belle étoile dans les combes solitaires, et chantent la gloire de la nature au milieu de leurs troupeaux, mais des bergers rusés et voleurs, murmure-t-on dans les parages, dont il faut craindre les mauvais coups. Mais ils répondent à l'appel des anges. Et ils chantent sur le chemin. Les pauvres, les moins que rien, ceux qui dorment sous le ciel, sont les premiers adorateurs. Dieu, du bout du ciel, réenchante le monde, voilà des histoires semblables à des contes de fées, des nuits magiques éclairées de diamants qui tracent la route, des histoires qui retournent les cœurs et les vies, c'est à peine croyable « Ne quittez pas la voie de lumière, leur dit-il, suivez-la à la trace, à la queue de la plus grosse étoile, il y a des nuits qui font changer le monde, qui trahissent l'ordre des vainqueurs et des puissants, des forts et des cyniques. Des nuits d'enfance qui remontent aux sources. » Les bergers, les pauvres, aiment ces contes et ces petites histoires. Qui sont donc ces fous qui vont plier genoux devant la crèche ? Cette nuit fait des croyants des hommes de foi : des naïfs et des crétins, diront les autres, sûrs de leur liberté absolue, farouches dans leur certitude. Qu'importe l'injure, dit la cohorte des bergers qui affluent au seuil de l'étable. Qui saura jamais la douceur de lait qui coule au cœur du nouvel homme ? Qui connaîtra la tendresse des larmes de qui se sait rejoint ?

Cela se passe entre 5 et 6 avant notre ère, peu avant la mort d'Hérode. Mais rien n'est moins sûr pour autant. C'est l'histoire d'un homme, Jésus, dont on ne sait presque rien, que cela, cette marche vers la lumière, cette naissance prodigieuse au milieu des bergers, et le tracé des étoiles pour leur servir de boussole. Théodore Monod, le savant aux yeux perçants d'aveugle, arpente les grands déserts. Dans les nuits glorieuses et solitaires, bien avant de rejoindre les coulées de palmiers dans les vallées miraculeusement fertiles, il mesure le poids des nuits étoilées et leur vibration, et l'impossible absence de Dieu. La grandeur des déserts, c'est d'avoir conservé sa présence, la sourate du guide qui chante Dieu traverse le silence et la nuit, assure du dialogue.

Jésus ne sait rien de toutes ces choses. Comme tous les à peine nés, il inspire à ses visiteurs respect et silence, idée de la pureté. Il émane de lui une lueur dorée, une réverbération de Dieu, quelque chose qui n'a pas de nom humain mais qui force la foi. C'est d'abord au nom de l'enfant que se jure la fidélité au Royaume, que naît le sentiment d'appartenance. « Je suis venu de toi, proclame le berger ignorant, j'avais cru te perdre et voilà que je t'ai retrouvé. Je croyais avoir oublié la nature de l'innocence, et toute cette confiance qu'il y a en toi et voilà que tu me les rends, que je les retrouve, intacts. Je ne croyais qu'en moi, qu'en la réalité de mes actes, et voilà que tu m'apprends à voir à la mesure de la simplicité et de l'ignorance. Non pas celles qui me font stupide mais grand et vaste, comme ce ciel au-dessus de moi. Toi-même tu es pauvre et réchauffé par des bêtes, comme nous, tu es Dieu fait homme pauvre et simple, tu es l'Autre que je ne voyais plus. »

Car Jésus qui naît, c'est aussi l'homme qu'on ne voyait plus, mais qui est comme soi, mêlé de solitude et de souffrance, d'amour et d'inquiétude, de pauvreté et de péché. Pas un dieu qu'on honore en courbant l'échine, non, Dieu qui vit et pleure, comme soi, comme toi.

Dieu le Père se frotte les mains en regardant toutes ces choses inouïes, il a rétabli la promesse de l'Alliance, il a redonné sens à l'espérance. On y croit si l'on veut, mais la nuit de Noël ranime l'or intérieur, l'or en soi contenu, non pas celui qui rend puissant et inspire la convoitise, mais l'or de l'amour, l'or des larmes qui ouvrent le cœur. Le petit Marcel Proust, qui n'a pas reçu d'éducation religieuse, est ébloui par l'or de Noël. Il a l'intuition que cette nuit-là fait traverser, qu'elle fait passer de l'autre côté du mur.

Noël comme une pause dorée dans le temps, Noël retrouvé dans la basilique San Marco quand, avec sa mère, devenu adulte, il acquiert la certitude d'entrer dans le lieu de Dieu, de Marie, de Jésus.

Quelque chose de nouveau s'est passé, qui n'était pas imaginable : la venue de Dieu dans un corps de bébé, quand tous l'attendaient dans le fracas des chars de feu, dans les orages hallucinés qui déchirent le ciel, quand sa colère ou son amour devaient forcément être du spectacle, avec grandes mises en scène à la Cecil B. de Mille, quelque chose de comparable à l'histoire de la mer Morte ouverte en deux et les chars du pharaon engloutis sous les vagues, juste après le passage des Juifs. Et dans les nuages rougeoyants, des pluies de cataclysme, et enfin Dieu triomphant, debout, dans son char illuminé. Mais rien de tout cela. Qu'une nuit froide de Judée, ordinaire et semblable à toutes les nuits d'hiver, et Dieu, disaient les bergers qui n'en croyaient pas leurs yeux, s'était manifesté là, dans cette pauvreté, dans cette banalité. Oui, quelque chose avait changé, Dieu se reconnaissait aux gestes des mères, tendres et attentifs, dans les silences des nuits, dans les berceuses à peine murmurées. Dieu n'était pas un monstre énorme et immense, mais il s'était glissé dans la misère des hommes, dans leur vie simple, il se plaisait dans la tranquillité des villages, il aimait entendre la corde qui racle le long de la margelle de pierre du puits, le pas des ânes, il aimait admirer la beauté des soirs, quand le soleil tombe sur la crête des petites dunes de sable. C'en était fini de ce Dieu de guerre et de vengeance, Dieu veillait autrement, par sa présence incarnée, visible, là, accueillante à qui le voulait.

Chapitre 5

Où Jésus, Marie et Joseph fuient en Égypte

Mais les forces obscures, jamais, ne désarment. Qui voudrait céder la place ? Renoncer au pouvoir ? Qui souhaite la lumière quand on la sait si exigeante ?

Hérode, le vieux monarque despotique, a demandé aux mages de lui rendre compte de ce qu'ils ont vu à Bethléem. « Moi aussi j'irai me prosterner devant l'enfant », rajoute-t-il. Mais les mages, avertis en songe de ne pas retourner au palais d'Hérode, ont regagné leur pays par d'autres routes. Leurs caravanes suivent les pistes des étoiles, elles avancent lentement, les mages sont soulevés d'une force nouvelle, ils chantent la gloire du messie, ils ont la grâce des premiers convertis. La colère d'Hérode est alors immense.

« Qu'on tue tous les enfants mâles en bas âge, tous les garçons de moins de deux ans. Qu'aucune mère ne se dérobe à mon décret ! »

Le souffle de l'ange de nouveau entre dans l'étable. Marie n'a plus peur de l'apparition. Elle sait qu'elle est entre les mains de Dieu, qu'il la veille et la protège. "Lève-toi, dit l'ange à Joseph, prends l'enfant avec toi, et sa mère, et fuis en Égypte, et restez-y jusqu'à ce que je te le dise, car Hérode va rechercher l'enfant pour le faire périr[1]." »

Joseph aussitôt prend la route avec Jésus et Marie. Ils sont tous les trois sur les chemins obscurs, le froid de la nuit ralentit leur pas, mais comme Marie porte l'enfant sous ses voiles, il ne grelotte pas, pelotonné contre sa poitrine. Ils longent la mer et croisent des campements de Bédouins qui feignent de ne pas les voir, ils ne demandent pas asile sous leurs tentes, ne se nourrissent que de lait de chèvre et de dattes que Joseph a achetées au bazar de Bethléem. Il faut aller, aller encore plus loin. Derrière eux, les soldats de Hérode sont partis à leur recherche. À Bethléem, personne ne sait que tous les bébés de la ville vont être égorgés. Ils dorment dans leurs berceaux, veillés par les mères, encore dans l'innocence de la nuit de Noël. Il règne un étrange silence, c'est le poids des étoiles accrochées au ciel qui semble figer le temps, lui donner son éternité. Mais le galop des soldats se rapproche. Ils entrent dans la ville, à fond de train, ouvrent du pied les portes des maisons, vont aux berceaux, tranchent les gorges. Des femmes hurlent, des enfants pleurent, puis c'est le silence, des mères emportent leurs petits dans les ruelles, mais elles sont rattrapées, jetées à terre, dépossédées de leurs enfants, égorgés sous leurs yeux. On entend des cris semblables dans les villages d'Espagne, quand les armées espagnoles hurlent *Viva la muerte* ! Vive la mort, oui, qui court et se rue dans les faubourgs. Pas de quartier non plus dans les douars kabyles quand les hordes du GIA, avinées, droguées, massacrent les enfants, en les faisant tournoyer au-dessus de leurs têtes, et les fracassent contre les murs. Pas de quartiers dans les antichambres funestes des camps de la mort, dans la vieille Europe comme aux alentours des villages rwandais ou dans les cours des fermes au fond des Balkans. Éteindre les étoiles, « assassiner Mozart », disait Antoine de Saint-Exupéry.

Marie, étrangement, n'a pas peur, ni Joseph, comme si Dieu avait glissé en eux de sa patience et de sa tempérance. Comme s'ils se savaient épargnés. Rembrandt, dans sa *Fuite en Égypte*, atteint l'apogée de son art du clair-obscur. Tout autour du motif, c'est la nuit la plus noire, un poing fermé qui ne laisse rien apparaître de l'horizon ni des étoiles. Seule la Sainte Famille est éclairée, étoile elle aussi, les ombres biaisées l'effleurent mais ne la touchent pas, elle est préservée de toute nuit, avance comme guidée intérieurement. Marie croit cela, qu'en donnant naissance à Jésus, elle a donné de l'innocence au monde, que toutes les mères ont ce don de la clarté, qu'elles sont la victoire sur la nuit, que fuir c'est aussi résister, et que Dieu est du côté des errants et des misérables, des sans toit, des bannis et des proscrits. Et qu'il leur délivre de la lumière en abondance, que les anges enfin les suivent sur la route risquée, comme ceux que Giotto a peints, rieurs et vigilants, précédant la monture. La fuite en Égypte, c'est l'une des toutes premières leçons de Dieu dans le grand dessein qu'il a conçu. La fuite ici est espérance, annonce de la lumière. Ceux qui fuient laissent toujours derrière eux l'ombre et la mort, ils fuient pour se sauver, rejoindre les rives des mers et les horizons de lumière, ils ont le regard qui va vers le jour.

Première partie

La vie cachée de Jésus

Chapitre 6

Où comment Jésus s'installe dans la paix de Nazareth

Marie a retrouvé Nazareth, la maison troglodyte, semblable à l'étable de Bethléem. Elle aime se savoir à l'abri du roc qui rassure, donne de la force et réchauffe. Depuis la naissance de Jésus, elle a acquis en elle une nouvelle énergie, une certitude pleine et tranquille. Elle qui n'a jamais douté a vu passer le souffle de l'ange, l'a senti sur sa peau. Qui pourrait la contredire ? Elle sait désormais ce qu'est la foi : cette évidence que nul ne peut entamer, cette pierre infracassable. Depuis elle chante son obéissance fidèle : « Mon âme exalte le Seigneur, exulte mon Esprit en Dieu mon Sauveur. » Elle répète les paroles en travaillant aux humbles travaux du ménage, Marie, la mère de Dieu, balaie, roule la graine, va au puits tirer son eau, donne à manger aux bêtes, berce l'enfant qui vient de naître. Nazareth est comme replié sur sa colline, à l'écart des routes de commerce, à l'ombre de la montagne du Nébi-Sahîn. Ce n'est pas à proprement parler une ville, mais plutôt une bourgade, moins prestigieuse que ses voisines, Tibériade ou Magdala ou encore Gennesareth. Mais tout autour c'est la Galilée féconde et luxuriante, verte par ses vallons, ses soubresauts montagneux cultivés jusqu'en leurs sommets. Le paysage est vaste, Marie le connaît bien, souvent avec

Joseph, portant Jésus dans ses bras, elle va se promener dans la douceur du soir, dans les odeurs suaves des plantes orientales, âcres et sucrées à la fois. Nazareth veut dire « la gardienne », elle est celle qui retient et protège, et par là sauve et empêche la dispersion des cités romanisées, lieux des Babel païens et profanes.

La petite enfance de Jésus reste un mystère. Nul ne sait comment il grandit, comment il joue, ses caprices de bébé et ses grâces enfantines, ses colères et ses éclats de rire. Elle est ce que sont toutes les enfances, les petites histoires secrètes et merveilleuses, les détresses et les larmes, les envies de se sauver, de découvrir le monde au-delà de la maison, et le grand refuge des bras de sa mère quand la peur de la nuit tombe comme une menace.

Marie a la grâce rustique des paysannes, des terriennes aux mains forcément calleuses, rien à voir avec ce qu'en feront plus tard tous les peintres de l'art chrétien. Rien à voir avec la grâce de fée qu'ont mise dans leurs tableaux les Bellini et les Van Dyck, les Vinci et les Raphaël, les Michel-Ange et les Tintoret. Elle n'a pas de rayons d'or qui s'échappent de ses doigts, pas de chair diaphane traversée par la lumière d'aube, pas de joyaux autour du cou ni de diadème car elle n'a pas d'autre royauté que celle du cœur et de l'amour. Pas d'autre royauté que celle intérieure, invisible, silencieuse.

Giotto peut-être pourrait bien être le seul à avoir vraiment vu Marie de Nazareth. Dans la chapelle dei Frari, à Sienne, il peint *a fresca* son visage rude et âpre. Elle ne sourit presque jamais comme si elle pressentait en son for intérieur des jours de malheur. Les mains sont pleines d'ocre, parce qu'elles touchent le blé et la terre, font du pain et des boulettes de céréales, comme on en mange ici, en Toscane. À la lueur de ses lampes à huile, Giotto peint

Marie à gros traits, son âme paysanne, sa fidélité à la terre, sa connaissance intuitive des germinations. La rudesse du peintre lui va bien, mais Giotto y glisse autre chose encore, de la pleine humanité, de la chair de mère, sauvage, qui craint pour son enfant, farouche pour ceux qui pourraient le lui ravir. Le corps de Marie envahit les murs, elle est présente partout, forte, indissociable de Jésus, liée à lui par ses mains, ses bras qui se tendent vers lui. Pas besoin de modèle à Giotto pour peindre le secret de Marie. Il connaît de quoi sont pétris les hommes, ça se voit aux mains qu'il prête à Marie, qui savent porter les seaux d'eau du puits, cueillir les dattes dans les oueds desséchés, en faire de la pâte qu'elle donne à son enfant.

Marie vit ainsi, dans la frugalité et la simplicité des campagnes, elle connaît aussi la paix des villages, ce que ça veut dire, ces maisons de cubes blancs rassemblées et comme pelotonnées, le lien des hommes entre eux, le village et la place centrale, et la fontaine un peu à l'écart, et la douceur des nuits quand elles tombent, tard, en commençant à rosir l'horizon, à le tendre entièrement de lueurs mauves puis violettes jusqu'à devenir noires et enfin le balancement des palmes qui fait un bruit doux, de caresse.

Parfois, Marie a trop chaud et elle monte, en pleine nuit, « boire », comme elle dit, tout ce ciel éclairé d'étoiles, cette immensité où vit Dieu dont elle a accepté le messager, et elle en est secrètement reconnaissante, les mots affleurent à sa bouche, elle ignore d'où viennent ces paroles qui s'échappent de sa bouche, elles jaillissent, joyeuses mais inquiètes quand même, parce qu'elles annoncent l'issue de l'histoire, le chant et la plainte.

Mais rien ne vient encore assurer son pressentiment. Jésus dort paisiblement, il joue et commence à babiller, à prononcer quelques paroles incertaines, il est doux et violent à la fois. Rien à voir avec l'enfant blond des images de Saint-Sulpice que les marchands du Second Empire vont répandre dans le monde entier. Il n'a pas de boucles blondes et un regard d'ange, il a l'œil sombre qui vibre d'un éclat particulier, presque irréel, et des boucles noires, très noires qui tombent sur ses épaules. Il joue et on le surprend quelquefois à ne rien faire, à fixer la terre, l'horizon de la terre, la ligne des montagnes violettes et pelées, le fil des palmiers, l'ocre de la terre, et le ciel et les étoiles. Marie l'emmène avec elle où qu'elle aille, au puits, au jardin, elle craint qu'il ne s'échappe, qu'il se fasse mal. Elle est comme toutes les mères mais plus encore, elle n'ose imaginer la suite.

Dieu regarde tout cela du plus loin de son immensité. Les voisines de Marie disent qu'il est dans sa cachette où il finira bien par les oublier, à force. Marie ne répond rien, elle sait que Dieu ne se cache pas mais qu'il est partout, comme une évidence qui crie, sur les chemins, dans les plantes et les bêtes, et dans toute cette humanité qui vaque et ne prend pas la peine de « faire silence ». C'est le secret de Marie, « faire silence » pour que tout s'ouvre et se donne, pour faire apparaître Dieu. Comment l'ange serait-il venu si, ce soir-là, elle n'avait fait silence, si Dieu n'avait pu trouver place pour s'installer chez elle et lui parler, lui dire tout ce qu'il avait décidé pour elle ? Si seulement elle voulait bien seulement ça ?

Le soir, quand le frais de la nuit commence à tomber, elle pense à ce oui qu'elle a prononcé, comme ça, sans réfléchir. « Acceptes-tu d'être le lieu de Dieu, celui qui va accueillir le Messie ? » et elle avait dit oui. Sur le coup, elle n'avait même pas réfléchi, tout semblait se dérouler dans un conte, une histoire à dormir debout, un beau rêve qu'elle se faisait avec des anges, du vent qui balaie tout sur son passage, et des lumières d'étoiles partout. Comment dire non ? Comment échapper au sortilège ? Elle avait dit oui, et puis elle avait laissé faire. L'ange n'avait pas pris le temps de débiter tout son message, et elle était déjà prête à recevoir, à rendre cet amour de Dieu.

Nazareth ne cherchait querelle à personne aux alentours, le village ne faisait pas la guerre, c'était un lieu apaisé, quiet, sans problème. La régularité des jours et des nuits s'appliquait aux gestes quotidiens, il y avait ceux qui travaillaient et ceux qui ne pouvaient plus travailler, les vieillards, les malades, il y avait aussi les enfants qui couraient dans les rues étroites, les mères essayaient de les rattraper parce qu'elles ne voulaient pas qu'ils se perdent ou qu'ils se fassent mal en jouant. C'était un lieu que Dieu connaissait bien, modeste, humble, pas fier pour un sou. Un lieu pour lui.

Le travail du bois commence à plaire à Jésus. Il joue avec les copeaux, les chutes de planches que son père, Joseph, découpe à la scie. L'atelier est silencieux, on y n'entend que le passage du rabot sur les bois. Jésus aime quand Joseph passe sa main sur son ouvrage et qu'elle glisse. Émanent de la pièce des parfums venus de très loin, des senteurs de résine, d'ambre, de fleurs quelquefois qu'il n'a jamais vues mais dont ses parents évoquent les noms en récitant les psaumes, des fleurs qu'il y avait jadis dans les jardins d'Éden et qui n'existent plus que grâce à la mémoire des poèmes chantés depuis des siècles. C'est ainsi que vit la famille de Joseph. Dans cette douceur retrouvée, dans ces traces d'un ancien temps. Peut-être n'a-t-elle jamais vécu comme ça, dans cette idée du bonheur, dans cette paix. Mais c'est ainsi qu'elle a traversé les siècles. Sa permanence atteste déjà de sa véracité. Il faut bien qu'il y ait quand même quelque chose de vrai dans toute cette histoire, il n'y a pas, comme on dit, de fumée sans feu... Dieu sourit quand il entend ça parce qu'il sait la force et la violence de ceux qui le nient, les mensonges et les dénigrements. Il connaît son parfait ennemi, qu'il appelle Satan, il sait tout ce qu'il emploie comme ruses et comme énergie pour saper son vieux rêve. Satan pour dire esprit retors, dérouté de son origine, fausse liberté, égoïsme, culte de soi, avarice... Mais, c'est étrange, cette idée du bonheur, tenace, rivée au cœur des hommes et des plantes et des animaux, cette rage de vivre, cette rage du vert que mettent toutes les plantes pour survivre, cette frénésie qu'elles mettent au printemps pour renaître et refleurir, cette volonté des hommes à ne pas mourir seuls, abandonnés, sans rien pour les consoler, la compassion, jamais enseignée, jamais apprise et qui s'exprime quand même à l'improviste devant le malheur commun. Il faut bien qu'il vienne de quelque part, ce désir d'amour et de lumière.

Chapitre 7

Où Jésus commence à vaquer à ses affaires

Il n'est pas l'enfant modèle du village, et Marie ne passe pas son temps à le couvrir de baisers et à le protéger, juste des mots habituels, ceux que toutes les mères de Nazareth prononcent pour évoquer leurs fils, des mots pour affirmer que leur enfant sera le roi du monde, qu'il est le plus beau de la terre, semblable à un ange. Des mots qui font rire les autres, qui n'en croient rien, mais qu'on ne cherche pas à dénoncer. Ils sont les faiblesses des mères et on les leur concède parce qu'on connaît trop leur malheur terrible de condamner à la mort ceux-là mêmes qu'elles ont mis au monde. On laisse faire la tendresse des mères, on ne veut pas faire tomber leurs illusions. C'est trop dur déjà, ces enfants qu'on élève et qui s'en vont un jour, loin de soi, et qui laissent derrière eux la solitude, toute la misère du monde.

Marie plus qu'une autre sait tout cela, ce qu'elle doit attendre du temps qui vient, de la promesse vite faite à l'ange et dont quelquefois, malgré ses prières et ses chants, elle regrette la vivacité. Mais Jésus ressemble trop aux garçons de Nazareth, il a cette tension et cette vaillance qui ne sont pas inscrites dans le corps mais dans l'esprit, cette énergie de vie qui force le regard, et ces yeux de braise, ce visage qu'on croise souvent ici, en Palestine, cette volonté surtout. Des Jésus, il y en a partout à Nazareth, qui guident les bêtes avec un bâton de roseau, qui font de la musique avec une tige de jonc, qui jouent à la balle avec une pelote de chiffons, qui courent dans les oueds. Sous la Restauration, dans les ateliers d'images pieuses des Bouasse, des Lebel, des Turgis, tous imagiers dans le quartier de Saint-Sulpice à Paris, un dessinateur met la dernière main à sa gravure. C'est Jésus en traîneau qui arrive, guidé par des anges. Il porte un flambeau allumé et de larges boucles pâles volent au vent, il ressemble à Louis XVII dessiné par Élisabeth Vigée-Lebrun, ou bien encore à un enfant peint par Greuze. La comtesse de Ségur raconte à ses petits-enfants dans le parc de son château de Normandie la vie exemplaire de l'enfant Jésus, elle l'appelle « le petit Jésus », il a une grâce d'ange et rien du visage de feu du petit Palestinien qu'il était, qui lançait des pierres dans l'oued pour chasser les chats et les chiens errants.

Donc, Jésus, le nôtre, ressemble à ceux-là, aux gamins des Intifadas qu'on canarde et qu'on massacre au gaz, à la mitraillette. Il a leur colère et leur violence, le courage de défier et de lutter, la rage de dire non. Depuis quelque temps déjà, Marie et Joseph ont observé son besoin d'indépendance, cette manière subreptice qu'il a de s'échapper des choses matérielles, de fuir les conversations et de se retirer seul. Avec qui, avec quoi ? Marie s'en inquiète, elle demande avis à sa cousine, à ses voisines. Elles lui disent que c'est une question de caractère, qu'il ne faut pas prêter attention à cela, que chacun est différent. Mais il y a des jours où Jésus est seul, Marie appelle ça « ses petites retraites » ; elle se demande ce qui peut lui passer par la tête. Et s'il lui prenait l'envie de partir par exemple, seul, sur la route ?

Quand il est dans ces jours-là, Jésus a l'impression de vivre pleinement. Non pas qu'il s'étiole ici, à Nazareth, non, mais il a le sentiment de ne pas être en accord avec lui-même, c'est difficile à raconter, cette sensation de manque, de vide, d'absence. Il dit qu'il lui faut rejoindre son père, la maison de son père, plus précisément. C'est très difficile à entendre pour Joseph, lui qui fut toujours le plus fidèle et le plus attentif des pères, même s'il a toujours su que ce moment arriverait, celui de l'abandon, du délaissement. Elle se réalisait donc, cette histoire de lumière qui aurait traversé le corps de sa fiancée et qui se serait installée en elle, aurait forcé son ventre, l'aurait fait grossir ? C'est bien ainsi que serait né Jésus et non pas de cette union des corps auquel il s'était lui-même dérobé parce qu'il avait été convaincu du choix de Dieu sur Marie et qu'il aurait laissé faire. « Comment cela pourrait-il ? » avait dit Marie à l'ange de la Visitation. Oui, comment comprendre cela et d'un autre côté, pourquoi ne pas admettre cela, la toute puissance de Dieu ? « Je serai là, ma fiancée, ma femme, pour t'aider dans ta tâche, pour vous protéger tous deux et je serai prêt au renoncement de tout, même de ma paternité. » Ainsi avait parlé Joseph quand il avait vu s'arrondir le joli ventre intouché de Marie, cette grâce d'enfant encore dans la chair, et cette certitude qui s'installait en eux que le Messie allait naître et que ce serait eux qui en auraient la charge.

Durant les jours irrépressibles auxquels Jésus se livrait au silence, à la solitude, il s'éloignait de la ville, rejoignait les collines qui entouraient Nazareth et seul, à l'abri des regards, il méditait, il chantait des psaumes, il priait en se mettant à genoux et en courbant son dos jusqu'à baiser la terre, et il s'abîmait dans cette posture, jusqu'à perdre la notion des heures : quelquefois Marie allait à sa rencontre, il n'aimait pas l'entendre qui criait son nom, mais il lui pardonnait tout parce qu'il la savait inquiète. Mais par ailleurs, comment résister à l'appel du Père qui veillait sur lui constamment, dont il sentait la vibration dans le corps, dans la tension du regard ? Car Dieu non plus ne le lâchait pas des yeux ; au contraire, aucune seconde de son temps n'était éloignée de son fils, Jésus était sa dernière carte, son joker pour ainsi dire, avec lui, il ferait don de ce qu'il a de plus cher pour que se répande l'amour infini. Telle était la mission qu'il avait élaborée pour son fils.

Pour l'instant, Jésus donne encore le change, il ressemble trop aux autres enfants pour qu'on le croie le Messie du monde, celui qui vient racheter les malheurs des hommes. Il court dans les fossés, les ruelles, il joue à la lutte avec ses camarades. C'était comme ça que le voyait aussi Renan : un garçon comme tous les autres, qui ne fait pas plus le malin qu'un autre. Marguerite Duras aimait bien aussi ce Jésus-là, pas confiné dans les jupons de Marie, pas si obéissant que ça, pas donneur de leçons. Elle disait qu'elle l'imaginait très enthousiaste, très bagarreur cependant, la connaissance millénaire logée au fond de lui. Quelque part c'est Jésus qui sert de modèle à Ernesto, le garçon de *La Pluie d'été* et de son film *Les Enfants*. Elle croyait surtout à ces enfants-là, pleinement dans le monde et lourds, très anciens d'un savoir qui était illisible en apparence, indéchiffrable aux yeux des autres. À eux seuls, ces enfants éclairaient les ténèbres, leur donnaient du sens. Doués de mystère, ils passent leurs journées entières dans les arbres.

Un jour, Marie l'a surpris tendant ses mains vers le ciel, c'étaient les mêmes mains que les hommes de la préhistoire plaquaient contre les parois de leurs grottes, des mains teintées de pigments rouge foncé et qu'ils offraient, paumes ouvertes, à la pierre, comme des cris d'amour. C'était au temps magdalénien, il y avait déjà des milliers d'années, des temps que Dieu avait pourtant déjà visités, et les hommes le craignaient, offraient leurs chants, leurs mains, pour lui dire qu'ils l'aimaient, qu'il ne les abandonne pas dans la nature cruelle.

L'enfance de Jésus se passe ainsi, étrangère au monde ordinaire, banale aussi.

Le soir, après le travail de Joseph, ils dînent tous les trois autour d'une table, la lampe à huile vacille et jette des ombres qui se tordent sur les murs, et Marie, avant toute chose, chante des psaumes transmis de mère en fille, où il est question d'aimer son Dieu, et de la délivrance de Jérusalem. Quand donc le peuple juif sera-t-il libéré de ses tyrannies, quand donc pourra-t-il se donner totalement à son Dieu ? Jésus écoute les paroles de sa mère, la longue litanie des louanges et il sait au fond de lui-même qu'il faut encore attendre avant de se lancer sur les routes, apporter la bonne nouvelle. Mais secrètement aussi il est saisi d'effroi, il voudrait que s'éternisent ces heures douces, cette tendresse qui les unit tous les trois. Mais comment dire qu'il faudra un jour tout quitter, et son père et sa mère, trouver sa voie, son chemin de vérité ? L'enfance de Nazareth s'en va à jamais, retenant une amère saveur, un bonheur tremblé, trop fragile, qui donne du poids aux choses les plus minuscules de la vie, le pain qu'il faut rompre, l'huile qu'on fait couler dans la lampe d'argile, l'odeur sucrée des jasmins qui s'échappent avec la nuit, le pas des bêtes dans les ruelles.

Mais rien de tout cela n'est innocent. Luc le sait bien qui dit que « l'enfant grandissait, se fortifiait et se remplissait de sagesse ». Tout petit déjà, il aime tracer avec son index des lettres sur le sable ou la terre sèche, il apprend à lire et à écrire à la synagogue, où l'amène tous les jours Marie. Il y passe des heures, on récite des textes de la Loi, on chante l'amour de Dieu pour ses créatures, on exalte la gloire de Dieu qui a promis un sauveur pour les Juifs. Jésus, comme les autres enfants de la synagogue qui est plus une école qu'un temple, porte un châle tissé de fils bleus sur les épaules comme le veut la tradition. « L'Éternel dit à Moïse : Parle aux fils d'Israël, dis-leur de se faire une frange sur les bords de leurs vêtements, de mettre un fil d'azur dans la frange qui borde le vêtement, en le voyant, vous vous souviendrez de tous les commandements du Seigneur et vous les accomplirez et vous ne vous laisserez pas entraîner par vos cœurs et vos yeux qui vous mèneraient à l'infidélité. »

Jésus reçoit ses paroles et les comprend très tôt. Joseph lui parle souvent d'elle, de la fidélité, de la vaillance qu'il faut pour la conserver, impeccable, comme un don qu'on fait à Dieu. Jésus écoute mais, au fond de lui, il sait déjà tout ça : que rien ne s'accomplit hors de la fidélité parce qu'il n'y a de vie que dans l'appartenance, de salut que dans la force du lien. Il dit, à chaque parole du prêtre, à chacune de ses bénédictions, « amen » en courbant son corps, oui, que cela soit ainsi. Il chante et danse avec les autres enfants la farandole de Simhat Tora, qui se termine toujours en rires et en bousculades. Après la synagogue, il rentre à la maison. Marie a tout préparé le soir, quand la nuit tombe, ils montent sur la terrasse. Et ils s'assoient sur des nattes de joncs tressés. Des effluves sucrés de figuiers viennent jusqu'à eux. Quand les nuits sont étoilées, les montagnes dessinent leurs silhouettes épaisses et réconfortantes. « Paix de Dieu sur nous », dit Joseph. Jésus chaque nuit s'assure que les étoiles n'ont pas bougé de place. Leur constance est promesse éternelle de leur éclat. « Il faudrait être comme elles, pense Jésus, des voies de lumière pour rejoindre mon Père. »

Dieu justement surveille de loin l'éducation de son fils. Il voit et il sait tout, il a voulu que Jésus soit semblable aux enfants de son âge, quelquefois il lui fait un clin d'œil en faisant filer une étoile vers la montagne. Son sillage de lumière attire le regard de Jésus, quand elle traverse la nuit et va sombrer derrière la ligne encore plus noire des collines. Ce que Dieu veut qu'il apprenne, ce sont d'abord les valeurs cardinales de la simplicité et de l'humilité, de la modestie et de la justice, de la compassion et de l'amour. La vie est dure au temps d'Hérode puis d'Archelaos, son fils, et de Ponce Pilate. En Galilée, la pauvreté règne un peu partout. Elle n'est pas ostensible parce que les paysans de Nazareth sont fiers et laborieux, mais une fois payés la dîme aux prêtres, l'impôt aux Romains, après avoir donné les premiers fruits de leur récolte au Temple, et le premier-né de leur troupeau pour les sacrifices, il ne reste rien. Jésus voit sourdre la colère, et le sentiment d'injustice germer. La solution pourtant n'est pas dans la révolte, quelque chose en lui garde la douceur et l'innocence des agneaux, la certitude d'une autre réponse.

Dieu n'a pas reculé ni oublié la promesse de l'alliance, il s'est mis seulement en retrait. Mais le lien est renoué. Marie le sait, et les Bergers aussi et les Mages. Ils ont quelque chose dans leur vie qui a changé, leurs yeux ne voient plus de la même manière, une sorte de déplacement des choses, une nouvelle façon d'envisager le monde, la vie, et cette lumière au fond d'eux, comme un feu qui ne s'éteint plus et qui embrase. Dieu appelle ça la conversion. Elle est la révélation de la Révélation. Elle est l'apparition, une autre lumière.

La grâce du don, Jésus la fait croître pour l'instant. Elle pousse lentement en lui. Ça explique ses heures de méditation et ses silences et tout ce qui l'éloigne finalement des autres. « Fais de moi, mon Père, ce qui te plaira, je me coule en toi, je t'aime dans la douceur violette du soir, je crois dans ta promesse de me ramener à toi, de vivre dans l'éclat des mondes inouïs, éclairés des étoiles. Je sens ta force en moi. Ta certitude. »

On entend d'ici les arguments des incroyants, de ceux qui ont renié Dieu de toute éternité, et qui l'ont écarté de l'Histoire. « Légendes dorées, disent-ils, contes de fées, hagiographies, fables et mythes, récits tout juste bons pour les crétins. » Et pourtant, répond Péguy, l'à peine converti, « quelles preuves m'apportez-vous ? Par quel implacable raisonnement grâce auquel je pourrais moi aussi me ranger me donnez-vous la preuve que tout cela n'est que récits merveilleux ? Et pourquoi retirez-vous de vous l'envie de Dieu ? »

Chapitre 8

Où Jésus sort de son silence

Chaque année, Marie, Joseph et Jésus vont à Jérusalem pour fêter la Pâque. La ville grouille de monde, de pèlerins, de voyous et de soldats, de miséreux et de mendiants ; dans les souks, c'est toujours la même foule qui se fond dans le labyrinthe, après avoir été faire ses prières au Temple. Marie aime se rendre dans la ville, aller y prier et céder pour une fois à l'ivresse du bruit et du commerce. Elle a bien recommandé à Jésus de ne pas se séparer d'elle, sous peine de s'égarer. Quoi qu'il en soit, elle ne le quitte pas des yeux : comment le retrouver dans la multitude grouillante ? On pourrait le ravir, l'envoyer en esclavage en Égypte ou ailleurs. Sur le chemin du retour, elle est rassurée. La caravane va bon train, lentement, elle amène les pèlerins chez eux, les guides font halte dans les villages, déposent les vieux et les malades devant leurs portes, puis on reprend la route. Parfois, on fait halte, on se repose sur le bas-côté, on se désaltère en se passant l'outre de peau de chèvre gonflée comme un énorme pis, on plaisante sous les figuiers. Marie croit que Jésus traîne avec les autres enfants. Et puis soudain, l'angoisse monte, où est-il, cela fait quelques heures déjà qu'elle ne l'a vu ? Ses intuitions se vérifient, Jésus n'est pas là. Le couple retourne en toute hâte à Jérusalem, Marie se morfond, invoque secrètement Dieu, chante dans son cœur, peut-être l'entendra-t-il dans sa détresse ? Elle refait le chemin du bazar, reprend toutes les ruelles qu'il a empruntées, mais cela fait des heures qu'elle les arpente comme une folle avec Joseph, qu'elle demande à tous s'ils n'ont pas vu un petit garçon de douze ans à peine, vêtu d'une chemise de lin blanc, ceinturée à la taille par une grosse corde de chanvre, mais il y en a des milliers qui lui ressemblent. Et toujours la même rumeur de la foule, ses criailleries et ses harangues, des hennissements d'ânes qui ploient sous les charges qu'on leur inflige, des chiens qui détalent dans les ruelles obscures, la folie marchande qui n'a que faire du malheur des autres. C'est la première épreuve de Marie. Elle avait accepté que cela fût, elle avait dit oui à l'ange. Maintenant commence l'histoire du Messie, ce qui l'attend.

Trois jours passent, aucun témoin n'a pu livrer une seule information, un seul indice. Trois jours que Marie connaît ce sentiment atroce de l'abandon, cette impression d'être perdue dans le flux anonyme du monde. Ses pas la guident pourtant, est-ce l'ange de Nazareth qui lui souffle de se rendre au Temple, elle ne sait pas, elle ne sait plus mais elle y va, en tremblant et en pleurant, « Va, lui dit doucement la voix, va le retrouver, il est là, ton enfant, dans le lieu de son Père ». Et Marie rit en pleurant, elle parle à haute voix et elle rit, ceux qui la croisent croient qu'elle est une pauvre errante, une folle qui n'a plus sa tête, elle aperçoit le Temple, elle court, va vers ce cercle qui se tient dans la cour principale, des rabbins, des hommes de Dieu qui entourent un jeune enfant et Marie reconnaît Jésus. Elle pousse les prêtres, se jette sur lui, le presse contre sa poitrine, mais Jésus n'aime pas cet afflux de tendresse, pas davantage les reproches que lui fait sa mère. « Mon enfant, pourquoi nous as-tu fait cela ? Vois, ton père et moi, nous te cherchons, angoissés.

— Et pourquoi me cherchiez-vous, répond Jésus, ne saviez-vous pas que je me dois aux affaires de mon Père ? »

Un vaste silence s'établit dans le cercle. Marie se tait, que répondre à Jésus ? Non, elle ne savait pas cela, mais à présent elle sait de quoi il parle, que l'ange ne l'a pas trompée dans le jardin de Nazareth, qu'elle a bien donné naissance au Messie.

Les prêtres aussi sont décontenancés. Qui est ce garçon qui les a éblouis ? D'où tient-il cette science qui les a surpris ? À quels débats subtils a-t-il été entraîné pour affronter la dispute ? « Dis-nous ton nom, enfant ? » Et il dit : « Je suis Jésus de Nazareth. — Tu dois venir ici poursuivre tes études, nous t'enseignerons. — Travailler le bois me suffit, répond-il, je serai charpentier. »

Il reprend la caravane avec ses parents. Elle ondule sur la route, lascive et lente, au pas des bêtes lasses de tant de monde. Un berger dans la troupe hasardeuse joue de la flûte avec un roseau de fortune. Les sons s'égrènent, rauques, et s'effacent dans les plaines désertiques. Marie est sombre, elle est heureuse d'avoir retrouvé Jésus mais elle comprend trop bien qu'il va se séparer d'elle, lentement, pour rejoindre son destin. Elle serre sa main, il la lui donne volontiers, sa colère à lui est déjà tombée ; la main de Jésus est chaude, il transmet cette chaleur, irradiante, à sa mère, cette ardeur de braise qui est en lui, cette violence de feu qui commence à souffler.

Mais les temps ne sont pas venus. Dieu le veut ainsi. « Rejoins, mon fils, ton silence obscur. Retourne à la paix de Nazareth, à ton existence banale, ne te fais pas remarquer par un quelconque éclat, ce n'est pas encore l'heure, vois le monde devant toi, regarde-le vivre, aime-le, garde-toi de toute ardeur. » Et Jésus reçoit secrètement ces paroles de son Père, il les accueille tranquillement, renonce à ses impatiences. La nuit est tombée sur Nazareth quand ils arrivent. L'odeur âcre des figuiers et des aloès envahit la cour de leur maison. Il faut entrer à présent dans le temps des heures noires et silencieuses, dans l'enfouissement de toutes choses, seulement dans l'obscurité du labeur, aider Joseph, polir les planches, raboter les poutres et affiner les solives, tailler les mortaises, balayer les copeaux dans l'atelier. Rien dire, que travailler, et retrouver le Père du ciel en s'éclipsant un peu, dans la campagne environnante, ne jamais plus inquiéter Marie. Apprendre à tout concilier, le ciel et la terre, accomplir la promesse qu'il a faite au Père d'en haut et dont il sera si fier, et aimer ses parents de Nazareth. Apprendre aussi le détachement, savoir qu'il faudra un jour partir, quand Dieu le Père le voudra, « mais je ne suis pas encore prêt, mon Père, j'ai peur, je ne sais pas tout de l'histoire, de là où tu me mènes ».

Les nuits de Nazareth sont comme des acceptations, de la même nature que le oui de Marie à l'ange annonciateur. Elles entrent en soi comme du miel qui coule, onctueux et doux, elles forcent à dire oui, « amen, que cela soit ainsi, mon Père ».

Chapitre 9

Où Jésus poursuit sa vie cachée

Les années passent et Marie reprend courage. Aucun signe messianique ne vient troubler la paix de Nazareth, tout semble oublié : le Dieu sorti de son silence, l'ange dépêché auprès de Marie, la hâte des bergers qui ont suivi l'étoile, la venue des mages, et la visite de Jésus au Temple. Dieu retiré dans son silence a tout son temps, il a prévu de grandes choses pour son fils, plus tard. Pour l'heure, c'est le temps de la vie cachée. De retenir en soi toutes les forces du monde, de faire peser tout le monde dans soi. De le comprendre et de l'entendre.

Jésus rabote et polit, découpe et cheville, en apparence il est le bon charpentier de Nazareth, pieux et solitaire, qui respecte la Loi, fait ses prières et bénit le jour qui vient. Aucun garçon du village n'est plus sage ni plus retenu que lui désormais. Mais aucun n'en viendrait à se moquer car il exerce une étrange attraction, certains disent qu'il semble couronné d'une auréole de paix, une vibration, une couleur même, dorée comme la lumière du couchant, l'entoure. Ceux qui l'ont suivi, ses disciples, dans le long déroulé des siècles, ont pu le voir dans cette nuée de lumière qui étonnait déjà les jeunes hommes de Nazareth. Il est question d'anges éclatants qui le suivent au désert et de cette clarté vive dont il est enrobé.

Dans le fond de sa cellule, Thérèse d'Avila, enfermée par les siens dans un cachot obscur, voit Jésus nimbé d'étoiles ; la lumière irradie de l'intérieur, elle éclate dans le regard, elle force l'attention. « Viens à moi, fiancé de lumière, dit-elle, éclaire-moi de ton feu intérieur, je t'aperçois dans la nuit de ma cellule, où pas une chandelle ne brûle dès que s'épuise le jour, et tu m'éclaires de ta lueur, et je n'ai plus peur. » C'est une histoire d'ondes, de vibrations cosmiques qui tremblent tout autour de son corps. Comment croire cela, disent les sceptiques ? Puisqu'ils ne voient rien, c'est que Thérèse est folle et Jésus un ange ! « Ne dites jamais plus ça, répétait Jésus, il n'y a rien d'extraordinaire à être un prodige. Chacun de vous est doté de cette lumière, il suffit de la tenir éclairée, parce que la lumière, c'est le souffle de la vie et la vie en nous se donne en plus à qui s'y abandonne. »

Hormis ces petites remarques, c'était une vie banale, de labeur et sans grande fantaisie, que Jésus menait. Il y avait bien de riches juifs qui s'étaient fait construire, dit-on, des palais sur les bords du lac de Capharnaüm, dans des palmeraies qui faisaient penser aux jours d'Éden, mais aurait-il été riche, c'eût été une vie trop visible, trop impudente pour lui. La gravité de son caractère s'exprimait jusqu'à devenir sombre pour les jeunes de Nazareth. Peu à peu Jésus fuit les sorties, les rencontres et se replie sur lui-même : il sent sourdre en lui le début de l'aventure. Il aime les déserts, il y va, à l'orée des espaces vides, il n'aime rien tant que cette solitude qui le met face à son « Père du ciel », comme il dit, dont il attend le signal pour partir. « Un jour, bientôt, lui avait dit Dieu, il faudra que tu prennes la route, que tu quittes la quiétude de Nazareth, et que tu affrontes le monde, que tu ailles au-devant de lui, car rien ne te sera épargné parce que tout te sera donné. »

Rien ne doit se dérouler dans l'éclat trop bruyant des choses merveilleuses. Ce n'est pas une légende qui doit se vivre, mais bien l'accomplissement des prophètes. Vient le temps de l'initiation intérieure. Elle se fait à bas bruit, dans le secret des cœurs. Jésus apprend le délaissement car pour tout rendre il faut tout quitter, il faut aller loin dans le courant du fleuve pour rejoindre l'embouchure. Il se défait lentement des siens, ne s'attache pas à Marie et à Joseph, ne recherche pas leur affection plus que nécessaire. Car c'est ainsi qu'il pourra mieux se donner à tous les autres. Il sent monter en lui quelque chose d'inouï et de violent qui est cet amour immense pour les hommes. En lui cette certitude naissante que seul l'amour peut sauver.

Et puis les étrangetés qui entourent sa vie commencent à l'interroger. Ceux que sa mère, à la veillée, sur la terrasse jonchée de branchages pour rafraîchir la pierre, lui racontait. Il était né dans une grotte qui faisait office d'étable, seuls les bergers l'avaient visité, et les rois mages qui étaient venus du fabuleux Orient. Qu'en était-il de toutes ces histoires incroyables ? À demi-mots se forge la conscience de son destin : sa naissance dans un lieu reculé et ignoré des puissants, des visiteurs qui ne sont que des miséreux et des simples et des mages qui, méprisés quoique redoutés des populations, sont des errants. Fallait-il prendre en compte ces signes incertains, ces circonstances hors du commun ? Jésus croit beaucoup aux signes de la divine providence : il sait que Dieu son père le nourrit d'enseignements, indirectement mais méthodiquement. « Oui, mon fils, tu fuiras les puissants qui vivent dans la richissime Césarée, dans le luxe et la débauche, tu n'aduleras pas leurs vices, tu écouteras le chant radieux des bergers qui jouent de la flûte pour rameuter leurs troupeaux et aiment le soir à les compter pour que pas une bête ne manque à l'appel, tu ne rejetteras pas les étrangers, ceux venus de très loin, tu aimeras particulièrement ceux que tous méprisent, ceux qui sont sur la route. » Ainsi parlait Dieu à son petit qu'il avait confié aux hommes.

Jésus lentement apprenait la leçon. Spontanément, il allait du côté des pauvres et des démunis, des errants, c'était, oui, cette révolution-là qu'il fallait faire, de l'amour et de la lumière, battre en brèche la nuit et le malheur. Il sent qu'il va aimer la route pour ça, pour rencontrer, pour se joindre aux marcheurs infatigables, à ceux qui fuient et se déplacent afin d'échapper à leur état.

Quelquefois, au camp de Sangatte, parmi tous ceux qui sont parvenus depuis l'Afrique à rejoindre le Nord, il y en a qui pleurent dans le noir les nuits étoilées de leur village, le bruit lourd et mat du pilon qui bat le mil, les piaillements des volailles qui fuient les jeux trop vifs des enfants, les mélopées lancinantes des vieilles femmes assises à l'ombre des palmiers. Qui pleurent encore les palabres interminables des aînés et les souffrances des enfants malades, la chaleur accablante qui s'abat sans faillir jusqu'au soir. Ils n'ont qu'une idée en tête, ceux-là, partir sur le ferry à Calais pour s'installer en Angleterre, il paraît qu'il y a du travail là-bas et des gens gentils qui vont les aider. Mais dans le camp, on entend le mugissement des sirènes des bateaux et les vigiles qui traînent leurs chiens muselés dans les baraquements, et la solitude éperdue. Il y a des centaines d'hommes rattrapés par la police, parqués là, qui attendent, et plus aucun ne se parle, chacun pour soi. « Il y a fort à faire, se dit Jésus, c'est là ma vie, là mon travail. Je ne serai bien qu'avec ceux-là, les oubliés dans le monde, les orphelins. »

La vie cachée, c'est la vie obscure, le lent cheminement des graines dans le secret de soi, la sourde maturation de l'éclosion. Jésus n'est pas encore prêt. Des années passent, banales, répétitives, sans grandes heures. Pas d'épopée ni de légende, seulement la vie qui va, avec ses jours et ses nuits et les malheurs habituels, et les fêtes régulières et les deuils, aucun accroc dans l'histoire parce que les pauvres qui habitent Nazareth ne la font pas, ils la subissent, tant bien que mal. Personne ne sait rien de ces années cachées de Jésus, aucun historien, aucune annale, aucun témoignage direct ou indirect.

Il est à présent un jeune homme. Il assiste Joseph dans son travail et devient le charpentier docile et fort de Nazareth. Il a acquis un corps puissant, une stature robuste, mais son visage exprime une douceur, un appel. Il possède plus que quiconque le don du silence, il est action de grâce, temps de prière intérieure. Quand il travaille le bois, il ne fait rien d'autre que de prier, il croit que prier est pour l'instant l'unique manière d'entrer en contact, de rejoindre l'illisible du monde, le secret du Père. Il n'y a rien qui ne le défausse de ses amis, mais peu à peu il s'en détache, non pas qu'il les rejette mais il a besoin de cette solitude habitée de la prière, de cette conversation intérieure à laquelle même Marie n'a pas accès. Il y aura un jour enfin où tout jaillira, l'élan vers la route, le début du véritable avent.

Chapitre 10

Où Jésus entend l'appel de Dieu

C'est ainsi tous les soirs. Jésus rentre du travail qu'il a accompli avec la certitude de la justesse. Il dit que dans cette régularité, semblable au retour des jours et des nuits, des saisons et des fêtes, c'est comme une autre prière qui se délivre, une autre manière d'approcher du Père.

Les nuits de Palestine sont douces et voilées d'une lumière qui éclaire le ciel, parce que tout l'éclat de la journée n'a pu se dissiper et nimbe le village et les collines alentour. Jésus est fatigué de sa journée, comme Joseph qui, chaque jour davantage, se courbe et sent ses forces décliner. Il sait que sa fin est proche, qu'il faudra laisser Marie s'occuper toute seule de Jésus. Il redoute les épreuves à venir, la douleur annoncée par les prophètes, le prix à payer.

La jeunesse de Marie s'est elle aussi lentement en allée, elle n'a plus cette grâce des femmes d'ici quand elles sont à peine fiancées, cette rondeur du corps qui alanguit leurs gestes, leur donne une féminité troublante, qu'accroissent leurs voiles. Marie est devenue plus grave, lourde d'un fardeau dont elle craint la menace. Elle s'abandonne plus qu'autrefois à la prière, se livre au Dieu qu'elle implore. Elle en aurait presque oublié la visite de l'ange, allant jusqu'à croire parfois qu'elle a rêvé toute cette histoire, mais une angoisse sourde monte en elle, qui assombrit le souvenir doré de l'ange, éteint son sillage de lumière et d'étoiles. Elle fait des rêves étranges et répétés où elle voit Jésus capturé par des soldats, jeté dans une fosse, mis à mort. Elle se réveille en sursaut, monte en hâte sur la terrasse, et boit l'air frais de la nuit, comme pour revenir à la vie. Non, Dieu ne veut pas ça pour son fils, Dieu n'est pas cruel, il a déjà sauvé du sacrifice le fils d'Abraham : comment accepterait-il de livrer à la mort son propre fils ?

Car c'est bien de cela qu'il s'agit toujours, de ce don du fils jusqu'à la mort terrible, jusqu'au martyre, pour qu'enfin il puisse rejoindre l'éternité du monde, et le sauver. Les psaumes chantaient cette promesse tragique, elle les a récités : elle en ignorait la portée. Pour se rassurer, elle chante alors d'autres psaumes, des chants d'allégresse et de louange, des chants composés par le roi David : « Yahvé est mon pasteur, Je ne manque de rien. Sur des prés d'herbe fraîche il me parque. Vers les eaux du repos il me mène, Y refait mon âme. Il me guide par le juste chemin pour l'amour de son nom[2]... »

Mais ni l'inquiétude sourde de Marie ni la violence intérieure de Jésus n'altèrent la paix de Nazareth. Chacun sait se contenir et se ramener à la simplicité des jours, à l'harmonie du foyer.

Puis Joseph mourut. Jésus veille son corps, Marie à côté de lui implore Dieu de lui donner les forces nécessaires pour surmonter l'épreuve, accompagner Jésus jusqu'au bout. Elle en a parlé avec Joseph, ce serait difficile d'entrer dans une voie qui la dépasse. De fait, Jésus voit un signe dans ce départ, celui de la route qui s'annonce à lui, une manière de lever le voile, de quitter le cocon. Tandis qu'il prie pour le repos de Joseph, sa pensée s'échappe vers l'irrépressible élan qu'il sent monter en lui, une énergie inconnue l'envahit. Comme si Dieu l'appelait enfin à se révéler, à se montrer. D'un père l'autre, le chemin est donc tracé. Il n'y a pas de douleur en lui, les morts rejoignent le Père du ciel, et c'est au contraire une grande joie pour les vivants de savoir que leur proche existe à tout jamais dans cette félicité tant espérée. Joseph a fait son temps sur la terre en homme de bien, il a vu grandir son fils, il a aimé sa femme, que peut-on réclamer de plus pour lui ? Ils l'ensevelissent sans apparat, il rejoint la terre et deviendra poussière de cette terre. « C'est ainsi, disait Jésus, c'est le grand retour de l'homme vers ses origines, il est passé sur terre, il a conquis les outils de fer et de bois pour survivre, il a joui des crépuscules et des aubes, il a connu la grâce d'aimer et d'être aimé, il s'est nourri des biens de la terre, et il n'a jamais offensé les autres hommes ni accompli d'actions mauvaises. C'est un juste qui nous quitte mais qui nous prépare la route. Ne soyons pas tristes, ma mère, car c'est une grande joie d'entrer enfin dans l'amour de Dieu. »

Marie entend ces paroles et elle les comprend. Elle ne doute pas de leur justesse. Jésus dégage une telle assurance, réverbère une telle lumière intérieure qu'elle irradie son visage, éclaire ses yeux d'une braise inaccoutumée. Les jours reprennent, mais Jésus sait que rien ne sera comme avant : il attend l'appel, il est prêt.

Et Dieu lui parle. « Oui, mon Fils, il est temps de partir, de t'accomplir. Va au Jourdain rejoindre Baptiste, va t'y faire baptiser, non pas que tu sois impur, comment pourrais-tu l'être, mais pour prendre le relais de Jean. Va, va à sa rencontre. Il te reconnaîtra dans la foule, car tu es unique par la lumière qui est en toi, et je saurai mettre devant tes pas un sillage de feu qui t'annoncera. »

C'est ainsi que Dieu parla à Jésus, des injonctions fermes et douces, promesses du feu et du ciel.

Jésus l'entend, tandis qu'il prie sur la terrasse à genoux, tard dans la nuit, et qu'il implore son père de l'envoyer enfin dans le monde. C'est la route qu'il veut, solitaire et vaste, avec son long ruban de terre à peine tracé, et des bornes pour se reposer et des villages pour annoncer la nouvelle : que Dieu veut aimer sans conditions les hommes qu'il a créés, qu'il y aura toujours de la place pour eux dans son plan, qu'il les a tous sauvés. Qu'aucun n'est perdu à jamais, et que Dieu saura tous les racheter.

Il ne sait plus comment remercier Dieu. Des chants de louanges s'échappent de ses lèvres, incontrôlables, une effusion sans fin. Il parle l'araméen, une langue aux sons rauques et graves, cloutée de silences et de paroles brèves, qui tombent comme des certitudes.

Il faut maintenant prévenir sa mère de ses intentions. Quand il les lui annonce, Marie ne dit pas un mot, mais en elle, elle murmure : « Les temps sont arrivés, protège-moi, ange de l'Annonciation, veille sur nous deux. » Et il vient, l'ange, drapé dans sa robe de lumière, elle le reconnait à cette clarté soudaine qui se fait dans la pièce, à cette heure de la journée, déjà assombrie, elle ne voit pas de forme, pas de silhouette, mais l'intensité d'une présence qui lui fait chanter à mi-voix un psaume des âges lointains, empli d'espoir. Il est donc venu, le temps de la révélation, de la pleine présence dans le jour.

C'est de cette manière que tout dut se passer, comment y croire et pourquoi ne pas y croire ? L'histoire résiste dans les siècles, orale et colportée d'un millénaire à l'autre, des pans entiers de la vie de Jésus restent dans l'ombre, livrée aux écrivains et aux artistes, aux pauvres et aux crédules que le démon de la raison n'a pas atteints. À eux, Jésus dit tout bas : « Laisse-toi amener, laisse-toi emporter, viens sur la route avec moi, n'aie pas peur, préfère la ferveur au dénigrement, choisis de croire plutôt que de refuser, et tu seras consolé, et fortifié. »

Chapitre 11

Où Jésus plie bagages et part vers le Jourdain

C'est plus fort que lui, quelque chose qui ressemble au vent, au souffle, à une immense respiration qui l'emporte et l'oblige. Cette force intérieure, il dit qu'elle vient de Dieu. C'est la présence de Dieu en lui.

Une fois encore, il monte au haut de la maison de Nazareth. La nuit l'entoure et le remplit de sa paix et de sa douceur bleue, presque noire. Il s'enivre de sa fraîcheur et de son silence, il a bien fallu ces années secrètes pour qu'enfin il se découvre et aille dire sa vérité. Celle à laquelle il croit, si évidente, si sûre.

Il n'a besoin de presque rien quand il fait son sac, il ne s'agit que d'aller sur la route et Dieu pourvoira à tout. Marie sait que le moment est venu. Elle ne dort pas sur sa couche. Elle entend les pas hâtifs de Jésus et la porte qui s'ouvre pour le laisser entrer.

— Viens, dit-elle, viens mon fils, ne me dis rien, je sais tout. Depuis toujours.

— C'est l'heure, mère, c'est mon heure. Ne sois pas en peine. Toi seule, toi plus que quiconque, sais où je vais.

Marie n'a plus de larmes pour pleurer. Elle étreint Jésus, à quoi servirait-il de l'empêcher de partir ? Elle sait qu'il refuserait, qu'il a cette idée en tête, depuis longtemps.

— Alors, va, mon fils, où te guide l'esprit. Va, lui dit-elle, va vers le Jourdain. Jean t'y attend. Il saura te reconnaître.

— Les affaires de mon père m'appellent, mère, je dois l'annoncer à ceux qui croient l'attendre en vain.

Il part sans se retourner. La douceur du foyer est une douleur dont il redoute le poids. Seule la route devient espérance. Elle s'allonge devant lui, il passe des étendues désertes et sèches, des hameaux de terre que la chaleur n'épargne pas, et des campagnes riantes, des îles de palmiers, des paysages divers et contrastés. Il va vers le Jourdain, vers ses rives, il sait aux terres vertes qu'il s'en approche, aux jardins qui le longent que les paysans arrosent de ses limons et de son eau. Le fleuve est fort et violent, il n'est guère navigable, peu de barques plates s'y aventurent, car le courant file vers la mer. Il y a cependant de petites bandes de terre qui forment des gués où croupissent des eaux chaudes et vaseuses. C'est dans ces mares incertaines que viennent se baigner les enfants, et les prophètes faire leurs ablutions. Des bêtes s'y désaltèrent et les caravaniers y font halte.

« Avez-vous vu, demandent-ils, Jean, le baptiste, Jean qui promet la venue du Messie ? Il rassemble des foules car il fait, dit-on, des miracles, il guérit les plaies et baptise dans l'eau les pécheurs, il redonne de la force à tous ceux qui l'ont perdue et la réclament. Il est Jean l'Annonciateur, qui précède le Messie. »

La rumeur court comme un lièvre dans le pays. Jean le Baptiste sait que le moment est proche, il le voit à cette clarté qui vient de la route, à ces faisceaux de lumière, vaste et rayonnante, qui éclairent Jésus. Il n'a jamais prêté attention aux vénérations dont il est l'objet : non, ce n'est pas lui, Jean-Baptiste, le fils de Dieu, dit-il. Il est celui qui l'annonce, qui prévient de son arrivée. Et ce Messie n'a pas d'armure étincelante ni de dons magiques, il ressemble à tous les pèlerins qui se pressent ici, sans sandales ni tunique, hommes sans pouvoir apparent, pauvres et les mains vides, uniquement fervents.

Jésus marche, on lui indique la direction du fleuve, il n'est plus très loin maintenant, il le devine, à l'horizon plus clair, plus vaste, aux couleurs indécises que prend le jour quand il se dilue dans l'eau, à cette pâleur étrange qui ressemble à une aube. Il aperçoit enfin les rives du Jourdain. Et ce rassemblement au loin, d'hommes, de bêtes et de chariots. Il va vers lui. Un homme prêche au milieu de la foule : il est très maigre, la barbe est longue, semble n'avoir jamais été taillée. Le regard de l'homme est vif et mobile, soudain leurs yeux se croisent. Jean le baptiste sait que Jésus est enfin venu.

— Il est là, celui que l'on attend tous, dit-il, il arrive dans sa lumière, il est précédé par le cortège des anges lumineux, regardez-le dans son éclat, il aveugle par sa vérité.

Jésus avance sans se presser. Il veut lui aussi être baptisé. Baptiste accepte de le bénir, de le recouvrir d'eau.

— Tu n'en as pas besoin toi, fils de Dieu, envoyé parmi nous pour nous sauver. Mais je te baptise pour accomplir les Écritures, parce qu'il a été dit que tu seras lavé dans les eaux du fleuve. Viens à moi, enfant de la lumière.

Jésus s'approche du gué. Il a de l'eau jusqu'aux genoux, Jean verse sur lui une coupe d'eau, elle coule sur ses cheveux, ses épaules, glisse le long de son corps. Jésus croise les mains sur sa poitrine, prie intensément. « Qu'il soit fait, ô mon père, comme tu l'as toujours voulu. Je ne ferai rien pour contrer ton projet. Je serai soumis à toi comme l'agneau du sacrifice, pattes liées, j'irai où tu me diras d'aller. »

Puis Jésus entre dans l'eau du Jourdain. Il s'immerge totalement. Les pèlerins, étonnés de son geste, comprennent que quelque chose d'imprévu se passe, quelque chose dont ils ne saisissent pas tout à fait le sens, mais qu'ils estiment quand même exceptionnel, unique. Certains croient voir une colombe voler au-dessus de sa tête. Une colombe blanche aux ailes déployées et qui aurait comme reconnu son lieu. Dieu, du haut de son perchoir, se réjouit. L'esprit souffle sur le fils, il va pouvoir avancer sans crainte.

Tout autour, ce ne sont que mendiants et pèlerins sans bagages, pauvres du monde, laissés pour compte, inutiles dans Babel. Les riches Juifs de Galilée ont des villas somptueuses qui rivalisent avec celles des occupants romains, ils se consultent et se croisent, ne se reçoivent pas mais maintiennent le pays dans la sujétion de l'argent et du pouvoir. Ceux des chemins n'ont pas d'asile ni de protection, ils sont dans l'espérance d'un monde meilleur. Serait-il donc enfin venu celui que l'on chante dans les psaumes ? Est-ce possible qu'il leur ressemble ?

Sur la route de nouveau. Jésus trace des repères, marque les lieux de repos, connaît ceux qu'il faut fuir. C'est toujours la même histoire de celui s'en va pour renaître, retrouver de l'air, chercher de l'espoir. Nerval part en Orient, quand tout en lui s'obscurcit, que la mort rôde et qu'il sait qu'il va aller vers elle. « Alors, viens à moi, bel Orient, portes dorées des terres inconnues, territoires immenses et jamais visitées, pour que renaisse en moi l'envie de vivre et d'admirer ! »

Nerval ne part pas au nom de Jésus, mais Jésus c'est aussi celui qui illumine d'or les routes et les ports, les chemins de l'espérance : « Guide-moi, Seigneur, pèlerin invisible, mène-moi vers... », chuchote le marcheur.

Bob Dylan chante et gratte sur sa guitare, le long des routes américaines, leur long ruban se déroule devant lui et il avance, il faut laisser les villes et leur chaos et retrouver l'esprit du chant, le silence intérieur. Il connaît la voie de Jésus, celle des bouddhas qu'il croise dans les temples, et qui disent la même chose, qu'il faut longer les voies, partir et tout laisser, s'appauvrir pour renaître. Dylan quitte San Francisco. Il faut retrouver le chant de soi. La voix rauque aux sons courts chante la douleur d'aimer et l'avenir des routes ouvertes devant soi. Au bout il y a des terres entières d'hommes qui dorment et qui aiment, des végétations luxuriantes où vivent les êtres innocents. On file vers les plages de Californie et les déserts du Nevada, on y va pour fuir le monde ruiné et les vieux souvenirs qui n'amènent plus rien que le désespoir et l'ennui.

Jésus ne parle que de ça : d'un jour où l'on doit accepter de partir, d'une voie qui empêche de s'installer, de l'espérance qui culbute derrière les montagnes. Mille ans qu'Israël pleure sa fortune et son bonheur, se lamente de sa ruine et de son malheur. Mille ans qu'elle attend. Qui viendra pour lui rendre l'espérance, qui ?

Il faut croire que c'est ça, la vie, cet éternel roulis de peines et d'espérances, ce manège tourbillonnant qui fait croire aux rêves et aux bonheurs, et vous lâche sur le quai sans vous regarder. Il faut croire que c'est le lot des hommes, cette attente mortelle qui viendra les sauver. Mille ans et puis Jésus arrive qui rétablit la promesse, mille ans et sa mort sur le gibet pour que beaucoup y croient, dur comme le cœur de chêne de la croix, que c'est lui le sauveur, et pourtant le manège qui recommence, et le roulis des malheurs et la chienne de vie qui reprend. Des centaines d'années après, il n'y a plus d'Égyptiens, de pharaons terribles, d'occupants romains violents et esclavagistes mais d'autres surgissent comme des têtes d'hydres, insatiables, infatigables dans leurs imaginations délirantes, leurs soifs de pouvoir et d'argent. Leurs victimes implorent Jésus de revenir. Mais il est déjà venu, il est mort et ressuscité, disent les apôtres, les seuls qu'on puisse croire pour l'avoir revu, touché après sa mort, et ils nous assurent qu'il ne reviendra pas comme ça tous les quatre matins car Jésus a habité cette terre, il y est resté. Resté ? Vraiment ? Jésus n'est plus un homme tombé du ciel, l'envoyé de Dieu, tout ce qu'on sait de l'histoire, des fables disent les autres, c'est l'esprit de Jésus qui est éternel, qui s'est dit dans le monde, s'est glissé dans la tête des hommes. Jésus, c'est plus que ce que sa vie en dit, c'est l'esprit d'amour qui s'est faufilé en douce dans les êtres ; s'ils veulent l'amour, alors Jésus les assure de leur éternité. Leur promet de grands jardins toujours verts et des vents calmes sur la terre. Avez-vous vu les paysages de Botticelli, dit-il ? Eh bien, ce serait comme ça, des forêts de pins parasols au fond desquelles s'étale la mer, où pas une brise ne vient effleurer l'onde, et cette douceur tranquille, paradisiaque...

Chapitre 12

Où Jésus est tenté dans le désert

Il va sans se retourner, il quitte Nazareth et part rejoindre sa vérité. Ils partent comme ça, les héros, voyez Perceval qui quitte le château de ses ancêtres : au seuil de la haute porte, sa mère pleure et se lamente, qui craint pour son enfant. Lui, part vers la forêt, inconnue, sombre et mystérieuse, il ne sait pas où le mènent ses pas, il marche. Jésus de même, il avance mais il est comme porté par la lumière du baptême, c'est étrange cette histoire, cette aspersion d'eau du Jourdain qui lave et sauve, l'investit de Dieu, l'assure de sa toute puissance. Il suffit que cette eau qui s'écoule des mains en forme de jarres sur le visage ruisselle sur les épaules, fasse luire tout le corps. Des mains de Baptiste, c'est comme le souffle de Dieu qui s'échappe. Jésus s'en souviendra plus tard, quand l'Esprit soufflera sur ses apôtres, le jour de Pentecôte, ce mystère du vent divin qui se faufile dans l'air et guérit.

Le baptême, c'est le jour retrouvé, la force acquise, non pas conquise, mais reçue, un don. Jésus sait cela, cette lumière que fait l'eau en soi, cette transfiguration de soi. Il peut aller vers le désert, le risquer...

Après Nazareth, il faut longtemps marcher, passer des champs et des vallées, surprendre enfin les premiers signes des terres arides, les butées de sable qui se logent contre les fossés et les talus, et les coulées de palmiers qui se raréfient, jusqu'à ce plus rien de la terre, où pas un ne s'aventure, entre les dunes et les rochers, à peine ces grottes aux parois desquelles il y a toujours des traces d'animaux disparus, des girafes et des zèbres, et des troupeaux de bisons, et des gazelles au souffle vif qui détalaient jadis dans les steppes et aussi des poissons énormes, comme des indices d'océans disparus, de vastes cataclysmes.

Plus rien désormais que cette étendue de terre sèche, et ce soleil de plomb, aucune source, que l'humidité, de la nuit, sous la voûte du ciel et des cavernes, les mains posées contre les parois pour sentir de la fraîcheur, la mémoire des oueds et des ruisseaux. Jésus s'avance dans cette nuit du désert, il sait ce que veut dire le désert : cette solitude innommée, ce grand lieu de nulle part, anonyme et illimité, et dont l'immensité justement finit par faire perdre la mémoire. Il faut, dit Jésus, l'épreuve du désert, le risque du rien, et le défilé incessant des jours sans emploi. Tout n'est que schistes bruns et terre craquelés, une solitude âpre et sauvage. Pas une lampe qui brille à l'horizon, pas de cris d'enfants ou de bêtes qui brisent le silence, seule encore la même nuée rose qui s'étire dans le ciel, quand arrive la nuit. Et là, à cet instant, attendre le poids noir de la nuit, et l'haleine des vents qui sifflent, s'effilent entre les corridors de pierre, se faufilent dans les cavernes, soulèvent et modifient les dunes.

Est-ce la grâce du baptême qui donne à Jésus cette maîtrise du désert ? Il s'y aventure : loin depuis longtemps déjà des vallées fertiles et vertes, loin du ruban d'eau du Jourdain, loin aussi des monts de Samarie et des plaines de Jérusalem, dans le fouillis des oliveraies. Quarante jours et quarante nuits, à jeûner, à n'être que dans la prière, dans l'absolu don de la prière, s'en remettre à elle comme nourriture.

Dans les monts du Hoggar, Charles de Foucauld connaît la même attente de Dieu. Il n'est pas Jésus, il se nourrit encore de quelques dattes et d'un bol d'eau, mais il n'est pas loin de son état, de ce moi délié pour être en état d'entendre. À l'Assekrem, Foucauld éprouve comme Jésus la mélancolie des crépuscules, le souffle mauvais du vent d'Arabie, quand il arrache le paysage à sa lumière, l'enfonce dans la rumeur des djinns, dans le concert des voix méchantes qui sifflent sans interruption jusqu'à la gloire du jour naissant, jusqu'à ce que l'aube vienne laver cette nuit. Voir imperceptiblement la lumière gagner le noir, le pâlir jusqu'à ce qu'il ne soit plus sombre, qu'il lâche prise et que le jour entier dévoile les pics acérés du Hoggar, le spectacle splendide que Dieu, en ses caprices, fit un jour premier.

Jésus sait que c'est au désert surtout que se découvre le mieux le chant clair des apparitions, l'intuition de Dieu. On croit qu'on est seul, on croit qu'on est perdu, sans eau ni pain, qu'il n'y aura plus jamais de source pour se désaltérer, qu'il n'y a plus de vie, que ce désordre sec et immuable, toujours changeant par le caprice des vents et il n'en est rien. On croit encore qu'on ne survivra pas à ce désastre, à cette solitude, et puis Jésus découvre que la source est en soi, qu'elle jaillit au plus profond de soi, et qu'il y a des forces de vie qui s'échappent d'ici, de la lenteur des choses immuables, de leur si discrète évolution. Et puis il y a encore, tous le diront, Foucauld et Monod, et les Touaregs, et les caravaniers, le baiser ineffable des anges, la nuit, quand tout s'écrase dans elle, qu'il n'y a plus rien à attendre ni à espérer, cette caresse étrange des anges, ce mouvement doux d'espérance, on dit les anges, ce pourrait bien être aussi le regard de Dieu qui se pose, quelque chose de tendre et d'apaisé quand tout semble hostile ou abandonné aux grands flux de la nature. Alors les anges, le regard de Dieu, du vent tiède, que sais-je encore, viennent bercer Jésus et lui redonner confiance. Il s'abîme dans la prière qui nourrit, il en a fait l'expérience déjà solitaire sur la terrasse de la maison de Nazareth, quand tout dormait, là, les anges, c'était la brise sur les palmiers qui les faisait se balancer et donnait toujours des raisons de croire et d'espérer. Qui comprendra cette histoire muette, invisible et là cependant, offerte, livrée pour rien ?

L'épreuve est vaste néanmoins, elle prépare des détresses, des désespoirs. Jésus sait que les déserts sont partout, là où on les croit les plus éloignés, dans Jérusalem c'est le désert, dans le temple lui-même c'est le désert, avec ses chants de peur, terribles et imprécateurs, dans Nazareth aussi, quand les voisins commencent à regarder d'un mauvais œil la solitude heureuse de l'atelier de bois, dans les fêtes des villages, aux noces et aux libations. Il a comme des visions qui se superposent devant les yeux, le Golgotha déjà devant lui, la montagne aux gibets, à l'écart de la ville, mais qui la domine de ses croix de bois, de ses suppliciés qui agonisent toute la nuit tandis qu'aux pieds personne ne se lamente, que les langues rêches des chacals et des chiens errants, et la solitude des râles, la plainte à peine perceptible de tous les suppliciés qui implorent, tous, la main de leur mère, pas un qui ne se souvienne de la petite berceuse de l'enfance, comment tout cela a-t-il pu arriver ?

Devant lui, le mont des Oliviers, la pauvreté nue de la nuit mal éclairée, la bande de voyous qui le cherchent et l'emportent vers son supplice et la nudité du Golgotha, la nuit de toutes les nuits, la boire jusqu'à la lie, pour retrouver le jour. Dans ce désert misérable et grandiose, Jésus s'avance, ses lacets se sont défaits, déliés de leurs sandales, il a peine à marcher, c'est à cause des cailloux qui le blessent, se fichent comme des aiguilles quelquefois dans ses chevilles, à cause des grains de sable qui fouettent sa chair et pénètrent dans les petites plaies qui se sont formées. Mais il avance, il a appris une chose au cours de son enfance : la prière isole de la douleur, la douleur même en brûlant mène à cet isolement, la douleur fait entrer ailleurs, dans un autre dialogue, une autre manière de parler au monde. À Jérusalem, les prêtres prient comme des moulins à moudre, ils répètent et ils répètent, il n'y a que cette litanie oisive qui tourne en rond et ne parle à personne, n'invoque personne, une prière d'aveugle et de fou et puis il y a une autre prière, un sillage, une flèche acérée, qui traverse et tranche, va comme la douleur qui fait tout oublier du reste, au vrai dialogue, à la rencontre. Oui, se dit Jésus, prier c'est rencontrer, sans détour.

Le monde maintenant n'a pas de prise sur Jésus, le désert l'a happé tout entier, il ne suffit pas seulement de se savoir envahi de Dieu, dirigé par lui, enfin appelé par le Père, il faut mettre à l'épreuve tout ce qu'il a prévu, tout ce plan qu'il a échafaudé dans son coin si retiré de l'univers, dans ce lieu inconnu encore des hommes et où il siège dans la splendeur de la lumière. Dieu d'ailleurs ne quitte pas Jésus, ne croyez pas qu'il laisse son fils tout seul dans sa détresse et sa solitude, dans cette arène mortelle où ne vivent que les pierres, dans ce néant minéral dont il faudra bien qu'il sorte vainqueur. Il n'y a pas d'autre choix pour Jésus, il le sait, ce désert. Ce passage.

Au fond des déserts, il sait qu'il existe toujours des sources, qu'il ne peut y avoir seulement cette existence abrutie de pierre. Il sait aussi qu'en fendant les pierres de la lumière peut jaillir, des étincelles de vie, des fusées de cendres. La nuit est fraîche, il se pelotonne dans sa grande chemise de lin que sa mère lui a tissée, il s'en enveloppe et se résume dans sa prière, dans son silence. Il n'aime pas entendre les frôlements des scorpions et des serpents, les chutes des pierres qui s'effondrent d'un coup sec se répandant comme un écho dans l'étendue illimitée. Il murmure des psaumes, ceux qu'il a appris dans son enfance, que chantait Marie en filant la laine, le soir, quand une lumière presque mauve tombe sur Nazareth. Ni faim ni soif, et pourtant son corps d'homme réclame un peu de pitance, il lape comme font les petits chiens des gouttes d'humidité qui perlent sur les parois de sa grotte. Les psaumes parlent de jardins verdoyants et de ruisseaux courant dans les prés ou bien de la solitude extrême des hommes, de leur détresse dans le grand tout de l'univers dans lequel ils ne parviennent pas à se situer. Dieu guide le chant des psaumes, souffle les mots et aide à les retenir. « J'espérais Yahvé d'un grand espoir, il s'est penché vers moi, il écouta mon cri, il me tira de la fosse fatale, de la vase du bourbier, il dressa mes pieds sur le roc, affermissant mes pas[3]. » Ceux qui les murmurent ont déposé leur ancre en Dieu leur sauveur, leur plainte les ramène à son amour. Le recueillement de Jésus, c'est une manière d'être près de son Père. Dieu lui a donné de se satisfaire du silence, il en connaît les forces intimes, secrètes. Il n'a pas peur dans le désert, il sait que Dieu veille sur lui, qu'une coulée infinie de vie le parcourra toujours. Il dit : « Éternellement. »

Il lui faut du temps pour se retrouver, pour faire le vide en lui, s'assurer de cet élan qu'il a toujours senti en lui, et que sa mère et Joseph l'empêchaient de prendre : « Mère », disait-il, le soir sur la terrasse, quand le frais de la nuit commençait à tomber, et que dans l'étincellement des étoiles il n'y avait plus qu'à leur parler pour qu'elles transmettent ses paroles à son « Père du ciel », comme il disait,

« mère, oh oui, mère, épargne-moi ta douleur et tes craintes inassouvies, laisse-moi prendre mon envol, laisse-moi partir, je sais, toi, que tu sais, le feu et le glaive et la douleur d'en mourir, et ma souffrance par laquelle il faudra bien que je passe, et cette plaie partout sur le corps, qui me traverse. Mais cette plaie béante, vois-tu, c'est aussi le cri de mon Père, fiché, là dans ma chair, ce flanc tranché des coups du glaive à venir, c'est mon Père qui appelle. Mais comprends-tu seulement cela, femme, qui est aussi ma mère ? En moi, cet élan, en moi cette force qui me dit d'avancer, de forcer la route et le temps simple de la vie. Cette marche qui s'ouvre devant moi, irrésistible, inévitable ».

Le jeûne ne le fait pas souffrir, comme si la prière remplissait tout, le nourrissait entièrement. Marthe Robin en fait elle aussi l'expérience, et tant d'autres déjà avant elle, ce cortège de saints et de saintes qui ne se sont plus nourris et que seules l'hostie et la gorgée de vin au ciboire satisfaisaient.

Marthe Robin, dans la solitude extrême de sa chambre, épuise son corps des mêmes souffrances que Jésus sur sa croix. Depuis qu'elle est entrée dans sa Passion, chaque vendredi cela recommence, faisant suite à la tentation du démon du jour précédent, et lui cause de terribles souffrances. Des pièces à côté, on entend le bruit du lit qui tape contre les cloisons et du corps qui se fracasse contre la tête du lit. Même après avoir triomphé du démon, la Passion ne faisait que commencer, c'étaient d'abord les coups de glaive dans le flanc et la couronne d'épines qui se fichait autour de sa tête et encore ces mains transpercées des clous du bourreau, et le sang coulait partout sur les draps immaculés, changés chaque jour, et la lingère de la communauté pleurait toujours en voyant le sang noir séché sur les draps de lin...

Pas de repas pour Marthe, non, jamais de gâteaux, de fruits juteux, de viandes onctueuses, fondantes, jamais de légumes, que cette hostie blanche, fade, pièce de monnaie comme un viatique pour traverser le temps et rejoindre Jésus, le tant aimé, pas de boisson, que ce vin clairet et aigrelet, dont on lui donnait seulement une gorgée, à l'aide d'une pipette parce qu'elle ne pouvait plus ouvrir les lèvres, comme Jésus sur sa croix, qui ne pouvait plus que sucer l'éponge imbibée de vinaigre tendue au bout d'une perche, oui, sucer, sucer, comme un bébé le sein de sa mère, pour apaiser la raideur de la langue, raide comme un morceau de carton sec.

Au désert, Jésus se retrouve. Seul aussi et face à lui, à l'immensité du monde. C'est étrange, cette impression de plénitude soudaine, cette liberté ouverte devant lui du désert, cette entrée dans son histoire. Il a laissé derrière lui sa famille, ses amis, dont il sait qu'il ne faut rien attendre parce que sa vie est ailleurs, promise à d'autres enjeux. Cela fait des jours qu'il est là, dans cette pauvreté du désert, qui ne demande rien, qui ne réclame que le chant au bord des lèvres, et que lui soient remises les ambitions, la volonté, car le désert n'accueille que le vent.

C'est une nuit pareille à celle qu'il a déjà vécue ici. Froide malgré la chaleur de la journée, malgré l'accablement du soleil sur la pierraille. Il a pris l'habitude de rester en prière, de ne pas se relever du coussin de sable sous ses genoux. Il médite, non pas en échafaudant sa vie à venir mais, comme le feront tous les ermites du monde à sa suite, en répétant : « Père, fais de moi ce que tu veux. J'attends ta parole, ton désir, je ne veux rien d'autre que de t'attendre. » C'est cette disponibilité-là qui plaît à Dieu, qui le veille du fond de son obscure retraite. Jésus donc attend et son attente est la prière que Dieu son Père veut. Aucune parole, aucune prière conçue, intelligible et façonnée de mots, seulement une effusion singulière qui s'échappent de ses lèvres, dans quelle langue, il n'en sait rien lui-même, logorrhée immense qui se déploie dans l'indifférence du désert de pierre. Jésus prie quand soudain il entend du bruit, comme font les bêtes entre les pierres, fouettant de leur queue le sable, un bruit mat et rauque qu'il ne connaît pas, d'intrus, presque étouffé, un cri bâillonné. C'est au désert que surgit toujours celui qui vient troubler la rencontre et veut rompre le lien. L'homme à la queue de crotale se glisse entre les pierres, il vient tenter Jésus. Il le surprend dans ses prières, quand l'esprit de Dieu est totalement sur lui, au point que Jésus ne le voit pas. Il n'est pas besoin cependant de le voir car c'est le vent du désert qui porte sa voix, venue de très loin, des abîmes de détresse et de mort, des terres abominables et désespérées. C'est presque la nuit. La montagne est faite de craie blanchâtre que traversent des corridors noirs où jadis roulaient des torrents. En haut du mont, l'haleine de Satan parvient à Jésus :

— Si tu es le fils de Dieu, commande que ces pierres deviennent des pains !

— Il est écrit, répond Jésus, que l'homme ne vit pas seulement de pain, mais de toute parole qui vient des lèvres de Dieu.

Satan résiste et feint de ne pas comprendre ; il use de tous ses sortilèges, de ses tours de magie qui transportent ses proies face à l'univers entier. Jésus voit s'ouvrir devant lui tous les paysages du monde, les forêts et les champs, les villes et les fleuves, et les trésors qui y sont contenus, et la rutilance de l'or et les pyramides, les temples immenses où les offrandes sont amoncellements de pierres précieuses, et les cirques où s'affrontent les fauves et les gladiateurs, et la puissance de tous les Césars de la terre, et toutes les cités de l'Iran et de la Mésopotamie, les royaumes de Ninive et de Babylone, d'Assour et de Pasargade :

— Cette puissance et cette gloire, je te les donnerai, car elles sont de mon obédience, je les livre à qui je veux. Prosterne-toi devant moi et elles sont à toi.

— Il est écrit, répond Jésus, « Tu adoreras le Seigneur ton Dieu et tu le serviras, lui seul ».

Satan ne cède pas, il connaît les hommes et la petite voie secrète de leurs désirs, l'instant inévitable où ils cèdent au pouvoir et à l'argent, à la puissance des rois. Il montre Jérusalem à Jésus, le vaste bosquet presque noir d'oliviers qui fait comme une oasis au bout du paysage, en bas de l'Hermon couvert de neige, tandis qu'au loin, encore plus vers le sud, scintille la mer de sel et d'eau morte.

— Si tu es le fils de Dieu, répète-t-il, jette-toi d'ici en bas. Car il est écrit : « Il a donné pour toi des ordres à ses anges ; ils te porteront dans leurs mains de peur que ton pied ne heurte contre la pierre. »

— Il a aussi écrit : « Tu ne tenteras point le Seigneur ton Dieu[4]. »

Puis Jésus n'entend plus rien que du bruit dans le sable, comme une bête qui détale. La nuit est complètement tombée sur le mont Qarantal. Il n'y a plus que les étoiles qui éclairent par intermittences le ciel, il les scrute car elles semblent s'agiter, filer dans le noir, faire comme une échelle de lumière qui descend vers lui. Quelque chose d'ample et de vaste, de libérateur se passe, il sent contre lui des ailes d'anges et le souffle frais de leurs bouches, et la tendresse de leurs plumes. Dieu ne perd rien de la scène, il sait ce qu'a enduré son fils : « Pour lui, ordonne-t-il, la douceur des anges, leurs ailes de plumes pour berceau, dans l'âpre dureté des pierres brûlantes qu'aucune nuit ne vient apaiser. »

Jésus sait que l'épreuve reviendra, que Satan ne lâche pas si facilement prise. Il est certain qu'il n'a pas rêvé, qu'il n'a pas imaginé la visite de Satan. Et pourtant, si tout ce cauchemar n'était qu'un simple délire accru par la chaleur intense de la journée ? Qu'importe la réponse car déjà toute sa pensée est en marche : sensualité, orgueil, puissance, tout ce qui organise cruellement la vie des hommes peut être vaincu si l'on s'abandonne à Dieu. Maintenant Jésus se repose dans les bras des anges, Dieu a soufflé un vent très doux, presque tiède pour qu'il puisse s'endormir. Un vent semblable à celui qu'il soufflait quand son fils allait prier sur les terrasses de Nazareth. Il dort dans l'amour de son père, vaste, sans mesure. Les anges n'ont pas de visage ni de corps. Ils sont la brise qui caresse, les étoiles qui gardent le ciel éclairé, comme des veilleuses pour les enfants qui dorment. Dieu non plus n'a de visage ni de corps, il est cette grâce qui tombe sur son fils, cette tiédeur qui le borde et lui murmure des berceuses à l'oreille.

Chapitre 13

Où Jésus redescend dans la vallée

Maintenant Jésus marche, comme libéré, le long des rives du Jourdain. Ce doit être au début du printemps 28 de son ère, dans la campagne de Jéricho. Il fait chaud déjà mais il va d'un bon pas, il n'ignore pas les élans de la marche, les forces qu'elle réclame et qu'elle délivre tout à la fois, ce qu'elle souffle dans le silence des pas, et la source intérieure à laquelle il puise pour progresser. Détaché enfin de l'haleine de Satan, de son remugle nauséabond, il peut avancer sans craindre les sortilèges. Loin des tours de magie et des tentations des trônes étincelants et des musiques assourdissantes qui proclamaient déjà sa puissance. La marche est pèlerine, il va vers quelque chose qui l'appelle, il sait qu'à son terme, il y a la promesse du lien retrouvé, indélébile. Maintenant Jésus doit annoncer la nouvelle. Il doit guérir.

Il traverse des champs de blé et d'orge, les moissons ne sont pas encore faites, les épis se couchent sous le souffle tiède qui vient, apaisé, du désert. Il traverse des villages et des groupes de paysans, il aime la terre et ceux qui la travaillent, il est de leur race laborieuse, farouche, sauvage. Il n'aime ni les grands discours ni les subtilités des prêtres des synagogues, il ne parle qu'un seul langage, ne connaît que très peu de mots.

Pasolini dans son *Évangile selon Matthieu* le décrit dans cette même tension du corps et de la parole, c'est qu'il ressemble à Jésus dans sa soif de comprendre, dans sa ténacité à avancer. Pasolini aime Jésus, il croit en lui, bien qu'il soit athée, parce que Jésus ne réclame de l'autre que sa foi, non pas des rites et des protocoles, mais ces pas qui vont, qui veulent avancer, ce désir de la route unie, pauvre et rocailleuse comme les chants des bergers de Sardaigne, rauques et bruts. Parce que sur la route tout peut arriver, l'apparition de la lumière comme des ténèbres, et qu'il n'en faut rien craindre. « J'ai peur, je sens la lumière tomber », dut dire Pasolini, cette nuit sur la plage d'Ostie, tandis qu'il se faisait prendre dans un traquenard, qu'on le frappait à mort, et qu'on le laissait agoniser dans son sang, « peur, oui. » Et il dut invoquer, c'est sûr, la lumière de Jésus, ses bras de lumière, et Jésus, ça aussi, c'est sûr, dut le relever de son martyre et l'emmener avec lui.

Sur la route, Jésus apprend la capture de Jean le Baptiste dans la forteresse de Macheronte. Un pressentiment l'envahit qui lui dit qu'il ne le reverra jamais plus. Mais c'est comme un relais dans la grande chaîne de Dieu, Jean a baptisé Jésus et Jésus maintenant va baptiser à son tour et, comme Jean, il sera capturé. C'est le plan de Dieu, il n'y a pas de doute, pas d'autre choix pour sauver les hommes. Jésus marche donc sur les routes qu'accable déjà la grande chaleur, il s'arrête quand la touffeur du jour fait vaciller les chemins, aux marches des maisons blanchies à la chaux qu'il connaît bien, juste sous l'auvent de bois, et il demande à boire. On s'interroge encore sur lui, on en a vu tant passer, des prophètes et des fous de Dieu, des délirants qui arpentent les chemins et qui finissent par croire à leurs délires ; les enfants des villages courent après eux en leur jetant des pierres mais les femmes leur donnent quand même de quoi continuer leur périple, de l'eau bien fraîche tirée du puits et quelques pains, des figues aussi et des dattes.

Mais là, ce n'est pas la même chose : d'où vient cette lumière dorée autour de lui, pas visible, non, comme une auréole, et cette lumière dans le regard, cette conviction qu'il a quand il parle et surtout cette douceur dans la voix, cette parole si simple que tous la comprennent ? Et si c'était le Messie qu'on leur a promis depuis des lustres ? Et si les Écrits avaient dit la vérité ? Parce qu'à force de perdre et de lutter, ils avaient tous fini par ne plus y croire à cette venue, et penser que la vie c'était ça, cette longue litanie des jours, médiocres et douloureux, cette histoire de séparations et de détresses, de maladies et de désespoirs, et cette dépouille finalement qui se détruisait en un rien de temps, en quelques heures, déjà les mouches qui attaquaient, rôdant sur les visages, effaçaient tout de ce qu'ils avaient été, beaux, jeunes, et les souvenirs qu'ils croyaient inoubliables et qui, en un jour à peine, à cause des grandes chaleurs, n'existaient plus, rayés de la carte, et toujours le beau paysage qui était comme une insulte à leur passage, les champs de céréales, souverains, qui répétaient leur moisson chaque année, sans se soucier d'eux, et le ciel capricieux et indifférent, pourtant mille fois invoqué et qui faisait la pluie et le beau temps, à sa guise, sans laisser entrevoir le moindre signe de ce Dieu féroce, plus tyrannique encore que les pharaons.

Jésus marche et prie. Dieu le suit du coin de l'œil, il ne laisse jamais son fils tout seul. Au milieu de sa prière, il a une vision, la tête de Jean est servie sur un plateau d'argent, le cou est sanguinolent, mâché par la lame de la hache, les yeux exorbités ne disent pas la splendeur du Royaume enfin révélé au martyr. Jésus prie pour ne pas céder au doute, il sent déjà l'haleine de Satan qui se rapproche de lui, il en connaît le sillage fétide, et sa parole suave, insinuante : « Vois le prophète du Jourdain, à quoi lui ont servi ses simagrées et ses grands discours ? À quoi lui aura servi l'eau prétendument bénie de ses mains et dont il t'a recouvert ? Jean n'est plus qu'une dépouille atroce abandonnée à la seule cruauté des hommes. Car il n'y a pas de Dieu, pour les sauver, non, rien que l'infâme cheminement vers la mort. Alors, viens avec moi, ne te fourvoie pas, à nous deux, nous gouvernerons le monde, nous le ferons aller comme on le voudra, et nous croulerons sous l'or, viens, viens... »

Jésus marche et prie obstinément, il sait très bien que prier éloigne le mal, qu'il n'y a pas de solution plus sage, plus juste. À ceux qui l'écoutent quand il fait halte, il commence à enseigner ce qu'il sait, sans apprentissage, sans leçon des grands prêtres de Jérusalem. « Prier, ce n'est pas débiter des paroles déjà toutes prêtes, c'est briser le mur épais des douleurs et des silences qui font mal, prier, c'est laisser entrer le flot des larmes, parce que les larmes sont l'eau vive de Dieu, le puits insondable d'où viennent toutes les réparations et tous les saluts. Prier, c'est se tendre vers Dieu, le reconnaître comme Dieu, et l'admettre. C'est revenir au berceau, au doux soupir des mères. N'écoutez que cela, ne vous préoccupez de rien d'autre, ne bâtissez aucun espoir sur l'or inaccessible et aveuglant parce qu'il vous ruinera. La prière apprend cette pauvreté-là. » Il parle et les paysans l'écoutent, font cercle autour de lui. Jésus est comme ces vieux conteurs des villages qui sont vénérés quand, le soir, ils apaisent les craintes des hommes en les charmant de leurs contes. Mais Jésus n'est pas vieux, « c'est donc toi, le charpentier de Nazareth, lui dit-on, ton père est Joseph et ta mère Marie, ta renommée est venue jusqu'à nous. Tu es robuste et tes mains sont larges, calleuses et puissantes. D'où tiens-tu ta sagesse ? »

Il aime s'asseoir à l'ombre des grands figuiers, dans l'odeur âcre de leurs feuilles palmées, les guêpes ne le piquent jamais, leur bourdonnement seul raye le silence. Sur les routes, il est seul mais à son passage des villageois accourent, des enfants, curieux, blagueurs, qu'il accueille aussi auprès de lui. Quand il repart vers Nazareth, des hommes, jeunes comme lui, lui demandent de l'accompagner. Ils ne savent pas encore qui est ce Jésus mais quelque chose d'inexplicable les a convaincus. Cet homme est sans nul doute le messie que chantent leurs parents à la synagogue, c'est le prophète annoncé venu de Dieu. Jésus ne les dément pas quand ils l'interrogent, il dit que cela n'est pas nécessaire de le savoir encore. Mais Jean et André, c'est leur nom, se souviennent du baptême de Jésus, ils y étaient, et comment oublier son visage et le cercle de lumière qui avait entouré son corps quand il était sorti des eaux du Jourdain, cette présence qui l'avaient fait reconnaître de Baptiste : « Oui, celui-là, c'est l'Agneau de Dieu, le Tant-Attendu. »

Depuis, Jean et André ont battu la campagne, mais l'étranger est resté introuvable. Fallait-il donc aller jusqu'au désert, dans l'âpre silence des pierres et des scorpions ? Et puis soudain, oui, c'est bien cela, ils l'ont reconnu, c'est lui, le tant recherché :

— Que me voulez-vous ? leur dit Jésus.
— Rabbi, où habitez-vous ?
— Venez, vous verrez bien.

Et c'est comme ça que tout commence. Deux déjà, les disciples, l'enseignement, la nuit, sous les palmiers, la marche triomphale jusqu'à Jérusalem, et leur abandon la nuit des Oliviers, et la mort promise de l'agneau, vécue seule, dans la nuit noire.

Jésus devient le maître. Il ne l'a pas voulu, mais les choses se sont faites comme ça, dans la marche qui recueille sur son passage ceux qui reconnaissent sa voix, atteignable au cœur seulement.

C'est étrange, cette voix de Jésus qui court dans les siècles, ce pouvait être il y a deux mille ans mais c'est aussi maintenant, cette voix sourde, secrète et douce. Peut-être que tout a commencé ainsi, par cet homme, paysan et rustre, doux, qui parlait avec la sagesse de Dieu, qui l'avait entendu, du plus loin de sa galaxie, et qui avait su la rapporter avec des mots tout simples jusqu'aux plus incultes des hommes. Peut-être aussi que cet homme n'avait-il fait que percevoir avec plus d'attention ce que Dieu dit à chacun des hommes ?

André rapporte à Simon, son frère, sa rencontre. Et Simon veut le suivre aussi, tout quitter, oui, ne pas perdre le chemin de l'étoile. Jésus regarde le nouveau venu, il le scrute, le pénètre de son regard clair, qui fait renoncer l'autre à tous les mensonges, il lui dit enfin :

— Tu es Simon de Galilée, mais tu seras Kephas, la pierre de notre foi, et sur cette pierre, je bâtirai mon église.

Ils marchent tous sur la route, ils longent la vallée du Jourdain, les petits villages de pêcheurs, Nazareth n'est pas trop loin, à portée de quelques jours. Bientôt Jésus reverra Marie, il se coulera dans ses bras, il lui présentera sa petite tribu de mendiants, ses fidèles, et Marie se souviendra de l'ange annonciateur, de l'éclat de sa lumière qui l'avait aveuglée et de la nuit qui s'en suivit et elle pleurera.

Toujours marcher pour rejoindre. Nazareth et aussi le ciel et la terre, faire se rejoindre Dieu et les hommes, restaurer l'alliance originelle.

Sur la route, à Bethsaïde, Jésus s'éloigne de ses compagnons. Il approche un jeune pêcheur, nommé Philippe : « Viens, suis-moi », lui dit-il impérieusement. C'est quelque chose d'étrange et de très fort, une attraction singulière, une certitude nichée au fond de soi, une émotion considérable car Philippe abandonne tout, quitte sa famille, et, déjà nourri de Jésus, fait le prosélyte auprès des siens : « J'ai rencontré le Messie, c'est Jésus, fils de Joseph de Nazareth.

— Que peut-il arriver de bon à Nazareth ? déclare l'un d'entre eux, nommé Nathanaël.

Jésus, qui n'assiste pas à la scène, la suit cependant en esprit. Il va, lentement, vers Nathanaël et, les yeux brûlants, lui dit :

— Nathanaël, bien avant que Philippe ne voulût te convaincre, moi, je t'ai vu.

Alors Nathanaël aussi s'abandonne à Jésus. Soudain, c'est comme une brisure en lui, une faille où s'épanchent ses larmes.

— Maître, dit-il, moi aussi je t'ai reconnu. Je sais qui tu es. Je sais où tu vas m'emmener.

— Viens, répond Jésus, en le prenant par l'épaule, tu verras de plus grandes choses que celles-là. »

La nuit commence à tomber sur le village. Ils partent tous les cinq, s'effacent sur la route. Les pêcheurs sont sans voix. « C'est comme une capture, dit enfin l'un d'entre eux. C'est irrésistible. »

Les nouveaux amis ne craignent rien de Jésus. De là où il les entraîne. Ils vont. Et aller, c'est espérer. Ils expérimentent la marche, eux qui sont toujours restés au village, à tendre leurs filets, à pêcher sur les eaux calmes du Jourdain.

Maintenant, ils apprennent l'incertitude de la route et obtiennent la récompense de la lumière, l'éblouissement des choses révélées quand le maître parle. Dieu, depuis le ciel, est satisfait de son plan. Jésus, c'est le témoignage de la marche, la leçon vivante du pèlerinage. Dieu apprend ainsi aux hommes le désir d'atteindre. Ils sont nombreux sur les routes du monde, ils ne savent pas toujours vers où ils vont mais ils y vont quand même. Jack Kerouac, le poète beat, roule en moto, en voiture, le plus souvent fait du stop, sur les grandes routes de l'Amérique, chaudes, désertes, pas même une bête sauvage ne s'y aventurerait. Il roule et il veut atteindre. Jésus est en lui, pas seulement Jésus, fils de Dieu, celui qu'il priait, petit enfant, mais Jésus comme signe de la marche, signe de l'en-allé. Rien n'arrête Kerouac, ni la soif, ni la crainte d'un mauvais coup, dans les nuits froides du Nevada, du Colorado. Ses héros sont Thomas Wolfe et Jack London, et son univers tourne autour des petites frappes interlopes des bas-fonds de l'Amérique des ghettos. Il cherche pourtant Dieu dans sa nuit éclairée d'étoiles filantes, il fonce à tombeau ouvert sur les routes, double à droite et torse nu, l'hiver quand il gèle, et s'enivre des départs. Il écrit des poèmes, courts, dessine dans ses carnets, note au passage des impressions, fugaces, vives comme les éclairs qu'il aime surprendre et les spirales des tornades, croisées au fond des campagnes solitaires. « Fuir, dit-il, fuir jusqu'au bout de l'horizon et, après lui, continuer encore car à un horizon s'ajoute une autre ligne de fuite, dépasser cette ligne, marcher, n'avoir toujours devant soi que le long ruban des jeunes autoroutes, où ne passent jamais que cent voitures à peine par jour, et voir filer la route, parce que Jésus est au bout de la route, mais c'est qui Jésus : seulement cet homme de Nazareth ? Non, pas seulement ça, Jésus, cet aiguillon qui fait avancer, qui délivre la clé. »

Kerouac ne connaît que cette fuite, où se glisse l'envie de Dieu, et celle d'en finir avec l'argent, avec le luxe, avec les riches. Avec les guerres. Et c'est toujours le même appel silencieux, nocturne et intérieur qui prend à la gorge et la brûle, et cette douce montée des larmes qui chauffent les joues, cette hâte qui balaie tout sur son passage, et cette nudité de pauvre qui s'impose. La route court sous ses yeux, elle file et il va, pas assez d'alcool, pas assez de drogues pour l'épuiser, il entreprend l'ascension du Matterhorn en Californie, haut de 4000 mètres, gravir, gravir jusqu'au point où se rejoignent la terre et le ciel, et puis écrire cette avancée, cette histoire de folie et d'amour qui devient *L'Écrit de l'éternité d'or* car c'est bien d'elle, l'éternité, qu'il s'agit, comme l'année suivante, en 1955, il accepte ce job de surveillant d'incendie dans la montagne de Desolation Peak, ne voyant personne, ne parlant à personne, mais face au ciel, au faîte des arbres, occupé à surprendre la moindre étincelle. Mais le feu, il l'écrit aussi sur ses rouleaux de papier collés les uns aux autres, comme des tables de la loi, sans ponctuation ni paragraphes, écrits dans le souffle de l'esprit, dans le passage du vent.

Les rouleaux d'écriture de Kerouac, les tables de la loi que les prêtres déroulent au Temple, c'est la même chose, encore la route, dire, psalmodier jusqu'à plus de voix, répéter inlassablement l'incroyable litanie des saints, et la parole de Dieu inscrite là, devant les yeux, c'est une manière aussi d'être sur la route : « Chante, continue de ressasser les mots de Dieu, sois sans état d'âme devant eux, dis-les, et tu avances, tu vas vers le point de lumière. »

Impossible aussi pour Jésus de rester à ce moment de la halte, impossible de revenir au foyer de Marie pour continuer le travail de Joseph, c'est le feu qui brûle en lui, cette braise qui le taraude : qui comprendra jamais autant l'exigence de Dieu ?

Au loin, des foyers de lumière brillent dans l'obscurité. Ce sont les maisons de Nazareth. Bientôt une à une elles s'éteindront et le silence s'installera. Jésus a le cœur qui bat, car bientôt il se blottira dans les bras de Marie. Depuis longtemps déjà, il sait qu'elle porte un plus lourd secret que le sien, il ne doute pas de l'intuition des mères qui n'ignorent rien du danger qui pèse sur leurs enfants. « Ne me fais rien regretter, mère, ne me donne pas l'amertume de m'arracher à toi, ne me capture pas au logis. Rends-moi libre de témoigner. Toi seule connais mon chemin. »

Deuxième partie

La vie publique de Jésus

Chapitre 14

Où Jésus accomplit son premier miracle à Cana

« Il faut que je revoie ma mère, et mon village, je ne vous brusque pas, restez encore sur vos terres, et rejoignez-moi à Cana, en Galilée, pour les noces auxquelles nous sommes conviés. Que la flamme reste sur vous. »
 Il parle ainsi et il s'achemine vers Nazareth. Il presse entre ses bras Jean, le fils de Zébédée, d'emblée il a compris qu'il serait le plus doux, le plus près de lui. La tendresse de Jésus se coule dans le corps de Jean, l'envahit entièrement, c'est comme une coulée de miel qui se répand en lui, une béatitude. Même impression de plénitude et d'envahissement quand Jésus ouvre la porte, Claudel, Huysmans, Verlaine, Charles de Foucauld et tous les grands convertis de l'histoire témoignent du même mystère, du même feu qui brûle et se répand dans le corps, vague chaude qui se noue à la gorge et rend soudainement poreux à Jésus. Car Jésus n'a pas d'âge ni de temps inscrit dans l'histoire du monde. Il est ici et partout, là et maintenant, sans avertir il surprend, il s'empare de celui qui est prêt à le suivre sur la route. Les chemins de terre de Galilée sont eux aussi partout, dans les villes, dans les faubourgs, dans les mauvais quartiers, sur tous les continents.

Blaise Pascal rentre chez lui. Après une soirée dans le monde, il ôte délicatement ses grands cols de dentelle ajourée, défait ses doigts des bagues qui les parent, enlève sa perruque, et se retrouve nu devant le miroir éclairé des lueurs falotes des bougies. Et puis soudain Jésus frappe à la porte, nuit de feu et de pleurs, abandon de Pascal. Comment la reconnaître, cette force secrète qui réclame de tout quitter, les honneurs et le luxe, les ambitions et la puissance ? Pascal pleure, c'est comme s'il se fendait en deux, et laissait pénétrer les larmes de Jésus, chaudes, qui coulent en abondance. Il prie et il pleure, des mots s'échappent de ses lèvres, ils viennent à son insu, se déversent de lui comme une fontaine. « Joie, joie, joie, pleurs de joie, je m'en suis séparé, *dereliquerunt me fontem*, mon Dieu, me quitterez-vous, que je n'en sois pas séparé éternellement... » Pascal ne comprend plus ce qui lui arrive, cet ébranlement total de lui, cet instant de feu qui le bouleversera à jamais. C'est que Jésus poursuit sa marche nocturne, s'arrête là où il veut, chez ceux qui sont prêts sans le savoir, débarque à l'improviste, et fait s'écrouler les certitudes : « Je suis là, ce point de lumière et de fracture, caché en chacun de vous, ce désir du lien, la fin de l'abandon. »

Il traverse de nouveau les campagnes et entre enfin dans la Galilée de son enfance, retrouve ses terres vertes et fécondes. Bientôt il parviendra à Nazareth où Marie l'attend : à l'heure où il arrivera, elle reviendra du puits et du lavoir, elle aura à peine posé son linge sur la table de la maison, elle entendra ses pas, à un murmure, à presque rien, parce que les mères ont des finesses d'antennes quand leurs enfants les rejoignent, et elle saura alors qu'il est revenu. Mais Jésus ne veut pas de transports trop sensibles, de démonstrations trop exubérantes. Il doit poursuivre sa tâche, serein, dégagé des liens si tendres de sa famille. Libre.

Marie l'étreint sans un mot. Elle sait que ce n'est qu'une halte dans le temps trop court de son fils, subsiste toujours en elle l'image d'une nuit terrible où Jésus va s'enfoncer.

Les jours passent dans le défilé paisible du temps. Nazareth répète ses gestes quotidiens, des jours banals que la lumière dorée des soirs glorifie. Jésus retrouve le silence de l'atelier de Joseph, le temps où il y travaillait encore est loin, il ne s'attelle à aucun morceau de bois, ne commence aucun ouvrage. Marie ne le questionne pas, elle le voit préoccupé : « C'est pour les affaires de mon Père », dit-il mystérieusement.

Pour les noces à Cana où il est invité, il part avec elle. Il va retrouver ses amis, Jean, Simon, André, Philippe, Nathanaël. Ces cinq-là ont déjà compris l'enjeu, avec eux il prendra la route. Jamais autant que dans la marche Jésus n'est aussi fort, aussi sûr de sa mission. C'est dans les campagnes, dans les villages des simples pêcheurs, auprès des pauvres et des malades qu'il est le mieux. Il dit que c'est eux qui peupleront le Royaume de Dieu.

À Cana, quand ils arrivent dans la grande pièce des noces, la fête a déjà commencé depuis plusieurs heures. Ce sont des instants de repos pour Jésus, elles reculent les heures dures et noires, celles à venir, celles du sang séché sur le corps meurtri, celles du sang qui s'écoule du flanc blessé, celles de la solitude désespérée pour lesquelles il réclamera de l'aide, fera des reproches à son père : « Pourquoi, dis, pourquoi m'as-tu abandonné ? »

Marie à bas bruit lui dit que le vin vient à manquer. Elle le souffle à son fils, mais qu'y pourrait-il ? Il n'est pas un magicien, pense-t-elle, pas un sorcier. Mais s'il est fils de Dieu, comme l'a dit l'ange, alors peut-être pourra-t-il convertir l'eau en vin. Des musiques répétitives, lentes et gutturales courent dans les pièces, les invités rient et dansent, mais le maître de maison sait qu'il n'y a plus de vin. Jésus a compris l'injonction de sa mère et la preuve qu'elle lui demande. Sans mot dire, il se lève, va vers les cuisines, demande aux domestiques qu'on lui amène les jarres vides.

« Remplissez-les d'eau à ras bord, leur dit-il. »

Comment comprendre cet ordre ? Les serviteurs hésitent entre le rire et la crainte. Que veut cet homme, Jésus de Nazareth ? De quoi parle-t-il ? Quel tour de passe-passe l'homme de Nazareth, qu'on sait un peu illuminé, veut-il accomplir ? Voudrait-il par hasard transformer l'eau en bon vin frais ? Mais n'est-ce pas blasphème que de tromper ainsi les invités ? De quel pouvoir magique se dote ce Jésus dont on prétend qu'il est devenu nomade, errant sur les routes de Judée ?

Les serveurs s'exécutent cependant. Ils remplissent les jarres jusqu'au bord de leurs cols retroussés.

Et soudain l'eau devient incarnate, d'un rouge flamboyant, semblable au sang qui coule sur les tauroboles du Temple, les jours de la Pâque. Tous ignorent la provenance de ce vin et sa saveur nouvelle, ce goût d'ambre et de fruits rares. Qui possède les terres d'où on l'a tiré ? Jésus ne répond pas aux questions. Il profite du brouhaha de la fête pour se glisser dans la nuit, se relier à son père, rejoindre son silence habité.

Marie, André, Philippe savent, eux, ce qui vient de se passer. C'est le premier miracle de Jésus, la première preuve de sa divinité. Ils sont saisis d'effroi et d'émerveillement. Marie sent tressaillir en elle l'enfant qu'elle portait jadis, se souvient de la visite de l'ange, et cette certitude qu'elle eut immédiatement, « que cela soit, oui, que cela soit ! ».

L'inadmissible vient maintenant de se produire. Comment imaginer que cette eau dans les jarres soit devenue du vin, du meilleur et du plus rare ? Comment y croire ? Pourtant le vin est bien là, il coule dans les vases, il enivre ceux qui le boivent. Mais Marie au fond d'elle-même voit se profiler le supplice de son fils. Elle a tout compris de ce qui l'attend, et que personne ne pourra empêcher.

L'eau transformée en vin, c'est le premier signe éblouissant et messianique de Jésus, lui-même veut garder raison, mais dans la nuit, seul, il est saisi de frissons, tout est trop vaste, trop lourd à porter :

— J'ai peur, mon Père, peur de ce que tu me donnes de faire. Fais-moi plus fort, qu'il ne me soit pas sans cesse demandé de prouver... Que je puisse proclamer ta vie sans preuves... Donne-leur de croire sans voir.

Chapitre 15

Où Jésus va dans la synagogue faire la lecture

C'est le jour du sabbat. Jésus entre dans la synagogue. C'est comme l'annonce de sa future entrée dans le Temple de Jérusalem où, il le sait bien, son Père le conduira. Il lui faut du courage pour affronter les prêtres, les servants, les fidèles. Mais la lumière de l'ange ne le quitte jamais et il avance nimbé de ce signe lumineux. Tous le reconnaissent, on murmure : « C'est le fils de Joseph, il est revenu, on dit qu'il fait des miracles. » Lui n'écoute personne, il se dirige vers la table où se trouvent les rouleaux sacrés. On lui donne le livre d'Isaïe. Il l'ouvre, sans faillir, au passage qu'il veut lire, se tourne vers l'assistance et proclame :
« "L'esprit du Seigneur est sur moi,
Parce qu'il m'a consacré par l'onction.
Il m'a envoyé porter la bonne nouvelle aux pauvres,
Annoncer aux captifs la délivrance,
Et aux aveugles le retour à la vue,
Rendre la liberté aux opprimés,
Proclamer une année de grâce du Seigneur[5]." »
L'intensité de sa voix saisit l'assemblée. Les mots du prophète résonnent en eux, comme des cymbales. Et si c'était vraiment lui le messie annoncé sur lequel l'esprit d'Isaïe

s'est posé ? Et si c'était lui que Dieu avait oint de ses saintes huiles ? Lui, l'envoyé venu porter la bonne nouvelle ?

Puis Jésus poursuit :

« Aujourd'hui s'accomplit à vos oreilles ce passage de l'Écriture. Mais ce n'est pas tout. Vous allez tous arguer : fais ici, de suite, ce qu'on dit que tu as fait, ici, là, à Cana et ailleurs. Va, montre-nous tes dons. Mais sachez-le, je vous le dis, aucun prophète n'est bien reçu dans sa patrie. Ni Élie, ni Élisée n'ont accompli les miracles que le peuple désirait. »

À ces mots, la foule commence à élever la voix. De l'admiration, elle passe à la perplexité, puis à la colère : « Qui est, dit-elle, ce faux prophète qui se moque de nous, qui blasphème dans la maison de Dieu, qui nous méprise ? Qu'il sorte, qu'il s'en aille ! »

Jésus sait qu'il a beaucoup osé, que les dés sont désormais jetés. Il sort de la synagogue, lentement, drapé dans sa lumière. Des hommes le poursuivent, l'entraînent par un chemin de pierre vers un belvédère qui domine des ravins où l'on jette d'ordinaire les bêtes mortes, les détritus. Il reconnaît devant lui la voie de Jérusalem, c'est une voyance qui s'accomplit, une vision de ténèbres et de haine, des hommes et des femmes qui assistent, impuissants, à son martyre, ces hommes implacables qui le conduisent vers une butte où s'élèvent des gibets et le ciel, sombre tout à coup, comme du sang séché. C'est la même chose en un instant qui se reproduit maintenant, la route est de rocaille, de la poussière se soulève, des bosquets d'aloès, épineux, bordent le chemin, il y a des cris, des crachats même, et ces enfants qui lui jettent des pierres. Il se ramasse dans son silence, s'abîme dans la prière, il n'entend plus rien de la foule. « Que ton esprit, Père, ne s'éloigne pas de moi, je suis en ton esprit, je ne te quitterai pas. Je suis consacré par toi, tu m'as choisi pour accomplir les Écritures, je t'obéis, mais prends pitié de moi, fais que je sente ton souffle derrière moi, toujours. »

Comme il ne répond pas aux injures ni aux sarcasmes, qu'il ne cherche pas même à s'enfuir, que ses pas sont réguliers, la foule se lasse de crier en vain. Et au fond d'elle, l'incertitude, la crainte de se tromper. De guerre lasse, elle l'abandonne à l'escarpement de la colline, déjà hors des murs de la ville.

Jésus s'assied sur une pierre, de son regard il embrasse les contreforts de la ville, la sienne. « Me trahiras-tu, Nazareth, ne parviendrai-je pas à te convaincre ? »

L'enfance, soudain, surgit, comme un spectre. Les promenades à cloche-pied dans le lit des ruisseaux asséchés, la cueillette des dattes et les menus travaux dans la maison, tandis que Marie trompe son angoisse en filant la laine, en allant au puits, en roulant la semoule, en faisant des galettes. Jésus pense à sa mère, Toute sa vie, elle a feint d'être sereine, sans accroc, sans écharde. Pas une nuit où elle ne songeait à lui, son enfant, différent, promis à des choses glorieuses, « mais à quel prix, à quel prix, mon Dieu ? », gémissait-elle jusque dans son sommeil. Tout cela, il le sait du fond de son cœur : comment revenir aux jours tendres ? Est-il même possible d'arrêter le cours du temps ?

Chapitre 16

Où le feu se répand

Maintenant Dieu a les choses en main, le feu est dans le monde, Jésus son fils va le propager. Il compte sur lui, sur le rayonnement qu'il a en lui, cette lumière dorée, la même que celle qui embrasait l'humble maison de Marie quand l'ange la surprit. Jésus connaît sa mission : il reprend la route, arpente les sentiers de rocaille et de caillasses sèches. À Capharnaüm, le lac de Tibériade apporte de l'air, une brise, presque rien, mais qui apaise la torpeur des pleins champs. Jésus parle avec les pêcheurs, il aime à les retrouver quand ils arrivent sur la berge, tirent leurs filets et lâchent leur pêche frétillante. « Ce que je veux, dit-il, c'est être avec vous, parmi vous. Ce n'est pas de rites dont vous avez besoin, c'est d'amour, c'est de ne pas craindre Dieu comme un tyran, mais comme un vrai père qui vous aime. Je suis venu pour vous le dire, soyez heureux car des temps nouveaux vont commencer. » Les pêcheurs, braves et bons, laissent dire, sans savoir au juste où veut en venir Jésus, ce qu'il prêche. Mais ils voient bien qu'il n'est pas tout à fait comme ces prédicateurs avec leurs boniments qui amusent les foules, les jours de marché, qu'il ne ressemble pas non plus aux prêtres du Temple, rigides et brutaux. Un jour où Jésus se mêle à la vie des pêcheurs, il ordonne à Simon, fils de Jonas, de monter dans une barque et de jeter les filets à l'eau.

— À quoi cela servirait-il, rabbi, puisque nous venons de rentrer nos filets et, vois-tu, ils sont vides. La journée n'est pas bonne, crois-nous.

— Va, Simon, va et jette tes filets.

Simon part avec André. La barque s'éloigne, les filets sont lancés. En quelques instants, ils se remplissent de poissons, tant que les mailles se rompent. Une première fois, une seconde et toujours autant de poissons. La barque revient enfin à la berge. Simon se jette aux pieds de Jésus :

— Je suis indigne de toi, Seigneur, car vraiment tu es le Messie, je suis pêcheur et tu m'as aidé.

Jésus le relève en souriant, lui prend la main, et lui dit :

— Tu es saint toi aussi comme chacun de nous. Maintenant tu as compris, viens avec moi, crois en ma parole et je te ferai pêcheur d'hommes.

Simon accueille sa parole, il se risque à pleurer devant ses autres compagnons, quelque chose l'a traversé qui est plus fort que la raison, quelque chose qui le pousse à tout quitter.

Il rejoint sa maison, en toute hâte, rassemble quelques affaires dans un baluchon, et part rejoindre Jésus.

Ils sont cinq en tout, cinq errants, cinq fous qui veulent conquérir le monde autrement que par les armes et la mort. C'est comme le début du monde, la même tendresse en eux, la même innocence. La même inconscience. Ils ne veulent parler que d'amour : qui donc pourrait leur vouloir du mal ?

Pendant les marches, entre deux villages, entre deux attroupements, Jésus et ses cinq compagnons marchent en silence. Parfois Jésus murmure un psaume, un chant qui implore Dieu, très ancien, venu du désir des hommes de trouver enfin la paix. C'est quand ils s'arrêtent pour faire une pause, sous les figuiers à l'âcre odeur, dans le bourdonnement des guêpes et des frelons, que Jésus parle à ses compagnons. Ils ne sont pas encore ses disciples, c'est trop tôt pour le savoir encore, mais tous sont prêts à le suivre, n'importe où, là où il voudra bien les mener.

« Vous serez des pêcheurs d'hommes, oui, vous connaissez déjà la patience du pêcheur, sa modestie, ce qu'il accepte quand la mer résiste, quand les filets sont vides, quand il ne croise aucun ban de poissons et qu'il revient bredouille à la berge. Vous avez cette humilité-là du pêcheur. Il vous faudra désormais témoigner sur toutes les terres que Dieu notre Père a faites pour les hommes, pas seulement la Galilée qu'on affectionne tant, mais partout au-delà des mers. Vous irez annoncer la bonne nouvelle à Chorazin, à Magdala, vous irez en Samarie, et plus loin encore à Bethsaïde, à Gadara, à Césarée, en Judée, à Béthanie, à Jéricho, en Phénicie, et encore plus loin. Il faut vous préparer à ce grand voyage, pour rejoindre les hommes, leur dire que Dieu a envoyé son fils, qu'il leur a donné la loi d'amour pour les sauver. »

Les cinq hommes regardent Jésus, émerveillés, déjà transfigurés. Il n'y a étrangement aucun doute en eux, pas l'ombre d'une suspicion, ils sont sûrs de Jésus, sûrs qu'auprès de lui ils se sont comme retrouvés, reconnus. Il y a une joie qui circule entre eux, Jésus l'apporte secrètement, sans faire apparaître sa mélancolie intérieure qui rarement ne le montre riant. La charge souvent est trop lourde, il n'est qu'un homme pour l'instant, promis à de grandes choses, mais seul, il se sent presque perdu et puis il y a le vin de Cana, le sang des jarres, abondant, qui réverbère. Le vin, le sang, le feu : « Fais-moi boire à ta source, mon Père, désaltère-moi, je suis assoiffé de toi et tu ne te montres guère. Allège-moi. Ne me laisse pas sur cette lame. »

Ils marchent et chaque jour, c'est plus de villageois, des simples, des pauvres, des mendiants qui viennent écouter le maître. Ils croient tous en cet homme de Galilée qui leur parle de choses si simples, compréhensibles, imagées. Chaque jour, c'est toujours plus de monde car la rumeur court vite, les enfants la colportent, de maison en maison, à cause des miracles que, dit-on, il fait. Jésus pourtant ne fait rien d'autre que d'écouter, de croire en ceux qu'ils croisent, les miracles ne viennent pas de lui mais d'eux, de leur attente, de leur profond désir, de cette force intérieure qu'ils possèdent, ignorée, cachée, prête à bondir. L'espérance.

Chapitre 17

Où Jésus survient dans un monde perdu

C'est une foule obscure, chaque jour plus dense, qui veut le rencontrer. Jésus redoute la colère des pharisiens, des nantis et des établis qui voient en lui un ennemi, un provocateur. Ceux qu'il recherche, ce sont les fous et les pauvres pour lesquels il rend vivante la parole des Écritures. Comme ses cinq compagnons ont le zèle des convertis, il leur dit qu'il faut se faire plus petit que l'enfant dans son berceau, car celui qui a cru ne peut imposer par la force sa croyance.

« Vous ne serez que des témoins, leur dit-il, c'est l'éclat de votre regard qui convertit les cœurs asséchés, c'est le rayonnement de votre être qui va emporter l'incrédulité. Vous êtes des rayons de lumière dès lors que vous avez cru, vous êtes transparents, lumineux et traversés. Il faut vous rendre disponibles à cette tâche, comme vous alimentez d'huile la lampe pour vous éclairer, il faut vous montrer dignes de l'oint qui vous a consacrés en Esprit. »

Jésus a confiance dans sa mission. Le soir, après une longue marche, et des haltes dans les villages, il se repose avec ses disciples sur les rives du lac de Tibériade. Une brise tiède souffle sur les voiles des barques de pêcheurs, la lune étincelle sur les eaux calmes du lac, et Jésus dit que la paix de son Père, enfin, s'installe sur eux.

Dieu, de fait, veille sur les marcheurs. Il connaît avant tous l'itinéraire, la voie glorieuse, la voie de douleurs aussi. Il sait que tout est chemin de croisées, qu'il n'y a pas dans le monde de voie unique, large, et qui se déroulerait comme un ruban. Tout n'est que carrefours et croisements, et il faut passer par eux pour l'atteindre. Il sait aussi que les hommes redoutent les croix que forment parfois les routes comme ils veulent ignorer leur propre point de contradiction. Des siècles durant, ils feignent de ne rien voir, de ne rien comprendre, refusent de partager. À Cana, les bombes israéliennes s'écrasent sur les immeubles de civils. Des cadavres d'enfants encore blottis dans leur effroi sont extraits des décombres. Il n'y a pas de miracle cette fois-ci à Cana. Toujours que la guerre, et l'envie d'en découdre. Jésus est passé sur ces routes où s'enfoncent aujourd'hui les blindés. Les oliviers et les palmiers explosent sur leur passage, des maisons s'effondrent, des vieillardes tendent les mains quand des cameramen filment les affrontements et réclament de l'eau, des enfants agonisent lentement sous les ruines. Dans toutes les églises du Moyen-Orient, Jésus est invoqué :

« Viens à nous, esprit de lumière, que de nos routes empruntées par tes pas naissent des lieux de paix et d'amour, partage notre malheur, fais descendre ton esprit. »

Mais rien ne s'exauce, que la mort et le malheur, que la souffrance et la traversée à pied du pays sous les bombes. Jésus reste muet, il n'accomplit aucun miracle, n'apparaît nulle part. Si c'était lui qu'on tuait ou qui râlait sous les gravats ?

Il naît cependant de l'attente, de la douleur, de l'humanité blessée. De l'impossible idéal, du malheur de l'imperfection. Il naît du désir du monde de changer la donne, de renverser les idées reçues, les ordres établis. Dans sa IVe églogue, Virgile annonce la naissance d'un enfant-roi qui sera l'annonciateur d'une ère nouvelle. À Sienne, au Duomo, au milieu de la nef, une mosaïque représente sur le pavement Hermès Trismégiste. Tout près de lui la sibylle de Cumes déroule un long rouleau où sont inscrits les vers de l'églogue. C'est dans cette attente, ce besoin de changement, que Jésus se révèle. Comment échapper à l'esclavage ? Comment accepter ce monde délétère et obscur ? Et ces rites orientaux, fondés sur la magie et la sorcellerie ? Comment restaurer la dignité de l'homme dans ce monde en crise, rompre avec l'argent, le luxe, le lucre et l'ambition ? Dans les pays asservis par Rome, les captifs pleurent et réclament justice. Ils en appellent aux chants obscurs des mages et des sorciers, souffrent de leur solitude et tendent dans leur nuit à un Dieu bon et unique qui les écouterait. Sénèque, lui, ne croit ni aux autres ni à Dieu, mais se forge une philosophie de vie où tout altruisme est banni : « Fuis la foule, conseille-t-il, fuis le petit nombre, fuis même la compagnie d'un seul. »

Alors Jésus vient, presque naturellement, comme un fruit mûr, comme une graine qui fait craquer sa cosse et surgit de la terre. Il dit aux passants :

« Avancez en eau profonde, ne craignez pas d'aller vers celui qui vous réclame et va vous consoler. Plus la mer est profonde, plus la pêche sera grande. Plus vous oserez avancer dans les profondeurs de la mer, plus vos filets se rompront de tant de poissons. »

Les foules se massent à son passage. Personne encore ne leur a parlé avec autant de force et de simplicité.

Marie, dans sa maison de Nazareth, continue de travailler, elle ne veut pas répondre à ses voisines qui la questionnent de peur de soulever des jalousies, des haines secrètes. Elle prie la nuit très tard, pour demander à Dieu d'épargner Jésus, de le rendre moins conquérant. Mais Dieu veut sûrement cela pour son fils. Lui aussi doit s'avancer en eau profonde, prendre le risque d'en mourir, sinon que voudrait dire un Dieu qui se protège ?

« Je suis avec vous, dit Jésus à ceux qui viennent l'écouter. Je ne suis pas un agitateur comme vous en voyez beaucoup ici qui passent et sèment des illusions en vous. Je n'ai rien qui ne m'appartienne, moins encore que vous qui possédez vos filets et votre maison de terre, mais je vous apprends ce que vous devez garder en vous, comme une manne précieuse, l'amour qui fait la paix, la foi qui fait la liberté. »

Quand il parle, il ne craint ni les occupants romains ni les servants des synagogues, pas davantage les prêtres. Il s'échappe de lui une telle assurance qu'il ébranle les plus sceptiques, raffermit les plus lâches.

Chapitre 18

Où Jésus guérit les corps et les esprits

Il n'y a que l'aube qui le trouve seul à prier. Le bruit court que Jésus guérit, qu'il suffit de lui présenter un malade et qu'il est sauvé. Chacun arrive avec sa misère, ses souffrances. C'est cette ferveur collective qui le porte, lui donne la force de continuer. De ne pas s'abstraire des autres. Un jour, un lépreux se jette à ses pieds. Le lépreux ne craint plus rien, ni son audace ni la foule qui, au loin, l'a évité. C'est comme s'il se mettait dans la main de Jésus.

— Seigneur si tu le veux, tu le peux, lui dit-il.

Jésus sent monter en lui cette chaleur intense, devenue habituelle désormais et qui surgit quand l'esprit de Dieu agit avec violence. Il tend ses mains vers l'homme, le touche et lui dit :

— Je le veux, sois guéri.

La lèpre aussitôt disparaît comme par enchantement. Les chairs se reforment, les mains retrouvent leur agilité, le visage son ovale, et tout le corps est poussé par une énergie nouvelle, brûlante, dynamique.

— Tu es guéri, homme, mais ne colporte pas ta guérison. Qu'elle soit intérieure, à toi seulement, ne t'en glorifie pas mais va au contraire te montrer au prêtre et fais pour ta guérison l'offrande telle que Moïse l'a prescrite. N'oublie pas que le feu de Dieu est passé en toi, qu'il t'a personnellement reconnu et qu'il t'a rendu à la beauté d'Adam. Prie-le désormais comme il se doit, car c'est par ta foi que tu seras sauvé.

Jésus le quitte, ses disciples le suivent.

— Il faut chercher, dit-il, des lieux de repos et de solitude. Pour retrouver en soi l'élan de Dieu, la flamme qui l'anime.

Sa réputation se fait de plus en plus grande. Il voudrait lui échapper mais comment être insensible au drame de la souffrance humaine, comment ne pas délivrer le feu ?

Les Pharisiens et les docteurs de la Loi commencent à s'inquiéter. Intrigués, ils se glissent dans la foule, écoutent Jésus enseigner, ils lui trouvent du talent, de la conviction. Les guérisons spectaculaires fascinent les foules et les rallient. Cela n'est pas bon pour eux.

Jésus ne veut pas cependant user de ses pouvoirs, il sait que le don de guérison est en chacun des hommes, donné par Dieu à chacun d'eux. Mais inexploité, renié, il croupit au fond de soi, sans emploi.

« Ce don, dit-il à ses compagnons, c'est la certitude de Dieu en nous, la puissance de Dieu qui se donne parce qu'il sait qu'il nous l'a donnée et qu'elle existe, toujours renouvelée, comme une source d'eau pure, inépuisable. Il suffit d'aller la tirer, elle est toujours là, dans les profondeurs de soi, et de la remonter comme les filets du pêcheur. C'est d'abord la guérison spirituelle qui, dans un second temps, transforme les corps et les rend à leur jeunesse, à leur pureté originelle. Il a fallu des choses fortes pour que cette foule comprenne enfin que Dieu est là, qu'il lui a donné une seconde chance, mais la guérison est intérieure, elle régénère les âmes et puis après elle embellit les chairs et les visages, fait étinceler les regards, redonne le don de l'admiration, la grâce de l'émerveillement. C'est votre ferveur qui emportera les hommes, le témoignage de votre foi, ardente, imbattable, et sans peur. C'est parce que les mains des lépreux étaient tendues et qu'elles rejoignaient les miennes que le miracle s'est accompli, elles étaient à leur façon pleines de foi et de ferveur. Mais il fallait d'abord les mains tendues.

Chapitre 19

Où Jésus défie les critiques

En chemin, il croise des foules émerveillées mais les critiques et les injures fusent aussi sur son passage. Il ne les écoute pas, ne juge pas ceux qui les profèrent. De son regard perçant, il les confond, leur fait baisser la tête, les rallie. Il sait que c'est difficile pour les hommes de croire en un dieu vivant, qui leur ressemblerait. Comment accepter les prodiges venus d'un homme en apparence ordinaire ? Comment croire aux guérisons miraculeuses venues d'un être aussi banal, aussi pauvre surtout ? Ceux qui croient ont entendu parler des prodiges passés, de la marche terrible de Moïse dans le désert, de la mer qui se sépare en deux, du déluge et de l'arche, tous ces récits dont chaque récitant redouble les effets, multiplie les miracles. Mais d'après Jésus, c'est Dieu, en chacun d'eux, qui peut faire de grandes choses. Il dit : renverser les montagnes.

— Mais comment, Seigneur, comment ?

— Par l'énergie divine qui est en vous, par ce feu qui vous anime que vous n'attisez pas assez, par la certitude que vous n'êtes pas seuls, que vous seuls ne pouvez commander le monde.

Tandis qu'il enseigne, on vient le rejoindre, des curieux, des inquiets, des fervents. Des hommes tentent en vain de faire entrer un paralytique sur sa civière dans la pièce ; comme ils n'y parviennent pas, ils le hissent sur la terrasse et le descendent avec des cordes dans le patio où Jésus se trouve. Jésus compatit au malheur du malade, à la souffrance des siens. Il interrompt sa parole et dit :

— Mon ami, tes péchés te seront remis.

Une rumeur parcourt l'assistance, non formulée, de réprobation. Jésus, qui lit dans les cœurs, déclare alors :

— Pourquoi ces pensées dans vos cœurs ? « Eh bien, pour que vous sachiez que le Fils de l'homme a le pouvoir sur la terre de remettre les péchés : je te l'ordonne, dit-il au paralysé, lève-toi, prends ton grabat et va-t'en chez toi[6] ! »

Un frisson parcourt alors l'assistance. Celui qui a osé remettre les péchés vient d'accomplir un prodige extraordinaire. Pour la première fois, au nom de Dieu, Jésus remet les péchés, évoque sa vraie mission. Ce qu'il doit enseigner, c'est l'amour qui efface tous les péchés. Plus question de Dieu vengeur, de Dieu qui comptabilise les péchés : uniquement l'amour qui purifie le mal.

— Il y a l'amour et ce dialogue constant que Dieu souhaite avec vous. Tant que vous serez dans ce lien de Dieu, vous serez sauvés.

Tous les jours il guérit, transmet ce feu qui le parcourt, pas même les sabbats ne le forcent au repos. Les Pharisiens, les Hérodiens crient à l'outrage, au blasphème.

— Tu ne dois pas travailler ces jours-là, à plus forte raison enseigner et tenter de guérir. Ce jour est à Dieu, disent-ils.

Mais Jésus n'écoute pas, il coupe à travers les forêts d'oliviers, il traverse des champs de blé, retrouve sa nature paysanne, son goût pour la terre ; avec ses disciples il arrache des épis, les froisse entre ses mains, les égrène pour se nourrir un peu.

— Tu outrages Dieu, tu es un sorcier, un falsificateur.

— Vous n'avez donc pas lu ce que fit David quand il eut faim ? Comme il entrait dans la maison de Dieu, il prit les pains de proposition, en mangea et en donna à ses compagnons, ces pains que seuls les prêtres ont le droit de manger. Et il leur disait : « Le Fils de l'homme est maître du sabbat. » En vérité je vous le dis, ne suivez pas des règles qui détruisent l'homme.

Un autre jour encore, de sabbat, il entre dans une synagogue. Les servants, les prêtres l'épient, attendant qu'il bafoue la loi pour le condamner. Osera-t-il guérir aujourd'hui ?

Un homme arrive qui tend sa main desséchée. Jésus regarde la peau flétrie, la main sans usage, morte, pendante :

— Viens, approche-toi, lui dit-il.

L'homme obéit, tandis que Jésus proclame :

— Vous, aux cœurs secs, je vous le demande, un jour de sabbat, est-il permis de sauver une vie ou de ne rien faire ?

Puis s'adressant à l'homme, il lui dit :

— Viens, étends ta main !

Jésus passe alors sa main sur celle du malade et la main soudain recouvre sa mobilité, les chairs se régénèrent, le sang y circule, la peau rosit doucement.

La stupeur saisit les assistants. Un lourd silence succède à la guérison. Mais tandis que Jésus sort de la synagogue, tous les Pharisiens pensent au moyen d'éliminer cet intrus, ce trublion.

Jésus ressent cette haine, il l'entend battre dans leur cœur, il la voit, cette haine, le recouvrir tout entier et l'alourdir. Chaque jour c'est le même accablement, ce doute jeté en lui, ce regret même de devoir incessamment faire ses preuves. La foule, elle, réclame toujours plus de lui. Elle transforme les événements, grossit les faits, à l'entendre, c'est tout un peuple que Jésus guérit, délivre des paralysies, des cécités, des lèpres. Lui voudrait que cette foule apprenne qu'il est venu, oui, pour guérir mais pas seulement les corps, surtout les âmes, les esprits dévoyés, oublieux de leur grandeur.

Dans ses paroles murmurées, la nuit, à Dieu, il lui demande de l'aider à enseigner cela, cette guérison des âmes, intime, mystérieuse.

« Mon père, apprends-moi à atteindre leur cœur, à les transpercer comme un glaive de ton amour. »

Dans l'Espagne livrée aux guerres et au lucre, le cœur de Thérèse d'Avila se fracasse au moment de son extase. L'amour de Dieu est entré en elle, il n'y a pas de limites à cet amour accueilli, à cette violente intrusion de Dieu, brutale, presque un orgasme, qui l'assaille et la rend pantelante dans les plis de marbre du Bernin. Le corps de Thérèse accueille le percement du glaive, un frisson agite sa bure de nonne comme un tulle quand Bernin la sculpte avec sa fougue de baroque. L'ange la transperce de sa pointe de feu, il atteint le cœur, qui cesse de battre, un trop plein d'amour que le corps ne peut supporter, et Thérèse s'affale sur le dallage de sa cellule, elle perd pied, elle crie et elle gémit, elle dit : « Mon Dieu, mon doux Jésus, perce-moi encore de ton amour, entre en moi, ne crains pas de me transpercer, car tu me donnes de te voir et de t'atteindre, de m'étendre sur ta couche. » « Hystérique Thérèse, proclament les sceptiques, les hommes de peu d'espérance. Ne voyez-vous pas qu'elle vient d'avoir un infarctus du myocarde ? » « Amour de toi en Dieu, bienheureuse Thérèse, répond Dieu, que j'entende encore proclamer ton amour. » « Viens, mon doux fiancé, dit-elle à mi-voix, pénètre-moi encore et encore, entre dans mon cœur et dans mon corps, fais de moi ce que tu voudras, car je connais à présent la nature de ton amour, viens, doux Jésus, enfonce le glaive et donne-moi le feu d'amour en moi. »

Chapitre 20

Où Dieu se réjouit de son plan

Ce que Dieu a voulu se déroule impeccablement. L'ange, la jeune Marie, la naissance à Bethléem, la fuite en Égypte, la vie obscure à Nazareth, et maintenant la marche vers Jérusalem, les miracles et les disciples, les foules subjuguées, et la rumeur du messie enfin venu sur la terre. L'histoire est parfaite, romanesque à souhait, avec des images fortes et des scènes incroyables, dignes des grands péplums d'Hollywood. C'est qu'il faut bien émerveiller les foules, emplies d'espérance en attente d'un sauveur qui les libérerait des tyrans et des mauvais, les arracherait à leur condition d'esclaves ou de soumis. Dieu a bien compris cela, ce besoin d'épopée, ce désir fou des hommes de se glisser dans le merveilleux, l'enchantement. Il fera tout ce qu'il faut pour les rassurer et leur rendre l'espoir, il ne négligera rien, ni les multiplications des pains et des poissons ni la guérison des malades qui se relèvent de leurs grabats et courent comme des gazelles. « Je vous promets une belle histoire, et un superbe héros, c'est mon fils, je vous l'envoie, je vous promets des actes inouïs et des moments incomparables, Jésus qui marche sur les flots, Jésus qui ressuscite d'entre les morts, je vous promets enfin l'incroyable, vous renaîtrez de vos cendres, et vous vivrez après votre mort, auprès de moi, dans la splendeur des cieux, et vous serez apaisés, délivrés de vos angoisses et de vos dilemmes, libérés de tous les jougs du monde. »

Mais déjà des sceptiques se manifestent. Ils ne croient pas à ces balivernes, à ces récits féeriques, ils ont bien vu les foules autour de Jésus, mais aucun miraculé, disent-ils, ou bien cet exalté qui s'est soudain levé de son brancard et que les paroles de Jésus ont si effrayé qu'elles lui ont fait comme un choc au cerveau qui l'a remis debout... Dieu n'est pas affecté par ces critiques, il les a prévues d'ailleurs : « C'est une question de foi, hommes au cœur sec et de peu d'espérance, leur dit-il, et la foi, c'est ce qui vous fend en deux, vous empêche d'agir avec vos règles et vos lois, c'est ce qui vous transperce le cœur, et vous délivre, dans les larmes. » Ce qu'il y a de bien avec Dieu, c'est qu'il connaît toute l'histoire, le début et la fin de toutes choses, les aubes et les crépuscules, la vie et la mort, il sait tout cela, pleinement, sans ombre nulle part. Les sceptiques ne lui font pas peur, il ne craint pas pour son plan, parce qu'il est plus fort que la raison et la science, puisqu'il est fondateur de tout, de l'inlassable spectacle des planètes, du mouvement incessant des cerceaux de lumière orange, bleue, dorée qui tournent autour des astres. Puisque c'est par lui et de lui qu'est né tout cet ordre qui n'a pas de fin. Lui sait que ses créatures, les hommes, ont besoin de Dieu, pas de ces idoles que des peuples entiers égarés invoquent en vain, mais d'un Dieu qui les aime, c'est ça la clé du mystère. L'amour. Et le plan ultime de Dieu, c'est ce fils tant aimé qu'il leur donne. « Tenez, écoutez-le, il est à vous, il est là pour vous dire tout ce que j'attends de vous, il vient vous le dire dans cette Galilée où vous habitez, dans ce petit coin du monde que j'ai choisi pour qu'il vous enseigne ma loi, il vous ressemble, il a votre apparence, il vient de vos villages et il parle votre langue, et ce qu'il a à dire, c'est soufflé par moi qu'il vous le dira, heureux ceux qui possèdent au cœur d'eux-mêmes l'amour car ils seront sauvés. Dieu vous dit cette évidence oubliée, bafouée, que j'avais mise pourtant au cœur de vos naissances et que vous avez négligée. L'amour. Car Dieu est amour. Dieu ne veut vivre que de l'amour. Tout le reste est invention des cyniques. »

Ainsi parle Dieu dans la musique des planètes. Jésus cependant avance sur sa route. Tout l'amour de son père est en lui, coule en lui comme un torrent qui ne se tarit pas. Il progresse selon les temps voulus par Dieu. Des lieux forts, des scènes puissantes, des élans d'espoir.

Dieu joue ici sa plus achevée partie. Il met dans la balance son fils, il l'installe sur la grande place du monde, au lieu où ça brûle, entre ses créatures spoliées ou perdues, vendues ou exploitées, sur l'étroite langue de terre de la Galilée. « Et va, Jésus, sur les tréteaux du théâtre d'illusions, va et décourage-les des mensonges, ramène au bercail mes âmes égarées ! »

Chapitre 21

Où Jésus apprend le martyre de Jean-Baptiste

Il faut encore plus de sang et de morts, plus de violences et de passion dans le péplum que Dieu a imaginé. Plus d'épreuves pour le fils. Des images fortes pour les hommes ivres de vie et de désirs. Des séquences de feu et de foudre pour marquer les imaginations car il sait leur paresse et leur insouciance. Il faut les sauver, tous, ne pas les laisser aux mains de Satan qui se les frotte joyeusement en voyant les chutes et les trahisons, les mensonges et les débauches, tous, récupérés dans le grand chaudron de Jérôme Bosch, brûlés comme des feuilles mortes, énorme bouillon d'âmes desséchées, réduites à néant. Et Dieu pleure en voyant le désastre de ses créatures : « Que vienne l'amour, hurle-t-il, afin qu'il les sauve tous, car rien n'est trop tard, hâte-toi, mon fils, poursuis ta route, Jésus, jusqu'à Jérusalem où je révélerai aux hommes la splendeur de leur destin, la résurrection infinie, le grand bond dans l'univers lumineux, dans les bras des saints anges ! »

Maintenant il est l'heure pour Jésus d'apprendre le martyre de Jean le Baptiste. On le lui murmure à l'oreille, on n'ose trop lui raconter l'orgie qui a présidé à la décapitation, la lâcheté d'Antipas, les esprits dévoyés d'Hérodiade et de Salomé, le plateau d'argent enfin où repose sa tête tranchée. « Tu ne seras plus, Jean, sur les rives du Jourdain, dans la clarté matinale des eaux, plus personne n'entendra tes prêches audacieux, tes mises en garde. Qui viendra à présent ondoyer le corps de ceux qui réclament Dieu, et veulent se laver dans son esprit ? »

Le silence tombe sur Jésus. Et cette solitude qu'il connaît bien maintenant, car personne, non, personne, ne sait encore, sinon lui, ce qu'il devra endurer pour retrouver la douceur du foyer, la paix qui inonde les corps et les âmes, cette douceur intérieure qui s'empare des élus de Dieu, cette joie aussi. Parce que Dieu l'a voulu ainsi, Jésus sait tout déjà de son destin. De cette douleur qui lui est faite d'être à la fois dieu et homme, de ne pas pouvoir être seulement homme dans son inachèvement et pleinement dieu, dans sa grandeur sublime et céleste. Seulement après, cette gloire, après les ténèbres.

Il apprend de ses compagnons la mort de Jean, colportée par la foule des pêcheurs. Dieu a frappé fort les imaginations, il y a du sang, des danses, des esclaves alanguies, de l'or et de la pourpre, du beau roman historique, comme Flaubert quand il cède à la tentation de l'antique et écrit *Salammbô*.

Acte I, planter le décor : Antipas, le fils d'Hérode, fait arrêter Jean-Baptiste. Depuis longtemps déjà il se méfie de lui, avec ses grands discours d'agitateur religieux, de réformateur du monde, d'annonciateur d'un messie qui viendrait fouler aux pieds les idoles et les corrompus. Mais quand Jean commence à critiquer la vie privée du souverain, Antipas décide de l'arrêter. « Comment tolérer, disait Jean sur les rives du Jourdain devant des foules muettes de stupeur, que votre roi ait rejeté sa femme légitime, Hareth, pour épouser sa propre belle-sœur, Hérodiade, oui, elle, la femme de son frère ? »

Fin de l'acte de présentation : Dieu en est satisfait, intrigue, décor. Sentiments et caractères antagonistes, tout y est pour que les foules frissonnent.

Acte II : Hérodiade aime l'amour et l'argent. Elle est ambitieuse, violente, dépravée, belle et manipulatrice. C'est la petite-fille de Hérode, le même qui avait fait tuer tous les enfants du royaume pour éliminer Jésus à Bethléem.

Dieu connaît bien les règles du jeu, les lois du théâtre historique.

Acte III : Hérodiade a épousé en premières noces Philippe, son oncle, mais le couple ne s'entend guère. Elle rêve de pouvoir et de luxe, et seul Antipas peut les lui donner. Elle entreprend donc de le séduire. Il n'en faut pas davantage pour qu'Antipas ne succombe à ses charmes et ne répudie Hareth, la fille d'un prince arabe.

Maintenant l'acte IV. Là, il faut jouer serré. Seul un coup de théâtre peut faire rebondir la machine : Hérodiade décide de se retirer en apparence de la partie. Elle va trouver refuge chez son père, laissant Antipas au désespoir. Antipas lui ordonne de revenir et l'épouse. Hérodiade est donc reine du royaume d'Antipas. Là même où le pauvre Jean-Baptiste, vêtu d'une peau de bête, harangue les villageois venus en foule entendre ses prédications. Entrée en scène de Jean le Baptiste. Il n'en finit pas de critiquer les mœurs royales, les soirées de débauche et les ivresses des femmes corrompues, toute la cour en prend pour son grade. Dieu écrit le *Satiricon* en Palestine avant Petrone... La garde royale arrête donc, sur ordre d'Antipas, le fou de Dieu.

À ce moment précis du drame historique, Dieu réfléchit à la suite qu'il va donner. Oui, il faut sacrifier Jean le Baptiste pour que la voie soit libre pour Jésus, pour que son martyre préfigure le Golgotha. Sang et ténèbres, Dieu aime encore cela avant de jouer l'ultime carte de l'amour.

Acte V : c'est le final. Dieu utilise toutes les ficelles des grands drames de Shakespeare et des romantiques. Hugo donc n'a rien inventé avec sa préface de *Hernani*. Il fallait lire la Bible...

Jean le Baptiste est enfermé dans la forteresse, au-dessus c'est la fête nuit et jour. Pourtant, Antipas est un brave homme, Dieu lui donne une chance de se sauver. Il a la capacité de s'ouvrir aux autres, d'écouter et de ne pas juger. Autrement dit, Antipas voudrait bien relâcher Jean et se convertir à la nouvelle religion enseignée par l'ermite. Il le fait venir jusqu'à lui, Jean continue à dénigrer son immoralité, et Hérodiade, qui l'apprend, devient folle de colère. Mais Antipas est faible, il cède aux charmes de sa nouvelle épouse. Au cours d'un grand festin, devant l'assistance médusée, danse la propre fille d'Hérodiade, la divine Salomé, encore adolescente mais déjà bien délurée. Antipas demande à la jeune fille ce qu'elle souhaiterait pour la remercier de ses contorsions orientales. « La tête de Jean sur un plateau », répond-elle aussitôt pour plaire à sa mère. Antipas, qui ne s'attendait pas à ce désir, ne peut publiquement le lui refuser et il ordonne à un des gardes d'exécuter Jean. Aussitôt dit aussitôt fait, la tête arrive sur un plateau d'argent dans les chants et les libations...

Voilà le bon scénario de Dieu qui, pour l'occasion, retrouve le souffle épique des anciens temps : une histoire de feu et de sang, de sexe et de sadisme. Du grand drame qu'aurait bien aimé George Sand.

« À toi de jouer à présent, mon fils. La route est libre. Tandis que Jean baptisait dans l'eau, tu baptiseras dans l'Esprit, car ton heure est venue de répandre l'eau vive sur toute la terre. »

Pourtant Jésus n'a pas besoin des paroles de son père. Mais Dieu insiste, enfonce le clou :

« Même drame pour toi aussi, mon fils, même scénario de feu et de sang, même douleur, même martyre. C'est le prix de l'amour. »

Jésus reconnaît son destin à cette souffrance qui l'accable soudain, à ce fardeau de douleur, à ce peu de résistance à la vie des hommes, à cette manière qu'il a alors de regarder le ciel et de respirer l'air du soir quand il fait frissonner les eaux de Tibériade, à ce poids qui pèse sur ses épaules. Il pense, une seconde peut-être, mais il y pense, à Marie, sa mère, il l'entretient dans le langage secret des enfants qu'il a conservé, à cette sorte de dialogue muet et secret qui défie les distances et le temps et qui fait que jamais une mère et son fils ne sont vraiment séparés.

« Mère, murmure-t-il, tu me manques tant, vois ton fils complètement seul dans les chemins, pas une lueur d'espoir au loin, parce que je sais que je vais vers les ténèbres, et que je ne pourrai plus longtemps me couler dans les blés de Galilée. Mère, pourquoi ne puis-je profiter un instant, un seul instant, du soir qui tombe, de la douceur des nuits d'été ? De celle de tes bras ? Et d'une autre femme que j'aimerais, à qui je donnerais des enfants, et qui me survivraient et se souviendraient de moi, de mon nom, inutile ? Ô mère, comme j'aimerais n'être que le charpentier de Nazareth, le fils de Marie et de Joseph, travailler aux charpentes de bois, sentir l'odeur de miel et de résine des pièces qui sèchent dans l'atelier ! Mais au lieu de cela, je sens en moi vibrer le feu inextinguible de Dieu, cette violence qui me parcourt, pour donner de la douceur au monde. Pourquoi moi, mère, pourquoi ? »

Pourquoi, oui, durent se demander frère Christophe et ses frères dans la claire solitude de Tibhirine, pourquoi craindrions-nous les soldats de l'ombre puisque nous portons la lumière du Christ en silence, sans prosélytisme, sans exubérance, seulement la même lumière de Galilée, quand, sur les rives du Jourdain, Jésus commençait à témoigner du vrai Royaume ? C'est le 27 mars, dans la nuit. Les amandiers sont déjà en fleurs et bientôt la même poudre blanche de pétales, odorante et floconneuse, se répandra sur les champs et les vergers. La chaleur est douce, les jours rallongent ; le frère jardinier n'a pas encore besoin d'arroser ses plates-bandes et ses bosquets de capucines et de belles-de-nuit. Cette nuit-là du 27, tout s'est passé comme d'habitude. Le dîner frugal, la prière pour les chrétiens d'Orient et les frères musulmans, et le vœu de frère Christophe, le moine-poète, qui résonne dans le réfectoire comme une prémonition : « Ami, tiens la table prête et belle, et ton regard sur le seuil en silence éveillé... » Puis c'est la prière du soir, et les laudes à Marie, « Oui, sauve-nous, Marie, de tout le malheur du monde, donne aux hommes de cette terre de demeurer à l'image de ton fils, Vierge Marie, sois notre mère à nous aussi, comble-nous de ta tendresse toute cette nuit et recouvre-nous de ton manteau de lumière. »

La nuit est profonde. Les assassins du GIA rôdent dans le domaine, on dit GIA mais personne n'en est sûr, les langues se délient très tôt, les soldats de l'armée régulière sont aussi mis en cause, qui donc a commis l'irréparable ? Les jours passent, longs et terribles, le monde entier prie pour les moines kidnappés, toutes les églises de la terre supplient Dieu et Jésus et Marie mais aucune réponse. Et puis le monde s'habitue à cette absence. Seules pleurent les mères comme dut pleurer la mère de Jean le Baptiste, parce qu'elles connaissent la peur de leurs petits, même quand ils sont devenus grands, elles seules savent ce qui les noue au ventre, cette angoisse de la mort, même s'ils savent, eux, les moines de Tibhirine, que l'heure du sacrifice est venue et que Jésus les attend dans sa résurrection. Pas une seconde, Christian, le prieur, Luc et Christophe, Michel et Bruno, Célestin et Paul aussi n'imaginent pas que là cesse à jamais leur existence comme si Jésus les avait assurés personnellement de la gloire qui les attend, celle d'être en Dieu. Il y a un moment, toujours, dans l'agonie, où celui qui sait qu'il va mourir lâche prise et se donne au temps, à ce qui pourrait bien ressembler au vide, à Dieu enfin. « Va, pauvre être, se dit-il, je suis prêt au passage. » La campagne de Médéa n'est pas prête pourtant à recevoir le terrible dépôt des corps mutilés, décapités. À Médéa, quand le printemps arrive, c'est une douceur extrême, une jeunesse qui s'élève, les arbres qui refleurissent, et des senteurs d'orangers et de citronniers, des champs reverdissent et des profusions de fleurs sauvages gagnent les terres en friches, pois de senteurs, bleuets, coquelicots. Et là soudain la stupeur des corps sans tête. Deux mille ans après Jean-Baptiste, même douleur, même violence pour qui annonce l'esprit de Jésus, et témoigne de son amour, sans partage, pour tous les hommes.

Jésus, qui voit toutes choses, connaît déjà le martyre des moines de Tibhirine. Il sait le sien et celui de tous les autres qui mourront après lui, pour lui, à cause de lui ou grâce à lui, ce qu'il faut en temps et en prières, en énergies vitales et en ténacité pour vaincre les assassins, briser la haine. Les meurtriers du GIA ou d'ailleurs n'ont aucune peine à égorger. Ils connaissent le geste antique des bergers de la Palestine, quand ils se rendent à Jérusalem pour faire sacrifier les bêtes. Dans la tendresse du mois de mai, ils passent la lame de leur couteau dans le cou des moines. Ça glisse comme une fleur, ça fait un grand sourire rouge au-dessous de leur visage, le père prieur a dû demander à mourir le dernier, comme la mère prieure des carmélites de

Compiègne à la Révolution dut subir jusqu'à la dernière de ses filles le spectacle de leur décapitation.

Dieu n'est pas absent de l'histoire. D'où viendrait la force des martyrs s'il ne la leur avait pas insufflée ? « C'est Jésus en vous qui vous donne le courage d'accepter, car toujours, pour entrer en mon Royaume, celui de l'invincible clarté, il faut passer par ce carrefour terrible, cette croisée des chemins et qu'enfin tout se dénoue. »

Les têtes des moines ont dû rouler sur la terre des maquis, on a dû les mettre dans un sac de toile et puis les jeter dans on ne sait quel ravin, données aux bêtes des bois ou bien peut-être brûlées pour qu'aucune trace de leur visage éveillé ne soit reconnaissable. Il n'y a pas de gloire du monde pour eux. Comme Jésus, comme Charles de Foucauld, ligoté devant son fortin et abattu tel un chien enragé, comme les petites carmélites de Compiègne, toutes dans la même charrette de l'infamie, trimbalées à travers les rues et huées par la racaille de l'époque, tous ces martyrs du monde assassinés parce que leurs bourreaux avaient la haine de Dieu en eux, qu'ils l'avaient renié et qu'ils voulaient diriger seuls le monde sans autre pouvoir que le leur, absolu et brutal. Et cependant pas la moindre haine chez les martyrs, comme Christian de Chergé, le père abbé de Tibhirine, qui, la veille même de son assassinat, le prévoyait et achevait son testament spirituel en s'adressant à son assassin pour lui dire : « Dans ce merci où tout est dit, désormais, ma vie, je vous inclus bien sûr amis d'hier et d'aujourd'hui et toi aussi, l'ami de la dernière minute, qui n'auras pas su ce que tu faisais. Oui, pour toi aussi, je le veux, ce merci, et cet "à-Dieu" envisagé de toi. Et qu'il nous soit donné de nous retrouver, larrons heureux, en paradis, s'il plaît à Dieu, notre Père à tous deux. »

Chapitre 22

Où Jésus reprend la route

Dieu a repris son fils en main. Il ne faut pas que Jésus soit tourmenté, impressionné par tant d'événements tragiques et flamboyants. Il faut lui redonner confiance dans sa mission, lui insuffler l'esprit d'avenir et de combat. « Tu es venu pour apporter le glaive, ne l'oublie pas. Et le glaive, c'est le désir de la vie, et l'espérance joyeuse au cœur de toi. »

Replié dans son domaine, Dieu supervise toute la création, quand il s'ennuie un peu, il admire le jeu constant, ébouriffant des planètes, les cerceaux de lumière qui tournent sur eux-mêmes et qui font un feu d'artifice tout le temps, mais il aime particulièrement cette planète Terre où il a envoyé son fils, ce petit coin de l'univers où ses habitants ont été conçus à son image et dont la turbulence ne cesse de l'inquiéter. Il commande à ses anges de réchauffer le cœur de Jésus, de lui donner tout l'élan nécessaire pour sa tâche. Les anges le veillent comme le font les mères. La nuit, dans la fraîcheur des terres de Galilée, ils le recouvrent de leurs manteaux de plumes si légères que nul ne saurait croire à leur présence. Douceur des légendes ! Il ne lui en faut pas davantage pourtant pour que les foules qui l'accompagnent se rallient à lui. Jésus n'ignore rien du sort fait aux prophètes et aux messies : crachats et malédictions, injures, lapidations et martyre. Mais il faudra bien prendre la route du sacrifice, puisque c'est à ce prix que s'obtient le Royaume. Plus il avance et plus il comprend que le Royaume justement se rapproche. Plus s'affirme la loi d'amour et plus il se devine à l'horizon. Les foules ne s'y trompent pas : elles suivent Jésus parce qu'elles espèrent, parce qu'il n'est pas possible d'en rester là, à ce royaume de ténèbres et de violences. Les Juifs et les Romains observent patiemment le cheminement de Jésus. Ils attendent la faille, le mot de trop. Pour l'heure, Jésus avance et, le soir, se retrouve dans sa solitude de nomade et d'errant. Il se nourrit de figues et de fruits secs, parce qu'il a faim non pas de cette faim d'humain mais d'idéal qui nourrit et emplit tout, et rassasie.

Il a gardé de ses premiers jours d'exil l'habitude de se retirer à l'abri de tous les regards. Là, il s'installe pour prier et parler avec son père. À ce moment précis de son histoire, il a choisi ses compagnons, il a percé leur cœur et il les connaît mieux que quiconque au monde : ils seront douze. Douze disciples. Certains sont très jeunes, à peine quinze ans, les plus vieux en ont vingt. Au matin de sa veille de prières, il rassemble ses disciples et parmi eux désigne ceux qui le suivront. « Vous serez avec moi, toujours, car jamais je ne mourrai. Je survivrai en vous, et je serai présent à tout moment de votre vie, parce que mon esprit revit et se ravivera en vous, comme l'eau des sources. Venez vers moi, Simon-Pierre, André, Jacques, Jean, Philippe, Barthélémy, Matthieu, Thomas, Jacques, Simon surnommé le Zélote, Thadée enfin, fils de Jacques, et Judas Iscariote. Vous serez mes frères en esprit, en infortune et en gloire. Car aujourd'hui, je vous le dis, commence la marche vers le Royaume acquis au poids de l'amour. Je vous le dis encore, croyez et vous aurez, soyez confiant et vous verrez le Royaume de mon père. »

Les disciples veulent arrêter le flot incessant des malades. Ils disent que Jésus va s'épuiser dans le don, perdre le fil d'énergie qui le relie à Dieu pendant ses grandes séances de guérison. Alors, ils l'entraînent à l'écart, lui donnent un peu à boire, l'installent sous un arbre. Mais sa force est infinie, et malgré sa fatigue, il leur dit à mi-voix des mots qu'ils recueillent comme des grâces, des pépites d'or qui vont changer le monde : « Croire, leur dit-il, c'est déjà guérir, c'est déjà combattre tous les germes mortels qui prospèrent en soi. Savez-vous à quel point la certitude de Dieu logée tout au fond de son cœur anéantit les forces du mal, redonne de l'esprit à ce qui ne peut être matière ? Savez-vous ce que signifie vraiment être en Dieu, s'en faire le dépositaire dans son propre corps et dans son propre esprit ? »

Désormais Jésus s'enhardit, ne cache plus ses intentions, il est le Sauveur, l'envoyé de Dieu, son fils tant aimé. Les prêtres et les Romains chargés de la sécurité du pays ont l'habitude de voir ces sortes de prophètes mendiants errer sur les chemins, délirer sur les places des villages. Ils laissent faire car ils savent que les foules ont besoin de ces êtres démesurés, mais jusqu'à un certain point. Jésus commence à dépasser les limites admises. Les rapports s'accumulent auprès des représentants de la loi. Bientôt il faudra réagir.

Lui ne s'en préoccupe pas. De toute manière il n'a aucun doute sur l'issue de sa mission. Elle finira sur la croix, dans le sang et la suffocation. Sa vie ne lui appartient plus, il avance, c'est tout. Dans la foule, Marie et ses cousins se sont glissés. Depuis des heures ils l'ont rejoint pour le mettre en garde, le réconforter, lui faire entendre raison. Seule Marie sait que tout ira à sa fin. Que cela est prévu de longue date, depuis le jour fatal où le vent de Dieu s'est faufilé en son corps pour l'ensemencer. Elle se révolte cependant, ne veut pas subir la loi terrible de Dieu qui a promis à son enfant le supplice et la mort.

« Pardon, dit-elle, pardon mon Dieu, de ne pouvoir dire oui comme en ce jour où ton archange est venu m'annoncer ta décision. Que cela soit, t'avais-je dit, imprudemment. Pouvais-je imaginer de te céder la chair de ma chair, de te rendre ce que tu m'avais donné, aussi facilement ? Pardon, Seigneur, de te trahir d'une certaine manière, car je veux garder Jésus vivant. Je veux qu'il revienne à Nazareth, qu'il assiste mes derniers jours, qu'il me donne des petits-enfants, qu'il continue la tâche de son père Joseph, qu'il oublie toute cette histoire, parce que Jésus, sais-tu, n'est pas un héros. C'est un homme jeune, fort et beau, fier et courageux. Ne me le prends pas. Rends-le moi, je t'en supplie. »

Mais nul n'a répondu à Marie. Alors elle a marché jusqu'à la foule qui se dessinait au loin, qui enflait de toutes parts, parce qu'on y venait des villages voisins. « C'est le Messie, le Messie, entend-elle en se coulant parmi les pèlerins, c'est lui qui nous délivrera du malheur. Il l'a promis. »

Marie se dirige vers ce qu'elle devine être un des disciples de Jésus.

« Va, mon fils, va dire à Jésus que sa mère est venu vers lui, qu'il lui faut rentrer à la maison, qu'on l'attend tous là-bas, que sa mère a peur pour lui, qu'il doit aussi avoir pitié d'elle. Qu'il ne poursuive pas sa route, elle est trop dangereuse, dis-lui qu'il en mourra, et que sa mère ne veut pas de cela. Qu'elle l'aime et qu'elle a peur, oui, surtout peur. »

Un des apôtres va vers Jésus et lui dit :

— Ta mère et tes frères se tiennent dehors et veulent te voir.

Jésus se retourne et aperçoit Marie. Un frisson le parcourt et toute la tendresse de son enfance remonte comme une lame. « Ô, ma mère, pourquoi as-tu fait cela ? Que viens-tu faire ici ? Il est trop tard et pourtant je voudrais tant moi aussi me retrouver dans la nuit de Nazareth. Comme autrefois, j'entends encore le bruit de ton rouet et tes pieds qui tapent régulièrement, telle une berceuse. Mais il me reste peu de temps, mère. Pardonne-moi. » Jésus dit ces paroles en lui-même, presque un aveu. Puis il se retourne vers l'apôtre et lui dit :

— « Va dire que ma mère et mes frères, ce sont ceux qui écoutent la parole de Dieu et la mettent en pratique [7]. »

Marie entend le message qui lui brise le cœur et le corps. Elle n'a plus qu'à accepter la longue marche vers la mort. Elle n'a plus de mots ni de larmes pour répondre à son désespoir, pour lui dire qu'elle le suivrait partout cependant, pour le relever quand il tombera, pour le protéger de loin, sur sa route hasardeuse.

— Je te redonnerai du courage, j'essuierai les larmes qui couleront sur tes joues, je laverai tes plaies, et mon cœur saignera comme le tien, parce que ton agonie sera forcément la mienne et ma détresse sera semblable à la tienne. Tu n'as rien voulu, Jésus, je le sais. C'est Dieu qui le veut, plus fort que tout, plus fort que nous.

Jésus est sûr de sa voie. Maintenant il n'y aura plus de fuite secrète, de retrait, d'échappatoire, de conflits intérieurs.

« Je suis à toi, mon père. Je suis ta proie. Vois, je quitte tout pour toi, je n'ai plus de mère ni de cousins que je reconnaisse. Tu m'as appris que tous les êtres vivants que tu as pu créer sont mes frères, qu'il faut tout abandonner pour bâtir ton Royaume. Me dépouiller de tout. Que c'est dans le dénuement que je m'enrichis, dans la pauvreté apparente des origines, qu'il y a tous les dons de la vie. »

Chapitre 23

Où Jésus révèle son enseignement

Des forces renouvelées saisissent Jésus. Poussé par son père, il n'a plus qu'à laisser se dérouler son plan. Dans la foule, chacun continue de se demander qui il est au juste, un prophète ou un messie, un imposteur ou un mage ? Un illuminé ou un délirant ? Mais la douceur de Jésus et la clarté de ses paraboles apaisent les inquiétudes, éloignent tous les doutes. Plus Jésus se détache de sa famille, plus il se sent appelé à porter les hommes, tous, pas seulement les pauvres mais les riches aussi qui, dans l'opulence de leurs demeures, sont à l'intérieur d'eux-mêmes pauvres de leur solitude, dignes d'être eux aussi aimés. Jésus sent en lui monter cette paternité universelle, qui est la marque de Dieu. Cette grâce coulée en lui qui se répand comme une onde, remplit tout. Sur sa route, s'étale un vaste plateau où la foule s'agglutine pour l'écouter parler. Il choisit un petit promontoire, une sorte de colline naturelle, pour se faire entendre de tous. Ils sont venus de partout, de Judée et de Jérusalem, du littoral de Tyr et de Sidon, tous avec leurs fardeaux de douleurs et de souffrances, leurs paralysies et leurs cécités, leurs détresses et surtout avec leur innocence. Car Jésus leur a déjà dit que rien ne s'accomplit sans cette naïveté du cœur, sans l'esprit de l'enfance sauvegardé. Sinon, ce n'est que dureté de l'âme, conscience de caillou, esprit de fiel.

— Laissez-vous envahir par la douceur, par l'amour, repoussez toutes formes de violence et d'agressivité, laissez de la place à Dieu.

Ils aiment entendre ces mots nouveaux, ces injonctions qui les relient à Dieu comme à un père.

— Vous n'êtes pas abandonnés, vous êtes, sans que vous ne le sachiez, toujours auprès de Dieu, dans sa béatitude.

Chacun veut toucher un peu de sa chemise, s'approcher de lui, sentir sur son front l'imposition de ses mains. À ce moment-là, Jésus accomplit pleinement le projet de Dieu :

— Tu seras semeur, mon fils, et ta parole ensemencera les foules, tu seras le soleil qui dore les grains de blé jetés en terre et ton enseignement sera comme une bénédiction.

Du haut de son promontoire, Jésus harangue les foules rassemblées autour de lui, il est devenu le guide et le maître vivant, celui qu'aucune force au monde ne pourra désormais empêcher de parler.

— Il faut, dit Dieu, que l'histoire ait ce rythme que rien n'arrête car rien n'est plus beau, plus grandiose, que l'activité secrète des germinations, la route obscure des conversions.

Pris dans son grand élan de messie, il prononce des paroles incroyables, jamais entendues, des paroles qui prennent à contre-courant toutes les idées reçues, tout l'ordre établi.

— « Heureux, vous les pauvres, car le Royaume de Dieu est à vous,

Heureux, vous qui avez faim maintenant, car vous serez rassasiés,

Heureux, vous qui vous pleurez maintenant, car vous rirez,

Heureux êtes-vous, si les hommes vous haïssent, s'ils vous frappent d'exclusion et s'ils insultent et proscrivent votre nom comme infâme, à cause du Fils de l'homme.

Réjouissez-vous ce jour-là et exultez, car alors votre récompense sera grande dans le ciel[8]. »

La foule reste muette, du même silence qui avait saisi les bergers de Bethléem quand ils avaient suivi les étoiles filantes qui les guidaient vers l'étable du Messie. Voilà que soudain Dieu s'incarnait et leur promettait, à eux, les pauvres, les abandonnés, les exclus, les laissés-pour-compte, toutes les richesses du vrai Royaume, car le Royaume, ils le comprenaient bien, n'était pas de ce monde. Et le monde ne pouvait pas s'arrêter à cette misère-là de la mort, à cette enveloppe charnelle, à cette dépouille ensevelie qui mettait fin à l'existence. Non, il y avait un sens à tout cela, ils le concevaient bien, tous ces hommes amassés là, pour écouter la parole de Jésus, forte et si puissante qu'elle parvenait jusqu'au plus éloigné, comme si la voix d'airain de Dieu s'était faufilée en lui. Et cette irradiance qui émanait de lui, le faisait presque immatériel dans la lumière, les nimbait d'une lueur étrangère, céleste.

Enhardi par la foule qu'il sent bienveillante, Jésus continue son message. Il ne se méfie pas des traîtres, des espions qu'Hérode a fait envoyer, il prononce des paroles de plus en plus dangereuses et menaçantes pour les pouvoirs politiques et religieux :

— « Malheur à vous, les riches : car vous avez votre consolation.

Malheur à vous qui êtes repus maintenant, car vous aurez faim !

Malheur à vous qui riez maintenant, car vous connaîtrez le deuil et les larmes !

Malheur à vous quand tout le monde dira du bien de vous[9] ! »

La foule applaudit, se sent reconnue.

— « Vous êtes le sel de la terre et la lumière du monde[10]. »

Jésus rassemble les siens, tous ceux qui se sentent touchés par sa parole. Il veut que cela soit toujours ainsi : une adhésion spontanée, évidente. Des retrouvailles.

Dieu se frotte les mains du plus loin de sa galaxie. S'accomplit enfin l'acte promis du début du monde, celui du lien retrouvé entre Dieu et ses créatures et qui avait été rompu.

— Oui, mon fils, tu as trouvé les mots les plus justes car c'est ainsi que j'avais voulu, jadis, que soient les hommes : sel de la terre, lumière du monde. Il y aura des ténèbres encore et encore et des tentatives d'obscurcissement, des actes effroyables et des guerres atroces qui décimeront mes pauvres enfants, mais qu'ils le sachent, en leur donnant mon fils, en suivant ses préceptes, ils seront tous sauvés, parce que touchés de la main de Dieu. Il en va seulement de cette filiation retrouvée, je vous le dis, quiconque coupe ce lien sera anéanti. Quiconque le rétablit et le respecte sera récompensé de ma paix.

Dans la paix justement de leur monastère, les petites sœurs des Béatitudes, partout essaimées dans le monde, vivent de cette douceur des paroles de Palestine. Elles répètent chaque jour que Dieu fait la litanie des Béatitudes prononcées par Jésus. Ses mots ont la force des évidences, ils s'installent en qui les profère et ramènent le monde à sa juste dimension. Au passage des saisons, à l'attention portée aux plus démunis, au regard du malade qui implore, à la douceur des villages, aux nuits de Noël qui sont nuits de naissance, nuits des enfants qui découvrent la splendeur du monde, nuits des apparitions.

Chapitre 24

Où Jésus accomplit des prodiges extraordinaires

L'invention de Dieu, c'est que Jésus ressemble à tous les hommes. Qu'il est un dieu vivant, mais qui ressemble à tous les hommes, les plus banals, les moins exceptionnels en apparence. Pas de surhumanité pour Jésus, il pleure et il éprouve lui aussi la solitude et le désespoir, le désarroi et l'abandon. Mais en même temps il est comme tous les dieux des épopées, toutes celles qui ont fait le monde, qui bravent les forces de l'univers, les lois de la gravité, défient les Goliaths et les géants des fables. Jésus pleure et souffre mais il sait remplir les outres et multiplier les pains à l'infini, il est trahi et se sent seul mais il guérit qui le veut de ses souffrances, il relève les infirmes et redonne à voir aux aveugles. Voilà la grande idée de Dieu, donner un dieu qui s'est fait homme et qui va gagner quand même contre la mort.

L'histoire de Jésus, c'est ce mouvement régulier entre prodiges et banalité, entre ordinaire et extraordinaire. Mais en étant homme comme tous les hommes, Jésus veut dire aussi que tous les hommes sont Dieu.

Cinq mille hommes suivent maintenant Jésus et ses apôtres. « Va, dit-il à chacun d'entre eux, que l'esprit de Dieu se pose sur toi et t'envahisse, qu'il t'inonde de sa clarté, qu'il te lave de tes impuretés et qu'il te délivre de tout mal. » Et à chaque fois, c'est une résurrection : « Je vous le dis, vous ressusciterez d'abord à la vie, si vous accueillez Dieu en vous, si vous restaurez le lien antique qu'il a conçu avec vous. Vous mourrez néanmoins comme la fleur inévitablement se fane un jour, mais dès lors que Dieu est en vous, vous reviendrez à la vie éternelle, vous serez auprès de Dieu, autrement, dans sa splendeur. » Les foules ne savent pas qui est exactement celui qui dit ces paroles inconnues : serait-ce Moïse auquel Dieu a redonné vie ou bien le prophète Élie ? Qui est ce Jésus doté de si surnaturels pouvoirs ? « Pour vous, dit-il à ses apôtres, qui suis-je vraiment ? » Pierre le premier répondit : « Le Christ de Dieu. » Et Jésus le pria instamment de ne le dire à personne.

Il veut aller près de la ville de Bethsaïde, dans un endroit isolé et désertique, car il sait que seul l'âpre désert refait les cœurs et sauve les corps. Le jeûne et la prière sont la voie de passage pour entrer dans la clarté de Dieu. Mais la foule le voit partir, le suit, et Jésus ne peut se refuser à elle. Il accueille ces milliers d'hommes, leur parle du Royaume, il les enchante avec ce lieu inconnu, invisible, « il est en vous et hors de vous, il est accessible aux fervents et inaccessible pour ceux qui doutent et se moquent. Il est la terre enfin promise par Dieu à toutes ses créatures, une terre de paix d'où sont bannis le mensonge et la haine, la jalousie et la violence. Où ne règne que l'amour, vaste, immense, qui accueille la nature entière, les aubes et les crépuscules, les bêtes et les plantes, les hommes, tous les hommes d'une égale tendresse ». Comme le jour a commencé à baisser, les apôtres demandent à Jésus de renvoyer la foule dans les villages avoisinants pour qu'elle aille se nourrir. « Donnez-lui vous-mêmes à manger », leur dit-il. Comme les apôtres restent perplexes, lui disant qu'ils n'ont que cinq pains et deux poissons, Jésus leur répond : « Faites-les s'étendre par groupe de cinquante. » Il prend alors les cinq pains et les deux poissons, les élève au ciel, les bénit, les rompt et les donne aux apôtres. La foule se nourrit à satiété et l'on ramasse même douze couffins de restes !

C'est presque la nuit. Les hommes lèvent le camp, émus, bouleversés, incrédules et éblouis par la grâce dont ils viennent d'être témoins. Par quel prodige sinon celui de Dieu Jésus a-t-il pu nourrir cinq mille hommes avec seulement cinq pains et deux poissons ? Il faut partir cependant, ne pas laisser trop de traces du phénomène, parce que la nouvelle croyance ne peut se satisfaire de miracles et de faits extraordinaires, « ce que je veux dire au monde est plus obscur et plus mystérieux encore, votre foi ne viendra pas des prodiges ni des guérisons miraculeuses, elle ne saurait se suffire de ces merveilles, votre foi naîtra d'une autre merveille, de la plus douce des révélations : Dieu qui est en vous ne vous abandonnera jamais, il sera un père pour vous comme il l'est pour moi, vous serez son fils, chacun personnellement, et vous vous parlerez, sans que vous ne vous voyiez, mais jamais il ne vous quittera car de ce jour l'ancienne alliance est rétablie. Il y aura des sursauts du mal mais le lien est indissoluble éternellement. »

Craignant que la foule ne le prenne pour en faire son roi, Jésus s'enfuit dans la montagne. Il échappe aussi à ses apôtres, réclame à son père un peu de repos et de silence. Ses disciples cependant prennent la mer et se dirigent vers Capharnaüm. Le vent grossit et fait enfler la voile, la mer se soulève et risque de faire chavirer l'embarcation. Soudain les apôtres voient une silhouette blanche s'avancer vers eux. Elle semble marcher sur les flots agités, nimbée d'une lumière éclatante. Ils sont tous effrayés, croient à des fantômes, à des esprits malins qui viennent les tourmenter : « C'est moi, n'ayez pas peur. » Pierre s'écrie : « Si c'est toi, Seigneur, fais-moi te rejoindre ! — Viens, dit Jésus, marche sur les flots. » Pierre s'avance, porté par sa foi, mais à peine a-t-il fait quelques pas qu'il s'enfonce dans l'eau, saisi d'un doute. « Incrédule, dit Jésus qui le rattrape par l'épaule, viens avec moi vers la barque. » Les autres apôtres veulent les hisser à bord mais aussitôt la barque rejoint la rive opposée, au lieu où ils ont prévu de se rendre.

Dieu, chaque jour de la route de Jésus, délivre un enseignement nouveau. « N'ayez pas peur, fait-il dire à Jésus, parce que la foi en Dieu défie les esclavages, fait tomber les murs, abat les montagnes, il n'y a pas de fatalité à votre misère et à votre solitude, n'ayez pas peur et ceux qui vous persécutent auront peur de votre audace et de votre foi, n'ayez pas peur et vous marcherez sur les flots car vous ignorez encore toute la force vive qui est en vous, tout le courant qui vous parcoure égal à celui qui anime les mers. »

Jésus se prête volontiers à la grande mise en scène de Dieu. Peu à peu il s'enhardit, trouve les mots pour assurer de sa filiation divine, ne craint plus de la proclamer. Les apôtres vivent dans sa réverbération, c'est sa lumière reçue chaque jour et chaque nuit passés avec lui qui leur est la plus impressionnante. Elle est tout intérieure, éclatante et cachée à la fois, profonde comme un foyer qui couve et ardente comme un incendie, étouffée et évidente. Quand il dort auprès d'eux, Jésus luit d'une lueur étrange, surnaturelle, qui veille. « C'est ainsi que mon père du ciel me veut, veilleur et lumière du monde, mais tous les hommes qu'il a créés sont voués au même destin de veiller ce monde qu'il leur a donné et de l'éclairer de l'esprit de Dieu, car sans cela, les hommes seront des loups entre eux et le monde ne sera plus que brasier mortel. »

Chapitre 25

Où chaque moment de la vie de Jésus
est une parabole

    Sous le Second Empire, à Saint-Sulpice, les grandes dynasties d'imagiers, de graveurs et d'estampeurs ont flairé le gros lot : mettre la vie de Jésus en images. L'inventivité n'est presque pas nécessaire tant Dieu y a déjà pourvu. Il ne reste plus qu'à forcer le trait des belles histoires qui se sont passées près de dix-neuf siècles auparavant. Les épisodes s'alignent sur les planches à graver, sur les bois, les plaques. Les imagiers rivalisent de détails et enrichissent l'œuvre des miniaturistes du Moyen Âge qui, dans leurs monastères, bâtirent pour les humbles et les enfants, mais aussi pour les rois, la légende dorée de Jésus. C'est avec des planches héliogravées, quelquefois rehaussées à la main, que l'école sulpicienne enjolive et exalte l'existence terrestre de Jésus. C'est à qui en fera davantage, fera surgir des images des bouquets de roses et de lis, des anges et Dieu logé dans ses nuages. Les scènes s'imposent comme des séquences obligées, alignées les unes à côté des autres, elles deviennent avant le XXe siècle des bandes dessinées, simplificatrices et stéréotypées, tirées à des milliers d'exemplaires pour les enfants du catéchisme et des écoles. Les images peuvent se détacher des planches et deviennent des bons points pour les élèves méritants, des intercalaires à glisser entre les pages des missels. Les séquences s'alignent sagement pour les Camille et les Paul, les enfants modèles que décrit avec grâce la comtesse de Ségur. Comme sur les chemins de croix qui recouvrent les murs des églises, les images racontent les faits et gestes de Jésus. Où est cependant la vie profonde et cachée de Jésus ? Que se passe-t-il entre les scènes théâtralisées ? Que fait-il entre Cana et l'épisode de Lazare ? Dieu ne se préoccupe pas de ces profondeurs-là. Ce qu'il veut, c'est donner son fils en exemple, rassembler un florilège d'images suffisamment puissantes et suggestives pour marquer les esprits. Mais Jésus, plus peut-être encore que tout homme, a ses abîmes et ses gouffres. Ses nuits et ses puits. Les apôtres ne veulent pas raconter sa vie, ce qui leur importe, c'est de propager l'enseignement de Jésus, ils suivent impérativement le plan de Dieu, simple et presque puéril.

Luc, Jean, Matthieu, Marc ne font aucun effort pour raconter les chutes inévitables de Jésus, ses découragements et ses angoisses atroces. Sur la route, ils ne veulent laisser aucune trace de cette misère intérieure, de ces liens perdus, retissés et de nouveau perdus, de ces secrets d'âme qu'il dut garder pour lui seul à ces moments intacts d'humanité. Il n'y en a que pour sa gloire en Dieu, ses miracles et ses prodiges. Mais si Jésus est aussi le Fils de l'homme, où est la trace inquiète de sa nature d'homme ? Il a murmuré pourtant dans la solitude des déserts et des taillis où il se réfugiait pour trouver un peu d'ombre des mots angoissés, il a souvent même dû regretter d'avoir pris la route, de s'être laissé à cette folie de la route, à ces marches implacables qui, chaque jour, l'ont amené au martyre. C'est qu'il fallait s'en convaincre de l'inévitable route, de l'obligé sacrifice. Rien ne pouvait donc contrer la force du destin.

Pas d'échappatoire à cette destinée, pas de trop longs regrets d'avoir accepté le sacrifice, seulement quelques craintes d'enfant, cette envie de reculer et de revenir au foyer maternel, de se lover dans les bras de Marie qui toujours l'a protégé et qu'il a surprise tant de fois à sangloter parce qu'elle savait la fin tragique de son enfant et qu'elle avait dit « oui » à l'ange, submergée par la splendeur de sa lumière qui l'avait nimbée à son tour et couronnée de sa gloire.

« Tu me souffles, mon père, qu'il ne faut avoir peur, dit-il à mi-voix. Que je sois le premier, digne de ton précepte, donne-moi le courage non seulement de le propager mais de le vivre moi-même, parce qu'à ce moment de mon chemin, j'ai peur d'avancer, les marches sur l'eau, les malades que je guéris. J'ai peur de ces prodiges, où veux-tu me conduire ? J'avance dans la vie pour annoncer ta présence partout dans l'univers, ta construction inouïe, irremplaçable, et je suis pris de panique devant cette solitude qui m'appelle sans me laisser de choix. Pardonne mes reculs et mes incertitudes. Fortifie mon ardeur à te défendre et à dispenser ton enseignement, j'en ai terriblement besoin, mon père, parce que je suis trop seul, un agneau parmi les loups. »

Les imagiers dessinent des scènes pathétiques pour les enfants sages, des nuées d'anges et de nuages où Dieu se repose, des crèches comme des maisons de poupées veillées par des ânes et des bœufs. Parfois, le petit Jésus, pendant sa période cachée, la nuit de Noël, s'élance en traîneau tiré par des anges dans les cieux pour aller porter la bonne nouvelle à tous les enfants du monde. Mais le sang et les larmes, les poitrines transpercées de glaives et le flanc éclaté par la hampe du centurion romain arrachent des plaintes et font naître la compassion. Dieu a toujours aimé les mises en scène stupéfiantes, les grands spectacles, auxquels ne résistent pas les producteurs d'Hollywood, parce qu'il sait qu'au fond de chacun des hommes qu'il a créés, il y a besoin de rêves et de sauveurs qui viendraient alléger le grand malheur d'être homme et la crainte de mourir, de ne pas savoir où l'on va, après. Alors Dieu fait tout son possible pour rassurer les angoissés, leur dire qu'avoir foi en lui c'est l'assurance que rien n'est perdu, qu'il y a des courses incroyables à accomplir encore dans l'univers, des balades inouïes dans la lueur azurée des astres. Tous les poètes savent cela parce qu'il y a en eux plus de dieu qui sommeille que chez les hommes ordinaires. Les poètes mais on pourrait dire aussi les musiciens, les enfants, les êtres sensibles qui ne sont pas lestés par l'argent et l'ambition et qui peuvent imaginer qu'ils ne sont pas seuls, qu'ils n'ont pas cette vanité extrême de se prétendre uniques de l'espèce. Ceux-là, les plus près de Dieu, ont déjà pris la route comme Jésus, ils marchent dans tous les déserts du monde, et sont convaincus durant leur marche de leur ignorance mais cette ignorance est un savoir exceptionnel qui est sûr que tout continue après, et que la résurrection promise par Jésus, c'est cette certitude que leur passage n'aura pas été vain, qu'il continuera, ce passage, à essaimer dans l'univers, à redonner du sel à la terre qui en manquait, à l'éclairer un peu plus.

Chapitre 26

Où Jésus se repose au puits de Jacob

La route est pénible et la chaleur sans répit. Quelle que soit l'heure, elle semble toujours à l'aplomb de midi quand toute vie s'arrête et que seuls les pierres et le sable vibrent et brûlent. Les disciples marchent derrière Jésus, assez loin pour le laisser méditer, et se chargent des provisions quand ils traversent des villages. Même harassés, ils n'osent interrompre sa marche. Il va, dépasse la ville de Sychar, ses compagnons font halte. Comment continuer plus avant et bien que le soleil décroisse ? Il s'arrête à un puits, des figuiers y prospèrent, jettent sur la place leurs larges feuilles d'ombre sous lesquelles il s'abrite. Une femme survient. « Donne-moi à boire », lui dit-il. « Tu es juif, et tu me demandes à boire, à moi, une Samaritaine ?

— Si tu savais le don de Dieu et « si tu savais qui est celui qui te dit : Donne-moi à boire, c'est toi qui l'en aurais prié, et il t'aurait donné de l'eau vive[11] ».

— Mais tu n'as rien pour puiser. Où donc prendrais-tu l'eau vive ?

— "Quiconque boit de cette eau aura soif à nouveau. Mais qui boira l'eau que je lui donnerai n'aura plus jamais soif. Elle deviendra en lui la source d'eau jaillissante en vie éternelle[12]." »

Dieu de son estrade suit la scène avec attention. Il lance son fils dans la bataille. Il faut qu'il avance maintenant, poitrine nue, à visage découvert, il est la lumière du monde, et il doit le faire savoir. Une voix intérieure pousse Jésus à parler. Plus de prudence, plus de détour. « L'eau vive, c'est celle qui, invisible et étincelante, étanchera ta soif. Elle a sa source dans les plus purs espaces de l'univers, elle est fluide et toujours fraîche, elle a la brillance des étoiles quand elle s'écoule depuis les torrents éternels, elle se répand en toi comme une onde, c'est presque impitoyable de douceur, elle s'écoule et tu es sauvée.

— Mais comment l'acquérir, Seigneur ? Qui peut me la donner ? J'ai soif de cette eau depuis toujours, je suis dans l'errance, dans le chaos du monde, je voudrais boire à ce puits introuvable, à ce mirage. Ne me trompe pas, Seigneur, ne m'illusionne pas, car je sais au fond de moi que l'eau dont tu parles existe, et qu'elle lave et rend la vie éternelle.

— Tu as en toi, dit Jésus, de quoi accueillir l'eau vive puisque tu crois, même confusément, à un Royaume plus vaste et plus juste qui ne fait pas de ses créatures des êtres mortels, mais régénérés par des forces venues de Dieu. Sois heureuse car est venu le temps où les sincères et les aimants adoreront Dieu en esprit et en vérité.

— Mais l'eau, Seigneur, l'eau ?

— Elle est déjà en toi, elle ne te quittera plus. Elle est le lien qui rassemble et réunifie toutes choses et les parties de ton corps retrouveront plus tard dans l'éternité, grâce à elle, leur intégrité et leur perfection. L'eau n'est pas seulement liquide et fluide, semblable à celle que viennent tirer les femmes en s'appuyant à la margelle de ton puits. Elle est esprit de Dieu qui fond sur toi, part de Dieu en toi, elle apaise ta souffrance puisqu'elle te réunit. L'eau vive guérit, elle vient des grands glaciers de l'univers, elle crépite comme l'or dans le creuset des alchimistes, elle apaise et elle réanime ce qu'on croyait voué à la mort. »

Dans les terres en friche près du Gave, à Lourdes, Bernadette ramasse du bois mort. C'est presque la nuit encore, des ombres et des brouillards flottent partout, les autres enfants lui disent de ne pas s'aventurer davantage, que c'est dangereux, que, de toute façon, le bois là-bas ne peut pas flamber parce qu'il est trop humide, à cause des eaux du Gave qui souvent débordent, mais elle ne sait pas pourquoi, elle y va quand même, attirée. « On rentre, Bernadette, reviens, reviens », mais elle n'entend déjà plus, le jour se lève, indistinct encore. Au fond, c'est la grotte, elle n'y est jamais allée, au-dessus de la roche, il y a des coulées de mousse et de lierre sauvage qui pendent, et toujours ce bruit énorme, roulant, de l'eau qui descend des montagnes, emportant dans son débit infernal des milliers de galets. Et puis soudain l'incroyable, l'apparition, une forme blanche, incandescente de lumière, une forme irréelle, féerique, qui lui parle, s'adresse à elle, l'invite à la rejoindre et qui lui dit des mots qu'elle ne comprend pas d'abord, mais si doux, si tendres qu'elle en est envahie. Elle est apparue dans un grand vent, un vent annonciateur, le même que celui que n'avaient pu identifier Abraham et Moïse, un vent léger, qui soulève à peine les peupliers. Bernadette n'entend plus les appels de ses compagnons. Elle est passée de l'autre côté du miroir. Au creux du buisson de ronces et d'églantiers sauvages, la silhouette fait signe d'avancer. Elle ressemblerait bien à une femme mais la lumière qui la nimbe efface les contours, la rend presque floue. C'est une lueur qui n'a pas de nom et qui accueille, qui attire et appelle.

Elle revient à la Grotte à plusieurs reprises, elle passe le morceau de terre entre le Gave et les replis de la montagne, elle y revient irrésistiblement, et la forme lumineuse, l'« *Aquero* », surgit du même buisson. Elle lui demande d'aller fouiller la terre, là, un peu plus loin et il en surgira de l'eau vive. Alors Bernadette y va, elle sait que sa famille s'inquiète de sa folie, de sa santé, elle tousse toujours et, malgré les recommandations de sa mère, elle se déchausse, trempe ses pieds dans la terre humide, marécageuse, il fait froid dehors, c'est le mois de février, elle a croisé son fichu sur sa poitrine et elle est allée là où la Dame lui a dit d'aller, entre des débris d'os et de bois séchés. La rumeur de l'apparition a déjà traversé toute la petite ville de Lourdes. Des gens, des curieux, des convaincus talonnent Bernadette, ne la laissent plus tranquille. Ils se mettent à distance de la Grotte, de l'autre côté du Gave, et la suivent du regard. Ne veulent rien rater de la scène. Elle, elle avance sur le terrain vague, elle va à l'endroit indiqué. Elle gratte de ses deux mains la terre encore sèche, elle remue des feuilles mortes et des détritus abandonnés, et, miracle, de l'eau sourd de la terre. Alors, elle redouble ses efforts, gratte à pleines mains, de ses mains de paysanne, fortes, rougeaudes, mal soignées et l'eau surgit enfin. La source vive jaillit, Bernadette pleure de joie, elle veut boire à même la terre, elle boit, elle boit, et son visage est plein de boue, de terre mouillée, elle se retourne, elle offre son visage maculé à tous ceux qui la regardent, et l'espionnent. Certains ont vu le miracle, ils s'agenouillent, se mettent à prier. Des cantiques montent de partout, et l'eau, l'eau miraculeuse continue de couler, de faire maintenant un vrai petit ruisseau, fluide, vivace.

« Eau de Jésus, eau de Marie, eau vive : qui croit en moi la boira et sera guéri. » Les mots de Jésus au puits de Jacob résonnent à Lourdes dix-neuf siècles plus tard.

« Viens vers moi, femme de Samarie, l'eau vive coule désormais en toi, ta prière naîtra spontanément de toi, tu n'auras besoin d'aucune autre parole ni de celles qu'on a voulu t'inculquer, parce que tu as accueilli l'esprit de Dieu en toi. L'eau vive t'épargnera les mauvais regards et les mauvaises pensées, elle te lavera et te revivifiera car l'eau vive est joyeuse. »

Chapitre 27

Où Jésus se proclame le pain de vie

On le rejoint, un jour, à Capharnaüm, c'est une foule inlassable qui le cherche et le traque. On monte dans les barques, on part à sa recherche, on le trouve dans la synagogue, en train de prêcher.

— Rabbi, que faut-il faire pour travailler aux œuvres de Dieu ? lui demandent des hommes.

— L'œuvre de Dieu, c'est de croire, leur répond-il, croire en celui qu'il a envoyé.

— Mais quel signe donnes-tu, rabbi, pour que l'on te croie ? Feras-tu comme Dieu fit pour nos pères qui ont mangé la manne au désert selon les écrits des prophètes : « Il leur a donné du pain venu du ciel » ?

Un moment de silence s'établit où Jésus sait que ce qu'il va proférer va induire la nouvelle route, entamer la voie de douleurs.

— En vérité, ce n'est pas Moïse qui vous a donné le pain du ciel, c'est mon père qui vous le donne. Le vrai. Car le pain du ciel, c'est celui qui descend de la maison du Père et donne la vie au monde.

— Donne-le nous alors, Seigneur, car nous avons faim de ce pain.

Le visage de Jésus se charge d'une force intérieure, son regard s'assombrit comme s'il voyait devant lui des images funèbres, des scènes de douleurs.

— « Je suis le pain de vie. Qui vient à moi n'aura jamais faim, qui croit en moi n'aura jamais soif[13]. »

Puis lentement, pesant ses mots, sa parole, il dit dans le recueillement ces paroles insensées qu'aucun prêtre ne peut imaginer, paroles blasphématoires à leurs yeux, paroles d'un fou :

— « Vous me voyez et vous ne croyez pas. Tout ce que me donne le Père viendra à moi, et celui qui vient à moi, je ne le jetterai pas dehors car je suis descendu du ciel pour faire non pas ma volonté, mais la volonté de celui qui m'a envoyé. Or la volonté de celui qui m'a envoyé est que je ne perde rien de ce qu'il a donné, mais que je le ressuscite au dernier jour[14]. »

Un frisson de stupeur parcourt la synagogue. Comment cet homme, ce Jésus fils de Joseph, ce Nazaréen, peut-il descendre du ciel ? Quel est ce prophète de théâtre ? Cet histrion ?

Mais Jésus, sans faire attention aux murmures, continue sa prophétie :

— « Nul ne peut venir à moi si le Père qui m'a envoyé ne l'attire. Et moi, je le ressusciterai jusqu'au dernier jour[15]. » « Je suis le pain de vie. Vos pères ont mangé la manne du désert et sont morts. Ce pain dont je parle est celui qui descend du ciel pour qu'on le mange et qu'on ne meure pas. Je suis le pain vivant, descendu du ciel. Qui mangera ce pain vivra à jamais. Et le pain que je donnerai, c'est ma chair pour la vie du monde[16]. »

— Mais comment peux-tu oser dire une telle chose ? Pour qui te prends-tu, prophète errant et va-nu-pieds ? Qui t'autorise à bafouer la parole de Dieu ?

— « En vérité, en vérité, je vous le dis, si vous ne mangez la chair du Fils de l'homme, et ne buvez son sang, vous n'aurez pas la vie en vous. Qui mange ma chair et boit mon sang aura la vie éternelle, et je le ressusciterai au dernier jour. Car ma chair est vraiment une nourriture et mon sang vraiment une boisson. Qui mange ma chair et boit mon sang demeure en moi et moi en lui[17]. »

Les paroles de Jésus font scandale dans le lieu saint. Les plus lettrés objectent, dénoncent sa hardiesse, les disciples eux-mêmes sont stupéfaits : « Ce langage-là est trop fort, disent-ils, comment l'accepter ? »

Alors Jésus qui voit en tous les cœurs, sonde tous les esprits, leur dit :

« C'est l'esprit qui vivifie, la chair ne sert de rien. Les paroles que je vous ai dites sont esprit, et elles sont vie. »

Dieu, de sa demeure lointaine, au plus loin de toutes les galaxies, applaudit : voilà, son fils a prononcé enfin les mots définitifs, l'objet même de sa mission. Jésus éprouve en lui le sentiment profond, amer et heureux, de l'accomplissement, mesure les conséquences de l'aveu inévitable.

« Par ces mots, je me suis révélé à vous. C'était par cette seule parole que je pouvais accomplir les Écritures. Tel est le sens réel de l'apparition. Il est un instant, nécessaire, obligé, où doit apparaître la vérité, où elle doit tomber plus vivement que le jour, fracasser les consciences, éclairer le chemin. Voilà qui est fait. Plus rien désormais ne sera comme avant. Plus personne ne me jugera autrement que comme un fou ou le Fils de l'homme que Dieu a envoyé pour prêcher sa parole. Je vous ai fait l'aveu de l'éternité et de la résurrection, car celui qui m'aura accueilli en lui sera promis à la résurrection. Non pas seulement celle où vous apparaîtrez dans votre corps glorieux de lumière auprès de mon Père, mais la résurrection déjà là, sur cette terre, dans la transformation qui s'empare de vous dès que vous entrez en moi et que j'entre en vous. Car la résurrection, c'est aussi ce mouvement intérieur qui s'accomplit en vous, dès que vous croirez en mon Père, c'est cette lumière soudain révélée qui vous fera voir le monde autrement. C'est une promesse, cette lumière qui chasse de son ardeur toutes les nuits. »

L'incroyable aveu bouleverse les disciples, les étreint et les presse de répondre à Jésus. Certains de ceux qui le suivent depuis longtemps, anonymes et las de leur condition, émerveillés par la fougue de Jésus et ses miracles, se retirent et cessent de l'accompagner. « Vous n'avez pas entendu la parole de Dieu qui demande de ne pas avoir peur. Vous êtes encore des hommes de peu de foi, Satan est encore en vous qui vous tient et vous tente. Partez, mais sachez que votre renoncement ne vous ferme pas la porte de mon Père. Au contraire, vous en êtes peut-être les plus aimés puisque les plus fragiles, ceux qu'il veillera le plus puisque les plus vulnérables au mal. Quant à vous, mes fidèles, voulez-vous partir avec moi ? La route est encore longue et s'assombrit. Vous serez persécutés à cause de moi, vous serez bafoués et trahis, mais c'est à ce prix-là que vous serez les premiers dans le Royaume de mon Père. »

Jésus se retire dans la campagne. Ses disciples le suivent. Il ne dort guère, comme si l'ombre de Dieu le maintenait dans cette ardeur intense, dans ce feu qui le brûle et l'attise. Il veille et il voit des lampes qui courent dans une vallée et montent vers son refuge, au pied des oliviers, il devine au pas des mercenaires qui montent vers lui qu'il a été trahi. Il ne doute pas qu'un des siens l'ait donné. Il sait seulement qu'il ne peut échapper à sa mission. Il a, logée au fond de lui, cette espérance de Dieu, cette force de l'esprit qui, seule, lui donnera de s'élever à l'heure voulue, vers son

Père. Parce que cette certitude-là allège tant le corps qu'elle l'élève vers Dieu.

Péguy, pelotonné comme un enfant dans la nef de Chartres, a la même impression de se noyer dans le grand vaisseau de pierre, éclairé de sa lumière bleue, comme une trace prochaine du Royaume. Il prie sans prier, sans formuler aucune parole, le silence est parole et prière. Lentement, il sent s'alléger son corps, jusqu'à n'être plus rien, jusqu'à ne plus le sentir, expérience mystique extrême, comme dépossédé de ses membres, de ses articulations, plus rien que cette prière qui monte et lui permet de mieux comprendre ce qu'est l'ascension, cette montée de l'esprit en Dieu. Il n'est plus que ce silence, ramassé, concentré, plus rien, dit-il, qu'un lit de feuilles que le souffle de Dieu emporte vers lui. Comme pour les Douze, il entend la demande de Jésus : « Voulez-vous partir, vous aussi ? », et Péguy répond : « Oui, Seigneur, je ne suis plus rien que ce souffle qui te rejoint, plus rien qui est plus que tout, et qui va vers toi. Conduis-moi sur ta route, éclaire-moi, trace une voie éclairée où mon esprit se dirigera, fais que ma prière te rejoigne, qu'au-delà de la profonde houle, au-delà de l'océan des blés, je voie ton regard. »

Chapitre 28

Où Jésus guérit inlassablement

Comme Péguy, Jésus voudrait lui aussi que le rappelle son père, que cesse cette mission à laquelle il l'a voué. Mais rien ne peut s'arrêter, la foule croît au fil des jours, refuse de partir, ne cède pas aux injonctions des disciples qui, quelquefois, prennent peur devant tant de bruit, de rumeurs et d'échauffourées. Elle présente à Jésus toujours plus de malades, d'infirmes, on se piétine pour accéder jusqu'à lui, ce cercle de silence et de lumière qu'il trace autour de lui, comme une auréole.

Les Douze craignent les représailles de tous ceux qui n'ont pas intérêt à ce que Jésus gagne la foule à sa cause, ils voudraient que tout se passe secrètement, ils recommandent pour cela de taire les miracles. Jésus affirme : « C'est une affaire de cœur, qui seuls vous concerne, une histoire entre Dieu et vous », mais chacun veut proclamer sa guérison, remercier Jésus en louant ses dons. Peu à peu sa réputation de thaumaturge, de mage, enfle. Elle se fait pressante, dérangeante, il est exhibé comme un objet de foire, une curiosité, un prophète aux mille et un tours dans son sac. « Mais la mission est loin d'être achevée, se dit-il, il y a encore des jours et des jours de douleur : comment laisser cette foule ignorante et fermée à l'amour de Dieu ? »

« Va, mon Fils, ne te décourage pas, lui murmure Dieu, je t'ai voulu Fils de l'homme pour que tu endures dans sa plénitude la condition de tous les hommes, tu connais l'absence et le lien défait, la douleur des séparations, tu sais ce qu'endurent les hommes depuis leur trahison originelle, les mille morts d'Ève et d'Adam que j'ai chassés du Jardin idéal. Mais tu vas connaître aussi la rédemption, je te sauverai de cette douleur, tu y échapperas pour me retrouver. »

Alors Jésus reprend courage, réinsufflé par Dieu, redonné à son esprit. S'en retournant du pays de Tyr, en plein territoire grec de la Décapole, il voit venir vers lui une de ces habituelles nuées d'errants et de mendiants. Toujours la même horde d'éclopés et de miséreux, d'aveugles et de fous qui veulent être guéris. Jésus n'est pas dupe : veulent-ils seulement être guéris ou entrer, grâce à cette guérison, dans l'amour de Dieu, revenir à lui ?

Les Douze le protègent de cette nuée disparate et gémissante. Mais Jésus veut aller jusqu'au bout de sa mission. Il écarte ses disciples, écoute les malheureux. On lui amène un sourd-bègue. Jésus ne lui impose pas les mains comme à son habitude, il lui met ses doigts dans l'oreille et prend de sa salive dans une main et lui touche la langue. Il lève les yeux au ciel et proclame en gémissant « *Ephphatha* !, Ouvre-toi [18]. » Aussitôt le malade entend la rumeur émerveillée de la foule, il ouvre sa bouche, émet quelques sons, prononce un mot puis un autre, il parle enfin, se jette aux genoux de Jésus qui lui recommande de n'en rien dire. Mais le miraculé n'écoute plus Jésus, il s'en va en proclamant sa grandeur, en le bénissant : « Il m'a guéri, clame-t-il, il m'a rendu la parole et l'ouïe, en vérité, je vous le dis, il est vraiment le Messie envoyé par Dieu. Il a bien fait toutes choses. Il fait entendre les sourds et parler les muets. »

Après les miracles, Jésus est soudain accablé d'une détresse immense, d'une solitude extrême. « Voilà cette foule qui a obtenu ce qu'elle réclamait et je suis maintenant seul après qu'elle m'a assiégé. Comprendra-t-elle enfin la leçon du miracle ? "Ouvre-toi" ai-je dit au malade. Oui, que l'on s'ouvre, que se dilate l'esprit en soi pour laisser entrer la lumière, que s'écartent les voiles de ténèbres qui obscurcissent la vue, éteignent les yeux, bourrent d'étoupe les oreilles ! »

Les disciples ont entendu les paroles qu'il a prononcées. Les paroles et le gémissement. Toujours l'obscur présage de Jérusalem, l'inévitable croisement. À cet instant, Jésus a tout vu, tout assumé. Jusqu'au gémissement sur sa croix à peine perceptible par les gardes, seulement de Marie, venue le rejoindre, confondre son gémissement au sien, « parce que tu crois, toi, ma mère, à la communion des souffrances et des peines, toi tu sais l'indicible secret de la compassion, ce qu'il faut d'amour, de don de soi pour entendre la douleur de l'autre ». Jésus voit s'éloigner lentement la foule, elle se fond dans la nuit, chaque homme de cette foule repart avec, logée en lui, l'annonce d'un bouleversement, une sorte d'émerveillement dans le cœur qui éclaire leur nuit de misère et de chagrin, c'est une parcelle de sa lumière à lui, Jésus, qu'il lui a donnée, il ne s'en sent pas dépossédé parce qu'il sait que le rayonnement qui est en lui est toujours renouvelé. Il sait que ces morceaux de lumière vont peut-être éclairer d'autres foyers, atteindre d'autres hommes, faire ce travail d'alliance pour quoi il est venu. Mais ce don constant n'est pas toujours serein et joyeux, il est aussi assombri d'une immense fatigue qui ressemble à la douleur d'une étreinte.

Chapitre 29

Où Jésus annonce sa Passion

Ce soir-là, Jésus réunit les Douze pour le repas. Il a l'habitude de se nourrir de peu de choses, de figues, de dattes, de caillé, de pain, de fèves, jamais de mouton noir ni d'autre viande. Depuis quelques jours, un sombre pressentiment l'occupe. Parmi ses compagnons, il y a Judas au regard sombre et hostile. Il sait qu'il sera celui qui le trahira. « Qu'y pourrais-je ? J'ai déjà donné ma vie, je serai livré aux Juifs comme l'agneau aux pattes ligoté qui a fini de braire parce qu'il sait qu'il va à l'abattoir et que rien ne pourra le sauver. » Judas observe, épie, s'irrite contre Jésus quand il arbore l'arrogance du glaive. « Mais qui est-il au fond, ce Nazaréen, qui se dit la lumière du monde, qui nous sermonne et nous déclare impropres au Royaume de Dieu si nous ne le suivons pas aveuglément ? »

Jésus a surpris les regards biaisés et les rancunes contenues dures comme des cailloux. « Celui-là me livrera à la mort, nul doute à cela, il conduira les soldats vers moi, il recevra en échange de sa forfaiture quelques pièces et son acte même le persécutera. »

Il rassemble cependant tous les siens, même Judas. Il leur demande de se réunir autour de lui. Devant eux, un feu allumé les éclaire de manière intermittente. Les visages se dessinent en clair-obscur, c'est le regard de braise de Jésus qui attire tous les disciples.

— Il est temps de vous indiquer le chemin que nous allons emprunter. Nous ne pouvons en rester là, à ces routes de Galilée, il faut annoncer plus loin la nouvelle, aller jusqu'à Jérusalem. Car c'est là que tout se jouera, le Fils de l'homme doit souffrir beaucoup, être rejeté par les anciens, les grands prêtres et les scribes, être mis à mort et le troisième jour ressusciter.

— Mais que veulent dire, Seigneur, ces paroles ? Nous t'avons suivi parce que tu es la vie, nous ne voulons pas t'accompagner au sacrifice ni à la mort.

— Je dois être livré aux mains des hommes. Ne craignez rien. C'est écrit.

Les disciples restent muets de stupeur. Ils n'osent insister pour comprendre.

— Il y a des choses que vous ne pouvez pas encore comprendre ni mesurer. Il y a des douleurs que vous ne pouvez soupçonner. Il vous faudra beaucoup de force et de courage pour me suivre.

— Où que tu ailles, Seigneur, je te suivrai, dit Pierre.

— Imprudent. Les renards ont des tanières et les oiseaux du ciel ont des nids. Le Fils de l'homme, lui, n'a pas où reposer sa tête. Es-tu prêt encore à me suivre ?

— Je te suivrai, Seigneur, mais permets-moi d'abord de prendre congé des miens.

— Quiconque a mis la main à la charrue et regarde en arrière est impropre au Royaume de Dieu.

Le feu lentement se consume. Il y a des braises qui rougeoient, font un foyer ardent, comme un cœur qui se dilate.

— Vous n'imaginez pas encore l'issue de la route ni ce qui vous est demandé. Vous devrez bientôt partir, seuls, sur les routes, sans moi, car je ne serai plus auprès de vous, je serai en vous, je vous suivrai, je vous veillerai, je serai en esprit autour de vous quand, le soir, vous mangerez vos maigres vivres, vous serez des moissonneurs qui devrez tout faire pour que la moisson soit abondante, vous serez des agneaux en apparence livrés à vous-mêmes, des agneaux parmi les loups, on vous persécutera à votre tour comme on m'aura persécuté, vous n'aurez rien pour vous défendre, ni armes ni bâton pour chasser les méchants qui vous harcèleront, vous n'aurez pas de bourse, pas de besace, pas de chaussures. Vous connaîtrez le désespoir et la solitude, l'ennui et la vacuité, vous vous demanderez tôt ou tard pourquoi vous faites tout cela, personne ne pourra vous répondre, mais vous sentirez lentement en vous quelque chose de doux et de chaud qui vous réconfortera, vous puiserez dans la prière et la louange toutes les forces pour survivre, et vous saurez alors que le Royaume de Dieu est tout proche. Il n'y aura pas du tout de magie, pas de ruses illusoires pour vous le faire apparaître, il n'y aura que l'aridité de la route, on vous jettera à la mer dans des barques en vous disant « à la grâce de votre Dieu » et vous partirez, seuls comme des naufragés. Mais je veillerai sur votre périple, je ferai souffler le vent de Dieu qui gonflera vos voiles vers des rivages bienfaisants, vous serez les vendangeurs de Dieu, où que vous serez, vous le proclamerez. Quant à moi, je sais que l'issue est proche.

— Pourquoi être parti, Seigneur, avoir quitté Nazareth et la douceur de votre famille ? réplique Pierre.

— « Passe derrière moi, Satan, tu me fais obstacle ! Car tes pensées ne sont pas celles de Dieu, mais celles des hommes [19]. »

Les disciples sont effrayés de la réaction de Jésus. Pierre se tait, Judas se lève, comme pour exprimer son mécontentement, il s'enfonce dans la nuit, rumine sa colère. Un silence profond s'abat sur le petit groupe.

— Comprenez bien cela, Dieu vous accueille en plénitude. Vous aussi devez vous rendre à lui, c'est dans cet échange absolu d'amour que vous acquerrez votre nouvelle liberté. Non pas celle des cités atroces où se tissent le malheur et la haine, l'envie et le désir insatiable, mais cette liberté donnée par Dieu qui apaise le regard, efface les jugements, se penche vers le malheureux. Alors vous sentirez en vous l'onction de Dieu qui apaise tout comme un baume. Et vous serez au plus juste, au plus vrai de vous-mêmes.

Chapitre 30

Où Jésus croise la femme pécheresse

Il se lève tôt pour reprendre sa route. Chaque jour, elle le mène plus près de Jérusalem, il est attiré par elle, inéluctablement il va vers elle. Il chemine à travers villes et villages, parcourt de longues étendues désertes, se désaltère à un puits, fait une pause, s'adosse à la margelle, croise des enfants qui jouent avec des ânes, sourit doucement à leurs cris insouciants, et puis repart. « La foi, dit-il à ceux qui le suivent, ouvre le cœur aux autres et renvoie sur soi des ondes d'amour, fait circuler comme une source d'eau vive toutes les bonnes énergies vitales. Car Dieu habite votre corps qui en est le tabernacle sacré. C'est pourquoi vous ne devez jamais le bafouer ni le trahir car vous êtes de Dieu, pleinement. »

Quelquefois des hommes se moquent de ce prophète qui arpente leurs terres et qui traîne à sa suite des loqueteux et des errants, et même des femmes. Une d'entre elles le suit partout, elle se souvient de ce jour où elle avait pénétré dans la maison d'un Pharisien qui avait invité Jésus à sa table. Elle était entrée, elle, la pécheresse, la courtisane, qui se donnait à tous les voyageurs, à tous les nomades contre de l'argent. Épuisée de sa vie, elle avait reconnu en Jésus le

Messie. Tout en pleurs, elle avait apporté un vase de parfum à ses pieds, et s'était mise à lui arroser les pieds de ses larmes. Puis les avait essuyés avec sa longue chevelure, les avait couverts de baisers et oints de parfum. Toute l'assistance en avait été interloquée, et le maître de maison avait aussitôt appelé ses serviteurs pour la chasser de la table. Mais Jésus l'avait arrêté :

— Tu vois cette femme ? lui dit-il. Je suis entré chez toi et tu ne m'as pas versé d'eau sur les pieds, elle au contraire m'a arrosé les pieds de ses larmes et les a essuyés avec ses cheveux. Tu ne m'as pas donné de baiser, elle, au contraire, n'a cessé de me couvrir les pieds de baisers. Tu n'as pas répandu d'huile sur ma tête, elle, au contraire, a répandu du parfum sur mes pieds. « C'est pourquoi, je te le dis, ses péchés, ses nombreux péchés lui seront remis, puisqu'elle a montré beaucoup d'amour [20]. »

Puis, se retournant vers la femme, il ajoute :
— Va, « ta foi t'a sauvée, va en paix [21] ».

Depuis ce jour, la pécheresse le suit, elle dit que Jésus laisse derrière lui un sillage de paix et de douceur, qui la sauve des violences d'autrefois. Tandis qu'elle marche, elle se souvient encore, de son attente d'une bonne nouvelle, enfin quelqu'un ou quelque chose qui vienne rompre le cercle infernal de sa vie sous la tente, disponible aux visiteurs, abandonnée à la luxure. Tous n'étaient pas mauvais, venant chez elle avec leurs poids de misères et de douleurs, des pauvres à leur manière, des abandonnés de l'amour, « même ceux, disait-elle, qui arrivaient en conquérants et qui, dans mes bras, se blottissaient soudain comme des enfants. Ils savaient que sous cette tente, ouverte aux grands vents du sable, il y avait de quoi guérir un peu de sa solitude, de sa souffrance. Il y avait les riches commerçants, les miséreux, les artistes, les pêcheurs, les artisans de toutes sortes qui trouvaient refuge sous la toile ouverte aux quatre vents. Et puis il y eut toi, Seigneur, que j'étais venue voir comme on regarde une curiosité, tiens, m'étais-je dit, voilà celui qui se prend pour le Messie, il est beau, il est grand, il a un visage d'amour incroyable, n'aime-t-il pas les femmes pour suivre la route avec douze compagnons ? Et j'avais deviné tant d'amour en toi, tant de douceur que tu m'avais conquise. Tu parlais de choses incroyables, de moissons et de pêches miraculeuses, de sources d'eau vive, de Royaume qui n'était pas de ce monde et qui, pourtant, était accessible, tu étais la nostalgie, et je te rejoignais dans ta quête parce que moi aussi, j'ai toujours été dans l'attente, dans la douleur de ne pas me sentir accomplie. Quelquefois oui, dans les bras de mes visiteurs, je m'approchais de la plénitude du monde, entre leurs bras, j'accédais à quelque chose d'absolu, et je me disais, c'est peut-être cela, cette paix que je recherche, sans creux ni vide, sans rien qui manque, comme un vase épouse l'eau qu'on y verse. Et toi, Seigneur Jésus, tu m'as fait entendre la musique de ton Royaume, on va tous les deux vers la même demeure. J'étais entravée et tu m'as libérée, j'étais dépravée et tu m'as rendue miséricordieuse. »

Jésus connaît le malheur des pécheresses, il sait que leur vie c'est d'attendre. Et attendre est encore une étape de la quête. C'est la halte de la route. Il accueille au grand dépit des disciples la femme maudite, il lui remet ses péchés. « De quel droit se le permet-il ? » murmure Judas. « Du droit que mon Père m'a donné, de remettre les péchés des hommes, de leur rendre la chance des origines. »

Il ne dit rien à la pécheresse, elle fait seulement partie de ses disciples, de ces convertis à lui. Il recueille cette femme parce qu'il sait qu'elle est, comme toutes les autres femmes, aux sources de la vie, qu'à ce titre-là elle est comme Dieu lui-même, associée à lui dans le grand élan de vie que Dieu a créé. Elle sait dire presque naturellement : « Ouvre-toi, ouvre-toi à la force de Dieu, à son amour. Mes cheveux s'entrouvrent pour t'essuyer, mes mains s'offrent à toi pour te masser et te caresser, mon corps est ouvert pour recevoir la vie et la rendre. »

Le dialogue muet entre Jésus et la pécheresse ravive des tensions nouvelles, puissantes, exalte l'œuvre de Dieu. Ils sont tous les deux comme des poètes qui ressourcent le monde, lui injectent des élans de vie, recouvrent la terre de grâces exceptionnelles. Ils marchent tous deux d'un même pas, il sait, lui, qu'il pourra toujours compter sur elle, même aux temps de solitude, funestes, quand les hommes le pourchasseront, qu'elle sera, elle, à ses pieds, et qu'elle lavera ses plaies, le parfumera, l'essuiera de ses longs cheveux. « Tu es, femme, l'œuvre de vie. Tu ruisselles de tout ton être, de larmes et de parfum, tu es la manne que Yahvé jadis a répandue sur son peuple qui traversait le désert, et pour cela tu seras sauvée parmi les premiers. Tu n'es pas le grain qui a été foulé au pied par les passants et qui n'a pas germé. Tu n'es pas le grain qui est tombé sur le roc et qui, une fois poussé, s'est desséché faute d'humidité. Tu n'es pas le grain tombé au milieu des épines et qui s'est laissé étouffer, tu es le grain semé en bonne terre puisque tu as entendu la parole de Dieu et que tu es venue à lui, avec constance. »

Chapitre 31

Où Jésus est transfiguré

Il va et c'est comme une manière de mourir déjà au monde, quelque chose en lui qui se retire et le rapproche de plus en plus du Royaume qu'il proclame. Il se sent las de la foule et même de ses disciples qui ne mesurent pas l'ampleur du drame qui se joue ici, et les temps de ténèbres qui s'annoncent. De plus en plus il s'enfonce et se ramasse dans la prière, abrité sous des fourrés de lentisques ou des buissons de caroubiers, loin de tous les regards. « Donne-moi, Père, le temps de l'alliance, ne me laisse pas dans ce monde incertain qui ne veut que des preuves et des miracles et dont la foi est aussi petite qu'un grain de sénevé.

— Avance et viens vers moi, fils bien-aimé, lui répond Dieu. Il reste peu de temps avant que tu me rejoignes et que tu resplendisses dans ma lumière. Ne te décourage pas, tu es le lien qui sauve les hommes et scelle l'alliance entre eux et moi. Par toi, par ton sacrifice, ils reviendront à moi. »

Au mont Thabor, où il veut se rendre pour prier, il emmène avec lui seulement trois de ses disciples, Pierre qui bâtira son église, Jacques qui le premier périra pour sa foi, et Jean le tant aimé, le confident, le fils qu'il aurait voulu. Il gravit la montagne, se faufile dans les sentiers de genêts et d'épineux, porté par l'eau vive. Derrière lui, les disciples peinent à suivre, s'essoufflent : « Doucement maître, attends-nous, pourquoi cette hâte ? » Mais Jésus n'entend pas leurs plaintes. Il se retourne et leur dit : « Vous seriez de peu de peu de foi si vous ne pouviez accéder au haut de la montagne. Mais si vous y accédez, alors vous serez au cœur du mystère que j'enseigne, vous vous serez allégés de tous les fardeaux, vous aurez souffert pour me rejoindre, mais vous aurez atteint à la lumière de mon Père. » Jean, Jacques et Pierre sont galvanisés par les paroles de Jésus. « Nous te croyons, maître, nous sommes sûrs de ta parole. Fais-nous les témoins de ton mystère.

— Vous avez compris que ce que j'enseigne est une parole en marche, que la foi en mon père est une foi qui veut atteindre et rejoindre. »

Quand ils arrivent au sommet de la montagne, les disciples s'allongent et prennent du repos. Jésus, qui n'aime que les hauteurs, l'air vif des montagnes, se met en prière. Elle est muette, pas même un murmure, mais c'est comme une fracture qui s'ouvre, dans laquelle il se précipite, une entrée en Dieu, une voie secrète où il pénètre. Plus il prie et plus son corps se nimbe d'une lumière étincelante, le fourré où il se trouve est irradié, comme le buisson ardent des patriarches. L'irradiation réveille les disciples qui se sont endormis. Ils voient le corps céleste de Jésus entouré de ceux de Moïse et d'Élie. Ils prennent peur, croient à un mirage, un songe, une diablerie. Pierre lui dit : « "Maître, il est heureux que nous soyons ici. Faisons trois tentes, une pour toi, une pour Élie et une pour Moïse[22]." »

Mais tandis qu'il parle, une nuée s'abat sur la montagne. Elle éteint tout, les étoiles et les corps célestes, et une voix surgit de l'obscurité : « Celui-ci est mon Fils, écoutez-le. »

Et quand la voix finit de parler, Jésus se retrouve seul parmi ses amis.

— Ne rapportez rien, dit-il, de ce que vous avez vu, avant que le Fils de l'homme ne revienne des morts. Ce qui est advenu signifie que l'heure n'est pas arrivée où je devrai rejoindre mon Père. Il y aura encore des temps de noirceur et de souffrance, des mains ligotées et des supplices dont il faudra connaître l'amer désespoir, avant que le corps humilié et torturé ne redevienne champ de lumière, puits de clarté.

Il redescend le mont Thabor avec ses disciples pour retrouver la foule qui l'attend dans la plaine avec les autres compagnons, jaloux secrètement de ne pas avoir été choisis pour partager la prière du maître.

— Vois cet enfant que cet homme nous amène. Nous ne parvenons à le guérir. Toi seul peux faire quelque chose.

L'enfant est saisi de convulsions atroces, il se roule dans la poussière, bave et gémit. Jésus passe sa main sur le corps en transes de l'épileptique. Il l'apaise et lui dit :

— Va désormais en paix car le démon ne te pénétrera plus.

Mais Jésus s'irrite de ce que ses disciples ne saisissent vraiment l'enjeu de la route.

— Vous êtes une engeance incrédule et pervertie et vous n'avez pas assez de foi pour guérir. Vous ne savez pas encore que chacun d'entre vous a une partie de moi-même en lui. Laissez ouverte la voie au Fils de l'homme et Dieu le Père vous envahira, vous emplira le cœur, vous insufflera l'esprit qui ressuscite les morts.

Comme les disciples ne comprennent pas toutes ces paroles, ils disent :

— Enseigne-nous encore, convaincs-nous, Seigneur, de tes certitudes, pour que nous devenions égaux à toi, messies nous-mêmes au monde.

— Quand vous aurez acquis ce souffle en vous, alors, vous le verrez, vous pourrez déplacer les montagnes.

Il profite du poids de ses paroles pour annoncer une nouvelle fois sa Passion.

— Ne restez pas dans l'émerveillement et dans le ravissement. Mettez-vous bien en tête que le Fils de l'homme doit être livré aux mains des hommes. Et qu'il sera condamné.

Les disciples ne cherchent pas à en savoir davantage, horrifiés par la prédiction. Seul Jésus connaît l'issue de la route. La capture au mont des Oliviers, le Golgotha, l'agonie. Mais cette douleur si entière, si pleine de toutes parts, si universelle dans son corps, finira par se transformer en béatitude. C'est la douleur au-delà de la douleur, un état qui cède la place à l'immensité de l'univers. Et fait passer sur l'autre rive.

Chapitre 32

Où Jésus accomplit la résurrection de Lazare comme
un signe de sa puissance sur la mort

C'en est trop pour certains qui voudraient voir cesser sa prédication. Jésus en est conscient, il risque la lapidation et échappe de justesse à ses ennemis après avoir déclaré : « Croyez les œuvres, afin que vous appreniez et reconnaissiez que le Père est en moi et moi dans le Père. » Il traverse le Jourdain, laisse se perdre sa trace sur l'autre rive. Là, il médite en solitaire, il ne craint pas les méchants. Mais on vient le chercher. C'est la maison de Marie et de Marthe qui l'envoie.

— Lazare, leur frère, est très malade. Seul vous, maître, pouvez faire quelque chose. Venez à Béthanie, venez le sauver.

Jésus attend deux jours pour y aller, apprend la mort de Lazare :

— « Lazare est mort, leur dit-il, et je me réjouis pour vous de n'avoir pas été là, afin que vous me croyiez[23]. »

Il arrive à Béthanie, accompagné de ses disciples, console Marthe.

— N'aie crainte, lui dit-il, je suis, moi, la résurrection et la vie. Celui qui croit en moi, même s'il vient à mourir, vivra ; Il est impossible que quiconque vit et croit en moi meure pour toujours. Crois-tu cela ?

— Oui, Seigneur, je le crois. Moi, j'ai la foi que c'est toi le Christ, le Fils de Dieu, celui qui vient en ce monde.

Jésus veut se rendre au sépulcre de Lazare, ordonne qu'on l'ouvre.

— Mais il doit sentir déjà, Seigneur.

— Va, obéis-moi, fais rouler la pierre pour qu'on aille jusqu'à lui.

Puis, d'une voix forte, il crie :

— Lazare, viens ici. Dehors !

Et Lazare vient, tout ceint encore de ses bandelettes.

— Déliez-le, laissez-le aller, dit Jésus.

Un silence stupéfait s'abat sur le sépulcre ouvert. La famille de Lazare le voit s'avancer sur le chemin, il ne dit mot, ne se retourne pas, mais il avance.

— Gloire à toi, Seigneur, disent Marie et Marthe, à ses genoux, tu es le libérateur, celui qui délie les corps et les cœurs !

Mais Jésus ne réclame aucun remerciement, aucune liesse. Une tristesse profonde l'envahit : cette guérison, c'est la preuve donnée aux Juifs qui le guettent et attendent son faux pas, c'est la voie tracée de Jérusalem. Et en même temps, il voit le sépulcre de Joseph d'Arimathie, son corps qui se redresse, ses bandelettes se délier, et lui aussi s'avancer sur la route, silhouette de lumière.

Il retourne au campement le long du Jourdain, il parle autour d'un feu avec ses disciples, approfondit son enseignement :

« Vous avez été témoins de la résurrection de Lazare, mais retenez surtout que la foi en mon Père vous déliera de vos angoisses et de vos peines. Que ce que je vous apprends, c'est que vos péchés, qui vous enlacent comme des bandelettes, se délieront dès lors que vous croirez. Que vos prisons s'ouvriront, et que vous verrez la lumière de ce monde. Vous ne trébucherez pas, parce que vous ne marcherez plus dans la nuit. Il y a des forces immenses en vous que vous délivrerez et qui vous donneront de guérir et de ressusciter. Maintenant, rejoignons Ephraïm pour nous mettre à l'abri des Pharisiens. La tâche n'est pas encore accomplie. »

Ils s'enfoncent dans la nuit, mais ils marchent comme en plein jour, sûrs de leur route, le regard dans les étoiles.

Troisième partie

La passion de Jésus

Chapitre 33

Où Jésus prend le chemin de Jérusalem

Maintenant il descend vers Jérusalem. Il longe le Jourdain, des villages samaritains, hostiles, toute cette Décapole peuplée de Grecs païens qui haïssent les Juifs, et la traversée de ces petites cités n'est pas sans risque pour lui. Il les évite, préfère parler aux hommes des champs, aux pauvres, aux humbles villageois qui subissent le joug des Romains. De tous ses disciples, c'est Jean qu'il préfère, parce qu'il lui ressemble, sa tendresse envers les simples, son regard lavé de tout mal font de lui le frère de confiance. Jésus, qui a le don de voir dans les cœurs et les esprits, sait que Jean sera auprès de lui au moment où tout s'écroulera, où il connaîtra l'abandon de toutes choses, où le désespoir cédera à l'espérance. Jean sera avec Marie, au pied de la croix, il sera en prière tout au long de son agonie, Jean le déliera de ses bois. Jean, c'est le secret de Jésus. Un amour au-delà de l'amour, une union parfaite et mystique.

Un jour, Jean a entendu au fond de lui ces paroles extravagantes de Jésus : « Je suis allé, ô Jean, jusqu'au fond de ton cœur, je sais la nature de ton âme, la naïveté de ton esprit, et cet esprit d'enfance qui va te donner d'être sauvé. Quand tous tes compagnons se disputaient pour savoir qui pouvait être le plus grand d'entre eux, j'ai bien vu que tu ne cherchais pas à dominer et à convaincre. Tu es le plus petit d'entre tes compagnons, et c'est parce que tu es le plus petit que tu seras le plus grand. Par ton émerveillement, ton regard neuf, tu es devenu celui qui appartient à Dieu. Dieu s'est faufilé en toi, il t'a rejoint et tu l'as reçu comme on reçoit à sa table le mendiant de passage. Souviens-toi de l'oiseau. Je vous disais un soir, à la veillée, qu'il suffisait de façonner une forme d'oiseau avec de l'argile, de souffler dedans, et un oiseau apparaissait qui s'envolait vers le ciel. Il en est de même pour toi et pour tous ceux qui se laissent pénétrer ; par votre cœur sincère, le souffle de Dieu entre dans votre corps qui est eau et argile et vous devenez oiseau du paradis. J'ai soufflé l'esprit de Dieu en toi, Jean, et désormais je suis toi, tu es moi. »

Jean reçoit ces paroles dans la prière. Elles le bouleversent mais ne lui donnent aucun sentiment de suffisance ou de vanité. Il a pris vie auprès de Jésus, par Jésus, il est peut-être de tous les Douze le seul à être déjà ébloui par la lumière de la résurrection. Il a à peine quinze ans, il a cette jeunesse dans le regard, cette manière émerveillée de voir encore avec des yeux neufs, défaits de toute envie.

La petite troupe avance dans les contrées de Samarie. Les disciples vont en avant pour préparer la venue de Jésus mais les bourgs hostiles aux Juifs lui interdisent leurs places. Alors Jésus, harassé, continue sa route, il a tout abandonné depuis longtemps, besace, vêtements chauds pour la nuit, il va comme les mendiants avec cette force et cette détermination dans le visage qui lui rendent quand même la marche légère, indifférente au désespoir. Il sent que l'heure est venue d'essaimer, de répandre sa parole dans tout le pays, il désigne soixante-dix autres disciples, leur ordonne de partir sur les terres voisines, d'être les témoins de la bonne nouvelle, les ouvriers de la future moisson.

— Je vous envoie comme des agneaux parmi les loups, leur dit-il. Soyez des artisans de ma paix. Car le Royaume de Dieu est tout proche.

— Mais quand, rabbi, quand le Royaume va nous apparaître ?

— Il ne surgira pas comme dans les rêves, ce ne sera pas un pays inventé par votre imagination, un nouvel Éden sorti d'une autre galaxie, car le Royaume de Dieu est en vous.

— Comment est-ce possible ?

— Parce que vous vous êtes ouverts à la parole de Dieu, et que vous avez cru en sa promesse, alors Dieu restera votre guide et vous conduira en son Royaume qui est d'abord son esprit en vous. Le Royaume, je vous le dis, n'est pas seulement où vous ressusciterez en Dieu après votre mort, mais déjà de votre vivant, le Royaume se révélera, par la paix qui se fera en vous.

Les nouveaux disciples sont stupéfaits de l'enseignement de Jésus.

— Alors ni loi inscrite sur les rouleaux ni rites obligés ?

— Non, je vous le dis, le Royaume de Dieu se passe des lois et des rites qui ne rassurent que les peureux et les nantis. Dieu souffle son esprit à qui lui a ouvert sa demeure. Par son verbe, il est le poète des âmes, par lui, on accède à l'émerveillement.

Le plan de Dieu se précipite. Jésus avance d'un pas plus audacieux. L'aveu du Dieu unique qui parle par sa bouche ne doit plus craindre les prêtres et tous les pouvoirs. Jésus sent en lui tressaillir son cœur d'allégresse quand Dieu, pour le réconforter, le berce de son souffle. Mais l'histoire trop huilée finit par déplaire à tous ceux qui croisent Jésus en Galilée et dans tous les siècles à venir. Comment accepter vraiment cette histoire digne des plus fastueuses mythologies, comment y croire ? Justement, croire, répondent ceux qui suivent Jésus. « Croire, disent-ils, ce n'est pas se soumettre et être naïf, c'est une grâce unique qui ouvre et unit. Elle donne accès au mystère, c'est-à-dire aux lieux les plus reculés de l'inconnu, aux rives de tous les ailleurs, là où la connaissance bute et renonce. »

Mais non, les paraboles, les contes à dormir debout, le coup des pains et des poissons multipliés, l'eau des outres qui se transforme en vin, les marches sur les flots, les paralytiques qui galopent sur les chemins, et la route de Jésus vers Jérusalem annoncée déjà par les prophètes, rien n'a pu se passer comme le rapportent les apôtres, propagandistes de la nouvelle religion. Et pourtant, comment comprendre que le bel album d'images pieuses que Dieu a conçu continue d'étinceler dans le monde ?

Jean, le très près de Jésus, le plus intime, retient l'ultime message de son maître : « "Je suis le chemin, la vérité et la Vie, nul ne va au Père que par moi[24]." — Tu es la voie, Seigneur, murmure-t-il dans sa prière muette, Dieu t'a donné au monde pour que le monde aille vers lui, tu es la clé du mystère, le secret de Dieu. »

Dans les cités modernes, des hommes taggent les murs, y écrivent rageusement *No future* parce que tout leur apparaît bouché, sans but, et que la vie leur semble irrémédiablement vaine. Mais Dieu ne lâche pas des yeux ses créatures. Il va les recueillir jusqu'au fond des squats, dans les lieux hostiles du monde perdu. Il a fait dire par Jésus que ce seront eux, les malheureux, qui entreront les premiers dans la gloire parce qu'il les aime. Peu sentent le souffle de Dieu qui les parcourt, trop fermés qu'ils sont à l'espérance. Mais Dieu ne désarme pas. Il a confiance parce que son joker, son incroyable pari, c'est que Jésus est toujours sur la route, il est toujours en marche pour consoler les déshérités. Il emprunte des formes multiples, il est doté de mille visages, il est Bach qui ouvre au Royaume, il est Van Gogh qui illumine Arles de milliers d'étoiles ou de cette lumière d'or qui coule sur les champs de Provence, il est Rilke qui retient le jour. Il est toutes ces petites religieuses de Calcutta qui ramassent sur le pavé des affamés et des malades du sida dont les familles ne veulent plus, et qui passent leurs mains sur les corps fiévreux pour les rassurer et les bénir. Jésus est tout ce qui permet d'ouvrir la voie, d'effacer les cloisons, d'imposer l'amour. Il accepte même qu'on ne l'appelle pas Jésus, qu'on ne le reconnaisse pas pour ce qu'il est, qu'importe si sa leçon d'amour est entendue ?

Chapitre 34

Où Jésus révèle la prière universelle

Une seule histoire a prise sur lui, celle de l'avènement du Royaume. Il sait qu'il ne peut plus reculer, de toute manière tout a été joué depuis l'étable de Bethléem, et le sillage de l'étoile qui indiquait la route aux mages et aux bergers. Il redoute les grands rassemblements parce qu'il a peur des Pharisiens qui l'espionnent et rapportent tous ses faits et gestes. C'est que l'illuminé, le ravi, inquiète sérieusement. Ne faudrait-il pas le faire arrêter ? Sa route se rétrécit, il voudrait être de plus en plus seul, guérir des malades dans la plus grande discrétion, redevenir l'enfant Jésus de l'étable. Mais le destin est en marche. Il n'y a que cette avancée terrible vers Jérusalem.

Il accepte l'invitation des femmes à se reposer dans leurs maisons, à l'abri de tous les regards. Là, il retrouve la douceur de Nazareth, et le temps simple, humain, la régularité des mois et des saisons passés à travailler, à aider sa mère, à prier avec elle et Joseph. Ce jour-là, ses amies Marthe et Marie l'accueillent. Spontanément, Marie, la cadette, s'est assise à ses pieds et l'écoute parler tandis que Marthe vaque aux travaux ménagers. Irritée de n'être pas aidée par Marie, elle laisse apparaître sa mauvaise humeur et demande à Jésus son sentiment :

— Cela ne te fait rien que ma sœur me laisse ainsi servir toute seule ?

— Marthe, Marthe, lui répond Jésus, tu t'inquiètes pour beaucoup de choses. Il ne faudrait vivre que de peu, du strict nécessaire. Apaise-toi. Prends exemple sur Marie, c'est elle qui a choisi la meilleure part. Elle ne lui sera pas enlevée.

Il va, de maison en maison, par petites étapes, égrener sa parole, des leçons de sagesse infime, qui recousent les liens.

Plus la voie est étroite, plus ses leçons s'alourdissent de sens pour ses disciples, comme s'ils comprenaient mieux la mission de Jésus, gagnaient plus de vision.

— Apprends-nous, Seigneur, apprends-nous à prier.

Jésus les rassemble tous dans un champ retiré des villages et leur dit :

— Il y a une prière qu'après mon départ vous devrez porter dans le monde, une prière universelle, sur laquelle toi, Pierre, tu bâtiras mon église. Une prière qui rassemble à elle seule tous les fondements de ma parole que mon Père m'a chargé de transmettre, une prière qui devra traverser les mers, être dite chaque jour, chaque nuit, sur tous les continents. Il faut faire silence en soi, être en état d'accueillir et de délivrer, être ouvert.

Doucement Jésus se coule dans sa nuit intérieure, les disciples sentent en eux cette vague de fond qui les parcourt, ils savent qu'ils nagent en eau profonde, qu'ils sont en train de rejoindre Dieu. Ils ouvrent leurs bras, comme ils voient faire Jésus, et attendent la prière. Jésus sort enfin de son silence et lentement prononce ces mots :

— Notre Père qui êtes aux cieux, que votre nom soit sanctifié, que votre règne arrive, donnez-nous chaque jour notre pain quotidien, remettez-nous de nos péchés, car nous-mêmes remettons à quiconque nous doit, et ne nous soumettez pas à la tentation. Voilà les mots qui ouvrent la route, qui traversent les frontières, effacent la douleur des hommes et éclairent les villes sombres. Souvenez-vous d'eux car ce sont les mots soufflés par mon père, qui instaurent le dialogue avec lui et vous relient à lui.

Les mots, de fait, s'inscrivent dans les siècles, Jésus croient qu'à les répéter tous les jours, jusqu'à la nuit des temps, ils apportent du divin sur la terre, apaisent les consciences, ne laissent pas ainsi les hommes orphelins de Dieu. Mieux encore, ses mots proférés, dans l'appel comme dans la détresse, dans la confidence comme dans la ritualité des offices immergent les lieux qui les accueillent et ceux qui les disent d'un manteau de lumière. Joris-Karl Huysmans parle d'un « capiton spirituel » qui recouvre alors la terre. Pas une journée depuis que la prière a été énoncée dans la fraîcheur nocturne de Samarie où elle ne soit récitée, et les murs des abbatiales et des lieux saints sont pénétrés de cette prière, elle les habite de sorte qu'elle change le lieu même, lui donne un poids, un reflet, une réverbération spirituelle intenses.

— Rappelez-vous, vous êtes la lumière du monde, et la prière est déjà trace de celle qui vous mettra en face de Dieu. Je ne vous promets pas seulement la résurrection à la fin des temps, mais dès aujourd'hui vous ressuscitez à vous-mêmes en rejoignant Dieu, en le reconnaissant, en approchant de sa lumière.

Dans Cracovie occupé par les nazis, le jeune Karol Wojtyla se livre à un étrange jeu. Il a rassemblé quelques amis chrétiens comme lui et jusqu'au couvre-feu, un chapelet dans la poche, selon un itinéraire bien défini, le groupe arpente la ville en la ceinturant de prière. Dans la nuit glaciale, Karol croise des camions, des voitures de SS qui roulent à vive allure, les Allemands ne se méfient pas de ces jeunes qui marchent d'un pas tranquille, ils vont sûrement rejoindre leur maison, ils ne savent pas qu'ils prient, prononcent les paroles apprises aux disciples en Samarie, font comme un cordon mystique autour de leur ville, empêchent à leurs yeux les forces mauvaises de s'étendre. Et la prière intérieure rejoint Dieu dans son lieu absolument inexploré. Le jeune Karol sait qu'il est entendu, dans ce lieu de la foi, indéfinissable, réel, incarné, qui répond et console. Il a en lui cette voix qui lui parle mystérieusement, impérieuse et douce, elle s'est fait entendre à qui a ouvert sa porte.

Chapitre 35

Où Jésus délivre ses ultimes conseils

Les évangélistes se sont souvenus de la vie de Jésus en portant au plus haut niveau d'excellence l'art de la parabole et de la fable. Ils ont négligé ce qui ne leur était alors pas apparu nécessaire pour leur enseignement, les faits et gestes de leur quotidien auprès de lui, ce qui se vivait entre les paraboles. Ils ont pris en cela le risque de la pétrification et du mythe mais quelque chose les en a sauvés. Quelque chose d'infiniment vivant qui s'échappe quand même de la fixité des histoires répétées dans la liturgie et qui fait de Jésus un être de chair et de sang, incomparablement plus vivant et plus crédible que les grands héros de l'Antiquité grecque, Œdipe, Ulysse, Antigone.

Des quatre évangiles, c'est bien celui de Jean qui est au plus près de Jésus, car il s'est éloigné de l'apologue et du prosélytisme. Jean donne la clé de ce mystère : Jésus lui souffle le secret. Il est en lui, par une sorte de communion invisible, et Jean se sent comme transporté, ressuscité par l'énergie vitale que Jésus diffuse en son esprit et dans son corps.

À ce point de la marche, seuls Jean, Pierre et Jacques ont saisi l'enjeu de l'histoire. Elle est publique, montrée devant des milliers d'hommes et de femmes, mais elle est aussi obscure et nocturne, car Jésus ne veut aucune publicité tapageuse, n'a aucune ambition du monde. Après avoir quitté la foule, tandis que le petit groupe se restaure de presque rien, les disciples découvrent la nouvelle parole, les mots de Dieu soufflés par lui à Jésus.

— Heureux ceux qui écoutent la parole de Dieu, leur dit Jésus, et la gardent !

— Mais comment être sûr de la garder, Seigneur ?

— Je vous le dis, il faut rester en éveil. Tant de fois, vous serez en butte au malin, au désir et à l'orgueil. Ne leur cédez en rien, fortifiez-vous et demeurez en Dieu en l'appelant à son secours, résistez ! Il faut garder la lampe toujours allumée. La lampe de votre corps, c'est votre œil. Lorsqu'il est sain, le corps tout entier est aussi dans la lumière. Mais dès qu'il est malade, le corps aussi est dans les ténèbres. Veillez à ce que la lumière qui est en vous ne soit ténèbres.

Les nuits s'allongent autour du feu. Jésus scrute le ciel, en lui cette hâte d'en finir, d'ensemencer. « Je t'ai obéi, Père, murmure-t-il, j'ai éclairé la route, je leur ai donné les moyens de la tenir éclairée, j'ai fait comprendre que ce que tu m'as donné est aussi donné à eux, que je ne suis que cette voie de passage, cette passerelle pour t'atteindre, maintenant laisse-moi venir à toi. »

Il rumine sa douleur de ne pas éclairer comme par magie la terre entière, de la soumettre à la clarté de Dieu, car il sait que la liberté de l'homme est le bien le plus précieux que Dieu a désiré pour ses créatures. « C'est d'eux-mêmes, lui dit Dieu, que les hommes devront se défier et s'abandonner à ma confiance. C'est en eux-mêmes qu'ils devront aller puiser la lumière mise en eux dès le premier jour. Je les ai rendus responsables de leur lampe. »

Jésus entend la leçon de son père. Il la rapporte fidèlement à ce qu'il appelle maintenant « son petit troupeau » dont il est le berger.

« Ne vous inquiétez de rien, ni de manger ni de boire, ni de savoir où vous logerez cette nuit ni si vous aurez des vêtements pour couvrir votre corps. Tout cela est affaire du monde. Dieu pourvoira à vos besoins car il ne s'agit que de s'abandonner à la Providence et de la laisser faire, le Royaume vous sera donné et le reste de surcroît. Vous partirez seuls et pauvres, et l'on vous vêtira, l'on vous donnera à manger et des femmes au puits vous donneront de l'eau. Vous trouverez des abris pour vous endormir. Dieu réclame ce retrait et il vous promet d'effacer vos tourments. »

La parole de Jésus résonne dans la nuit de Palestine. Des hommes l'espionnent et rapportent tout aux autorités du monde car il faudra bien le faire taire, celui qui affaiblit les nantis et interdit les faux bonheurs, tout ce dont « les païens de ce monde, dit-il, sont en quête ». Les autorités de Jérusalem attendent le faux pas, un moment viendra où Jésus se trahira et l'imposture apparaîtra au grand jour. Jésus n'ignore rien de l'embuscade. Il va comme les moutons au sacrifice. Il a confiance dans son père. Comme s'il prévenait déjà sa Passion, il demande aux disciples de rester éveillés.

« Vous êtes les sentinelles de ma vérité. Vous ne devrez pas rester assoupis tandis que je serai parti vers mon père. Vous êtes la lampe allumée parce que la foi que j'aurai mise en vous sera de l'huile inépuisable. Et quand je reviendrai, heureux serai-je quand je vous verrai éveillés, à m'attendre. Soyez toujours prêts, ne vous laissez distraire par aucune illusion, je vous confie la maison, mon église et son mystère. »

L'incompréhension, les doutes sur l'apparition du Royaume pèsent sur ses disciples. Il les sent saisis d'un soupçon atroce qu'il devine dans leur cœur. « Et si tout n'était que bavardages et imposture ? Et si Jésus n'était qu'un faux prophète, ou encore un délirant ? Nous t'en supplions, Seigneur, donne-nous encore des preuves. Des preuves pour te suivre jusqu'au bout.

— Vous êtes de peu de foi et vous ranimez ma colère. Vous doutez de moi parce que je vous révèle le signe de contradiction qui dit que la vie passe par la mort, qu'il n'y a de vie que par le passage de la mort, mais ce que vous avez appris auprès de moi, l'aviez-vous déjà entendu ? Vous voulez des preuves et vous en aurez. Je rebâtirai le temple de Jérusalem en trois jours et je ressusciterai d'entre les morts. Cela, vous le verrez, et vous irez le proclamer après moi. Mais la preuve, elle est là surtout, dans votre regard ouvert à la lumière. Aiguisez-le et regardez avec un esprit pur. Vous me trouverez alors et je vous renverrai ma lumière et vous aurez déjà accès à une part du Royaume et au concert des anges. Ouvrez votre regard et alors vous verrez Dieu. »

Il se retire pour faire un peu de silence en lui, apaiser le feu qu'il a allumé. Plus que la lumière, il se veut le feu qui embrase tout, qui renverse le monde, punit les riches et détruit leurs biens, brûle les idoles et ravage les cités maudites. Il n'a plus peur de rien, « je ne suis que d'un temps, dit-il, je ne suis pas de ce monde, je ne fais rien de moi-même », alors il ose tout, « n'amassez rien, parlez ouvertement et sans crainte, vendez vos biens, faites l'aumône, malheur à vous, Pharisiens, légistes, hommes de piètre foi ! "Faites-vous des bourses qui ne s'usent pas, un trésor qui ne vous fera pas défaut dans les cieux, où ni voleur n'approche ni mite ne détruit[25]" ».

Chapitre 36

Où Jésus approfondit son enseignement

L'enseignement de Jésus se poursuit dans sa marche aléatoire vers Jérusalem, aléatoire et en même temps décidée, sûre d'un accomplissement. Jésus se rapproche du terme, il a accepté l'issue de la mission. Il parle souvent du Royaume, celui à venir mais aussi celui qui est déjà là, dans la conversion à Dieu.

« À quoi puis-je le mieux le comparer, dit-il ? Il est semblable à du levain qu'une femme a pris et enfoui dans trois mesures de farine, jusqu'à ce que le tout ait levé. C'est à cette naissance-là que je vous appelle. Il y a en vous tous les ingrédients pour que lève la pâte, car vous êtes, vous aussi, des habitants du Royaume, et vous l'ignorez. Vous avez en vous le grain de sénevé, il ne s'agit que de le faire lever, comme le jardinier a jeté le grain dans son jardin et qu'il l'a vu pousser, devenir un arbre et les oiseaux du ciel s'abriter dans ses branches. Dieu vous promet cette terre à lui, paisible et harmonieuse. Car que cherchez-vous tous au fond de vous-même, sinon cette douceur ancienne logée mystérieusement en vous dont vous avez gardé la nostalgie, irréparable, obsédante ? »

Les jours passent, ils se font longs et lourds, en avançant vers la Passion. La parole de Jésus se fait plus âpre, non pas amère mais plus sauvage, quelquefois plus violente. Il dit qu'il faut renoncer à tout ce que l'on a de cher, jusqu'à sa propre vie, renoncer en particulier à tous ses biens, ne rien attendre du monde et de sa propre famille, ne pas s'affadir.

« Vous êtes le sel de la terre, je vous l'ai déjà dit, le sel et la lumière du monde. Mais pour que la lumière garde son éclat de nuit comme de jour, il faut que le sel qui est en vous, la source d'eau vive, ne perde jamais de sa saveur. Gardez en vous l'amour de Dieu, ne vous laissez jamais égarer par les illusions du monde. Vous êtes né d'un homme et d'une femme, mais en vénérant Dieu, vous êtes né de lui. C'est une seconde naissance. Vous êtes né de nouveau. Rendu à la lumière divine, ramené dans ses bras, non pas soumis à lui mais auprès de lui, dans la réverbération de son amour. »

Jour après jour, l'attachement de ses disciples à son enseignement, à sa propre personne, s'accroît et se fortifie. C'est comme un lien qui les rejoint, fort et secret, une affection singulière, presque exclusive, qui leur fait oublier leur famille, leur village, leurs amis et leurs occupations de pêcheurs ou de pauvres ouvriers.

« Par quelle étrange parade, disent les sceptiques, suivent-ils ce prophète ? Par quel envoûtement satanique ? À coup sûr, c'est le démon qui parle en cet homme ! » Jésus n'écoute pas. Il sait qu'il a donné à ses compagnons de route la force de guérir, de soulager les malades et d'apaiser leurs angoisses, il les a instruits pour qu'ils préviennent de la promesse de Dieu de les réunir, tous, il leur a insufflé le don de la parole qui convainc et rend la confiance. « D'où vient, dit-on pourtant, que ces miséreux que les prêtres n'ont pas choisis aient le don de guérir et de soulager ? D'où leur vient cette parole inspirée ? D'où vient que dans leurs paroles, on entende battre leur cœur ? »

Il n'y a cependant pas que les grands rassemblements autour de lui et les craintes soulevées par les disciples, pas seulement les menaces à peine voilées qu'il entend sur son passage. Il y a aussi toute cette humanité donnée à lui par Dieu qu'il faut bien aider à vivre, les doutes et les nuits, les vertiges du néant et l'idée confuse, obscurément tenace, que cette histoire n'est qu'un cauchemar, un mauvais rêve, une sombre farce qu'on lui fait jouer. Il aurait voulu plus de légèreté, plus de disponibilité pour contempler le paysage, regarder passer les femmes des villages qui vont au marché, vénérer Dieu simplement.

Dieu justement, dans sa tour d'ivoire, se frotte les mains. Ce qu'il voulait dire aux hommes est en passe d'être proclamé, en faisant de son fils un homme, il dit aux hommes qu'ils sont tous divins. Voilà la grande leçon qu'il veut donner. Il dit bien : « Il n'y a pas d'élus, mais tous sont sauvés. Tous sont en situation d'être dans le Royaume. »

À la suite de Jésus, tous ceux qui ont accepté de le suivre jusqu'au bout connaîtront les mêmes nuits que les siennes. C'est la nuit la plus obscure pour Jean de la Croix dans son cachot de Tolède, pour Thérèse d'Avila, pour tous ses imitateurs, à travers tous les siècles, tous le même désarroi, la même solitude, le même délire, le même embrasement, les mêmes ténèbres. Tous quémandent à Dieu de leur accorder un peu de lumière, de ne pas les laisser tomber, car ils deviendraient alors fous et ils en mourraient, tous disent les mots de Jésus : « Pourquoi m'as-tu abandonné ? » La petite Thérèse Martin dans sa cellule de Lisieux ne vit plus dans la lumière, elle n'est plus rien qu'une lampe éteinte, sa vie n'aura été qu'une illusion de bout en bout, elle s'est égarée, voilà tout, c'est un transport de son esprit affaibli, débile, à cause de cette enfance trop mystique, qui lui a dérangé l'esprit. Elle est sur son lit d'agonie, elle réclame à boire, tout autour d'elle ses sœurs se relaient pour prier, elle entend leur prière, d'un revers de main elle les écarte, elle dit que ça ne sert à rien, que tout le monde ici s'est trompé, a bâti sa vie sur des illusions, sur des rêveries insensées, les religieuses se signent, croient à l'assaut de Satan, font brûler de l'encens autour de son corps, mais rien n'y fait. Thérèse a sombré dans la nuit, elle veut la traverser cependant, elle se démène, elle crie même, puis elle pleure doucement, parce que tout est trop injuste, trop dur à vivre, alors elle appelle la mort, qu'elle l'emporte et qu'on en finisse puisque Dieu n'existe pas. Thérèse respire à peine, empesée dans l'agonie, et puis soudain, cette lumière sur son visage, cet éblouissement dans ses yeux, comme une résurrection, ce feu qui se rallume, cette tension du regard qui redonne des couleurs à son teint de cire, et ces paroles qu'elle murmure à peine audibles : « Merci, mon Dieu, de me rendre l'eau vive, merci de m'avoir répondu, car je vois à présent que tu es là, que tu ne m'as jamais quittée, et que tu viens me chercher avec tes anges. »

Mêmes paroles, curieusement prononcées dans la bouche du rebelle Rimbaud à l'oreille de sa sœur Isabelle. D'une certaine manière, Isabelle et son frère sont tous deux Jésus, elle accueille et apaise Rimbaud et lui, après le reniement, cède sa colère, rend les armes, se coule dans le divin dont il avait déjà touché de son vivant les rivages et pour quoi il avait été rejeté et nié. « Je viens dans ton sillage, toi Jésus, l'innommé, l'inconnu, toi qui as ce nom et aucun nom, qui parles au nom de Dieu, et qui es peut-être Dieu, je te suis parce qu'auprès de toi, je veux voir l'or dont j'ai rêvé, et la rivière de lumière que je pourrai descendre pour atteindre au trésor qui m'a été révélé. »

Chapitre 37

Où Jésus ranime le feu

Jésus aime prendre à rebours la morale établie, parce qu'il veut remonter toujours le fleuve de la vie à la source, revenir à la promesse des origines, quand le monde était encore dans cette lactance d'opaline, quand il ne devait y avoir que de vastes étendues apaisées et des terres vierges. Quand la lumière était toujours d'aurore. C'était avant le temps, juste après les grands bouleversements cosmiques, quand toute l'organisation intelligente du monde s'est mise en place et que la grâce de Dieu planait sur toutes choses. Il dit à ses disciples qu'il veut défendre la vie, qu'il risque tout pour cela, même la mort, parce qu'il sait que de cette mort renaîtra la vie, ainsi vont les saisons et les âges dans ce cours perpétuel et dynamique qui rend toujours le souffle après qu'il a cédé en apparence à la mort.

« Celui que Dieu aime et chérit, qu'il préfère à tout autre, même à ses plus fidèles serviteurs, est celui qui, l'ayant abandonné, veut revenir dans ses bras. Il est la brebis égarée du troupeau, le fils infidèle qui est parti dépenser l'argent du père pour des femmes, et qui, seul et malheureux, veut rentrer à la maison. Rien n'est plus doux à Dieu que de voir sur la route son fils rentrer chez lui. Pour lui, il tuera le veau gras, avant la Pâque, il fera un festin, il engagera des danseurs et des musiciens pour égayer la fête. L'autre frère fidèle ne sera pas content, lui qui est resté auprès du père et qui l'a servi honnêtement. Mais le père lui dira : "Toi, mon enfant, tu es toujours avec moi et tout ce qui est à moi est à toi. Mais il fallait bien festoyer puisque ton frère que voilà était mort et qu'il est revenu à la vie ; il était perdu et il est retrouvé."

Je vous le dis, Dieu mon père ne veut entendre que des paroles de vie parce qu'il l'a créée, et croire que la mort vaincra tout, c'est croire aux forces de Satan. De la vie naîtra la vie qui engendrera de nouveau la vie. »

Il est repris par ce grand souffle que Dieu a mis en lui, il presse ses disciples de marcher vers Jérusalem, il veut atteindre au plus vite la vallée du Jourdain. Il y a comme une joie retrouvée, qui ressemble à l'allégresse de la Pâque, comme une naïveté qui traverse le peuple. À ceux qui croient que le Royaume de Dieu va surgir dans des temps très courts, Jésus leur dit : « Sa venue ne se laisse pas observer. On ne saurait dire : Le voici, le voilà ! Car sachez-le, le Royaume de Dieu est parmi vous. » Il leur dit encore que seuls ceux qui accueilleront le Royaume en petit enfant y entreront.

Pour la troisième fois, il évoque avec ses disciples sa Passion. Ils se taisent quand Jésus leur dit qu'il sera livré aux païens, bafoué, outragé, couvert de crachats, flagellé et mis à mort.

« Et le troisième jour, rajoute-t-il, je ressusciterai. »

Jean et ses amis prennent peur. Ils voient la nuit tomber en plein jour, des temps funestes où ils devront prendre la relève du maître. Ils ne savent pas s'ils auront ce courage de partir témoigner sans Jésus.

« Mais je serai toujours avec vous, mon esprit vous pénétrera et vous avancerez, vous irez porter la bonne nouvelle, celle qui dit que Dieu aime son troupeau et qu'il veille sur lui. »

C'est aux miséreux et aux égarés qu'il s'adresse, à tous ceux qui sont perdus, lâchés dans le monde sans comprendre. Ils n'ont rien demandé, bafoués par tous ceux qui les exploitent, les mettent en esclavage, et puis les jettent comme des objets usés. Mais ils connaîtront les vraies richesses, parce qu'ils n'auront pas trahi, pas thésaurisé, pas détruit l'harmonie de l'œuvre divine. La Palestine est comme la métaphore du monde, elle recèle pour tous les siècles ses pauvres et ses nantis, ses miséreux et ses opulents, ses humbles et ses orgueilleux. C'est le monde entier qui est comme ça. La nature humaine. Le plan de Dieu renverse l'ordre établi, bouscule les conventions et les lois, déroute les tribulations des forces mauvaises puisqu'il n'y a que l'amour qui sauvera les hommes, la seule voie possible pour accéder au Royaume. Plus ils montent vers Jérusalem, plus les disciples font corps autour de Jésus. Il s'est passé de telles choses entre eux depuis les jours où Jésus les a choisis, comme une tendresse secrète qui les a rassemblés. Il n'était souvent pas même question de parler pour qu'ils ressentent ce mystère : désormais rien pour eux ne sera comme avant, ils sont marqués d'un sceau indélébile, habités d'un feu qui ne s'éteindra plus, d'une foi qui leur donne des ailes. Ils éprouvent en eux la force inouïe de l'espérance, celle d'un monde à bâtir, qui préfigurera déjà le Royaume. Car le secret de Jésus, c'est le mystère de la communion.

« Vous êtes, leur dit-il, un petit foyer de lumière. À vous douze, vous êtes le feu qui va embraser le monde, lui révéler la vérité de Dieu. Soyez des veilleurs de nuit, ne profanez pas votre temple intérieur, cette vérité logée au fond de votre cœur, ne la conservez pas pour vous tout seuls, car cette vérité flamboie et jette ses rayons qui éclairent le monde. »

Les disciples se sentent transportés. Ils étaient il y a peu encore des pêcheurs, des jeunes hommes forts et solides, qui n'avaient pas d'états d'âme, qui ne finassaient pas, mais leur robustesse était leur seule richesse. Et voilà qu'ils acceptaient toutes ces choses extraordinaires que leur disait Jésus ! Par quel étrange prodige cela était-il possible ? Par tous les siècles, les sceptiques refusent de jouer les niais, craignent de paraître naïfs. Ils ont au fond d'eux pourtant la même espérance que celle des disciples, quelquefois ils disent même qu'ils les envient. Qu'ils aimeraient croire eux aussi. Céder un peu de leur certitude, car elle est dure et fine la lame de rasoir de ceux qui ne croient pas, elle les fait danser sur son fil, elle les oblige à ne croire qu'en ce qu'ils voient. Souvent, en silence, dans leur désespoir, ils appellent Dieu, mais qu'importe le nom, Dieu, enfin quoi, quelqu'un qui écoute, qui protège et fait espérer, quelqu'un qui leur dise que tout n'est pas achevé, qu'il n'y a pas cet ordre implacable qui régit l'univers mais qu'il y a aussi des bras ouverts qui acceptent les larmes et qui les consolent. Nietzsche, dans sa vallée de douleurs, réclame un peu de cette douceur : « Je suis la brebis égarée du troupeau, le fils prodigue qui l'a quitté, mais je suis si seul, si perdu dans ma raison, moi aussi je suis dans la nuit obscure, quelle flamme au loin peut encore me guider et me faire marcher ? Quelle espérance me reste-t-il ? »

Chapitre 38

Où Jésus atteint enfin Jérusalem

Maintenant il est à l'orée de la ville sainte. Des souvenirs de son enfance remontent lentement, ces heures passées au Temple à enseigner, à douze ans, devant les meilleurs docteurs de Jérusalem, cette foule innombrable qui se pressait sur le parvis des Gentils et ces animaux de partout qui bêlaient, pressentant le sacrifice, les béliers, les agneaux mâles que l'on achetait pour les offrir à Dieu, et cette odeur d'encens, de plantes aromatiques, de cèdres et de réséda, qui flottait partout pour combattre celle des chairs et des entrailles brûlées, et les rigoles de sang qui s'écoulaient sur les pierres polies, ces bruits, ces cris, ces marchandages de toutes sortes, ces litanies proférées, ces incantations qui finissaient par donner le vertige. Pouvait-on même prier dans ce caravansérail, dans ce chaos qui faisait penser à une cité corrompue plus qu'à une ville sainte ? Jésus se souvient aussi de l'angoisse de sa mère, des heures qu'elle dut passer dans le labyrinthe de la ville, pour le retrouver, il n'ignorait pas sa plainte mais il avait conscience qu'il fallait d'abord s'occuper, comme il disait, des affaires de son père. Déjà, il savait que pour le rejoindre, il devait tout quitter, même elle, sa mère.

Il aborde Jérusalem empli de sentiments confus, inexprimables. La ville se découpe à l'horizon, vaste, avec ses maisons en terrasse, cubiques et blanches, qui grimpent jusqu'au rocher du Moriah vers lequel convergent tous les pèlerins. On y devine une activité intense, des ruelles qui serpentent, et cette agitation qui règne partout, si loin de ce silence où il sait que se retrouve et se délivre son Père. Il embrasse de son regard Jérusalem tout entière, il se lamente et pleure sur elle car elle n'a pas su, dit-il, reconnaître le temps où elle fut visitée.

« Si tu avais compris, toi aussi, le message de paix ! Mais hélas, il est demeuré caché à tes yeux. Oui, des jours vont fondre sur toi où tes ennemis t'environneront de retranchements, t'investiront, te presseront de toutes parts. Ils t'écraseront sur le sol, toi et tes enfants qui seront dans tes murs. »

Les disciples entendent la prédiction. Ils sont horrifiés, comprennent que l'issue du drame va à présent se jouer ici. Il faut bien avancer cependant, aller au bout de la route. Se mêler aux pèlerins venus de partout, d'Alexandrie, de Babylone, d'Italie et d'Asie mineure, toute cette foule qui campe sous des tentes de fortune, qui se presse au milieu des païens, des hommes et des femmes, indistinctement, des hérétiques même, des excommuniés par les grands prêtres, des marchands qui négocient des passereaux, des veaux, des moutons, des pigeons. Et toute cette foule anonyme qui grouille, prie et crie à la fois, achète et revend, blasphème et adore, se piétine et vocifère.

« Nous sommes nous ici des pèlerins, dit-il à ses disciples, nous avons connu les affres de la route, la solitude et l'amertume des jours difficiles, le doute et la crainte des mauvaises rencontres, mais nous avons été conduits par l'amour de Dieu, en cela nous sommes des pèlerins qui accomplissons notre devoir et nous donnons à Dieu tout ce fardeau de désespoir, d'angoisses mais aussi d'espérance. Le pèlerinage a un but, entrer dans la chambre de Dieu, se loger chez lui, donc chez nous, puisqu'il nous a promis que sa demeure était celle de tous les hommes. Jérusalem est la clé de la route. Dieu l'a habitée mais tous ces hommes ne le savent plus, occupés à d'autres tâches. »

Il se faufile dans le dédale, il n'y est pas reconnu, il leur ressemble, avec son visage mal rasé, son profil de Sémite, sa peau burinée par le soleil et la marche. Seule peut-être cette ardeur dans le regard, ces yeux qui brillent d'un feu trop ardent, et que ceux qui savent voir redouteraient de croiser parce qu'ils y verraient les ardeurs d'un incendie. Il se hâte vers le Temple, vers la demeure de son père, il sait qu'il est transformé en lieu de foire, on y entend sonner l'or et l'argent aux étals des changeurs qui fournissent de la monnaie « pure » pour acquitter l'impôt du Temple. On y entend les marchandages pour acheter les bestiaux, des bêtes affolées souillent le parvis, tentent de pénétrer plus avant. Comment a-t-on pu en arriver à ce degré de blasphème ? À ce tapage ? Il sait que son père ne se livre que dans le silence retrouvé de celui qui le prie. Jésus voit bien qu'il a quitté depuis longtemps le Temple, qu'il préfère se retirer dans ces espaces introuvables de l'univers, dans ses galaxies inconnues, loin de ce chaos. Mais tous ici continuent de penser qu'il est présent. Ils ne savent pas qu'il ne reste que des gesticulations, des rites dépourvus de sens, des actes inventés par le monde.

La colère le saisit, il a toujours gardé au fond de lui cette impatience, cette brutalité primitive, cette sauvagerie qui bouleverse ses plans, lui donne soudain le courage de tout oser. Il saisit un paquet de cordes à un étal, des cordes qui servent à ligoter les bêtes sacrifiées, il les rassemble, les noue à leur base et en fait un fouet. Il balaie la table d'un changeur, les pièces de monnaie se répandent sur le dallage, roulent dans la foule. Aussitôt les badauds arrivent, la foule se précipite, on avertit des gardes, on croit à une émeute. Mais Jésus ne craint plus rien, il continue à renverser les étals, les cages d'oiseaux et de volailles : « Il est écrit, dit-il, ma maison sera une maison de prières. Et vous en avez fait, vous, un repaire de brigands ! »

Les scribes, les grands prêtres accourent. Qui est cet homme qui fait un tel scandale ? Est-ce ce Jésus de Nazareth, cet errant venu de Galilée, qui vient semer le trouble et dont la réputation est parvenue jusqu'à nous ? Mais Jésus n'est déjà plus là. Sa colère est tombée, transformée en une immense douleur. Il s'est glissé de nouveau dans la foule, comme s'il éprouvait la vanité de son acte, cette nécessité et cette folie à la fois d'accomplir son devoir. Il se perd dans les ruelles, atteint les collines voisines, se réfugie sur le mont des Oliviers, il s'adosse à un de ces troncs trapus, sous le feuillage bas et vert sombre, et murmure : « Me voici près de toi, mon père, je suis au dernier acte de l'histoire, il n'y a plus de route, plus de carrefour, que le croisement des bois auxquels ils me cloueront. J'ai besoin de ta consolation, de ton souffle chaud sur moi. »

Dieu recouvre alors son fils d'un manteau de vent tiède, il demande à ses anges de l'apaiser par leur présence diaphane, d'installer plus que d'ordinaire d'autres étoiles dans le ciel pour que la nuit lui soit douce, de faire brûler des essences rares. « Refaites la nuit de Bethléem, leur dit-il, il connaît sa douceur et sa lumière, dressez au-dessus de lui un dais de lin brodé, qu'il entende le chant des bergers. » Il monte, le chant, comme dans la nuit kabyle, des gardiens de moutons soufflent dans leur flûte de roseau, une musique âpre et chaude à la fois, et des sourates lentement s'élèvent, prononcées, il monte, comme la prière chaque jour répétée des moines de Jérusalem, devenue le lieu prédit de Jésus, fait de guerres et d'affrontements, où les bombes explosent à deux pas des lieux saints, et cependant le chant continue sa psalmodie. « La nuit tombe, Seigneur, viens à mon secours, je vois venir les ténèbres et j'ai peur. Viens me sauver. »

Chapitre 39

Où Jésus défie les Juifs

« De quel lieu parles-tu ? Au nom de qui ? D'où viens-tu ? » questionnent les Juifs mais Jésus ne répond pas. Il préfère parler au peuple, en paraboles si claires que tous le reconnaissent comme un maître. On l'espionne, on envoie des hommes de main pour prendre en défaut sa parole, on espère qu'il tombera de lui-même, que ses paroles le piégeront et alors on l'arrêtera enfin et on l'exécutera. Jésus sait tout cela, mais sa parole est au plus juste de celle de Dieu et nul ne peut y trouver à redire. Encouragé par la foule qui l'écoute avidement, il retrouve ses accents guerriers, sa parole de feu, ses prophéties apocalyptiques. Il est celui qui vient et qui voit.

« Continuez à veiller et à prier par tous les temps, afin d'avoir la force d'échapper à tout ce qui doit arriver, car il y aura des guerres et des bouleversements, des pestes et des famines, et dans le ciel des phénomènes effrayants, et de grands signes. Pour cela, soyez toujours dans le Père, vivez en lui, ne vous laissez pas séduire par d'autres forces, elles sont maléfiques et ne veulent que votre perte, soyez comme Loth fuyant Gomorrhe. »

Une sourde inquiétude règne parmi les prêtres et les scribes du Temple. « Que veut dire Jésus en annonçant la fin de Jérusalem et la ruine du Temple ? Quel oiseau de malheur est-il pour vouloir nous effrayer autant, nous tourmenter ainsi ? Nous sommes sans péché, nous avons prié comme la Loi nous le dit, nous avons fait scrupuleusement nos actes rituels, pourquoi Dieu nous punirait-il ? » Des prophètes, ils en ont vu, mais pas comme Jésus le Galiléen. Aucun n'avait sa force de persuasion, sa sagesse, sa justesse dans la parole. Aucun n'était apparu aussi dangereux. À ceux qui veulent lui tendre un piège, le livrer mains liées au gouverneur, à ceux qui lui disent : « Mais nous est-il permis de payer le tribut à César ? », Jésus leur répond comme à son habitude, avec clarté : « De qui porte l'effigie de vos deniers ? De César, n'est-ce pas ? Alors, rendez à César ce qui est à César et à Dieu ce qui est à Dieu ! »

Personne encore ne peut ruiner sa logique de simple, ils disent tout bas qu'il est protégé par Dieu, qu'il a Dieu avec lui.

Jésus a besoin de la solitude du mont des Oliviers. Chaque nuit, il s'y réfugie seul tandis que ses disciples forment un peu plus loin une garde rapprochée mais discrète. C'est à ce moment surtout qu'il se sent auréolé de la grâce de Dieu, loin de ces polémiques et de ces disputes qui l'assiègent et l'accablent. Il voudrait qu'on le laisse aller seul à la mort comme les bêtes du Temple vont au sacrifice, pattes liées, hébétées. Il a des visions qui le traversent, Jérusalem écrasé sous les assauts des ennemis, les dômes et les maisons, le temple lui-même, à peine reconstruit, tout sera détruit, les éléments eux-mêmes seront déchaînés, les mers submergeront les continents, les nations du monde entier seront dans l'angoisse, il n'y aura plus de lieu pour prier Dieu, il sera rejeté de la terre, nié et bafoué. Puis Jésus voit encore la gloire de son Père apparaître dans les nuées, il sera à ses côtés, élevé auprès de lui, et alors son règne sera éternel.

Les disciples dorment profondément, ils prétendent que ce n'est que d'un œil, mais Jésus sait qu'ils n'ont pas encore assimilé la leçon. Jean et Pierre ressentent pourtant une angoisse sourdre en eux, ils feignent de ne pas y prêter attention, la nuit est si claire, si douce. Comment les ténèbres pourraient-elles s'abattre sur eux ? Jésus ne leur laisse aucune illusion.

« Bientôt, dit-il, je vous quitterai, puisque mon terme est presque arrivé. Je suis d'une infinie tristesse de vous laisser mais ce n'est pas un abandon, vous êtes baptisés dans l'esprit et ma présence sera constante. Le plus dur vous appartient, il faudra rendre compte, témoigner de ce que vous avez vécu, annoncer ce que je vous ai appris, le dire sur toutes les terres, même les plus infidèles. Qu'un seul foyer y soit et Dieu bénira cette terre. »

Au petit matin, après quelques heures à peine de sommeil, la foule vient chercher Jésus au mont des Oliviers pour le ramener au Temple. Il est épuisé de fatigue, ne récupère plus, mais se rend à sa mission.

Elle est de plus en plus provocante, quelques mots de plus peuvent allumer l'incendie. Tous les nantis font cercle autour de lui pour le faire tomber. Lui continue sa route. La foi est plus forte que la peur, plus inconsciente que tous les raisonnements. Il est sûr de lui, de sa foi, sans pouvoir l'expliquer, le mystère lui est apparu d'une limpide clarté : comment s'y opposer ?

Mais la voie de Dieu est aussi voie de douleur. Elle n'épargne pas ceux qui l'empruntent, comme la nature tout entière, elle sait qu'il faut passer par la mort, en connaître les affres et les terreurs pour renaître à la lumière. Que reste-t-il du figuier les jours de givre et de froid ? Qu'un tronc torturé et sans feuilles. Et pourtant, à la fin de l'été, il croule sous les fruits, onctueux comme du miel. « Donne-nous, Seigneur, à notre tour, d'atteindre ta vallée de miel, tout ce que tu as promis à Israël ! »

Pour oublier le désastre et les images atroces de son supplice qui le traversent, pour fuir un instant l'itinéraire du sacrifice dont il connaît pas à pas déjà tous les arrêts, il se remémore les psaumes de l'ancienne Loi, les chants d'allégresse et d'espérance, que sa mère, chantait, doucement, en bonne servante du Seigneur. « Yahvé est ma lumière et mon salut. De qui aurais-je crainte ? Yahvé est le rempart de ma vie, devant qui tremblerais-je ? Quand je crois, tu me réponds, vous les hommes, jusqu'à quand ces cœurs fermés, ce goût du rien, cette course au mensonge ? Sachez-le, Yahvé fait merveille pour son ami, Yahvé m'écoute quand je crie vers lui, en paix je me couche, aussitôt je m'endors[26]. » Loin de lui Nazareth et la tiédeur du foyer familial, loin les nuits de son enfance qu'il croyait infinies, toutes ces heures qu'il passait à contempler la voie lactée, dans l'innocence des étoiles, et qui faisaient dire aux siens, à ses voisins qu'il était décidément différent, qu'il ressemblait sans leur ressembler aux garçons de son village, que quelque chose échappait pour mieux le connaître, quelque chose qui se disait à son insu même, une gravité surtout, un sourire triste, inexprimable, une distance et une proximité à la fois, et l'intuition d'un savoir vaste, sans mesure, dont il était possesseur, mais inconnu pour lui. C'est tout ce poids qu'il ressent dans ces nuits de Jérusalem, la certitude d'avoir été envoyé pour témoigner du Père et en même temps les limites de son humanité, vécues dans ses doutes, ses désarrois, ses peurs.

Chapitre 40

Où Jésus amorce la chute de l'histoire

On est au temps des vendanges. L'automne est encore tiède, à Jérusalem la chaleur est forte, pas un brin d'air, de la poussière partout, soulevée par le passage des bestiaux, par le défilé continu des pèlerins, et toujours cette odeur âcre du sang, ces cris d'animaux effrayés, égorgés, ces odeurs de bois brûlé et ces senteurs aromatiques qui s'engouffrent dans le dédale des ruelles. C'est aujourd'hui la fête des Tentes. Jésus s'est glissé dans le Temple en évitant de se faire voir. Ensuite vient le moment où il se met à enseigner. Tous les prophètes, tous les errants, ont le droit de parole sous les portiques. Des Pharisiens, des grands prêtres, toute l'administration du Temple, lui demandent :

— Au nom de qui parles-tu ? Qui es-tu ?

— Ma doctrine n'est pas de moi mais de celui qui m'a envoyé. Pourquoi voulez-vous me tuer ?

C'est la première fois que Jésus s'exprime aussi brutalement. C'est lui-même qui annonce son martyre.

— Je ne suis pas venu de moi-même, dit-il. Mais il m'envoie vraiment celui qui m'a envoyé. « Vous, vous ne le connaissez pas, moi je le connais, parce que je viens d'auprès de lui et que c'est lui qui m'a envoyé[27]. »

Une rumeur de désapprobation parcourt l'assistance. On crie au blasphème, on veut l'arrêter. Jésus ne fait aucun geste, son heure n'est pas venue.

— Vous voulez m'arrêter, mais je me déroberai à vous et vous ne me trouverez pas. « Où je suis, moi, vous, vous ne pouvez venir [28]. »

Plus tard, il en reparle à ses disciples. Dans cette paix du soir qu'il affectionne, quand tous sont partis, que Jérusalem continue de vivre dans l'impureté, que la nuit est aux prostituées, propice aux mauvais coups.

— Ne croyez pas que je m'enfuirai en Grèce ou ailleurs pour continuer à instruire les hommes. Mon savoir est entre vos mains. À vous d'être le vent. Ceux qui ne me comprennent pas ne pourront pas saisir le sens de ce que j'ai dit au Temple : « "Là où je suis, moi, vous, vous ne pouvez venir [29]." » Oui, ils ne pourront venir ceux qui ont le cœur dur et les oreilles bouchées, ceux qui jugent sur l'apparence et conservent tous leurs biens. Car le Royaume dont je parle est ouvert à ceux qui aiment les autres et font circuler leurs richesses. Leur or et leur argent sont l'amour, la compassion. Ils n'ont pas d'autres richesses mais ce sont les seules vraies richesses.

Dans la nuit de Jérusalem, il pense soudain à Jean le Baptiste. « Je viens vers toi, Jean, toi qui m'as baptisé, qui m'as oint d'eau bénite, qui m'as transmis le fil sacré du reliement, mon heure n'est plus lointaine, j'entends déjà les cris et les injures, je vois déjà les torches qui se faufilent entre les oliviers, j'entends les cris des agneaux à l'heure du sacrifice et la plainte douce de ma mère, à Nazareth, qui connaît depuis toujours l'issue de l'histoire. Elle s'apprête à partir, à prendre elle aussi la route, à dos d'âne, pour me rejoindre, mais tout est inutile, je le sais, car tout est déjà écrit. »

La fin de la fête des Tentes s'achève. Elle a duré huit jours, de libations, de chants et de processions. On y célèbre l'eau vive jaillie du bâton de Moïse et on implore Dieu d'accorder au peuple des pluies généreuses pour les champs. Seul Jésus sait que la pluie d'eau vive, c'est l'amour de Dieu qui rejaillit sur les hommes quand ils le reconnaissent et le prient. Puis vient la procession des femmes à la fontaine de Siloé. Les chandeliers immenses, en or, sont tous éclairés, le Temple entier en est tout illuminé, les musiciens et les femmes jouent et chantent des cantiques du temps de Moïse, de la libération de leur peuple. « Que ces lumières allumées rappellent la nuée qui étincela dans le ciel et guida Moïse et les siens ! » proclament-ils.

Depuis le mont des Oliviers où il s'est réfugié, Jésus dit à ses disciples :

« Les rites n'ont de sens et de force que s'ils sont animés d'une foi intérieure, mais je vous le dis, il n'est pas besoin d'eux pour aimer son père, car le père préfère la parole secrète du cœur. Il n'est pas besoin d'éclairer Jérusalem de torches mirifiques parce que vous qui m'entendez et croyez en moi êtes déjà des êtres de lumière. Pas besoin de ces cérémonies pour affirmer que Dieu existe, vous êtes, à vous seuls, la lumière du monde. Et vous l'éclairerez parce que le monde en a besoin, et qu'il connaît la nuit plus que le jour. Vous, vous ne demanderez pas à Dieu des pluies d'automne pour féconder vos terres, vous demanderez la pluie d'eau vive, et elle tombera pour vous, sous la forme du feu. Car le feu, c'est l'esprit. »

À ce moment de l'histoire, les incroyants du monde entier, par-delà les siècles, explosent de colère et d'indignation. Ils disent que les légendes ont la vie dure, que Dieu se moque de la raison des hommes, qu'il les prend pour des naïfs prêts à tout gober. Il y en a qui se révoltent, proclament la mort de Dieu, déclarent que tout n'est que fables et légendes, que la mythologie chrétienne n'a fait que frustrer les hommes et les culpabiliser, que les hommes sont libres, essentiellement seuls et libres. Il n'y a rien à dire à ce processus biologique qui éteint leur vie et les dissipe dans la terre ou dans le feu. C'est bien triste, tout ça, il aurait mieux valu que ça se passe comme prétend Dieu, la vie, la mort, la résurrection, et la vie de nouveau auprès de lui et de tous les saints, le concert des anges en prime et l'affection de Marie, elle aussi élevée au rang de déesse, et tout le saint frusquin, mais comment y croire vraiment ?

Donc, l'histoire de Jésus n'est qu'une immense manipulation, d'ailleurs y a-t-il une vie de Jésus possible ? Comment s'en sortir pour un biographe ? Imaginez : Jésus est un Juif né en Israël sous le règne d'Hérode le Grand, il est un prédicateur charismatique entouré de quelques disciples, il est crucifié à Jérusalem (il n'est pas le seul) tandis que Ponce Pilate est gouverneur de Judée. Il a à peine trente-trois ans.

Toutes les sources écrites viennent après sa mort, les Évangiles comme les récits d'historiens, Pline le jeune, Tacite et Suétone.

Les contempteurs de Jésus estiment que tout est faux, au mieux un joli conte. Comment bâtir là-dessus ?

Jésus résiste aux attaques. Il passe dans l'histoire antique et il exerce une étrange fascination, il dispense une telle foi qu'elle rayonne dans tous les siècles à venir. D'où viens-tu ? Oui, d'où, pour que ton enseignement soit si vivant, si intimement présent pour tant et tant de fidèles ? Impossible biographie de Jésus, que des trous, des lacunes, des absences, des récits de seconde main, des rêveries éthérées. De la science-fiction.

« Je te cherche, Jésus, dans ma nuit noire, balbutie Edith Stein. Je suis seule et abandonnée. Tu combles mon vide et mon ennui. Je pourrais vivre comme ça, sans toi, rien qu'avec mes forces humaines, mais elles me lâchent et mon esprit me dit confusément qu'il y a autre chose. Je perçois au fond de ma nuit une lumière qui pourrait être toi. Je cherche à te rencontrer. D'où que tu sois, fais-moi signe. Parce que je suis aveugle et que je veux voir. »

Chapitre 41

Où Jésus s'accorde une pause

Le peuple vit dans l'attente de la promesse. Il en a vu défiler, des prophètes et des Christs, mais pas un comme Jésus. C'est cette lumière qui irradie son visage, cette certitude ancrée en lui. C'est à cela qu'ils se prennent à croire qu'il est envoyé par Dieu. Ses paroles les ébranlent, ils ont l'impression qu'il décille leurs yeux d'aveugles, que quelque chose de grand va se passer. D'irréversible. Jésus ne leur promet pourtant ni le Royaume pour demain ni la facilité. C'est un retournement des esprits qu'il opère, une autre manière d'envisager le monde.

Mais la violence des Pharisiens le submerge d'angoisse et de solitude. Il veut se réfugier de l'autre côté du Jourdain, attendre encore quelques jours avant de se jeter dans l'arène, avant de s'offrir en martyr à ses ennemis. Avec lui, toujours cette petite troupe de fous d'amour, les Douze qui ne le quittent pas depuis des mois, et quelques femmes, Marie de Magdala, et des errantes, des mendiantes qui vivent d'épluchures ramassées dans les poubelles des riches, et tous ces anonymes en exil mais qui croient avoir trouvé quelqu'un qui les ramène enfin chez eux. Jésus prend seulement quelque distance avant la tombée de la nuit parce qu'il a besoin de retrouver son père, de lui demander le chemin. Depuis des jours donc, on ne le voit plus à Jérusalem, on s'en inquiète, on fait des plans. On pense qu'il est peut-être parti, qu'il a pris peur, « un fou, juste bon à lapider », disent les Pharisiens. Jésus est accueilli à Béthanie qui se trouve à quelques kilomètres à peine à l'est de Jérusalem.

Marie reste auprès de lui, il ne l'éloigne pas parce qu'elle est une femme, il cherche au contraire sa compagnie, lui demande de lui raconter sa vie, il lui apprend à prier. Souvent elle chante pour lui des psaumes de l'ancien temps, des chants d'espérance et de certitude qu'elle-même avait entendus, autrefois, dans son enfance. Sa mère peut-être, elle ne sait plus. Ils lui reviennent sans qu'elle en cherche les mots, c'est une mémoire très vieille. Inoubliable. Elle lui lave les pieds comme elle a toujours su le faire avec les hommes qu'elle recevait, jadis, sous sa tente. Elle y mettait tout son cœur parce qu'elle voulait donner le meilleur à ses visiteurs, elle était une sorte de mère qui remplaçait celle qu'ils avaient perdue ou délaissée. Et tous revenaient se blottir entre ses seins, dans la mer de ses cheveux. Elle lave les pieds de Jésus avec les parfums les plus rares, des essences d'Orient, et Judas, qui nourrit intérieurement un ressentiment toujours plus grand envers Jésus, fait observer qu'on aurait pu vendre ce nard au moins trois cents deniers pour les donner aux pauvres.

« Laisse-la, lui dit alors Jésus, car moi, elle ne m'aura pas toujours. »

Entre Marie et Jésus, c'est comme une histoire d'amour, un autre baptême. Du gué où se trouvait Jean-Baptiste et qui, étrangement, s'appelait aussi Béthanie, jusqu'à l'onction de Marie, c'est la même histoire qui se déroule. C'est Jean qui oint Jésus, l'intronise et l'élève au rang de Messie et c'est Marie, l'ancienne vénale et libertine, qui oint ses pieds, les purifie de son amour. Elle vide tout le précieux flacon, tout est pour Jésus. L'huile parfumée pénètre sa peau, la sanctifie car l'essence est sainte, vouée à Dieu. Elle la répand dans ses cheveux, qu'elle essuie lentement, comme si elle voulait tempérer la violence de son Verbe, ou peut-être le contraire, car le feu peut embraser l'huile et répandre l'incendie. C'est pour quoi Jésus aime Marie : à eux deux, ils sont l'huile et le feu, l'âme et l'esprit, ils sont inséparables, car l'huile sans feu ne peut garder la lampe allumée et le feu sans huile s'étiole et dégénère.

Judas n'écoute plus que sa rancœur. Comment supporter cette intimité entre Jésus et Marie ? Comment s'attirer les grâces de Jésus pour lui tout seul ? Car il en est sûr, il aime Jésus d'un amour terrible, atroce, démoniaque et exclusif. Et Jésus ne voit rien ou feint de ne rien voir. Judas ne dit pas un mot, mais tout son visage parle pour lui. « Ne vois-tu pas, Seigneur, que je t'aime ? Que je voudrais te protéger, t'éviter les malheurs où tu te jettes ? Pourquoi m'avoir donné ce dernier des rôles, celui de tenir la bourse de notre misérable troupe d'errants, tu ne me regardes même pas, comme si je ne devais pas comprendre ce que tu enseignes. Mais pose, ne serait-ce qu'un instant, qu'une seconde, tes yeux sur moi et tu verras de quelle nature est mon amour pour toi, tu verrais alors le feu, sauvage, qui court, que je ne peux contenir parce qu'il me déborde et me dévore. Mais toi qui vois tout, tu sais que je suis jaloux des onze autres, et de Jean surtout qui n'hésite pas à se blottir dans tes bras, à te parler à mi-voix et que tu écoutes, comme s'il était un ange venu du ciel, tandis que je ne suis que le comptable de ta misérable église, pour moi seul les soucis d'argent. À toi, aux Onze et même à Marie la pécheresse, les questions de l'esprit. Seigneur, tu m'as déjà renié. Je te tromperai, je te donnerai à tes ennemis et je serai alors le dernier, le maudit, le fils prodigue qui aura tout dilapidé de ta vigne, ton enseignement et ton amour, mais je t'acculerai à me pardonner, je serai le dernier et tu m'accueilleras quand même et je serai alors le premier dans ton cœur, je t'aurai trahi et tu m'auras pardonné, je serai le plus égaré du troupeau et tu m'y ramèneras, tu appliqueras pour moi ta parabole du fils prodigue. »

Jésus entend les paroles secrètes de Judas. Il faut bien un traître qui dénonce, un des siens qui n'aura pas su aller jusqu'au bout de son amour, et qui le donnera. Et ce sera lui, Judas l'Iscariote. Et alors tout sera accompli selon les anciennes Écritures.

À Jérusalem, les grands prêtres se sont réunis. Toute cette agitation, ces rumeurs de miracles et de guérisons, ces injures proférées par ce fou de Jésus, bouleversent la vie bien réglée du Temple. La foule est en émoi et ne prie plus selon la Loi. Il faut faire cesser au plus vite ce scandale. Pour la première fois, dans leur esprit, est née l'idée de le tuer. Pour s'en débarrasser à jamais. Oui, c'est cela la bonne décision, le faire crucifier avec les voleurs, les tueurs, au gibet du Golgotha.

Chapitre 42

Où Jésus est trahi

Le lendemain de l'arrivée à Béthanie, Jésus veut défier de nouveau les Pharisiens, les scribes et les grands prêtres.
« Vous fermez aux hommes le Royaume de Dieu, leur dit-il. Vous ne laissez même pas entrer ceux qui le voudraient ! Malheur à vous, scribes et Pharisiens hypocrites, qui acquittez la dîme de la menthe, du fenouil et du cumin, après avoir négligé les points les plus graves de la Loi, la justice, la miséricorde et la bonne foi ! Malheur à vous qui ressemblez à des sépulcres blanchis : hypocrites qui purifiez l'extérieur de la coupe et de l'écuelle quand l'intérieur en est rempli par rapine et par intempérance ! »
Puis, revenant vers ses disciples, il ordonne :
« Allez me chercher un âne à l'entrée du village voisin, il y en a un à l'attache que personne n'a encore monté. Prenez-le et dites à son maître que le Seigneur en a besoin et qu'il le lui rendra. »
Les disciples s'y rendent et trouvent en effet un ânon qui paît dans une cour, attaché à un pieu. Ils le délient et le portent à Jésus. Il monte sur l'ânon et entre dans la ville. Aussitôt des hommes et des femmes le reconnaissent, se prosternent sur son passage, jonchent le sol de feuillages et même de leurs vêtements pour faire une voie royale à celui

qu'ils appellent maintenant ouvertement le Messie. « Hosanna, disent-ils, béni soit celui qui vient au nom du Seigneur. Hosanna au plus haut des cieux[30]. »

Lui ne dit mot. Il sourit doucement et pense à cet étrange cortège, à tous ces pauvres et à ces simples qui le louent, tandis que les Pharisiens l'observent et l'épient. Le voilà monté sur cet ânon, comme autrefois quand Joseph et Marie durent s'enfuir en Égypte à dos d'âne pour échapper aux massacres d'Hérode alors qu'il n'était encore qu'un nourrisson. Plus que jamais il se sent proche des plus faibles, des plus démunis, des plus fragiles. À César l'aigle impérial, à lui, le Fils de Dieu, l'animal le plus méprisé, le plus esclave de la vie domestique !

Les disciples font corps autour de lui, ils craignent toujours un incident, une arrestation. Ils n'approuvent pas cette nouvelle initiative de Jésus, la jugent trop dangereuse pour lui et pour eux. Mais Jésus manifeste tant de calme, tant d'assurance : comment ne pas lui faire confiance ?

Seul Judas apprécie le geste ostentatoire de son maître. Il pestait jusqu'alors contre les disciples qui voulaient rester discrets : « Est-ce ainsi, dit-il souvent, que le Seigneur va rassembler son Royaume ? » Lui ne voit que la gloire et le pouvoir, il ne veut pas vraiment comprendre les paroles de Jésus qui affirment que tout est ailleurs, dans le Royaume de Dieu, que le passage sur terre n'est qu'une transition, que le pouvoir y est une réalité aléatoire, et qu'il éloigne irrémédiablement de Dieu parce qu'il est lié à Satan, à toutes les forces sombres qui sont constamment à l'œuvre dans le monde. Il déteste Jean pour sa clarté et cette lumière qui l'auréole, repérée très vite par Jésus. Et lui, pourquoi Jésus ne l'a-t-il pas remarqué ? Il l'aime pourtant, à eux deux, pense-t-il, ils referaient le monde, ils auraient tout le pouvoir possible. Et lui, Judas, serait un bon serviteur, il tiendrait bien les comptes et il saurait faire fructifier l'or et l'argent. Il veillerait à ce que la cour de Jésus ne soit pas encombrée de prostituées et de mendiants, il lui donnerait de bons conseils pour conserver le pouvoir, renoncer à ses discours enflammés et dangereux, et déclarer au contraire que ce sont les Pharisiens et les grands prêtres qui iront les premiers au Royaume et non pas les publicains et les filles des rues. Marie de Magdala est aussi aux côtés de Jésus, elle suit le cortège et elle chante la gloire du Messie. On ne l'écoute pas, on sait qu'elle est prostituée, et folle, et l'on trouve que Jésus est bien bon de parader avec tous ces errants et tous ces miséreux.

Marie ne cherche à convaincre personne, elle accompagne Jésus sur sa route, elle va avec lui sur la petite voie qu'il s'est choisi. Elle aime cette modestie de Jésus, cette naïveté qui lui vient de l'enfance. Elle l'aime encore parce qu'il a chassé d'elle les sept démons qui la tenaillaient, la contraignaient de se donner comme un objet à tous les hommes qu'elle recevait. Elle avait fini par en prendre l'habitude, d'accepter. Il y avait la luxure, la séduction, le rire outrancier, l'impudeur, la trahison, le poison et, logé au fond d'elle, le plus terrible des démons, le désespoir que Jésus mit tant de temps à extirper de son corps pantelant, car c'était surtout ce démon-là auquel Satan tenait le plus, le désespoir qui chevillait sa proie, la retenait à lui comme une bête de somme, l'obligeait à se détruire, ce désespoir qui empêchait de s'ouvrir à Dieu, de lui dire qu'elle est là, misérable et abandonnée, seule au milieu de tous ces hommes qui attendaient leur tour à l'entrée de son lieu. Et Jésus s'était acharné à faire surgir au-dehors de son corps ce démon atroce, cette douleur qu'elle croyait inguérissable. Par quels prodiges ? Marie s'était-elle soudain décidée à rencontrer Jésus ? Quel miracle avait fait qu'elle l'avait reconnu comme son frère, presque son double en tout cas celui qui lui ressemblait le plus sur cette terre ? Lui, Jésus, l'avait vue nue, intégralement nue après qu'il l'eut débarrassée de ses démons, et sa nudité ne l'avait pas outragé parce qu'elle était sans péché, vierge. Oui, Marie de Magdala se sentait vierge à travers Jésus, et elle pouvait maintenant entrer la première à sa suite dans le Royaume. Tout les unissait dorénavant : comme elle s'était offerte à tous les hommes sans exclusion, lui aussi s'offrirait à tous les hommes de la terre. N'allait-il pas subir lui aussi le châtiment qu'Ézéchiel prédisait aux filles de Babel ? « Ils t'arracheront tes vêtements, proférait le vieux prophète, et ils te prendront tes bijoux, ils te laisseront toute nue puis ils exciteront la foule contre toi, on te lapidera, on te percera à coups d'épée, on mettra le feu à tes maisons. » Même lapidation pour Jésus, mêmes coups de lance dans son corps outragé, mêmes injures et même lynchage pour lui. Ils se retrouvent côte à côte, tous deux nus et abandonnés, la prostituée et le fils de Dieu, et personne ne peut vraiment comprendre ce que signifie ce couple retrouvé, cette union si insolite du péché et de la grâce.

C'est de tout cela dont Judas est jaloux, jusqu'à en être malade, jusqu'à la nausée. Lentement, comme la nuit quand elle succède au jour, se forge en lui l'idée de se venger, de trahir son maître, de le donner aux prêtres du Temple. Il s'y rend, demande à être reçu.

— Je suis des proches de Jésus de Nazareth. Que me donnerez-vous si je vous le livre ?

— Trente pièces d'argent, lui répondent les prêtres.

— Soit, je reviendrai bientôt pour vous le livrer.

Il revient vers Jésus et les Onze. Quelque chose d'indicible lui noue le corps et le ventre, il a peur, il tente de se rassurer, mais la souffrance l'étreint de plus en plus. Il éprouve une étrange impression de vide et de chute, de tétanie et d'oppression, il veut les rejoindre et il s'égare, arrive à la géhenne, l'immense décharge publique qui brûle de nuit comme de jour, où rôdent les bêtes sauvages et les rats. Une odeur âcre de braise et de cendres, de chair décomposée brûlée infecte l'air :

— Pardonne-moi, Seigneur, je ne voulais pas cela, c'est que je t'aime, que je te voulais pour moi seul, à nous deux nous aurions été les maîtres du monde mais tu m'as renié avant même que je ne te trahisse. Je voudrais revenir sur ma faute et je sens bien que je ne le peux plus, pardonne-moi, qui t'ai mis sur la voie des prophètes.

Quand il arrive au campement de fortune, Jésus sait déjà qu'il a trahi. Il ne dit rien, il le regarde et Judas baisse les yeux, il ne peut soutenir son regard de feu.

— Nous allons bientôt manger la Pâque, dit Jésus, et tu dois venir toi aussi. Prépare-toi au repas de vérité.

Chapitre 43

Où Jésus entre dans sa Passion

Jérusalem n'a jamais aimé les prophètes, Jésus le sait, il retarde l'heure où il y entrera de nouveau et que personne ni même Dieu ne pourra suspendre. Il faudra alors aller au sacrifice, s'y résigner comme l'agneau qui a fini de bêler. Il aime se rendre sur les rives du Jourdain, y puiser la paix de Jean-Baptiste, y retrouver le silence lustral du baptême, ces journées d'onction que Jean accomplissait pour tous ceux qui voulaient alors s'en remettre au Dieu qu'il annonçait. Il est dans les pas de Jean, dont la force et la foi ont comme habité le lieu. Jean n'est plus là, mais Jean est déjà ressuscité, et tout ici lui parle et parle de lui. Jésus vient prendre des forces avant l'épreuve. « Me voilà seul devant elle, et je m'en remets à ta prière, Jean devenu saint parmi tous les aimés de mon Père, Jean auprès de lui, je me nourris de la force que tu m'as insufflée il y a peu encore sur ces mêmes rives, ta prière remonte des grands fonds de ma mémoire, je la récupère et la renvoie à Dieu, pour qu'il ne cesse de me porter dans le sacrifice, pour qu'il ne m'abandonne pas. »

Des Grecs, gagnés au monothéisme d'Israël, demandent à Philippe s'ils peuvent rencontrer Jésus. Accompagné d'André, il se rend auprès de lui et lui fait part de la demande. Jésus frémit d'une angoisse nouvelle, le destin est en marche, se dit-il, c'est le moment.

« Je m'y rendrai parce qu'il le faut, mais voici l'heure venue. Je ne peux m'y dérober davantage. Si le grain de blé ne tombe en terre et ne meurt, il reste seul. S'il meurt, il en renaîtra quand même beaucoup de fruits. Qui aime sa vie la perd. Et qui hait sa vie en ce monde, la conservera en vie éternelle. »

Pour la première fois, Jésus annonce son entrée dans la Passion. Les disciples sont perplexes, ne savent quoi penser de toute cette histoire, leur esprit qui s'est ouvert depuis des mois déjà aux miracles, qui s'est émerveillé devant des prodiges dont ils étaient les témoins directs, est saisi d'incertitude et de terreur. D'une manière ou d'une autre, que tout soit mensonge ou vérité, des jours funestes vont s'abattre sur eux. « Seigneur, implorent-ils, donne-nous l'espérance qui fait tomber les doutes et les peurs, raffermis notre foi qui chancelle. »

Jésus parle à haute voix, il ne craint pas que ses propres angoisses soient entendues de tous. Depuis que les disciples sont venus le rejoindre, des hommes sont arrivés de toutes parts, ils forment cercle autour de lui, attendent des preuves, des signes merveilleux, quelque chose de surnaturel qui viendrait du ciel ou des ténèbres, qu'importe, mais quelque chose qui leur donnerait la certitude qu'ils ne sont pas seuls, abandonnés à eux-mêmes. Alors, oui, ils prieraient Dieu, ils l'imploreraient, et ce ne seraient pas que des gesticulations, des rites bien huilés, bien codifiés, qui deviendraient routine. Mais tous voient Jésus douter de sa mission.

« Ne prenez pas peur, je serai saisi de la même angoisse au mont Gethsémani, je connaîtrai la même solitude qui me fait blasphémer, douter de mon père. Mon âme est troublée, je l'avoue, Que dire, à présent : "'Père, sauve-moi de cette heure[31] ?'" Trop tard puisque tout le chemin parcouru n'a tendu qu'à cette heure. Comment m'y soustraire ? Comment ne pas accomplir les Écritures ?

Le prodige attendu de la foule survient enfin. C'est une voix, immense, « un coup de tonnerre » qui déclare : « "Je l'ai glorifié et je le glorifierai à nouveau[32]." » Puis Jésus déclare :

« Je ne serai avec vous que pour peu de temps. Marchez dans la lumière, conduisez-vous en fils de la lumière et vous me retrouverez. Car celui qui marche dans les ténèbres ne sait pas où il va et n'a aucune chance de retrouver la route du Royaume. Croyez en la lumière, suivez son sillage d'étoiles, sa nuée d'argent, revêtez-vous de cette lumière, que votre esprit éclaire le monde, qu'il lui donne de l'air, de la clarté. Vous êtes cette lumière. »

En proclamant ces mots, Jésus disparaît. On ne savait jamais dans l'assistance comment il faisait pour se dérober à sa vue, par quel nouveau miracle il s'effaçait. Était-il venu ce moment où il disait qu'il allait être élevé de terre ? Partait-il rejoindre le Dieu du ciel ? Les disciples font un cercle très resserré autour de Jésus. Ils craignent non seulement pour sa sécurité mais ils veulent rester au plus près de lui, s'imprégner de son énergie, réclament des dons. Judas sent venir l'heure plus que tous les autres disciples. Il murmure en lui-même : « Il est trop tard, n'est-ce pas, rabbi, pour t'implorer de m'accorder un regard. La nuit avance et j'ai peur et tu n'atténues pas ma terreur, tu sens mon âme troublée et tu ne viens pas me consoler, tu entends ma plainte mais tu refuses de l'accueillir. Que t'ai-je dit, rabbi, pour que tu me renies ainsi ? Est-ce Dieu qui m'a choisi pour que le divin dessein se réalise absolument ? Suis-je condamné à trahir quand je t'aime ? Ou bien crois-tu que je suis la clé qui ouvre la porte de ton mystère, celui qui te fait entrer dans ta Passion et te donne l'accès au Royaume ? »

La nuit tombe sur Jérusalem. Non pas celle qui succède d'ordinaire au jour, mais une nuit qui pénètre les esprits et les cœurs, une sorte de malheur intérieur, un doute et une peur profonde qui s'installent. Inconnus au monde. Inévitables.

Chapitre 44

Où Jésus se prépare à quitter les siens

« Je vous aimerai jusqu'à la fin. Il n'y aura pas de répit pour cet amour, je m'en irai et je serai avec vous, dans l'amour, vous croirez être seuls mais vous ne le serez plus, car je vous veillerai. Là où je vais, vous ne pouvez aujourd'hui aller mais je vous promets que vous me rejoindrez. »
Jésus est grave, il accomplit les derniers gestes que son père lui a commandés. Il dresse la table. Quand il devra partir, il repliera la nappe, tout sera en ordre, il n'y aura pas de bruit, pas de violence, pas de cris ni de larmes, mais ce baiser d'adieu et d'amour qui les scellera à jamais. Il lave les pieds de ses disciples, ils s'y refusent mais Jésus insiste. « "Si je ne te lave pas, tu n'auras pas de part avec moi[33]" », dit-il à Pierre qui résiste. La scène est très douce et très calme. Il n'y a que du silence tout autour ; les disciples savent que l'heure est venue. Ils ne s'y sont pas assez préparés.
« Je vous ai demandé d'être toujours dans en état d'éveil. De ne jamais vous laisser surprendre. Je suis rabbi et je m'en vais. Vous le saviez mais vous n'y croyiez pas vraiment. À présent, c'est le moment, il faut s'y résoudre. Parmi vous, il y en a un qui m'a trahi. Qui a cru me servir en me livrant. Il est impur mais il sera pardonné. »

C'est le dernier repas pris en commun. Ils ne partageront plus ensemble les fruits secs et les poissons séchés achetés sur les places des villages, rien ne sera plus comme avant. Pierre, Jean et les autres disciples sentent en eux comme un souffle qui les balaie, qui leur dit que l'heure est aussi venue pour eux, celui de la mission. De leur éclatement dans le monde. Cette annonce incroyable, féerique, à transmettre à tous les peuples.

« Je vous confie la nouvelle alliance. Vous devrez la faire connaître. Rien ne sera impossible à vous. Vous prendrez la mer et vous irez sur tous les continents dire la nouvelle. Vous m'avez reçu et à votre tour vous avez reçu celui qui m'a envoyé. Ceux que vous convaincrez me recevront à leur tour et l'annonce du Royaume se fera ainsi, dans la contagion de l'amour. »

Judas ne peut supporter son forfait. Il regrette déjà son geste, esquive le regard de Jésus.

« "Ce que tu as à faire, lui dit-il, fais-le vite[34]." »

Judas quitte le repas. Tous croient que Jésus lui a demandé d'aller porter l'aumône à des pauvres, dehors, puisque c'est lui qui tient la bourse. Judas s'enfuit dans la nuit. Il est pris de vomissements, de nausées, il sent en lui quelque chose qui grouille et le blesse. Il dit :

« C'est Satan qui entre en moi, je suis à lui maintenant. Je t'ai aimé, Jésus, et je t'ai quitté, je t'ai trahi quand je ne le voulais pas. Je ne sais où aller puisque je n'ai plus de chemin, plus de guide pour me conduire. Satan est en moi, il m'entraîne vers la géhenne, je le sens à l'odeur âcre des bêtes crevées, je t'ai aimé, Jésus, mais pas de l'amour que tu voulais, je t'ai aimé exclusivement, je voulais que tu sois tout à moi comme j'aurais été tout à toi, d'un amour sans partage, mais toi, tu voulais le contraire, donner de ton amour au monde entier, le dilapider dans l'univers. »

La nuit est profonde. Dans la décharge brûlent toutes les ordures de Jérusalem. Elle est repérable au lit de braises ardentes où se consument à petit feu les viscères des animaux sacrifiés et tous les déchets de la ville, toutes ses immondices jetées dans le ravin où viennent mourir les bêtes agonisantes, où se donnent la mort les sans-espoirs.

« Tu m'entraînes, Satan, dans la géhenne. Tu me guides vers ma mort. J'ai vendu l'espérance contre trente deniers d'argent. Misérable que je suis ! Perdu ! »

Jésus pendant ce temps rassemble autour de lui tous les siens. Il est au milieu de la grande table rectangulaire, il préside le repas. Il appelle ses disciples « mes petits enfants ».

— Vous connaissez le chemin de mon Royaume. Je m'en vais le premier vous préparer une place. Je reviendrai vous prendre avec moi.

— Mais, Seigneur, comment connaîtrons-nous le chemin ?

— « Je suis le Chemin, la Vérité, la Vie[35]. »

Les mots de Jésus s'incrustent dans les siècles. Les disciples les entendent, mais pas seulement eux, tous les hommes après eux, la terre entière. Jésus livre le Grand Secret, celui des alchimistes et des poètes, le Graal, l'or du monde. Il n'est pas Jésus seulement, physiquement, dans sa vie aléatoire, incertaine et en pointillés, il n'est pas Jésus à l'existence confuse, presque mythique, il est d'abord la vie et tout ce qui contribue à elle. Il est l'énergie qui fait avancer, l'amour qui fait s'attirer les êtres entre eux, il est la chlorophylle des herbes et de toutes les plantes, il est le sang qui parcourt les hommes, il est le chant qui s'élève dans la nuit, dans la guerre, il est le feu qui court dans les esprits et qui résiste, il est le maquis sauvage, le vent ardent qui efface tous les miasmes, il est la semence de vie, le sperme qui féconde, l'embryon et l'enfant, il est la vie, au premier mouvement, à la première pulsation, au premier tressaillement, fût-il à peine perceptible, il est la colère et la tendresse, le baiser et l'étreinte. C'est ainsi, Jésus de Nazareth qui naquit en l'an 4 avant notre ère, chargé de cette mission de rappel. « Aimez-vous les uns les autres. » Plus besoin de vie réelle, alors, plus besoin de dates précises, que cette leçon qui reste, le Grand Secret, divulgué, sitôt oublié, renié. Dehors, celui que Jésus appelle le « Prince de ce monde », dont il ne sous-estime pas la force et la vaillance, s'emploie à effacer ce commandement de l'amour. Il s'agite comme un diable qu'il est à détruire l'œuvre de Vie, à dévier le Chemin, à répandre le mensonge. Judas traîne dans la géhenne, personne dans la montagne d'ordures, il s'enfonce dans les viscères décomposés, ramenés du Temple, celles des bêtes sacrifiées, une odeur infecte plane partout.

« Aie pitié de moi, Jésus, fais-moi revenir vers toi. Envoie-moi tes anges. »

Mais Jésus laisse aller son disciple sur sa pente de douleur. Il est le fils de division, il a tenté de le convertir car, depuis le début, il a vu que son esprit était disponible à la convoitise, au gain et à l'ambition. Mais il croyait lui insuffler cet amour qui sauve le monde. Il n'y a plus que les Onze et lui-même. Sur la table de la Cène, Giotto a peint *a fresca* tous les acteurs du drame mystique. Jésus a la rudesse des paysans de Toscane, et Jean la douceur de ses paysages. Il ressemble à un jeune éphèbe, presque une jeune fille. Il est très jeune en tout cas, fragile aussi. Jésus fait le geste de rompre du pain. Mais avant le pain, il a porté à ses lèvres une coupe remplie du vin nouveau :

— « Prenez ceci et partagez entre vous, car je vous le dis, je ne boirai plus désormais du produit de la vigne jusqu'à ce que le Royaume de Dieu soit venu[36]. »

Il prend ensuite le pain, il le rompt et le bénit, le donne à ses disciples en disant :

— Ceci est mon corps qui va être donné pour vous, faites ceci en mémoire de moi.

Giotto, Michel-Ange, Vinci, Raphaël, Rembrandt, Veronese, Lotti, tous les maîtres de la peinture rejouent à leur façon la Cène. Partout dans le monde, les mots de Jésus sont répétés chaque jour, à chaque heure, ils montent comme un lien tendu vers Dieu, ils font de chaque fidèle, un disciple de Jérusalem. C'est cette constance qui trouble et fascine, cette litanie dans le monde comme un cordon qui l'entoure. Du fond de leur lit de douleur, les grands mystiques du christianisme, avec la même régularité, demandent à boire à la coupe le vin de Jésus et à manger du pain. Plus que tous les autres fidèles, ils sont les disciples de Jésus, leurs successeurs, ils sont dans la même proximité d'âme qu'eux, et par un étrange enchantement, ils deviennent le sang et le corps du Christ. Il coule ce sang, dans leur Passion du vendredi, au travers de leurs plaies qui se rouvrent et suintent d'un jus clairet et rosâtre, c'est la chair du Christ qui s'éventre et s'éclate, sous les coups de fouet invisibles mais bien réels que le martyre leur inflige.

C'est le temps des adieux. La nuit est tombée. Des lampes à huile éclairent la pièce de lueurs falotes, elles éclairent par intermittences les visages, des gestes, la coupe de vin, la corbeille de pain azyme. Puis Jésus dit encore :

— J'ai prié pour toi, Pierre, parce que je sais que ta foi sera défaillante.

Et comme Pierre s'en défend farouchement, il rajoute :

— « Je te le dis, Pierre, le coq ne chantera pas aujourd'hui que par trois fois tu auras nié me connaître[37]. »

À la fin du repas pascal, Jésus dit encore :

« Vous n'êtes plus seulement mes disciples, mais des apôtres à présent. Je vous donne au monde, je vous y envoie, vous le sillonnerez et vous l'ensemencerez, et du Royaume de mon Père je verrai vos récoltes. N'usez pas du nom de Dieu pour l'imposer, ne forcez quiconque à croire, car c'est par l'amour que vous témoignerez de lui. Mais je vous le dis parce que je sais qu'en mon nom l'on accomplira des forfaits et des crimes. Ceux qui vous suivront flétriront mon nom par leurs exactions. Il y aura des massacres au nom de Jésus, des conquêtes atroces, des conversions forcées, des mensonges et des hypocrisies, mais la vérité finira par triompher, pour peu que vous vous souveniez que Dieu est amour et compassion. Vous êtes donc mes apôtres, mes brebis dans les vastes champs du monde, vous avez en vous la lumière que je vous ai insufflée, et le vent pour vous déplacer. Vous n'avez plus de maison ni de famille, de votre petite troupe faites des légions, faites lever la pâte. »

Il quitte enfin la table que personne n'ose desservir tant elle apparaît sanctifiée, immuable. Jésus est sur le seuil de la maison, il boit l'air de la nuit, regarde la voûte céleste illuminée et disparaît. La nuit, lourde dans son cœur, étincelle pourtant de toutes ses étoiles, les rumeurs de la ville l'atteignent à peine, il entend des sons de flûte, des musiques lascives et rauques qui disent la douleur d'aimer et d'avoir été abandonné, des musiques d'exil, répétitives et qui, inlassablement, reprennent la même mélodie. Le mont des Oliviers forme une masse noire au milieu du halo lumineux de la ville. Jésus s'y enfonce par des chemins étroits, au passage il est griffé par des épineux, des figuiers de Barbarie vifs comme des herses, il va s'abriter sous un olivier, au feuillage si bas qu'il fait une grotte.

« Ce n'est plus l'heure de dormir, Père. Je veux cette nuit pour toi entièrement de prières. Qu'elles t'atteignent dans ton refuge ! »

Chapitre 45

Où Jésus veille au mont des Oliviers

C'est une nuit d'incertitude, personne ne vient à son secours, il a l'esprit troublé, il n'est plus sûr de rien, ni du Royaume ni de la vie éternelle qui y est promise, peut-être pas même du Père. Il sait que les jours de chair s'achèvent, qu'à présent vont s'abattre les ténèbres. Il ne voit pas de lumière au bout des ténèbres, et si tout n'avait été qu'illusion ? S'il s'était lui-même laissé prendre au piège de son imagination ? Et si Satan ne lui avait pas soufflé son destin de Messie pour mieux le faire retomber à terre ? Au mont des Oliviers viennent le plus souvent des hommes, des femmes, pour se rencontrer. Ils se cachent dans les fourrés, parlent à mi-voix, gémissent de plaisir. Jésus marche sur les sentiers de fortune, se faufile entre les oliviers, fuit les bosquets d'où s'échappent des murmures et des plaintes. Il va plus loin encore, presque au faîte de la montagne, là où plus personne ne se rend. Les disciples le suivent mais à distance, Jésus veut être seul cette nuit, la dernière de sa vie d'homme. Après commencera celle de sa vie divine. En bas, dans la vallée, Jérusalem brille de ses foyers éclairés. Ils forment comme une guirlande de lumière, mais ils n'attendent personne, n'éclairent aucune venue. La quête était-elle donc vaine ?

Jésus va jusqu'à ces petites grottes qui dominent le mont, il s'y réfugie pour prier, être à l'abri de tous. Là, il s'allonge sur le sol et entre dans sa première Passion. Dieu, du fond de sa retraite, est particulièrement attentif à l'issue du drame qu'il a fixé. Pour que Jésus comprenne tout à fait le dessein de sa mission, il faut lui faire parvenir des visions effroyables de ce dont sont capables les hommes. Jésus voit autour de lui des cercles de démons et de fantômes qui le harcèlent et veulent l'entraîner dans une sarabande infernale. Il résiste, il a froid, il tremble de tout son corps. Par cercles concentriques, il descend dans son agonie. Il y a des cataclysmes et des bouleversements marins, des tours effondrées, transpercées par des avions, des camps d'extermination où des hommes martyrisent d'autres hommes, démunis, abandonnés, il voit des gouffres qui s'ouvrent devant lui d'où surgissent des scènes atroces, des carnages, des massacres collectifs, des femmes, des enfants, tirés par les cheveux, lancés comme des volailles contre les murs, des hommes qui égorgent et qui émasculent d'autres hommes, d'autres victimes alignées le long de fosses ouvertes passées par les armes et qui viennent combler les charniers, pire encore, des chrétiens poursuivis par d'autres chrétiens dans les rues de Paris, assassinés tandis qu'au Louvre, le roi de France orchestre le massacre, des terres conquises, exubérantes, des jungles remplies d'oiseaux sauvages et multicolores où se sont installés des indigènes dans des huttes de joncs et de palmes, traînées en esclavage en son propre nom, lui, Jésus, des génocides, des peuples entiers déportés, des tribunaux d'exception où les juges sont des prêtres, les descendants de ses apôtres, et qui envoient au bûcher des femmes, toute une humanité détruite, blessée, souffrante, méprisée, et qui croyait aussi, sûrement, en la venue d'un monde meilleur, toute cette humanité qui connut l'enfance et qui a été trahie, reniée, et qui, dans ses yeux d'enfance, avait connu les étincelles de l'espérance. Jésus voit toutes ces scènes horribles que lui impose son Père qui lui tend le calice. « Bois, mon fils, bois la coupe jusqu'à la lie car c'est par ton sacrifice que tu feras advenir l'espérance. En la buvant, tu portes avec toi tous les péchés du monde, et par là, tu libères les hommes de leur poids de péchés. »

Jésus accepte le martyre. Dehors, Judas a déjà rencontré les archers qui arrêteront Jésus. En tête de la petite troupe, des Pharisiens, des grands prêtres qui veulent enfin que s'achève le scandale. Ils sont encore à Jérusalem, Judas est auprès d'eux, réclame ses trente deniers d'argent à l'avance, les prêtres veulent d'abord qu'il leur livre Jésus. « Je m'approcherai de lui et je l'embrasserai. Vous saurez alors que c'est lui, Jésus le Galiléen. »

Ils atteignent le mont des Oliviers. Ils se faufilent dans les sentiers. Des couples enlacés dans les taillis retiennent leur souffle, croient qu'on vient les arrêter. Mais la troupe cherche autre chose, ce soir-là. Elle avance, guidée par Judas qui connaît la cachette de Jésus. Près de la grotte, les apôtres qui devaient veiller se sont endormis. Judas dit que Jésus n'est plus très loin maintenant. Ils vont tous à pas de loup, ils avancent comme des maquisards dans la nuit, ou bien des voleurs, ils se mettent en embuscade, Judas seul avance dans la nuit, éclairé par des torches. Jésus ne les entend même pas arriver. Des visions nouvelles l'accablent. Celles de sa propre mort, il voit tout, les crachats et les cordes autour de ses mains, la croix qu'il porte lamentablement dans les rues de Jérusalem, les injures à son passage et les clous qu'on plante dans ses mains, dans ses pieds, et tout son sang qui s'écoule de son ventre, et son visage meurtri, et cette douleur intolérable qui secoue son corps tout entier, broie ses os, raidit ses muscles, cette douleur, si immense, qu'elle finit par ne plus même exister, fondue dans une sorte d'abîme gigantesque, insondable.

Alors de nouveaux prodiges surgissent. Comment y croire vraiment sans avoir l'œil émerveillé des enfants qu'aucun miracle n'arrête ? Comment ne pas y croire si Dieu existe vraiment et qu'à lui tout est possible ? Des anges en nuées viennent pour soulager la douleur de Jésus. Ils s'approchent de lui dans leur auréole de lumière, ils n'ont pas de forme humaine, seulement un nuage lumineux, quelque chose d'indicible, qui apaise la douleur, peut-être de la musique seulement ? L'un d'entre eux, sûrement un archange, apporte un calice et le présente à Jésus qui le porte à ses lèvres et boit le vin qu'il contient. Maintenant tout est consommé. La nuée d'anges disparaît, Jésus se retrouve seul, de nouveau, il se relève, rajuste sa robe de gros lin, et va rejoindre les disciples. Ils dorment.

« Ainsi, vous n'avez pu veiller une heure avec moi ! leur dit-il. Pourquoi dormez-vous ? Levez-vous et priez ! L'heure est venue où le Fils de l'homme doit être livré aux mains des pécheurs. Celui qui doit me livrer approche. Mieux vaudrait pour lui qu'il ne fût jamais né. »

Puis Jésus, d'un geste de la main, montre la petite colonne éclairée de flambeaux qui monte vers eux.

« Je ne résisterai pas, je me livrerai à eux, et tout sera alors accompli. »

Il quitte ses apôtres sauf trois d'entre eux qui l'accompagnent et va vers ses ennemis.

Du fond de son lit de douleurs, Catherine Emmerich, la petite stigmatisée du XVIIIe siècle qui vécut en Westphalie, voit dans ses yeux meurtris par la souffrance la Passion de Jésus. Elle voit qu'il s'éloigne des apôtres et reprend en sens inverse le chemin de Jérusalem, le sentier d'épineux bordé d'oliviers. Elle dit qu'il a fait un miracle que le temps a oublié mais que son don de voyance à elle ramène de la nuit. Jésus a prié, les mains ouvertes posées sur la paroi de la grotte. Quand les apôtres y allèrent après son passage, les mains étaient comme imprimées dans le rocher. Mains ouvertes, données au monde, mains tendues, faites pour relier. Sait-elle, Marguerite Duras, en écrivant *Les Mains négatives*, qu'elle reprend le même propos que Catherine Emmerich ? Elle écrit un long poème sur ces mains peintes et imprimées, elles aussi, sur les parois des grottes magdaléniennes de l'Europe Sud-Atlantique. Les mains partout courent et crient sur la roche, elles disent, raconte Duras, qu'elles sont un geste d'amour : comme aucune explication n'a été trouvée à ce jour, rajoute-t-elle, elle imagine que ce sont des messages d'alliance et les mains diraient à peu près cela : « Je t'aime plus loin que toi

J'aimerai quiconque entendra que je crie que je t'aime,
Trente mille ans
J'appelle
J'appelle celui qui me répondra
Je veux t'aimer je t'aime
Je suis celui qui criait qu'il t'aimait, toi. »

L'inconnu des grottes d'avant l'histoire rejoint Jésus dans la conscience confuse et obscure du lien irrésistible qui rattache l'homme à un dieu aimant, dans l'espérance qu'il n'est pas seul dans le grand tourbillon des planètes et dans la rumeur des astres.

Chapitre 46

Où Jésus est arrêté

Jésus avance dans la nuit de Gethsémani, il dit que son âme est triste à en mourir, mais que c'est ainsi, qu'il faut avancer, sans craindre le supplice car le Royaume est au bout. Il va à la rencontre de la troupe qu'il aperçoit à travers les fourrés et les arbres bas, une colonne qui se dirige vers lui, éclairée de torches. Il arrive enfin à la croisée de deux chemins. La troupe le rejoint, c'est une bande de brutes qu'accompagnent Judas et les serviteurs des grands prêtres et des anciens du peuple. « Celui que je baiserai, ce sera lui », a déclaré Judas. Alors il se détache seul de la troupe et va directement à Jésus. Il s'approche de lui, Jésus ne recule pas, ne fait pas un geste de dénégation ou de reproche, sur son visage aucune trace de peur ou de mépris à l'encontre de son disciple. Judas s'avance, tend ses deux bras vers lui, veut l'enlacer, puis il se penche vers Jésus et dépose un baiser sur sa joue.

Quel sentiment agite alors Judas ? De quelle nature est son baiser ? Accomplit-il la promesse faite au grand prêtre ou bien un ultime acte d'amour, désespéré, qui préfère les perdre tous deux plutôt que de renoncer à Jésus ? Il baise sa joue et Jésus ne se retire pas, il accepte son baiser, Judas appose ses lèvres fiévreuses sur la peau mal rasée de Jésus, il voudrait que son baiser lui dise tout l'amour qu'il lui a porté, et ce pardon qu'il réclame de lui, confusément, il l'embrasse et il lui dit intérieurement : « Maître, j'implore ton pardon, dans ta miséricorde immense, vois ton disciple qui a péché, ne lui tiens pas rigueur, tout était inscrit, déjà accompli, c'est Dieu qui m'a choisi pour accomplir le mauvais travail, mais toi, rabbi, tu sais combien je t'ai aimé, combien je voulais que tu m'accordes ton unique attention, comment effacer l'irréparable ? »

« Ami, lui dit seulement Jésus, fais ta besogne. »

De même, à celui qui va l'égorger, le père abbé de la communauté de Tibherine dit doucement : « Ami, que nous nous retrouvions tous deux auprès de Dieu, amis et frères. »

Les gardes et les brigands qui les accompagnent s'emparent alors de Jésus. Ils le ligotent et le ramènent à Jérusalem par les chemins sinueux et rocailleux de Gethsémani, ils tirent sur les cordes, blessent déjà ses poignets. Tous les disciples qui suivent de loin la scène reculent, horrifiés. Ils se cachent et profitent du désordre pour s'enfuir. Jésus est seul avec les gardes. Derrière la troupe, Pierre n'a pas suivi les autres apôtres. Il veut savoir où l'on amène Jésus. Dans la nuit noire, il va sur leurs pas, jusqu'au palais du Grand Prêtre où l'on dépose Jésus. Sur son passage, des hommes et des femmes crient et l'insultent, ils hurlent contre le blasphémateur, le faux messie qui a eu l'audace de défier le Temple. « Je le détruirai, avait-il dit, et je le rebâtirai en trois jours ! » Comment cela pouvait-il être possible ? Comment imaginer cette farce ? Ces sornettes ? Personne encore ne peut comprendre ce que veut dire Jésus. Trois jours, oui, c'est-à-dire après sa résurrection, le temple sera rebâti, parce que le temple, désormais, ce sera chacun de ceux qui se seront convertis à Jésus, à la nouvelle foi, chaque disciple de Jésus sera un apôtre nouveau et son corps comme son âme seront un temple inviolable où Dieu pourra séjourner sans être l'objet d'un culte factice et ostentatoire, mais un Temple où Dieu parlera au cœur de son nouvel élu, dans le silence et dans l'intimité de son amour.

— Dis-nous enfin, dis-nous si tu es le Christ, le Fils de Dieu ?

— Tu l'as dit, répond Jésus. « D'ailleurs, je vous le déclare, désormais vous verrez le Fils de l'homme siéger à droite de la Puissance et venir sur les nuées du ciel[38]. »

— « Vous venez d'entendre le blasphème, exulte le grand prêtre. Il mérite la mort[39] ! »

Pierre, qui attend Jésus sur le seuil du palais, est pris à parti par des serviteurs :

— Lui, c'est un disciple du Nazaréen.

— Est-ce vrai ?

— Non, par pitié, je ne sais pas ce que tu veux dire, répond Pierre.

Passe alors un autre serviteur :

— En voilà un qui était avec le Nazaréen !

— « Comment cela pourrait être possible ? Je ne connais même pas le nom de cet homme[40]. »

Pierre passe son chemin, arrive dans la rue mais il est poursuivi par d'autres serviteurs :

— Tu en es, tu en es !

— Je vous le jure, je ne connais pas cet homme, laissez-moi !

Et soudain, comme il dit ces mots, lui reviennent les paroles de Jésus : « Avant que le coq chante, tu m'auras renié trois fois. »

Il erre dans la rue, effaré et terrifié. Mais il ne cherche plus à se cacher, comme si tout désormais lui était devenu inutile et vain. Il va dans la ville, à l'aveuglette, il pleure mais personne ne le console, il est seul dans la grande fourmilière des bazars. « Seigneur, pardonne-moi, car je t'ai trahi trois fois. Tu connais ma faiblesse, fortifie-moi pour que je puisse te servir complètement. »

Judas, pendant ce temps, erre de nouveau dans la géhenne. Il marche dans les cendres incandescentes, il s'enfonce dans les détritus et dans les déchets d'animaux sacrifiés, de ses pieds à peine retenus par des sandales de cuir s'élève une fumée noirâtre, il n'a plus rien dans ses poches, pas même les trente deniers que lui ont donnés les grands prêtres, il les a rendus, mais comme personne ne voulait de l'argent parce que c'était le prix du sang, il a jeté à terre sa bourse et les pièces d'argent ont filé sur le pavement du Temple. Il va vers un petit monticule où se dresse un arbre à moitié calciné. Il trouve un vieux linge dont il entoure son cou et va se pendre. Son corps flotte dans l'air noirâtre et brûlé. Où est partie son âme ?

Marie est partie de Nazareth car elle sait que la fin est proche. Son corps entier de mère souffre, traversé de douleurs, elle a rejoint Jérusalem. Elle est déjà dans les faubourgs de la ville, elle va jusqu'au temple, se glisse dans le dédale des ruelles, se repose un moment sur une place. On dit que Jésus de Nazareth a été arrêté, qu'il est en ce moment même interrogé. Elle a ce don d'ubiquité qu'a donné Dieu à toutes les mères. C'est un miracle qu'elles connaissent toutes parce qu'elles le vivent à chaque fois que leur enfant est en danger. Elle apparaît dans la lumière intérieure de Jésus. Il la reconnaît. Elle lui demande de ne montrer aucune émotion, mais elle est auprès de lui, tout contre lui, « que je t'éclaire de mon amour, mon fils bien-aimé, que je souffre en même temps que toi tes mille morts, que je sois moi aussi transpercée de tous les glaives, car tu es ma chair et mon sang, et tu ne souffriras aucune douleur sans que moi aussi je ne l'éprouve ».

Jésus soudain est comme illuminé, nimbé d'une douce clarté.

— Viens, ma mère, que je me repose contre toi, que je redevienne ton enfant de Bethléem, que ton haleine me réchauffe, je m'en vais rejoindre mon père où je sais que tu viendras, toi aussi, dans ta gloire. Je te la préparerai.

— Voyez cette lueur autour de lui, disent les gardes. Est-il bien vrai qu'il faille le condamner ? Qu'a-t-il fait au juste de si répréhensible ?

— C'est Satan en lui qui s'agite et qui vous trompe. Ne prêtez pas attention à ces faux prodiges. Vous offenseriez ainsi votre Dieu.

Marie bénit son fils, elle lui donne de sa tendresse de femme, de sa douceur. Elle caresse son visage, son cou, ses mains. Elle dit qu'il est son petit, que nul ne pourra le lui ravir. Et tous autour sont étonnés de la paix de Jésus. De son calme.

Marie maintenant ne quittera plus Jésus. Il n'est plus le messie annoncé par l'ange, il est son fils qu'on a arrêté et qu'on maltraite dans la maison de Caïphe, le grand prêtre. Elle a ce don de voyance qui lui permet de tout partager de lui, de le soutenir dans l'épreuve, d'éponger la sueur qui coule de son visage, d'essuyer ses larmes. Quand Van Gogh peint sa *Pietà*, rare sujet religieux dans son œuvre comme s'il se souvenait de ses années d'enfance passées auprès de son père pasteur et de cette époque où il faisait le prédicateur en Belgique, il est à Arles. Comme lorsqu'il peint les blés, les iris ou la place de sa ville, il choisit deux couleurs, le bleu et le jaune, qu'il utilise en longs traits discontinus qui déforment la réalité, qui font vibrer la toile, trahissent l'exaltation de ses motifs. Marie est derrière Jésus, les deux bras tendus, lui, est abandonné, l'enfant de la crèche sans défense. Elle sait ce qui l'attend, elle veut l'en prévenir, l'assurer de sa présence, de toute manière, elle souffrira avec lui, chaque blessure infligée lui reviendra, parce qu'elle l'a enfanté, porté dans sa chair, et qu'elle ne se pardonne pas d'avoir accepté le message de l'ange. La demande de Dieu est insoutenable, elle voudrait mourir à sa place, mais ce n'est pas ainsi que Dieu a voulu l'histoire. « Dieu implacable, murmure-t-elle, délivre-moi de mon consentement. »

Jésus, qui l'entend dans le mystère de l'amour, l'abjure de ne pas céder au désespoir. « Ne reniez pas, Mère, ce que vous avez consenti dans la lumière de l'ange. Tout s'accomplira comme mon père l'a voulu. Mais soyez quand même au moment du passage, aux heures difficiles et cruelles de l'abandon, quand je n'aurai plus la force de me porter moi-même, et que je demanderai à Dieu d'envoyer ses anges pour m'emmener jusqu'à lui. » Marie éprouve ce qu'est la douleur pure, un abîme, un puits, une vaste plaine déserte où le corps et l'esprit se fondent dans la même souffrance, jusqu'à ressentir une non-existence, un état de vide et d'absence, meurtrie, anéantie. C'est la douleur des mères devant le corps agonisant de leur enfant, leur douleur, une colère, quelque chose d'indicible qui arrache et n'a plus de conscience. Van Gogh la connaît, cette douleur, Marie comme une ombre couvre Jésus, elle veut lui porter secours, le protéger de son manteau bleu d'iris, et l'emporter comme quand, jadis, à dos d'ânesse, elle a fui Bethléem, Hérode, le massacre des enfants, la traque atroce des tueurs d'innocents et l'exode pour mettre à l'abri son fils. Mais la douleur, c'est aussi la vanité de tout cet espoir, de toute cette foi chantée dans les psaumes quand elle vaquait au ménage de sa maison de Nazareth. « Alors quoi, tout est-il donc vain, la prière et la ferveur, pour que l'issue soit aussi fatale ? Je t'ai prié, Dieu, pour que tu reviennes sur ton projet, pour que ne s'accomplissent pas les Écritures, et j'ai cru que tu ferais un geste, que tu t'apitoierais sur ton enfant abandonné, mais non, rien que ce destin qui doit se réaliser. »

Chapitre 47

Où Jésus entre dans son agonie

Maintenant Jésus se tait. Il n'est plus que ce bloc de silence en attente de la rencontre suprême, appelant de tout son corps le retour vers les origines du monde, le voyage interstellaire qui va l'entraîner dans les mondes galactiques où pourrait bien se trouver le Royaume. Vous voyez, on est bien dans la féerie, dans les contes les plus débridés, où tout est possible. Et cependant quelque chose d'incroyable se passe. Par quel miracle, par quel tour de passe-passe, aussitôt après la mort de Jésus, imminente, son histoire va-t-elle se pulvériser dans le monde, se disséminer sur tous les continents, croître et convertir, rassembler des milliards d'hommes quand il n'y avait en tout que treize illuminés qui proclamaient la venue d'un hypothétique royaume ? « Je suis pauvre et malheureux, je suis seul, Jésus, dans ma vie et dans la vie de tous les hommes, cette terrible certitude de la mort sans promesse. Tes mots me donnent la force de croire, ils m'apprennent un mot surtout, qui n'était pas envisageable, parce que la mort dévore tout sur son passage, tu m'as appris le mot espérance et depuis que je l'ai éprouvée en moi, mon regard s'est éclairé, et la lumière m'a habité. » Voilà un peu la prière de tous ceux qui suivent Jésus. La petite prière de nuit, enfantine et modeste, sans bla-bla, sans grandiloquence, ce tutoiement secret, cette proximité qui vont rendre le temps plus supportable.

Jusqu'à la lie, la coupe sera donc bue, c'est Dieu qui l'a voulu, et rien ne dérogera à son plan. « Tu boiras, mon fils, la coupe amère et douce de la solitude et de l'amour. Et tu sauras qu'à la dernière goutte du breuvage, quand tout sera achevé, que la nuit tombera sur tes yeux, qu'il n'y aura plus rien à espérer de la terre, tu la quitteras, tu entendras le frôlement des anges et tu sentiras sur ton corps le vent t'envelopper et te mener dans une autre lumière. Non pas un autre monde avec des villes, des dômes et des édifices grandioses, avec des êtres qui jugent et travaillent, mais un monde rempli d'âmes voltigeantes, animées d'un souffle divin, qui vivront toutes ensemble, des milliards de parcelles d'âmes, d'esprits, qui joueront harmonieusement de la musique, et tu en seras le centre ardent, la note extrême qui orchestrera le chœur immense, innombrable, des hommes, charriés depuis des millénaires dans le grand tout de l'univers. Et ce sera alors comme une aube douce, lumineuse et radieuse, quelque chose qui s'élèvera sans bruit et éveillera tout le royaume, et ce sera l'avènement d'une immense conscience, nourrie des milliards d'humains et de leurs esprits. C'est cela la résurrection, mon fils, dont tu seras le premier à découvrir la lueur. Tu cesseras de respirer, mais, une seconde après, tu plongeras dans le jour immense, sans douleur ni amertume, et tous les hommes connaîtront cette élévation. »

C'est encore la route qui continue. La même voie empruntée depuis son départ de Nazareth, la route chaotique et sinueuse, mais obstinément tracée, vers Jérusalem. C'est un fou qui a achevé son errance. Muré dans son silence, il semble ailleurs. Les brutalités commencent, il ne les sent pas. Les gardes croient qu'il se moque. « Pourquoi ris-tu ? Crois-tu ton sort si enviable ? » Mais Jésus ne les voit ni ne les entend. Sa mère pleure à son oreille, il lui sourit. L'amour de Marie recouvre la douleur, anéantit la souffrance et la peur. À ce moment de l'histoire, le visage de Jésus se fige pour l'éternité. Il était homme, il devient icône.

Roublev, et tous les moines oubliés dans leurs monastères glacés de l'ancienne Russie, peignent son visage comme il devait l'être alors : des yeux surtout, qui parlent à celui qui les dessine, un regard qui traverse. Séraphin de Sarov, le petit starets vénéré du peuple, a tout connu lui aussi de la douleur de Jésus. Il a dans son ermitage un rocher appelé Golgotha, un carré d'arbres qu'il appelle son mont des Oliviers, son Gethsémani. Il s'abîme en prières et Jésus lui apparaît au fond du jardin dans sa lumière immense. Trente-sept années de sa vie dans l'ascèse et le désert, broutant l'herbe, sorte d'Adam revenu aux origines, adossé au rocher pour prier comme Jésus dans le tableau d'Andrea Mantegna, Jésus priant tandis que dorment ses apôtres. Séraphin voit apparaître Jésus dans le flamboiement de sa lumière, elle inonde le jardin, ruisselle partout. Il lui promet la résurrection. Et elle vient après son silence d'ermite. Comme ressuscité, « starets », il revient à la vie publique, mais corps de Jésus déjà, avant sa propre mort, il marche dans la rue et les femmes pleurent parce qu'elles le voient marcher « une aune au-dessus du sol, sans même toucher l'herbe ». Et il leur disait : « Mes joies, ne le dites à personne, tant que je serai vivant ; lorsque je vous aurai quittées, vous pourrez peut-être le dire. »

Séraphin est toute prière, il n'est plus que cela, il a la grâce de la vision, il est en Christ.

À Jérusalem, dans son prétoire, l'épouse de Pilate lui dit de ne pas se mêler de cette affaire. Elle flaire des ennuis et peut-être un sacrilège. Elle est romaine mais se méfie des Juifs et plus encore est saisie de doute quand un Juif annonce la venue du Royaume. Pilate aussi ne voit pas pourquoi il devrait condamner Jésus. Mais les Juifs insistent, alors il ruse, il dit : « Préférez-vous que je relâche l'abject Barabbas, ou que je libère Jésus ? » Et la foule crie : « Barabbas ! Libère Barabbas, à mort Jésus, le blasphémateur, qu'il soit crucifié ! »

Alors il prend de l'eau dans une coupe qu'on lui apporte, il se lave les mains, et déclare : « "Je ne suis pas responsable de ce sang, à vous de voir[41]." » Puis il relâche Barabbas et, après avoir fait flageller Jésus, il le livre aux bourreaux pour être crucifié.

Tout va très vite maintenant. Et pour Jésus commence l'agonie. Il est porté par Marie, soutenu dans l'invisible par elle, Dieu aussi murmure à ses oreilles, promet la cohorte des anges, et toute la musique glorieuse des *putti* grassouillets qui l'accompagneront sur la voie de lumière. Les gardes s'emparent de Jésus, lui mettent une tunique rouge, tressent une couronne d'épines qu'ils placent sur sa tête, le font s'asseoir sur une pierre, lui mettent dans la main un sceptre dérisoire, une branche de roseau et mettant genou en terre, lui disent : « Salut, roi des Juifs ! » Ils crachent sur lui, le frappent à la tête, l'obligent à se redresser. « Hâte ma mort, ô mon père, je suis submergé de douleur, de détresse aussi, parce qu'ils n'ont pas entendu ma parole. Je suis seul comme au désert, c'est l'heure âpre de minuit, quand viendra ta musique ? »

Mozart, du fond de son lit, agonise lui aussi, il est transi de froid, traversé de convulsions, il écrit pourtant, il se hâte car il sent qu'il va mourir, il inscrit toutes les notes du requiem qui s'ordonnent dans son esprit, le chant de Jésus, sa complainte atroce. Les mots du supplice s'inscrivent sur sa partition, Mozart écrit, biffe, gomme, remplit des pages, lui aussi saigne et souffre, va au calvaire. « Voici donc l'homme. » « *Ecce homo* », clament les gardes. Voici celui qui va renverser le Temple et le rebâtir en trois jours. Voici le dieu du monde qui veut se faire homme et mourir comme eux, risquer les mêmes outrages. » L'image, forte, puissante, mythique, s'inscrit dans les imaginations. Il y en eut tant qui marquent la vie de Jésus, comme des chapitres d'un roman, voici maintenant une nouvelle lame du jeu de tarots : Jésus aux liens. Partout, les peintres de l'Europe chrétienne reprennent le motif. Les Flamands et les Italiens, surtout, et plus tard aussi Daumier, qui peint Jésus de profil, debout, ligoté, surplombant la foule hystérique, dans des couleurs fauves et sourdes, qui font comme un bûcher. On dirait toutes les victimes du monde, tous les bannis et les sacrifiés, tous ces peuples détruits, fauchés sous la lame des fous et des tyrans, toutes ces charrettes de victimes qui vont à l'abattoir, Jésus aux liens, c'est Marie-Antoinette croquée sur le vif par David, du haut d'une lucarne, et se dirigeant vers l'échafaud, c'est le train plombé bourré de Juifs qu'on va gazer dès qu'ils arrivent au camp, c'est le déporté torturé dans les laboratoires des médecins psychopathes et jeté par terre, soumis aux pires sévices, aux expériences les plus abominables, c'est l'Arabe électrocuté dans les caves des villas d'Alger, attaché lui aussi, humilié, toute cette humanité trahie, déniée, condamnée à périr.

Chez Giotto, le mal et le bien sont face à face, beaux tous les deux. Les gardes, ainsi que Jésus, ont la fraîcheur de l'innocence et de la jeunesse, comme si le peintre voulait dire par là que c'est au cœur de tout homme que s'affrontent des violences contraires. Mais seul Jésus garde la lumière autour de lui, il est protégé par elle, elle l'irradie tandis que se déchirent les méchants et les bienveillants. Jésus est déjà ailleurs, comme à l'agonie, tout près de Dieu, les hommes le sont déjà. C'est l'heure des comas et des sommeils profonds, des veilles étranges, que nul ne peut rapporter, cet état de suspension et de lévitation, ces heures étranges où le temps s'est arrêté, où la main du mourant ne cherche même plus celle du vivant mais où déjà commence la marche vers l'ailleurs. La petite flamme du corps s'amenuise au fil des heures, elle vacille, chandelle qui n'aurait plus que quelques larmes de cire, elle tremble comme un papillon effrayé, mais c'est tout seul qu'il va, l'agonisant dans sa lumière. Tout autour on croit qu'il entre dans la nuit, qu'il ne verra plus d'aube se lever, que son corps s'anéantit mais il va, il se dirige vers l'inconnu.

Rimbaud qui ne croyait en rien appelle la lumière avant de mourir et Baudelaire, qui n'attend plus rien du monde, réclame « du nouveau »... Jésus et l'homme se retrouvent dans la même posture, dans le même instant fragile et grave du passage. Il y a encore des heures, peut-être des jours avant de céder sa vie, avant de renoncer à la lumière qui se lève, aux babillements des enfants, aux splendeurs du monde, les fleurs, les bêtes, les champs et les forêts, les ciels étoilés et la mer immense avec ses houles toujours différentes. On croit qu'ils ne pensent à rien, les agonisants, qu'ils subissent leur malheur, des médecins, des familiers parlent tout haut de leur mort prochaine, demandent quand ils vont passer, eux, ils entendent tout cela, ils ont de la peine de laisser le monde mais ils doivent veiller aussi à prendre la route promise, pas un homme qui ne meure et qui ne soit conscient encore, qui n'espère contre toute attente apercevoir au loin, la lumière du Royaume et le chant des anges. Pas un.

Les femmes se rejoignent dans la maison de Marthe et de Marie. Il y a Véronique et Marie-Madeleine, et Marie, la mère de Jésus. Elles aussi ploient sous la douleur, dehors, elles entendent la rumeur monter des ruelles de Jérusalem et toute cette foule en délire qui crie et s'apprête à conduire Jésus au Golgotha. C'est un bruit immense, d'une rare violence, une rumeur qui se propage comme une onde, qui ne s'arrête pas, une rumeur d'émeute. Marie implore Dieu du fond de sa douleur, elle y puise les mots entrecoupés de suffocations. « Redonnez-moi, Seigneur, la confiance de Bethléem, la douceur de cette nuit-là, et faites-nous entendre le chant des anges et tous les anges musiciens qui les accompagnent. » Elle doute soudain, ne croit plus à la promesse.

Il n'y a plus rien que la mise à mort de son fils, que cette nuit qui s'affale sur la ville, lentement, sans espérance. Elle dit encore, dans un souffle, que c'est à présent son ultime déchirement de mère. Elle en a tant vécu, depuis la fuite en Égypte et la fugue dans le Temple et le grand départ de Jésus dans la vie publique. Et, aujourd'hui, son enfant n'est plus à elle, il se sépare définitivement d'elle. Elle cherche à lui parler par la grâce de leur amour mais elle n'y parvient pas, c'est que Jésus ne veut plus de cet attachement, qu'il est déjà parti. Le déchirement de Marie est celui de toutes les mères, car la maternité ressemble à sa douleur, elle est fusion et exil. C'est une vie de déchirements successifs dès le premier tressaillement dans leur ventre, un don et un abandon tout à la fois, la chaleur et le froid qui les saisissent, cette confiance et cette trahison.

Chapitre 48

Où Jésus est crucifié

Marie est impuissante à soulager son fils. Jésus n'entend plus rien, accepte l'agonie jusqu'à l'humiliation. Une angoisse mortelle le submerge, elle provoque en lui un trouble physique intense, une sueur de sang le recouvre gagne lentement tout son corps, se répand par tous les pores de sa peau. C'est comme une immense plaie qui se répand, l'hémorragie gagne ses cheveux qui suintent et deviennent plus pâles, presque blonds, puis blancs en quelques heures, lui, le Sémite aux cheveux noirs. Les experts du Linceul de Turin notent dans leurs conclusions la présence de cette sécrétion rougeâtre qui a envahi le corps du supplicié, et les pigments capillaires sont blancs.
Il est attaché par les deux mains à une colonne, puis on le flagelle. Deux longues lanières de cuir auxquelles on a ajouté à leurs extrémités deux petites boules de plomb. La chair éclate sous les coups, plus de quarante, juste assez pour qu'il ne meure pas sous leur violence. Le cœur, la plèvre et les poumons sont envahis d'un flux de liquide organique, des douleurs thoraciques pressent Jésus comme dans un étau, son cœur bat très vite puis s'arrête, et reprend, il a soif, une mousse blanchâtre sort de sa bouche, mais personne n'a pitié de lui, le bruit sec des lanières sur

la peau claque dans la salle dallée de marbre, la couronne d'épines s'enfonce dans sa tête, sa nuque. Les bourreaux ont choisi les branches les plus épineuses, elles crèvent la peau du front, des gouttes de sang coulent dans ses yeux et toujours cette sueur rouge qui colle déjà sur son corps, forme une fine pellicule crevassée. Marie erre dans les rues, se rapproche du lieu de supplice, elle joue des coudes pour passer parce que tous les habitants veulent voir la mise à mort du « roi des Juifs ». Elle ne pleure pas, elle a cette gravité dans le visage au-delà de la douleur, farouche. On apporte enfin le *patibulum*, cette pièce de bois horizontale qu'on met sur ses épaules meurtries, il a les pieds entravés par des cordes, il avance à petits pas. Jésus se dirige vers le Golgotha.

Pas un mot ne sort de sa bouche, pas une plainte. Marie parvient enfin à le rejoindre. Partout des injures, des railleries, des jets de pierre. Les apôtres se sont fondus dans la foule, craignant le même sort que leur maître, Marie-Madeleine pleure et suit le chemin de croix en suffoquant, Jésus marche en titubant. Il s'effondre une fois, face contre terre. « Je suis là, rabbi, murmure Marie-Madeleine, que ta souffrance me rejoigne, qu'elle se fonde en moi, qu'elle m'atteigne jusque dans le tréfonds de mon corps, jusque dans mon sein, tu n'es pas seul, rabbi, prends de ma vie, de ma force. »

On atteint enfin le mont Golgotha. On l'étend à terre, on le fixe sur la croix. Les prêtres se sont rendus chez Pilate car ils ne sont pas d'accord sur l'inscription placée au haut de la croix : « "Celui-ci est Jésus, le roi des Juifs[42]." » Mais Pilate est irrité, il ne leur donne pas satisfaction, les renvoie à leur meurtre. On le cloue par les poignets, entre les os carpiens et l'os du radius du bras. Ce sont des clous forgés d'au moins douze centimètres de long. On place le pied gauche sur le pied droit et on les cloue. La tétanie est immédiate, Jésus est saisi de crampes, des douleurs atroces s'élancent de ses mains, rejoignent chaque muscle, chaque organe, pas une seule partie du corps qui ne soit touchée, les battements de son cœur se ralentissent, des hémorragies internes parcourent comme des houles son corps. Il sent son corps qui lâche, il ne peut entendre le bruit de la foule, il est devenu sourd, aveugle, son souffle est rauque, haletant. C'est midi ou la sixième heure. Le début des ténèbres. Un vent sifflant se lève. Des nuages s'amoncellent dans le ciel, c'est pourtant une journée de printemps, à l'air encore vif certes mais les amandiers sont déjà en fleurs, et les bougainvilliers ont éclaté sur les murs de chaux, flamboyants, mauves comme du sang séché. Un orage menace, inquiétant, inhabituel.

Une stupeur muette recouvre le Golgotha. On se prend à douter, à avoir peur, à craindre des calamités. Jésus s'avance dans sa Passion. La voie est de plus en plus serrée. Elle se rétrécit, ressemble à un étroit corridor noir et solitaire, il s'y engouffre. Certains tentent de scruter ses lèvres, pour voir s'il va dire quelque chose. Vers trois heures de l'après-midi, à la neuvième heure, il clame d'un grand cri : « *"Eli, Eli lema sabachtani* ? Mon Dieu, mon Dieu, pourquoi m'as-tu abandonné[43] ?" » On lui tend une éponge fixée en haut d'une perche, elle est imbibée de vinaigre : « Bois, fils de Dieu, désaltère-toi, Élie va venir te sauver ! » Puis Jésus dit à Jean qui est au pied de la croix : « Fils, voici ta mère », dans un second cri, il expire enfin.

Quelque chose d'extraordinaire se passe soudain : le ciel s'ouvre, les nuages éclatent, la terre tremble, la tenture qui sépare le Saint du Saint des Saints se déchire en deux, des rochers se fendent, des morts ressuscitent, entrent dans Jérusalem et se font voir, et le jour réapparaît. Les prêtres se souviennent de la prophétie d'Amos, le berger de Teqoa, des visions qu'il eut à propos d'Israël au temps d'Ozias, roi de Juda, et de Jéroboam, fils de Joas, roi d'Israël : « En ce jour-là, oracle du Seigneur, je ferai coucher le soleil en plein midi, je couvrirai la terre de ténèbres en plein jour, je changerai vos fêtes en deuil, tous vos chants en lamentations. Et ce sera jusqu'à la fin comme un jour d'amertume. » Les soldats se sauvent, pris de panique, abandonnent le lieu, laissent les femmes s'approcher de la croix. Il y a Marie, la mère de Jésus, Marie-Madeleine, Marie, mère de Jacques et de Joseph, Marie, mère des fils de Zébédée. Toute la foule a fui le prodige, il ne reste plus qu'elles et Jean. Marie de Nazareth s'écroule au pied de la croix. Elle n'a plus de voix, plus de vie en elle, c'est un état absent, intemporel, où se loge la rencontre avec son fils.

Un garde revient sur ses pas, il veut s'assurer que Jésus est bien mort, qu'il ne s'agit pas d'une feinte, d'un évanouissement simulé, alors il prend sa lance et transperce le côté droit, l'enfonce entre la cinquième et la sixième côte. Du liquide pleural et péricardique s'en échappe, il coule comme du sang clairet, on dit que Jean l'a recueilli dans un calice de terre cuite. « Que la terre d'Israël, disent les croisés, tremble car voici venu le jour où nous arrivons d'Europe, de la sainte Europe chrétienne, pour retrouver le divin calice, qu'aucun Maure ne se mette en travers de notre chemin car nous apporterons le feu et le glaive jusque dans les maisons, nous les brûlerons, jusqu'à ce que nous le leur reprenions pour l'adorer chez nous. »

Marie est robuste, elle se souvient du regard qu'ils ont échangé, elle et son fils, sur le chemin de croix, regard muet, seulement saisi, compris, éprouvé par eux deux, ignoré de tous les autres, pourtant nombreux et qui n'ont rien vu de cet amour silencieux. Elle se nourrit maintenant de ce regard croisé, elle dans les yeux de son fils, lui immergé dans le sein de sa mère, comme autrefois, avant de naître. Elle veut se souvenir de cela seulement, de ses derniers mots adressés à Jean : « Voici ta mère. » Il l'a appelé femme autrefois et elle en avait souffert, mais au dernier moment de sa vie terrestre, il est revenu à elle, elle comme mère, pour lui confier Jean, et tous les autres fils de la terre, et du monde, parce qu'une mère, pensait-il, a cette vocation-là, extrême, indestructible, d'être la mère de tous les hommes, vouée à cet unique amour.

Chapitre 49

Où Jésus est mis au tombeau

C'est Joseph. Un homme riche d'Arimathie. Il s'est fait disciple de Jésus, croit en sa divinité. Il demande à Pilate le corps de Jésus. Pilate le lui accorde, quelque chose en lui dit toujours qu'il pourrait bien être le messie mais il doute et puis le poids de sa fonction, la trahison envers sa religion, et la peur d'apparaître coupable d'apostase, le renvoient à son silence. Mais Pilate ne cesse de penser à Jésus, il le porte comme un fardeau, une croix dont il ne parvient pas à se défaire, la grâce est lourde pour lui, elle le frôle, un froissement d'aile d'ange, une musique fine, céleste, inconnue, il voudrait la saisir mais que diraient Rome et César ? « Donne-moi, dit-il comme une prière, si tu es vraiment le fils de Dieu, le courage de l'aveu, et celui du martyre, ou bien alors reste où tu es, dans ce tombeau de pierre où comme nous tous, tu te réduiras à toi-même, cendres et poussière, mêlé à la terre. »

Il faut maintenant descendre le corps de Jésus de la croix. Vers cinq et demie de l'après-midi, juste après que les gardes se sont assurés que Jésus était bien mort, en lui donnant le coup de lance, et après avoir achevé les deux autres condamnés qui se trouvaient à la droite et à la gauche de Jésus, ses amis entreprennent la descente de croix. Joseph d'Arimathie est allé au bazar de Jérusalem pour acheter un linceul, il a choisi un beau sergé de pur lin pour l'envelopper. Il est de couleur crème, d'une pâleur presque immatérielle, soyeuse. La toile, lui a assuré le marchand, vient de Syrie, de la ville de Palmyre. Joseph n'a pas lésiné sur le prix, rien, dit-il, n'est trop rare ni trop beau pour envelopper le corps du rédempteur. On commence lentement le travail de dépose. Joseph, accompagné de Nicomède, décloue d'abord les pieds, le corps de Jésus est pendu au *patibulum*, la pièce de bois horizontale à laquelle sont cloués ses poignets. Joseph monte à une échelle, il décloue patiemment le poignet gauche, puis taille la corde qui soutient le corps à l'épaule gauche, puis décloue le poignet droit.

Au pied de la croix, Marie de Magdala et Marie de Nazareth sont prostrées, elles n'osent lever les yeux vers le corps livide de Jésus, blanc comme une nacre, exsangue. Le corps s'affaisse cependant de tout son poids, Joseph le descend, Jésus n'est qu'une chose inerte, molle et abandonnée. Joseph a entouré le corps du suaire, vaguement, à la hâte, c'est ainsi que les femmes l'accueillent dans leurs bras. Marie repousse le drap d'un geste et prend son fils dans ses bras. Tous s'éloignent, forment un cercle de silence autour de la *pietà*. La mère et le fils restent ainsi indissolublement liés l'un à l'autre une heure entière. Il est presque six heures et demie. La nuit va bientôt tomber. L'air est frais et Joseph dit qu'il faut faire vite, car les premières étoiles vont briller dans le ciel, et le sabbat va commencer. Cette heure de silence, c'est aussi celle de Bethléem, dans la même nudité des corps et de l'amour, dans la même indifférence au monde extérieur. Eux deux, la mère et le fils, sont dans cette unité absolue, offerte à tous les regards. Et c'est tout le poids de la terre qui les traverse, tout l'amour du monde qui passe entre eux, la complicité des jours heureux, la tendresse des promenades qu'ils faisaient ensemble autrefois, les déjeuners frugaux de galettes de son et de poissons grillés, toute leur histoire secrète et intime qui se déroule comme le fil du rouet qu'elle faisait tourner à Nazareth en attendant l'heure du coucher, jusqu'au dernier regard que Jésus lui jeta, en montant au Golgotha, au petit signe, invisible aux autres, ce regard éperdu pour lui dire de ne pas s'avancer davantage, mais qui l'assurait que l'amour était là, que rien n'était rompu.

Marie porte Jésus sur ses genoux, elle le tient, là, en travers de son corps, comme un énorme poisson mort, elle a les jambes écartées, semblables au moment de l'accouchement, pour laisser passer le corps de son enfant, en se tenant ainsi, elle donne à Jésus plus d'assise, plus d'équilibre, on dirait qu'elle le berce. Tout autour, des hommes s'affairent, des gardes près des autres croix dressées délient les derniers crucifiés, ils les maltraitent comme des paquets inutiles, les projettent à terre. Leurs visages sont ceux que Jérôme Bosch a peints : hideux, grotesques, obscènes. Marie n'entend rien, elle parle à son fils, Marie de Magdala s'approche d'eux, elle voudrait apaiser la douleur de Marie, mais qui pourrait y parvenir ? Elle s'agenouille aux pieds de Jésus, commence à les lui laver comme elle le faisait il y a peu de temps encore, elle verse sur lui de l'eau des jarres, le baptise à son tour de l'eau lustrale, de l'eau bénite qu'elle a elle-même sanctifiée par sa prière, parce que Jésus lui a toujours dit que ceux qui auraient foi en lui seraient aussi doués de cette grâce de bénir, de recouvrir de la musique de Dieu le corps délaissé, livré à la mort pour que justement il accomplisse son voyage vers sa résurrection. Marie de Nazareth s'égare dans sa douleur, elle parle à son fils comme s'il était encore vivant, petit garçon détalant dans les ruelles de Nazareth. « Vois-tu je te rhabille, je te refais tout beau et tout propre. Tu as les cheveux emmêlés. Où donc es-tu allé traîner ? Avec quels gamins es-tu allé jouer ? Quel ravin as-tu dévalé ? Tu ne dis plus rien. Parle-moi, dis quelque chose, seulement ton souffle sur mes mains, comme autrefois quand je m'assurais de ton sommeil paisible et que je me penchais sur toi pour savoir si tu étais toujours en vie, pas encore arraché à moi. »

Des chiens sauvages lèchent au pied de la croix le sang à peine séché. Une odeur de mort partout règne. Une heure à peine doit se dérouler après le coucher du soleil pour que le sabbat commence. Joseph n'ose retirer le corps de Jésus des genoux de Marie. Elle s'en détache enfin, laisse faire les hommes, elle dit seulement ces mots : « Que cela soit fait comme à l'arrivée de l'ange, autrefois, il est maintenant, je vous le dis, le messie, plus à moi mais à tous, il est l'hostie vivante. »

Marie laisse le corps de Jésus à ses premiers disciples, Jean la prend dans ses bras et la ramène à Jérusalem. Ce n'est plus qu'une femme portée par la douleur, brisée dans son corps, incapable de proférer une seule parole, murée dans son silence. On porte le corps nu de Jésus jusqu'au sépulcre, on le dépose sur une dalle de pierre lisse, on l'enveloppe du linceul de Palmyre. Du sang, clair et mêlé à du liquide biologique, de la lymphe, s'étale sur la toile, imprime des traces, suit les contours du corps. Le mystère se met en place. Il est adoration intérieure, élan vers l'invisible, supplique à Dieu pour qu'il aille au bout de son plan, au bout de la promesse de l'ange.

Jusqu'à ce moment de l'histoire, qu'auraient donc à redire ceux qui dénient à Jésus sa réalité sur la terre ? Qui pourrait contredire cette scène ? Comment la réfuter ? Dès le début du sabbat, des prêtres acharnés à dénier Jésus vont refuser de croire à ce qui va suivre. Onfray et toute sa bande ne sont pas les premiers à exploiter la petite boutique de la libre pensée, le petit commerce virulent de l'athéisme militant. Tout est haine, disent-ils, dans l'histoire de Jésus : « Haine de la raison et de l'intelligence, haine de la liberté, haine de tous les livres au nom d'un seul, haine de la vie, haine de la sexualité, des femmes et du plaisir, haine du féminin, haine des corps, des désirs... » Tout le contraire, disent les tenants de Jésus. « Tout est amour de l'intelligence, de la lumière, des arts auxquels il a servi de modèle comme aucun autre sujet, amour de la vie, de l'eau courante, du sang dans les veines, amour des femmes, amour du féminin, par quoi naissent tous les hommes de la planète, femmes, sentinelles de l'invisible, comme disait le pape Wojtyla, dans le creux de la grotte de Lourdes. »

Tout est prêt pour que s'épaississe le secret. En 1898, la photographie est dans sa jeunesse, on effectue le premier cliché du suaire de Turin, livré depuis des siècles à la dévotion populaire. Divine surprise : surgit en négatif la silhouette d'un homme crucifié. Et si c'était Jésus ? On s'obstine depuis cent ans à croire ou à réfuter le prodige. L'examen au carbone 14 affirme qu'il date du début du Moyen Âge, mais il y a des doutes, et l'examen n'est pas totalement fiable. L'imaginaire se replie dans les zones incertaines. Comme les astrophysiciens qui ne peuvent certifier que tout l'univers a été cartographié, laissant ainsi une place au repli de Dieu dans son lieu mystérieux, les plus pointues avancées technologiques ne peuvent affirmer que le Linceul est postérieur à Jésus.

Une dernière découverte, énoncée au symposium de Dallas en 2001, affirme que la présence des pollens prélevés dans la toile, le *Gundelia tournefortii* et le *Zygophyllum dumosum*, permet de dire avec certitude le lieu et la saison où ils se déposèrent sur la toile : à Jérusalem et au printemps !

Joseph et les saintes femmes embaument Jésus selon la coutume juive. Elles doublent le linceul de myrrhe et d'aloès, mais le jus qui s'en échappe permet au sang de se coaguler, de fixer la trace du corps sur la toile. Puis les femmes, après avoir pilé des morceaux d'essence solidifiée qu'elles ont incorporée dans de l'huile d'olive, parfument le corps, l'honorent ainsi d'un oint de lavande et de citronnelle, d'ambre et de romarin. Les femmes assemblent de nouveau le corps, lui redonnent la grâce des jours anciens, lui rendent la peau lisse et blanche, colmatent les blessures, les plaies. C'est le temps de l'étable qui revient, du corps réchauffé par l'haleine des animaux et des bergers, des langes qui emmaillotent le bébé de bandelettes blanches jusqu'à ce qu'il soit immobilisé, et qu'il s'endorme dans la chaleur diffuse des céréales séchées. À l'oreille, ce bruit des débuts du monde, ce remuement des bêtes, régulier, paisible. L'eau des éponges ruisselle sur la peau meurtrie de Jésus, Marie de Magdala lisse les cheveux d'une crème qu'elle passait jadis dans les cheveux de ses amants, dont elle enduisait chaque mèche, et tout le corps brille de cette pâte d'amour, comme brillaient les corps des princes d'Égypte, des paysans, des poètes affamés, des pauvres qu'elle acceptait quand même dans l'anse de son propre corps. Entre les bras et le corps, entre les jambes, elle place des rames de romarin, des branches encore vertes de myrrhe, et Jésus n'est plus qu'une couche de fleurs, qu'un arbre en fleurs. Un insecte pris dans la dentelle d'une branche bourdonne près de ses hanches, et c'est déjà la vie qui revient. Il faut faire vite maintenant, ne pas risquer de troubler le repos sabbatique. On le lie aux deux extrémités d'une corde de chanvre et on le porte à mains d'homme dans le tombeau tout neuf que Joseph a fait tailler dans le roc. Marie de Magdala pleure et murmure des prières incompréhensibles, ce sont des paroles fiévreuses, haletantes, qui soulèvent sa poitrine. Dans la hâte, tout le rituel n'a pas été exécuté. « Vous reviendrez demain », dit Joseph. Ils descendent le corps dans le tombeau tout neuf, passent d'abord par l'antichambre avec son banc en pierre taillée dans le rocher pour que les parents puissent venir prier et pleurer leur mort et passent dans la seconde salle, la chambre funéraire, où ils déposent enfin le corps de Jésus. Ils roulent la pierre taillée qui glisse sur son rail.

En sortant, ils entendent résonner les trompettes du Temple. Le sabbat a commencé. Tout est suspendu à l'adoration de Dieu.

Dieu, qui veut aller jusqu'au bout de son dessein et renvoyer dans la géhenne les grands prêtres du Temple, les réduire à leur haine et à leur conformisme. Dieu, qui va souffler bientôt le grand vent de la liberté. Il en connaît la force, la vivacité. Le souffle des poètes, le grand fleuve des mots et de la musique, bientôt, irrésistible. Comme une porte immense qui s'ouvre et aère le monde. L'espérance.

Chapitre 50

Où l'on découvre que le tombeau de Jésus est vide

Le lendemain, les femmes veulent revenir au sépulcre, accomplir les derniers gestes rituels sur le corps de Jésus : pratiquer les sept ablutions, couper ses cheveux et sa barbe, habiller le corps et le remettre dans son linceul. C'est leur intention lorsqu'elles passent sur la route du tombeau de Joseph d'Arimathie. C'est le petit matin, il fait encore frais mais la lumière est déjà douce et dorée, comme une promesse. Elles vont, désolées, sur la route, quand, en arrivant à proximité du tombeau, elles aperçoivent une grande lumière blanche. Une lumière magnésique, étincelante, presque aveuglante. Une silhouette d'homme jeune s'en échappe, va vers le sépulcre, fait rouler la grosse pierre sur ses rails, et entre dans le tombeau. Les gardes que les grands prêtres ont obtenus de Pilate, parce qu'ils craignent une ruse des disciples, s'enfuient, épouvantés. Les femmes sont elles aussi pétrifiées, et l'Ange de lumière, vif comme un éclair, leur dit :

« Ne craignez rien, vous, je sais bien que vous cherchez Jésus, le Crucifié. Il n'est pas ici, car il est ressuscité d'entre les morts, et le voilà qui vous précède en Galilée. C'est là que vous le verrez. Voilà, je vous l'ai dit. »

Marie de Magdala, Marie Jacobé et Salomé retournent vers Jérusalem pour annoncer la bonne nouvelle. Mais qui les croira ? Comment concevoir ce prodige ?

Tout s'accomplit, tout ce qui a été annoncé se réalise. Isaïe, la genèse, Jérémie, Michée, Osée, Malachie, Zacharie, Daniel, le Livre de l'Exode, Amos, et tous les psaumes ont déjà dit ce qui allait arriver : « Après les épreuves de son âme, il verra la lumière et sera comblé. Par ses souffrances mon Serviteur justifiera des multitudes, en s'accablant lui-même de leurs fautes... Prêtez l'oreille et venez à moi, écoutez et votre âme vivra. »

Les femmes pleurent de joie : « Béni soit Dieu qui n'a pas écarté ma prière ni son amour loin de moi. » Elles courent sur le chemin, ceux qu'elles croisent ne comprennent pas leur hâte, elles crient et elles chantent, elles pleurent et elles rient, et Jésus leur apparaît dans sa robe de lumière. « "Je vous salue, leur dit-il, ne craignez point, allez annoncer à mes frères qu'ils doivent partir pour la Galilée, et là ils me verront[44]." Ne m'approchez pas, car je ne suis pas encore monté vers mon Père, mais allez vers mes frères, et dites-leur que je remonte vers mon Dieu qui est aussi votre Dieu. » Marie-Madeleine se prosterne sur la route, elle voudrait l'étreindre, mais Jésus la repousse doucement : « Nous nous reverrons un jour, Marie de Magdala, nous nous retrouverons, je t'attendrai dans la maison de mon Père et je t'y accueillerai, je te préparerai une tente où je viendrai te visiter, il n'y aura pas de guerre dans ce Royaume, pas de divisions, mais une éternité d'amour. Tu vas prendre la mer, Marie, tu vas aller très loin sur d'autres terres où tu te réfugieras, où tu finiras ta route terrestre, ne me touche pas, non, parce que tu es l'amour et la tendresse, non pas le mal qui tente, mais l'amour et je sais que seul l'amour retient à la terre. Et je suis homme encore, pas encore monté vers mon Père. Tu me vois dans ma lumière, dans ma nudité intégrale, dessaisie des bandelettes, tu vois mon corps sans blessure, sans plaie apparente, parce qu'entre toi et moi, c'est la même compréhension de l'amour. Ne pleure plus, Marie, ni sur moi ni sur la tombe descellée, car tu es bienheureuse, toi qui hériteras de tout le Royaume de la lumière, tu es le parfum sublime, et tu vas voyager dans une barque sans rame ni voile, tu iras à l'aveugle, poussée par le vent, et tu accosteras sur une terre chaude et parfumée. » Marie de Magdala écoute Jésus, elle seule le voit, elle l'aime tellement qu'il lui apparaît, elle croit tellement en lui que cette masse de lumière ne peut être que lui. Voir, c'est être dans l'état de l'apparition. Y être prêt.

Jean et Pierre, que les femmes croisent en chemin, ne peuvent croire la nouvelle. Ils se précipitent au sépulcre. Pierre seul entre dans la chambre mortuaire, Jean l'observe par un rayon de lumière qui tombe dans la pièce, tous deux voient le linceul vide, les bandelettes qui reposent à terre, le linge n'est pas froissé au sol, mais comme redressé sur lui-même, comme si Jésus s'était mis debout, défait de ses vêtements et levé vers le jour.

Alors Jean se met à pleurer, surgissent les larmes de l'amour, elles s'épanchent doucement, coulent sur tout son visage, il pleure comme une enfant. « Je me remets entre tes mains, Seigneur, que ta lumière me recouvre et trace ma route. »

La nouvelle atteint les autres disciples. Ils sont au Cénacle, Marie de Nazareth est avec eux, elle est encore nouée dans sa douleur, dans cet infini de l'amour qui ne l'a pas rendue au monde, elle entend la rumeur d'espoir, elle n'est pas surprise, elle sait déjà tout, depuis longtemps. Les apôtres décident de partir pour la Galilée, ils vont refaire la route de miséricorde, ils vont reprendre à rebours le même itinéraire qu'ils ont déjà emprunté avec Jésus, ils vont remonter les mêmes chemins comme on revient à la source, traverser les mêmes villages, ils s'arrêteront la nuit aux mêmes croisements, ils retrouveront la trace de leurs campements, les bois calcinés autour desquels ils écoutaient les enseignements de Jésus, et puis ils attendront sa venue. Ils savent qu'il surgira comme le vent, peut-être même tandis qu'ils seront assoupis, car ils sont conscients aussi que Jésus aime bien les prendre en faute, lampes éteintes, occupés à dormir plutôt qu'à veiller. Peut-être apparaîtra-t-il, lors d'une forte brise, dans une lumière indépassable, inconnue pour des yeux humains, une lumière qu'ils seront bien obligés, faute d'autres mots, d'appeler divine. Et ils pleureront pour avoir douté de sa promesse. Pour avoir cru qu'il ne s'échapperait pas du sépulcre.

Et pourtant Jésus les avait prévenus : « Vous ressusciterez à votre tour comme je ressusciterai moi-même, mais vous ressusciterez deux fois, la première par l'espérance qui vous convertira, par l'amour qui vous possédera, et ce sera déjà une nouvelle vie, celle en Dieu, et la seconde après votre mort où, libéré du poids de votre corps, votre esprit s'échappera, ne craindra aucun obstacle, aucune pierre tombale et fluide, s'en ira dans les airs, rejoindre d'autres esprits, et tous, rassemblés dans la même ronde universelle, vous referez le monde, vous le soutiendrez de nouveau, vous maintiendrez en équilibre le jeu des planètes, vous serez par la vibration de vos esprits, par le frottement de tous les esprits entre eux, vous serez la musique des planètes, tant il est vrai qu'il est impossible que vous mourriez pour toujours. Dieu vous reprendra dans ses mains comme il vous a déposé sur la terre, en naissant, il vous rattrapera et vous donnera de l'air et des ailes, et vous ne serez plus liés à cette terre, vous serez libres. On vous traitera de fous pour cela, pour croire en cela, mais vous ne prêterez pas attention à leurs blasphèmes et à leurs injures. Vous saurez, vous, que rien ne s'arrête, que vous participez à la mélodie secrète du monde, qu'il n'y a plus de mort à cause de l'amour, que le moindre caillou, que le moindre fil d'herbe concourt à l'amour, à l'éternité. Ne craignez pas la mort quand vous verrez l'acharnement du monde à détruire et à renier. Faites confiance à l'infinie compassion de Dieu, à son incroyable patience. Il lui en faut plus pour se décourager, pour abandonner le monde et cette fois à jamais. Croyez et vous serez sauvés. »

Devant l'annonce de la résurrection, les apôtres baissent la tête, non pas qu'ils soient accablés devant la mission à venir, mais parce qu'ils accueillent la nouvelle comme une onction qui les recouvre. Ils savent que maintenant commence la vraie tâche, celle d'avancer sur la route, seuls en apparence, mais accompagnés cependant, et même certains de n'être plus jamais seuls. Ils arrivent en Galilée. Ils pressent Jésus de venir, de les rejoindre, mais ils attendent toujours en vain. « Il viendra, dit Jean, c'est sûr, il reviendra, il suffit d'être entièrement dans sa foi et alors il se fera entendre. »

Chapitre 51

Où Jésus apparaît aux apôtres et
où il n'y a pas d'épilogue à l'histoire

Ils ont repris la route. Ils vont vers la Galilée. Ils croient et ils sont sceptiques à la fois. Ils ont le vent en eux, le feu et la braise, l'eau vive, tout ce que Jésus leur a donné, mais ils ne peuvent échapper au doute amer, aux échardes des questions, à la tentation de l'abandon. Ils ont bien vu, tous, les bandelettes défaites, posées à même le pavage de pierre, le suaire encore dans sa forme humaine, et Marie de Magdala qui les a assurés du retour du maître. Mais comment croire Marie, exaltée, fantasque ? Et si elle délirait ? Si elle simulait une vision ? Thomas surtout se méfie. Il voudrait croire complètement et il ne peut pas : il ne sait pas encore ce qu'est la foi, cette roche inébranlable, cette certitude ancrée au cœur du cœur. Cette vérité inscrite en soi, donnée par grâce et qui échappe à toutes les raisons, contre toutes les évidences. Ce mystère. Il observe Matthieu, Luc, Pierre, Marc et surtout Jean, ils ont confiance, ils commencent déjà à entrer dans la foi. Ils portent en eux un indéfectible amour en Dieu, sans quoi ils ne sont rien que de pauvres errants, des fanatiques, des fous, de purs accidents de la matière. Ils ont été visités par une grâce, ils ignorent comment ça s'est produit, par quel hasard organisé, forcément, mais ils sont confiants. Un jour il y a eu une rencontre et cette rencontre ne peut pas être fortuite, comme dans l'amour, comme quand la plaine épouse la forêt, quand la fleur se plaît dans le jardin, quand une attraction se produit, pour quelque chose ou pour quelqu'un et qui est étrangère à sa propre volonté et qui se fait malgré soi. Qui pourrait avoir organisé cette Rencontre ? Qui a mis sur leur route de pêcheurs ignorants ce marcheur inouï qui les a ralliés à sa cause, les a convertis ? Comment expliquer ce basculement ?

Les apôtres font le chemin seuls, Marie de Magdala ne les a pas suivis. Elle est restée à Jérusalem, on dit qu'elle est devenue folle, qu'elle parcourt les rues et les jardins à la recherche de Jésus, elle insulte ceux qui sont sur son passage, les accuse de l'avoir laissé crucifier, elle n'est douce qu'avec les fleurs, les arbres et les fontaines, elle leur parle et elle trouve seulement auprès d'eux un peu de consolation. Le peuple s'habitue à la folle de Jérusalem, à ses imprécations et à ses chants mélancoliques, ils la prennent pour une délirante que le crucifié aurait ensorcelée, ou bien mettent sa folie sur le compte de son passé luxurieux, de ses débauches. Elle les ignore, toute attachée à retrouver Jésus. Elle n'a qu'une hâte, c'est de partir loin d'ici pour aller à sa rencontre, de l'autre côté des océans, vers l'horizon où la mer justement le rejoint.

Marie de Nazareth non plus n'a pas suivi les disciples. Elle n'en a ni la force ni le goût. Elle préfère rester encore à Jérusalem, suivre les pas de son fils, refaire le même chemin qui l'a conduit au Golgotha. On peut la voir emprunter les ruelles, se glisser entre elles, rejoindre la *via dolorosa*. Mais comme certaines stations du chemin de croix ont été bouchées par des palissades afin d'éviter des scènes de fanatisme ou un culte sauvage, elle part dans la campagne. Elle sait parfaitement le nombre de haltes que Jésus a faites et le nombre de pas qu'il a effectués, elle les reproduit mentalement, abîmée dans la méditation. De toute façon, elle n'a pas besoin d'aller à la rencontre de son fils car il ne lui appartient plus, il est aux autres, au monde, à l'histoire des hommes, jusqu'à la nuit des temps. Elle sait bien sûr que Jésus a ressuscité, c'est-à-dire qu'il s'est glissé dans ceux qui se sont ouverts à lui, à l'amour de Dieu, dans ceux qui admettent l'hypothèse folle qu'il y a un Dieu, malgré son silence et son apparente indifférence, qu'il est partout, dans les yeux des enfants et dans l'absolue perfection des fleurs et des papillons, dans l'incroyable élaboration de l'univers, dans la rencontre de l'amour humain, prémices de l'amour divin, dans tout ce qui est aussi savamment organisé et qui ne peut n'être né de rien, surgi du néant, comme ça, sans projet ni regard.

C'est ce défi-là qu'elle lance depuis le Golgotha où elle va chaque jour, mentalement ou réellement, comme un défi à l'absurdité et au non-sens de Sisyphe.

Les Onze marchent toujours obstinément. Jésus leur apparaîtra sûrement malgré les heures obscures. Ils vont vers la montagne où Jésus avait conduit trois d'entre eux, peut-être se présentera-t-il à cet endroit ? Le soir, ils refont les mêmes gestes qu'avec lui, ils allument un feu, se mettent en rond autour de lui, prient avant de manger, appellent Jésus, l'invitent à leur table. Cela fait plusieurs nuits que la Pâque est passée, reviendra-t-il vraiment ?

Jean le premier déclare qu'il n'a pas besoin d'avoir la preuve de sa résurrection, que sa foi en Jésus suffit et que Jésus est en lui, que ses actes désormais seront vécus en lui, qu'il faut le chercher ailleurs que sur la route, mais en soi, dans sa vie intérieure et que c'est peut-être cela la résurrection : cette certitude que Jésus occupe tout l'être, qu'il n'y a pas besoin de réclamer des preuves visuelles mais que l'amour, seul, inspire l'existence. Et que donc l'amour, c'est Jésus.

Et puis un soir, juste avant la nuit, du vent se lève. Et une intense lumière, une forme étincelante, apparaît, éblouissant les disciples. Et Jésus se présente à eux. Ils se souviennent alors de la barque, un grand vent soufflait, soulevant la mer. Jésus marchait vers eux, ils l'ont invité à monter dans la barque mais aussitôt elle est arrivée à terre, là où ils se rendaient, comme si Jésus n'avait pas voulu monter auprès d'eux. Il leur avait dit seulement : « C'est moi, je suis, n'ayez pas peur. » Et aujourd'hui, il paraît de nouveau, de son habituelle manière, faite de feu et de lumière, qu'attisent des vents, et il leur dit encore une fois : « C'est moi, je suis, n'ayez pas peur. » Est-il vraiment apparu dans son char de lumière ou bien a-t-il surgi comme une évidence dans leur esprit ? Est-ce par l'esprit qu'il les atteint de nouveau ? Ils savent qu'il est là, que c'est une certitude. Seul Thomas, encore effrayé, ne le voit pas.

— Où es-tu, rabbi, montre-toi ? Je sens ta présence et je ne te vois pas.

— Seule la foi fait voir, répond Jésus. Tu as des yeux et tu ne vois toujours pas. Que faut-il te dire et te montrer pour qu'enfin tu t'abandonnes à Dieu ?

Alors Jésus se montre vraiment à lui, il est là, tel qu'en lui-même, tel que Thomas l'a toujours vu et considéré, en homme, sans apparente blessure, avec sa robe de lin salie par la poussière de la route, avec sa barbe de Sémite et son regard de braise, et cette chevelure qui descend sur ses épaules, Jésus comme il l'a toujours vu, au repas du midi et du soir, dans la prière, dans l'enseignement qu'il lui prodiguait. Mais comme Thomas prend peur, Jésus s'avance vers lui, lui prend la main, soulève sa tunique, et plonge la main de son disciple dans la plaie béante.

— Vois, Thomas, qui ne sus pas croire sans voir, vois et crois maintenant.

Thomas s'affaisse sur lui-même et dit seulement ces mots :

— « Mon Seigneur et mon Dieu[45]. »

Jésus se retourne vers les dix autres disciples. Il les couvre de son regard, il les entoure et les nimbe de sa lumière. Il les regarde intensément, presque avec douleur. Tout autour, la campagne semble transparente, presque invisible tant sa lumière éblouit le groupe. Il leur dit :

— Voyez comme je vous aime, allez maintenant de toutes les nations faire des disciples, allez les baptiser. Je vous en donne le pouvoir et aussi celui de guérir. Et moi, je suis avec vous, pour toujours, jusqu'à la fin du monde.

Le vent, vaste, inconnu, chaud et vif à la fois, fait vibrer la lumière qui entoure Jésus. Les apôtres ont juste le temps de le voir bénissant de sa main droite chacun d'entre eux. Il leur murmure : « Vous êtes onze et vous serez des multitudes, vous êtes onze et vous rejoindrez le monde, vous l'enserrerez de vos mains, vous embrasserez les foules et vous les vouerez à Dieu. » Puis Jésus s'efface, s'évanouit dans l'air, la lumière disparaît, comme si Jésus désormais ne devait plus être que cette brise. Quand tout est achevé, que le paysage a rétabli ses contours, ses points d'équilibre, que les champs et les chemins redeviennent visibles, que tout est comme avant, ils aperçoivent au sol une marque, une empreinte, ils se penchent et voient la trace d'un pied, celui qui servit de tremplin à son ascension.

Dès lors, ils le savent, Jésus ne reviendra qu'à la fin des temps, bien après eux, bien après des millénaires peut-être, au moment où tout sera accompli, que le monde aura usé son feu jusqu'à la dernière étincelle, que les aubes ne pourront plus se lever faute d'énergie, et que le soleil se sera éteint. Quand ? Cela, ils ne le savent pas. Mais il y a quelque chose en eux qui a changé, qui a bouleversé leur destin, quelque chose que personne ne pourra leur ôter, même pas les martyres, les persécutions ou les pogroms à venir, quelque chose en eux d'inaliénable, pour lequel ils accepteront de mourir, cette certitude de Dieu qu'ils vont s'employer à transmettre et à révéler malgré les moqueries et les évidences scientifiques, cette foi si peu définissable, si étrangère à tous les mots humains, et qui pourtant les cheville et les oblige.

Cette nuit-là, les disciples ont appris que leur foi ne sera pas vaine, puisque Jésus est avec eux. Qu'il ne cesse d'être auprès d'eux. Ils le sentent, ils le voient à des signes imperceptibles, à des détails infinitésimaux, à cette espérance que tout ne peut être comme le déplorait le roi David, « vanité ou poursuite du vent ». Déjà, ils ressentent la Pâque en eux, Jésus relève et éveille. En plein désert, en plein désarroi, ils savent qu'il viendra les relever et les éveiller. Et il faudra bien reprendre la route puisque c'est cela qu'il a demandé : marcher, péleriner, arpenter le monde et le tenir en éveil et debout.

Un jour, Rainer Maria Rilke raconta que ce qui tenait le monde en vie, c'était la capacité qu'avaient les hommes de l'ouvrir, de le laisser ouvert, et de s'aventurer ainsi au-delà de ce qu'il donne à voir, dans l'ouvert invisible et soudain infiniment visible. Mais pour cela, poursuivait-il, il fallait avoir la foi des roses et de la lumière, et qu'alors seulement, on pouvait entrer dans ce qu'il n'appelait plus que « l'Ouvert », qui va vers le Royaume. Jésus n'est en fait pas autre chose que cela, cette incitation à ouvrir le monde, à le laisser en état d'effraction pour que les hommes puissent, eux, être justement dans l'état de l'apparition.

Jésus est une aube, une lumière qui se lève, une lumière qui clame qu'il n'y a aucune solitude irrémédiable pour peu qu'on lâche les amarres, qu'on se livre au large de Dieu. Jésus, c'est cette flamme, cette musique, un nom qui veut dire « salut », c'est Mozart, c'est Bach, c'est tous les poètes et le vent qui souffle et qui mène à Dieu, à l'origine, aux clartés du premier jour, à la force de la vie, aux étoiles, à ce nom de Dieu. Cette absence. Cette arrogance et cette tyrannie. Cette consolation aussi. Cet amour qui permet à ces hommes d'écrire tant de choses incroyables, ce nom de Dieu rejeté ou adoré, et toujours au cœur de tous, cependant, comme une douleur sans cesse rouverte, contre quoi bute toute existence, et qui a tant de mal à se faire accepter, à cause de cette liberté que Dieu a donnée aux hommes. Même Sartre, du fond de sa rancune, du haut de sa posture altière et implacable, invoque Dieu, un jour de doute, Dieu qui vient contredire ses thèses, grain de sable qui grippe la belle machine théorique. Même Duras qui écrit, qui boit, qui souffre « en l'absence de Dieu », dit-elle, l'appelle dans sa douleur ramassée comme un immense sanglot et balbutie des mots, d'aube et de source, pour ne pas croire que tout est vain, atrocement vide.

« Ne croyez pas au vide, dit Dieu, croyez à l'Ouvert plutôt, car le vide vous précipite dans les abîmes tandis que l'Ouvert vous fait traverser et rejoindre. » C'est cela que commencent à comprendre les apôtres sur les routes ouvertes devant eux, la Galilée d'abord, et au-delà la mer, les océans, l'imprévisible, et d'autres côtes où il faudra bien annoncer la nouvelle, celle d'un dieu d'alliance qui a envoyé son fils pour enseigner aux hommes. Une histoire d'amour en quelque sorte, comme celle qu'ils tentent de vivre dans la misère de leurs existences, et dans l'amertume de leurs chants. Dieu, ils en avaient déjà l'intuition – car comment expliquer alors leurs étreintes et la protection qu'ils manifestent envers leurs enfants ? –, est le lien absolu, celui qui boucle l'humanité en une grande chaîne d'amour et de lumière. Dieu, c'est le lien qui ne se rompt pas et qui fait se rejoindre les êtres entre eux, et les apôtres savent désormais qu'il n'y a rien d'autre à faire que d'aller vers ce mystère, que s'avancer avec ce qu'ils sont, dans leur dénuement absolu, pour ne plus être des hommes défaits, déliés.

Se repassant en boucle l'histoire que Dieu leur avait envoyée, les apôtres n'en finissaient pas de s'émerveiller comme des enfants à qui on a raconté des contes extraordinaires. Mais c'était pourtant bien de cela qu'il s'agissait : d'un conte de Noël, de nativité, d'une histoire abracadabrante, qui faisait rêver et espérer. Alors ils riaient et se disaient qu'il fallait garder cette naïveté-là de l'enfance, elle seule pouvait conserver leur capacité d'espérance et leur donner le courage d'affronter la route, ses épreuves et ses aubes splendides. Tout au fond d'eux, ils avaient cette certitude-là que tout était possible grâce à Dieu, et même le pouvoir de dépasser la mort, de guérir de soi et de ses égoïsmes, parce qu'il y aurait toujours une force en eux qui ne se tairait pas et qui, aussi forte que le vent, inciterait à dépasser les frontières, les sentiers balisés. Ils riaient comme des enfants, oui, et Dieu avec eux, parce qu'il était fier de son nouveau plan, même s'il savait qu'il y aurait encore beaucoup de ténèbres qui tenteraient d'empêcher l'alliance.

Il ne doutait pas de la vaillance des apôtres. Après eux, il y en aurait d'autres et d'autres encore, aussi fous, aussi intrépides et nul n'y pourrait rien. Il y veillerait personnellement, c'est certain.

Notes
(Source : la Bible de Jérusalem, éditions du Cerf, Paris, 1955)

1. Matthieu, **2**, 13.
2. Psaume **23**, 1-3.
3. Psaume **40**, 2-3.
4. Matthieu, **4**, 1-12.
5. Luc, **4**, 18-19.
6. Marc, **2**, 11.
7. Luc, **8**, 21.
8. Luc, **6**, 20-23.
9. Luc, **6**, 24-26.
10. Matthieu, **5**, 13.
11. Jean, **4**, 10.
12. Jean, **4**, 13-14.
13. Jean, **6**, 35.
14. Jean, **6**, 36-39.
15. Jean, **6**, 44.
16. Jean, **6**, 48-51.
17. Jean, **6**, 53-56.
18. Marc, 7, 34.
19. Matthieu, **16**, 22.
20. Luc, **7**, 47.
21. Luc, **7**, 50.
22. Matthieu, **17**, 4.
23. Jean, **11**, 14.
24. Jean, **14**, 6.
25. Luc, **12**, 33.
26. Jean, **13**, 33.
27. Psaume, **27**.
28. Jean, 7, 16.
29. Jean, **13**, 33.
30. Jean, **12**, 13.
31. Jean, **12**, 27.
32. Jean, **12**, 28.
33. Jean, **13**, 8.
34. Jean, **13**, 27.
35. Jean, **14**, 6.
36. Luc, **17**, 18.
37. Luc, **22**, 34.
38. Matthieu, **26**, 64.
39. Matthieu, **26**, 66.
40. Matthieu, **26**, 72.
41. Matthieu, **27**, 24.
42. Matthieu, **27**, 38.
43. Matthieu, **27**, 46.
44. Matthieu, **28**, 10.
45. Jean, **20**, 28.

N.B. : À de nombreuses autres occurrences, l'auteur s'est librement inspiré de l'éminente traduction de la Bible de Jérusalem, source inépuisable d'inspiration.

Table des matières

1. Où il est question du début du monde et du refuge de Dieu dans un trou noir 13
2. Où Jésus le Fils est annoncé à Marie 19
3. Où Joseph et Marie quittent Nazareth pour rejoindre Bethléem 25
4. Où se découvre la splendeur de cette nuit 31
5. Où Jésus, Marie, Joseph fuient en Égypte........... 37
6. Où comment Jésus s'installe dans la paix de Nazareth 43
7. Où Jésus commence à vaquer à ses affaires 49
8. Où Jésus sort de son silence 57
9. Où Jésus poursuit sa vie cachée 61
10. Où Jésus entend l'appel de Dieu...................... 67
11. Où Jésus plie bagages et part vers le Jourdain...... 73
12. Où Jésus est tenté dans le désert...................... 79
13. Où Jésus redescend dans la vallée..................... 91
14. Où Jésus accomplit son premier miracle à Cana.. 103
15. Où Jésus va dans la synagogue faire la lecture 109
16. Où le feu se répand..................................... 113
17. Où Jésus survient dans un monde perdu 117
18. Où Jésus guérit les corps et les esprits................ 121
19. Où Jésus défie les critiques............................. 125

20. Où Dieu se réjouit de son plan............................ 131
21. Où Jésus apprend le martyre de Jean Baptiste 135
22. Où Jésus reprend la route 143
23. Où Jésus révèle son enseignement........................ 149
24. Où Jésus accomplit des prodiges extraordinaires.. 155
25. Où chaque moment de la vie de Jésus est une parabole... 161
26. Où Jésus se repose au puits de Jacob 165
27. Où Jésus se proclame le pain de vie..................... 171
28. Où Jésus guérit inlassablement............................. 177
29. Où Jésus annonce sa Passion................................ 181
30. Où Jésus croise la femme pécheresse.................... 185
31. Où Jésus est transfiguré.. 189
32. Où Jésus accomplit la résurrection de Lazare comme un signe de sa puissance sur la mort 193
33. Où Jésus prend le chemin de Jérusalem............... 199
34. Où Jésus révèle la prière universelle 205
35. Où Jésus délivre ses ultimes conseils 209
36. Où Jésus approfondit son enseignement 213
37. Où Jésus ranime le feu... 217
38. Où Jésus atteint enfin Jérusalem 221
39. Où Jésus défie les Juifs 227
40. Où Jésus amorce la chute de l'histoire 231
41. Où Jésus s'accorde une pause................................ 237
42. Où Jésus est trahi 241
43. Où Jésus entre dans sa Passion............................. 247
44. Où Jésus se prépare à quitter les siens.................. 251
45. Où Jésus veille au mont des Oliviers.................... 259
46. Où Jésus est arrêté.. 265
47. Où Jésus entre dans son agonie 273
48. Où Jésus est crucifié... 281
49. Où Jésus est mis au tombeau 287

50. Où l'on découvre que le tombeau de Jésus est vide... 295
51. Où Jésus apparaît aux apôtres et où il n'y a pas d'épilogue à l'histoire 301

DU MÊME AUTEUR

Marguerite Duras, Seghers, 1972.
Anthologie de la poésie fantastique française, Seghers, 1973.
Bonaventure, Stock, 1977.
Amore Veneziano, Stock, 1979.
Introduction au journal de ma vie de Thérèse d'Avila, Stock, 1979.
Vivre en poésie, entretiens avec Eugène Guillevic, Stock, 1980.
Maman la Blanche, Albin Michel, 1981.
Alger l'amour, Presses de la Renaissance, 1982.
Tant que le jour te portera, Albin Michel, 1983.
La Vie, la vie, Albin Michel, 1985.
Là Nuit de Mayerling, Plon, 1985.
Le Petit Frère de la nuit, Albin Michel, 1988.
Séraphine de Senlis, Albin Michel, 1986.
Le Monde merveilleux des images pieuses, Hermé, 1988.
Le Roman de Jacqueline et Blaise Pascal, Flammarion, 1989.
Introduction à Sainte Lydwine de Schiedam de Huysmans, Maren Sell, 1989.
J.-K. Huysmans, Plon, 1990.
Duras, François Bourin, 1991.
La Tisserande du Roi Soleil, Flammarion, 1992.
Introduction à La Cathédrale de Huysmans, Le Rocher, 1992.
Naissance d'un père, Le Rocher, 1993.
Saint-Exupéry, Julliard, 1994.
Devenir Venise, Lattès, 1994.
Actes du Colloque de Cerisy-le-Salle sur Marguerite Duras, sous la direction d'Alain Vircondelet, Écriture, 1993.
Jean-Paul II, Julliard, 1994.
Pour Duras, Calmann-Lévy, 1995.
La Princesse de Lamballe, Flammarion, 1995.
Là-Bas, souvenirs d'une Algérie perdue, Le Chêne/Hachette, 1996.
Marguerite Duras, vérité et légendes, Le Chêne/Hachette, 1996.
Je vous salue, Marie, représentations populaires de la Vierge Marie, Le Chêne/Hachette, 1997.

Charles de Foucauld, Le Rocher, 1997.
Le retour des sources, in *Une enfance algérienne*, Gallimard, 1997.
Jean-Paul II, naissance d'un destin, Autrement, 1997.
Marguerite à Duras, Éditions 1, 1998.
Mortel amiante, Anne Carrière, 1998.
Albert Camus, vérité et légendes, Le Chêne/Hachette, 1998.
Alger Alger, Éditions du Laquet, 1998.
Actes du Colloque de l'ICP sur Marguerite Duras, sous la direction d'Alain Vircondelet, Le Rocher, 1998.
Rimbaud ou La Terreur des chiens, Le Rocher, 1999.
La Maison devant le monde, Desclée de Brouwer, 2000.
Marguerite Duras ou l'émergence du chant, La Renaissance du Livre, 2000.
Saint-Exupéry, vérité et légendes, Le Chêne/Hachette, 2000.
Les Chats de Balthus, Flammarion, 2000.
Bernadette, celle qui a vu, Desclée de Brouwer, 2002.
L'Enfance de Jean-Paul II, Le Rocher, 2002.
Sagan, un charmant petit monstre, Flammarion, 2002.
Les Enclos bretons : chefs-d'œuvre de l'art populaire, Flammarion, 2003.
Journal de résistance d'un chrétien dans le monde, Flammarion, 2003.
Nulle part qu'à Venise, Plon, 2003.
Jean-Paul II, Éditions First, 2004.
Jean-Paul II : la vie de Karol Wojtyla, Flammarion, 2004.
Une passion à Venise : Sand et Musset, la légende et la vérité, Plon, 2004.
La passion de Jean-Paul II, Presses de la Renaissance, 2005.
Antoine et Consuelo de Saint-Exupéry : un amour de légende, Éditions des Arènes, 2005.
Les Derniers Jours de Casanova, Flammarion, 2005.
Sur les pas de Marguerite Duras, Les Presses de la Renaissance, 2006.
Éloge des herbes quotidiennes, Le Rocher, 2006.
Venise, sous la direction d'Alain Vircondelet, Flammarion, 2006.

Composition et mise en page

CET OUVRAGE
A ÉTÉ REPRODUIT
ET ACHEVÉ D'IMPRIMER
SUR ROTO-PAGE
PAR L'IMPRIMERIE FLOCH
À MAYENNE EN FÉVRIER 2007

N° d'éd. L.01ELJNFF8871N001. N° d'impr. 67503.
D. L. : février 2007.
Imprimé en France